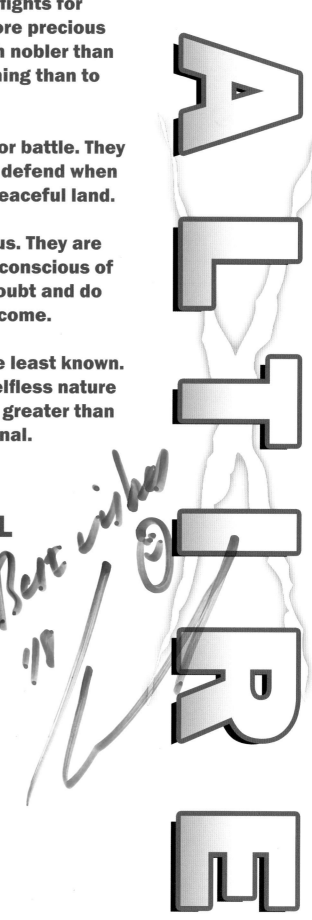

Foreword

For a name to echo through the ages, they must conquer worlds. But the true hero fights for something greater than glory and more precious than remembrance. To defend is much nobler than to attack. To protect, a much finer thing than to persecute.

The greatest warrior shall not agitate for battle. They are content to be there for those they defend when the conquering foe steps forth onto peaceful land.

A hero does not consider himself thus. They are selfless and just. Noble of cause and conscious of consequence. They will rise above doubt and do what is right no matter the outcome.

The finest warrior of an age is often the least known. Their achievements confined by the selfless nature of their actions. They serve a purpose greater than legacy. They are legend. Eternal.

LEGEND ETERNAL

WRITTEN BY
JOHN FERGUSON

ART BY
LYDIA PRAAMSMA
ALVARO FELIU GUTIERREZ
TONI DOYA HEREDIA

COLOURS BY
KASEY SCHIAVONE
LAUREN KNIGHT
REBECCA HORNER

LETTERS BY
PHILLIP VAUGHAN

PREVIOUSLY...

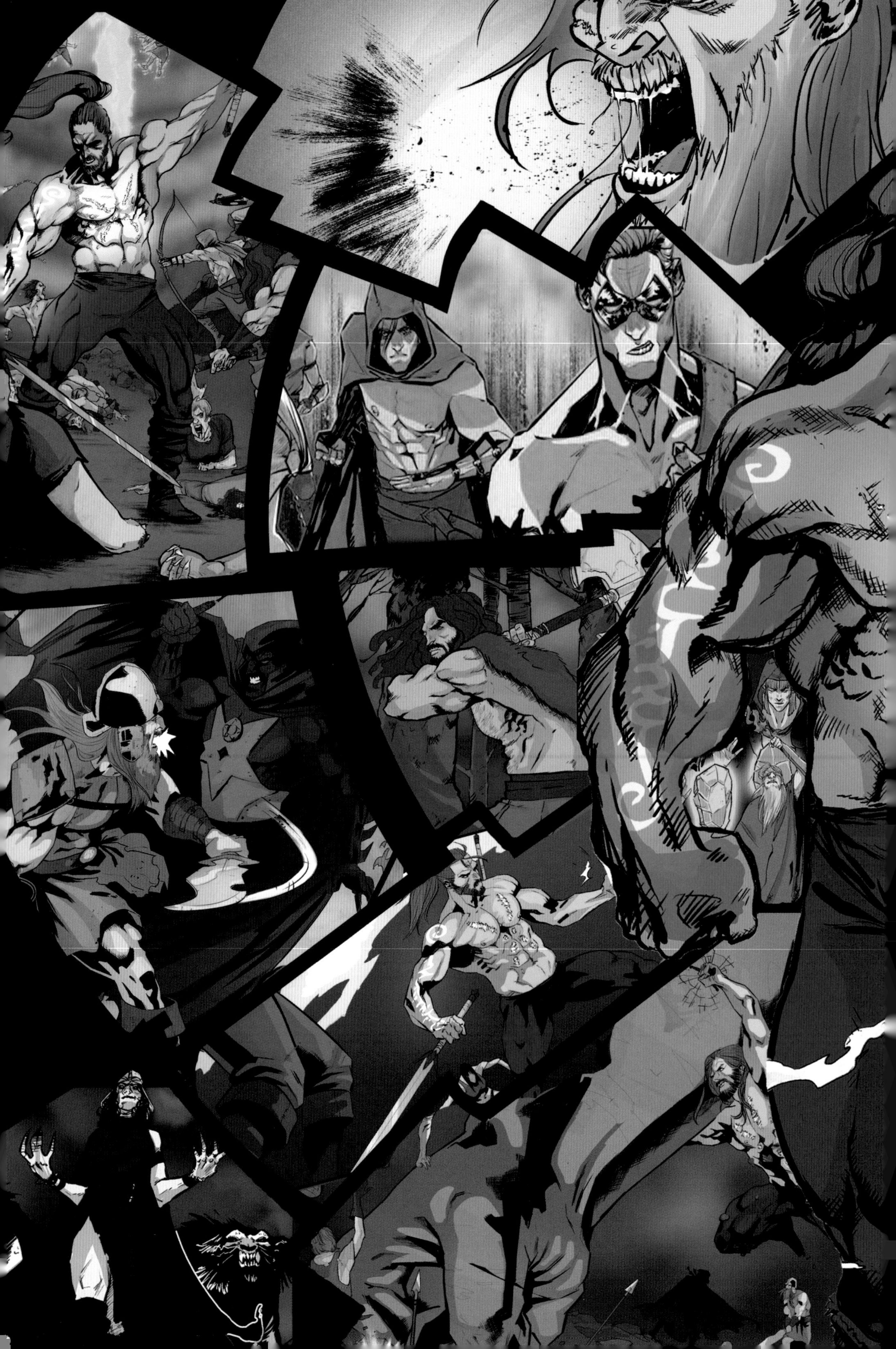

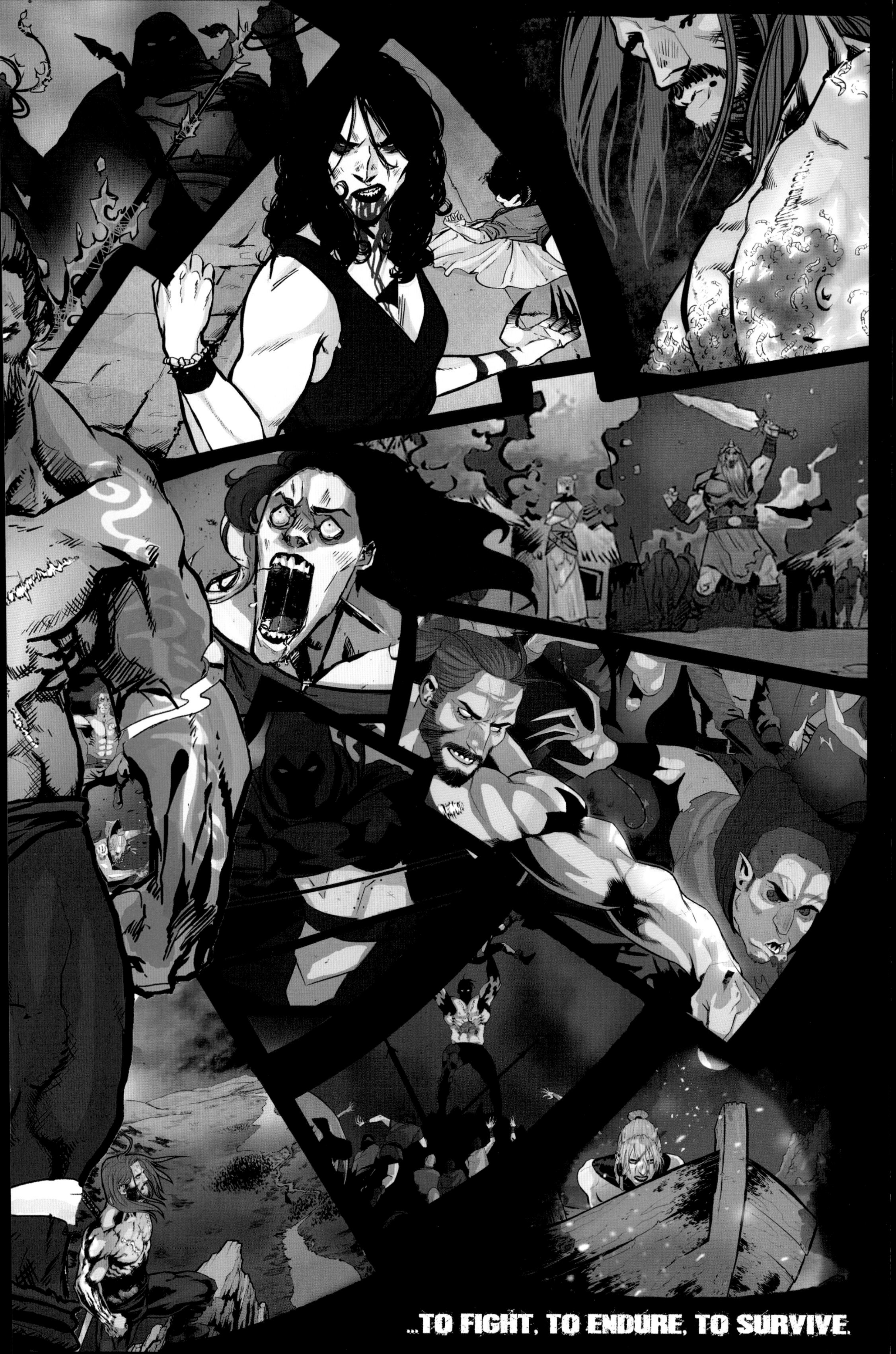

...TO FIGHT, TO ENDURE, TO SURVIVE.

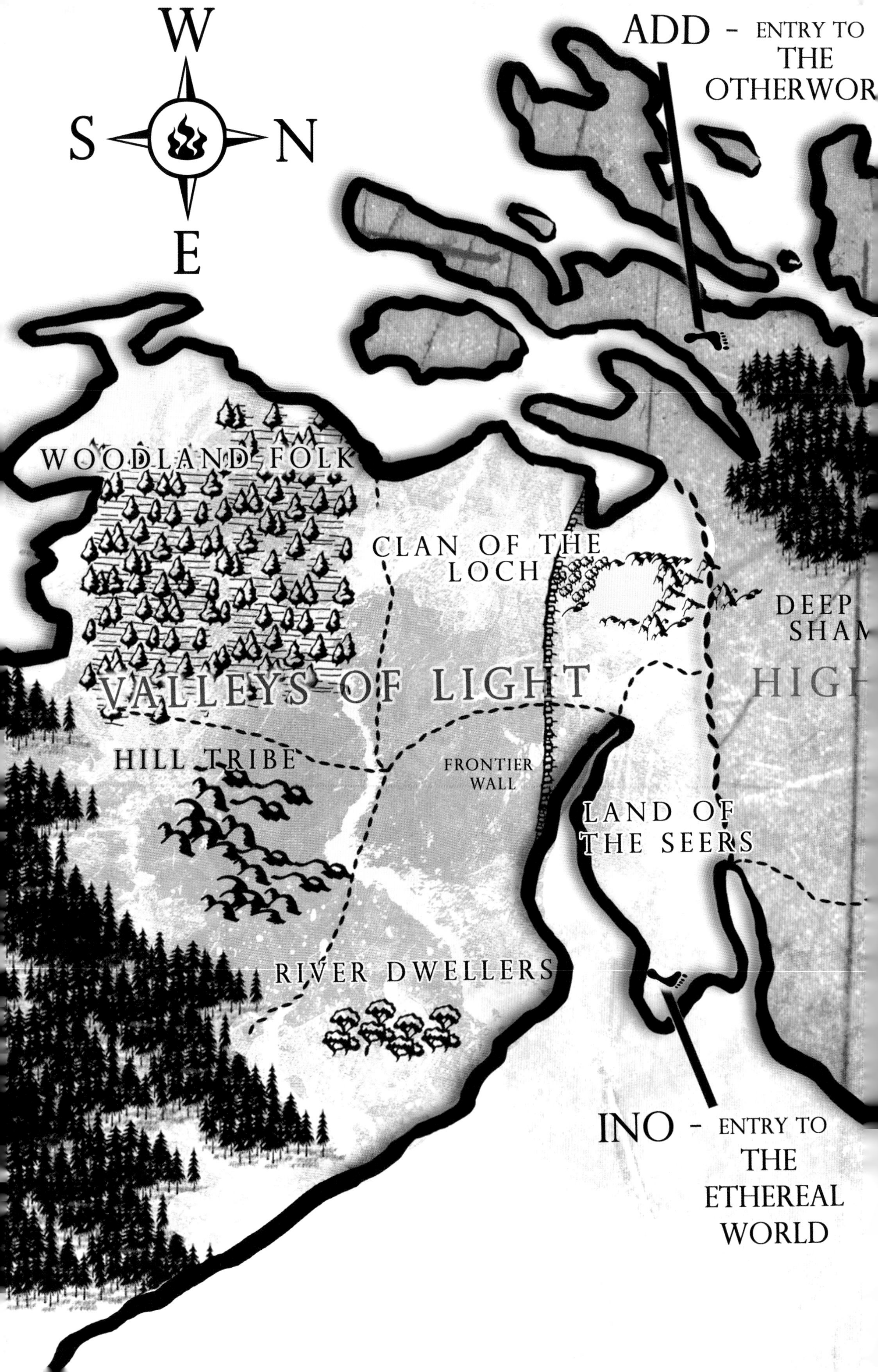
W
S
N
E
ADD - ENTRY TO THE OTHERWOR
WOODLAND FOLK
CLAN OF THE LOCH
DEEP SHAM
VALLEYS OF LIGHT
HIGH
HILL TRIBE
FRONTIER WALL
LAND OF THE SEERS
RIVER DWELLERS
INO - ENTRY TO THE ETHEREAL WORLD

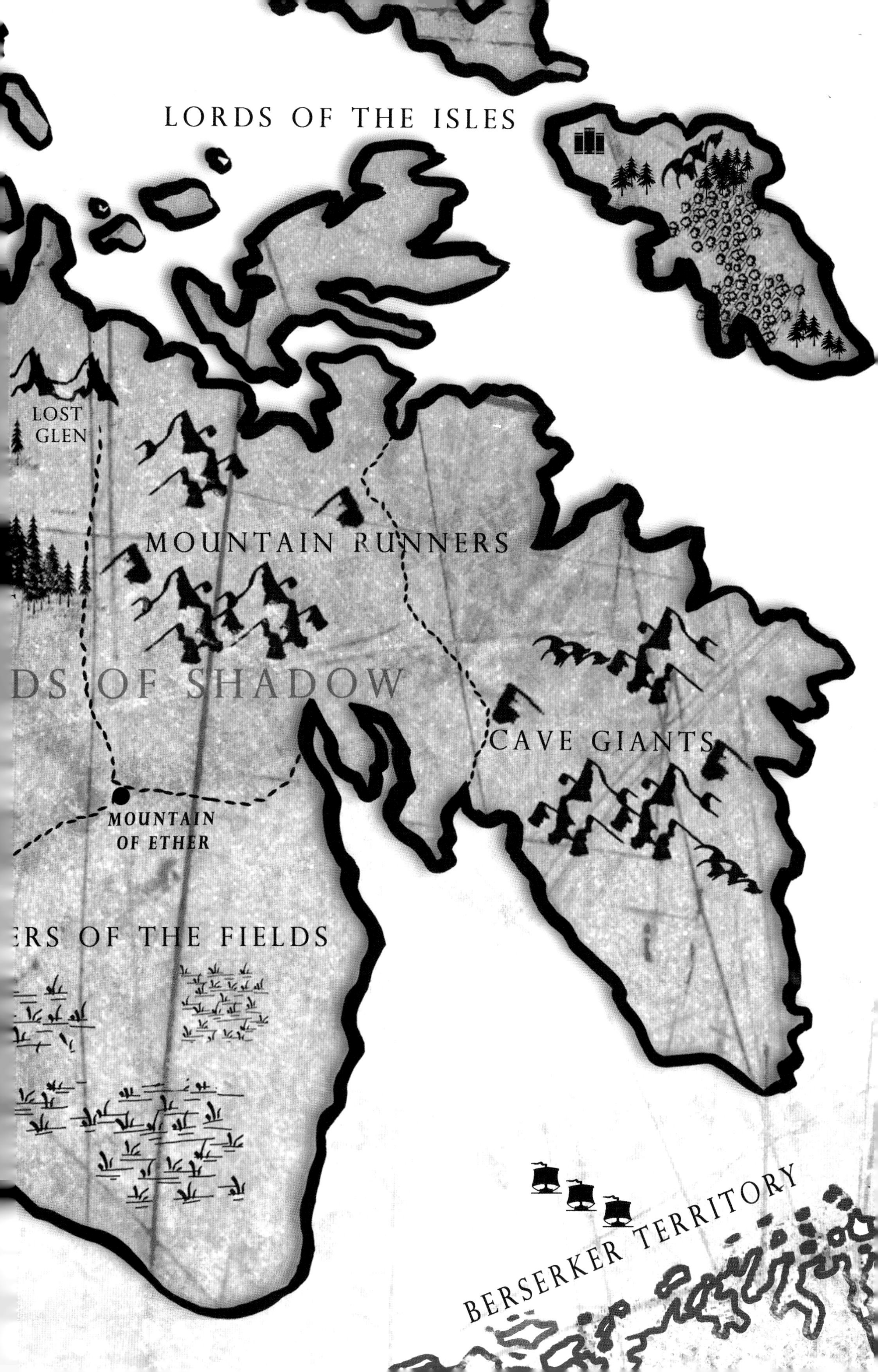
LORDS OF THE ISLES
LOST GLEN
MOUNTAIN RUNNERS
DS OF SHADOW
CAVE GIANTS
MOUNTAIN OF ETHER
ERS OF THE FIELDS
BERSERKER TERRITORY

Chapter One

Script: John Ferguson
Art: Lydia Praamsma
Colours: Kasey Schiavone
Letters: Phillip Vaughan
Editor: Clare Ferguson

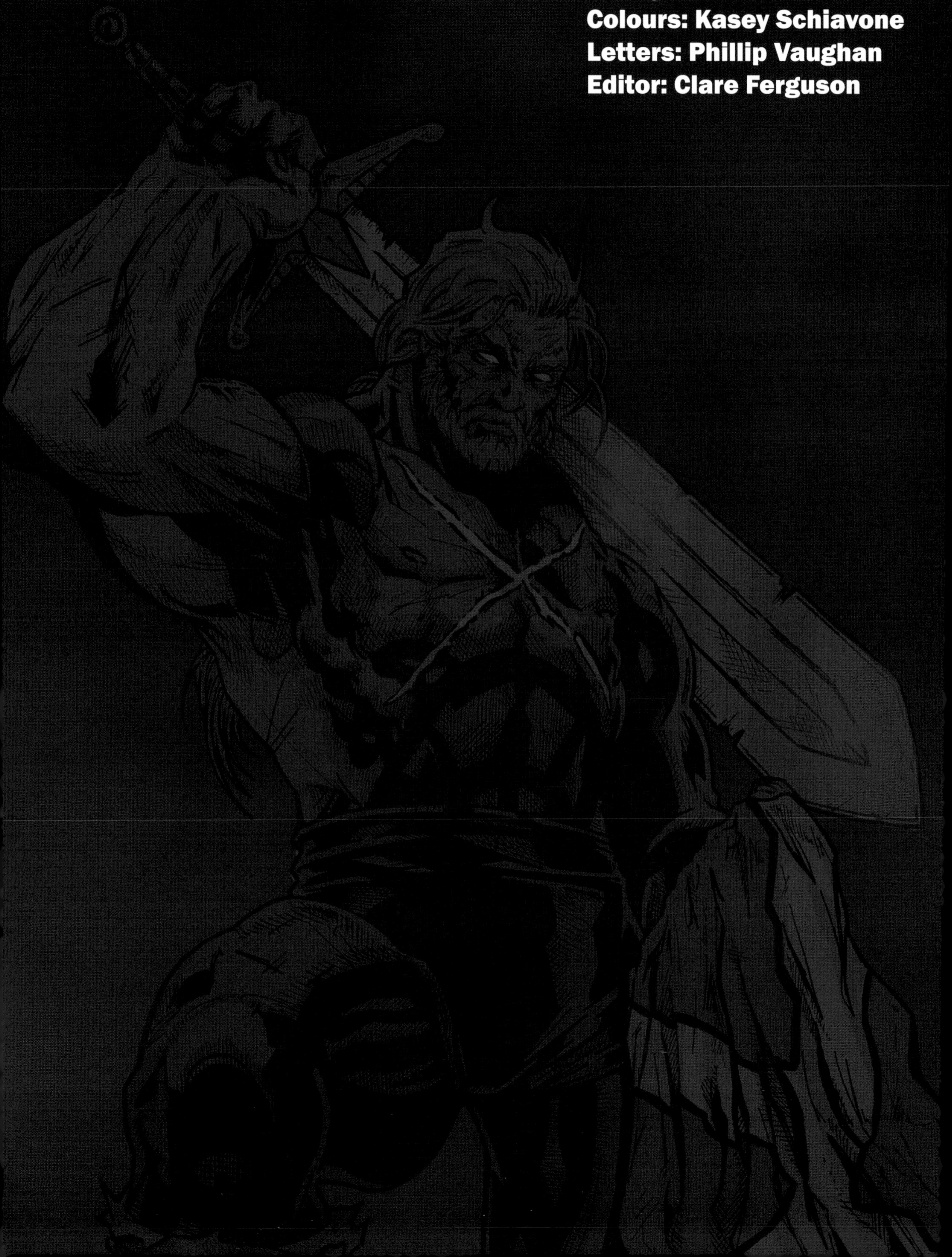

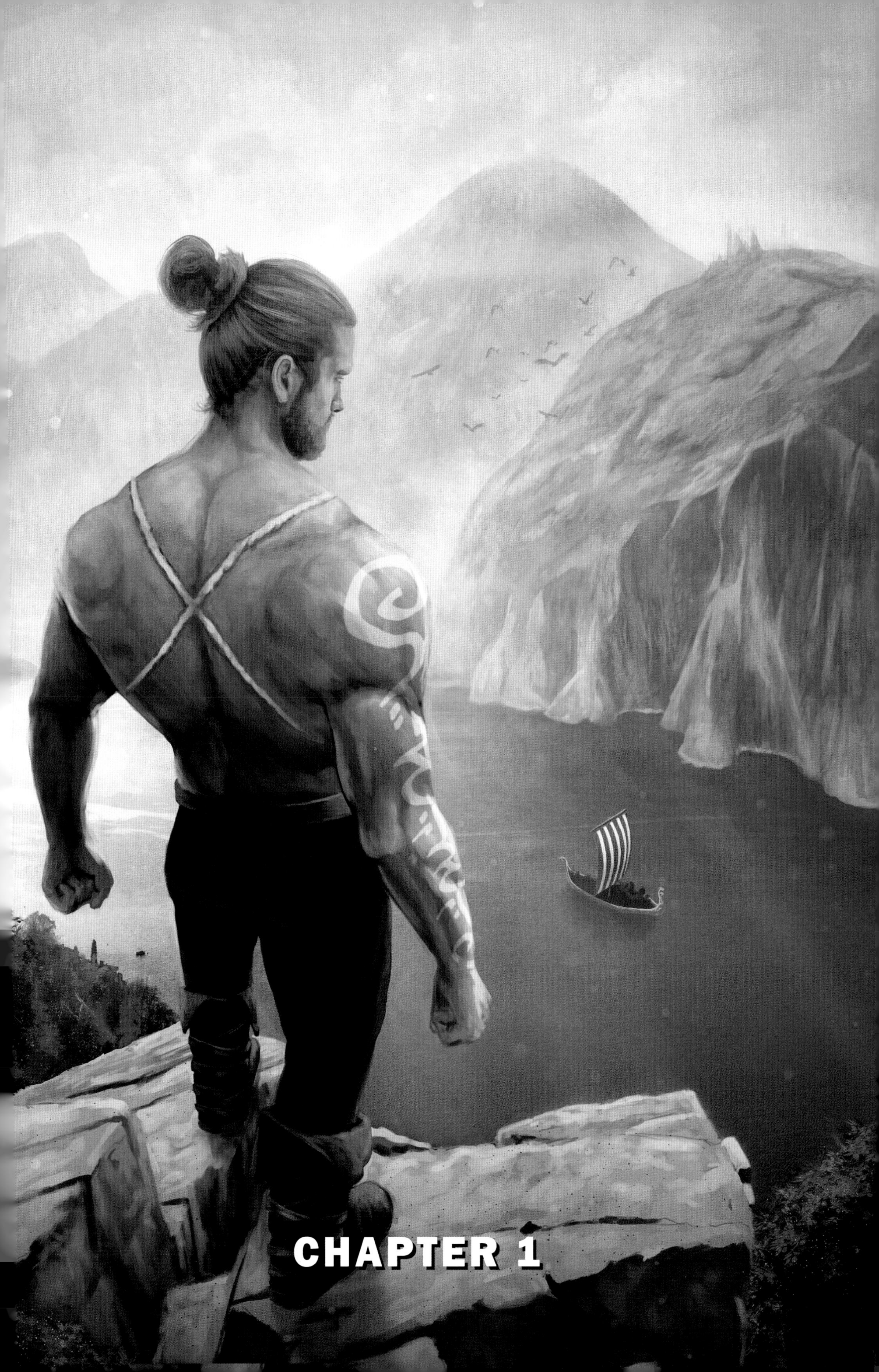

CHAPTER 1

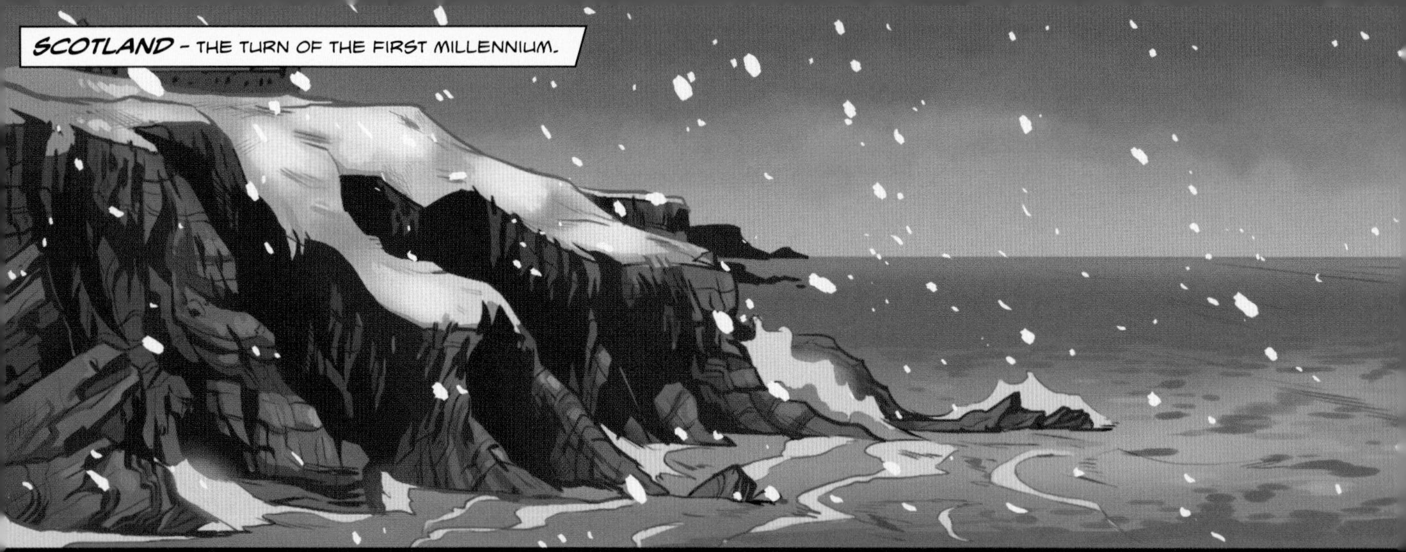
SCOTLAND - THE TURN OF THE FIRST MILLENNIUM.

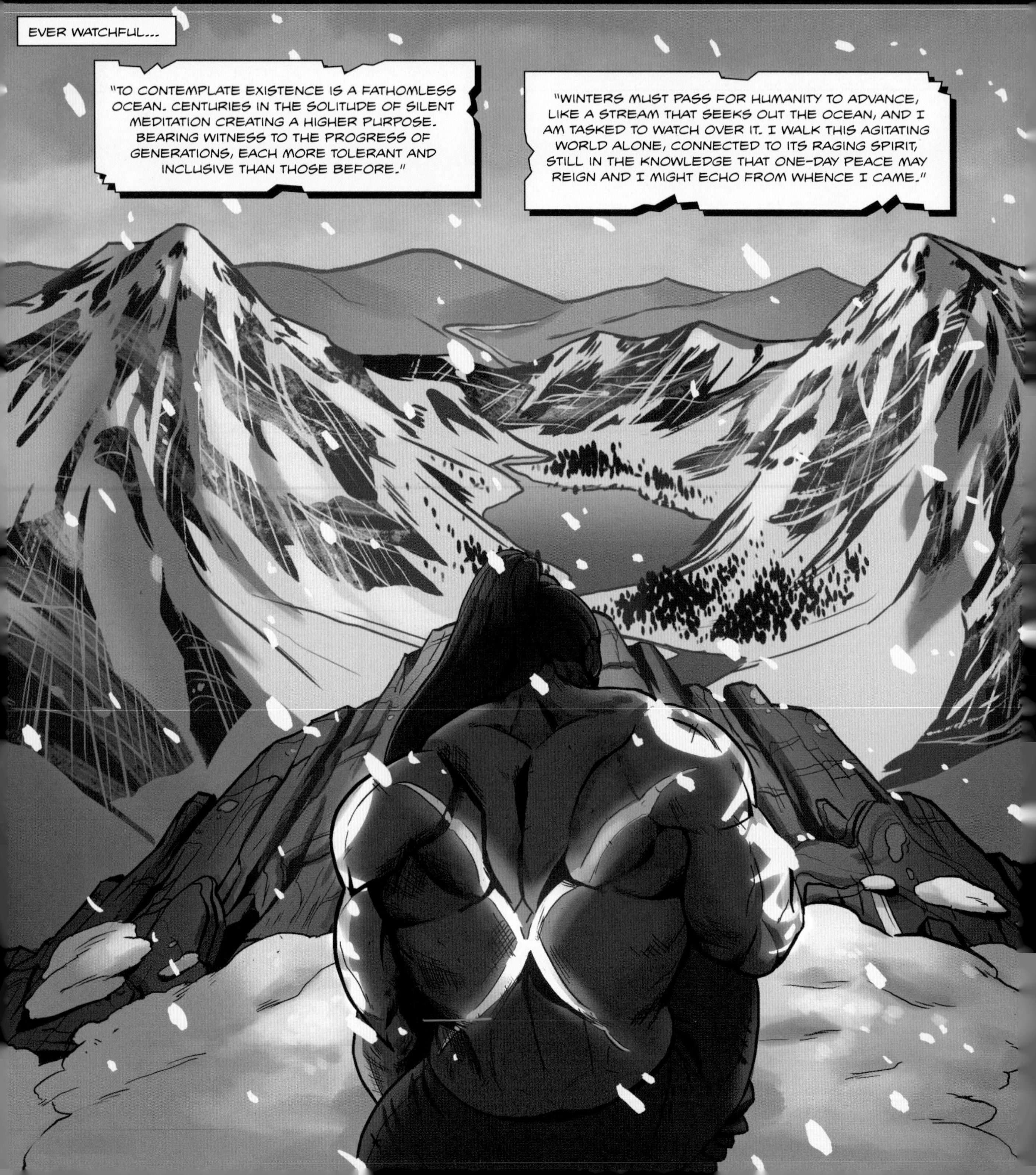
EVER WATCHFUL...
"TO CONTEMPLATE EXISTENCE IS A FATHOMLESS OCEAN. CENTURIES IN THE SOLITUDE OF SILENT MEDITATION CREATING A HIGHER PURPOSE. BEARING WITNESS TO THE PROGRESS OF GENERATIONS, EACH MORE TOLERANT AND INCLUSIVE THAN THOSE BEFORE."
"WINTERS MUST PASS FOR HUMANITY TO ADVANCE, LIKE A STREAM THAT SEEKS OUT THE OCEAN, AND I AM TASKED TO WATCH OVER IT. I WALK THIS AGITATING WORLD ALONE, CONNECTED TO ITS RAGING SPIRIT, STILL IN THE KNOWLEDGE THAT ONE-DAY PEACE MAY REIGN AND I MIGHT ECHO FROM WHENCE I CAME."

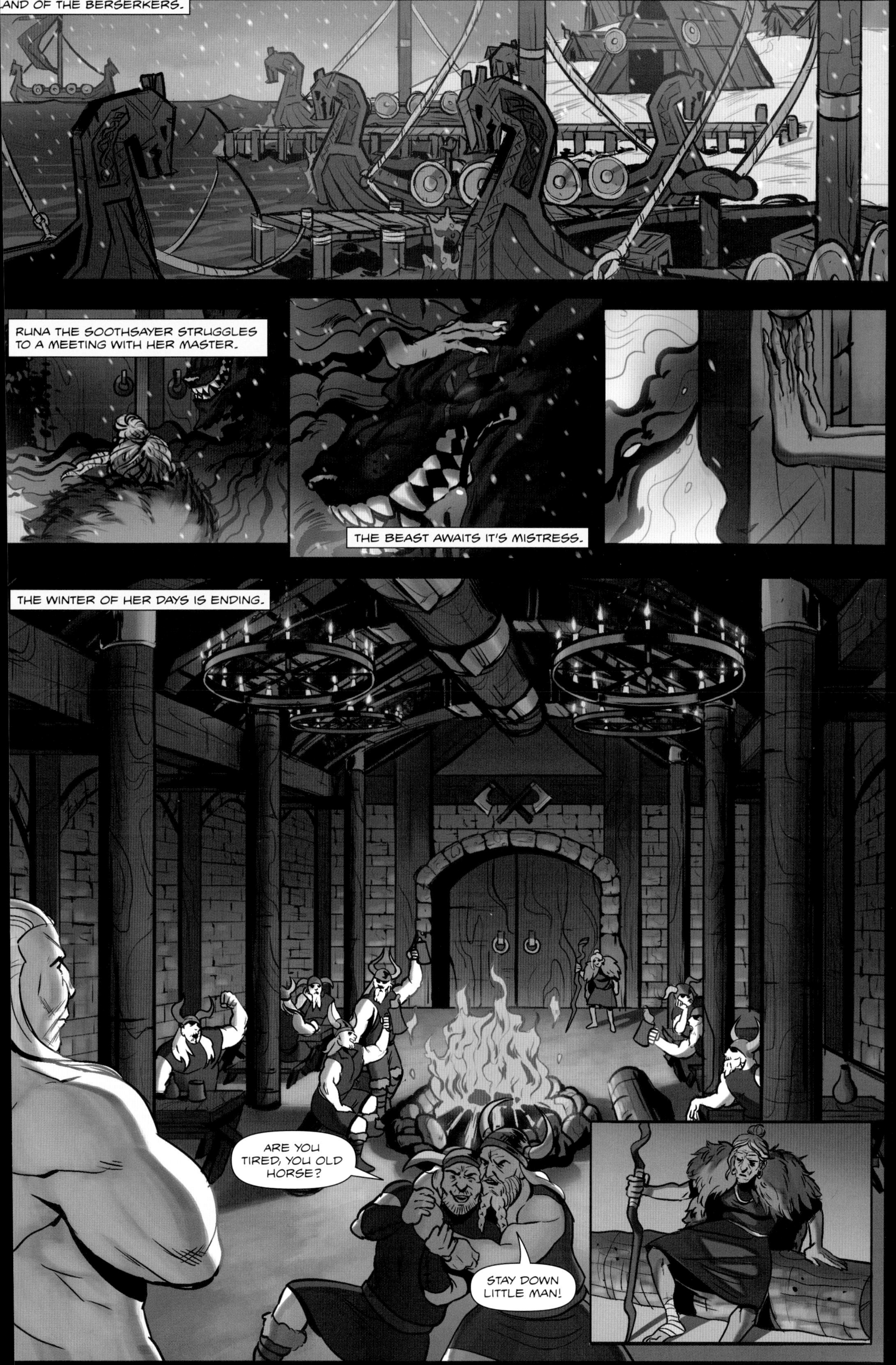
AND OF THE BERSERKERS.
RUNA THE SOOTHSAYER STRUGGLES TO A MEETING WITH HER MASTER.
THE BEAST AWAITS IT'S MISTRESS.
THE WINTER OF HER DAYS IS ENDING.
ARE YOU TIRED, YOU OLD HORSE?
STAY DOWN LITTLE MAN!

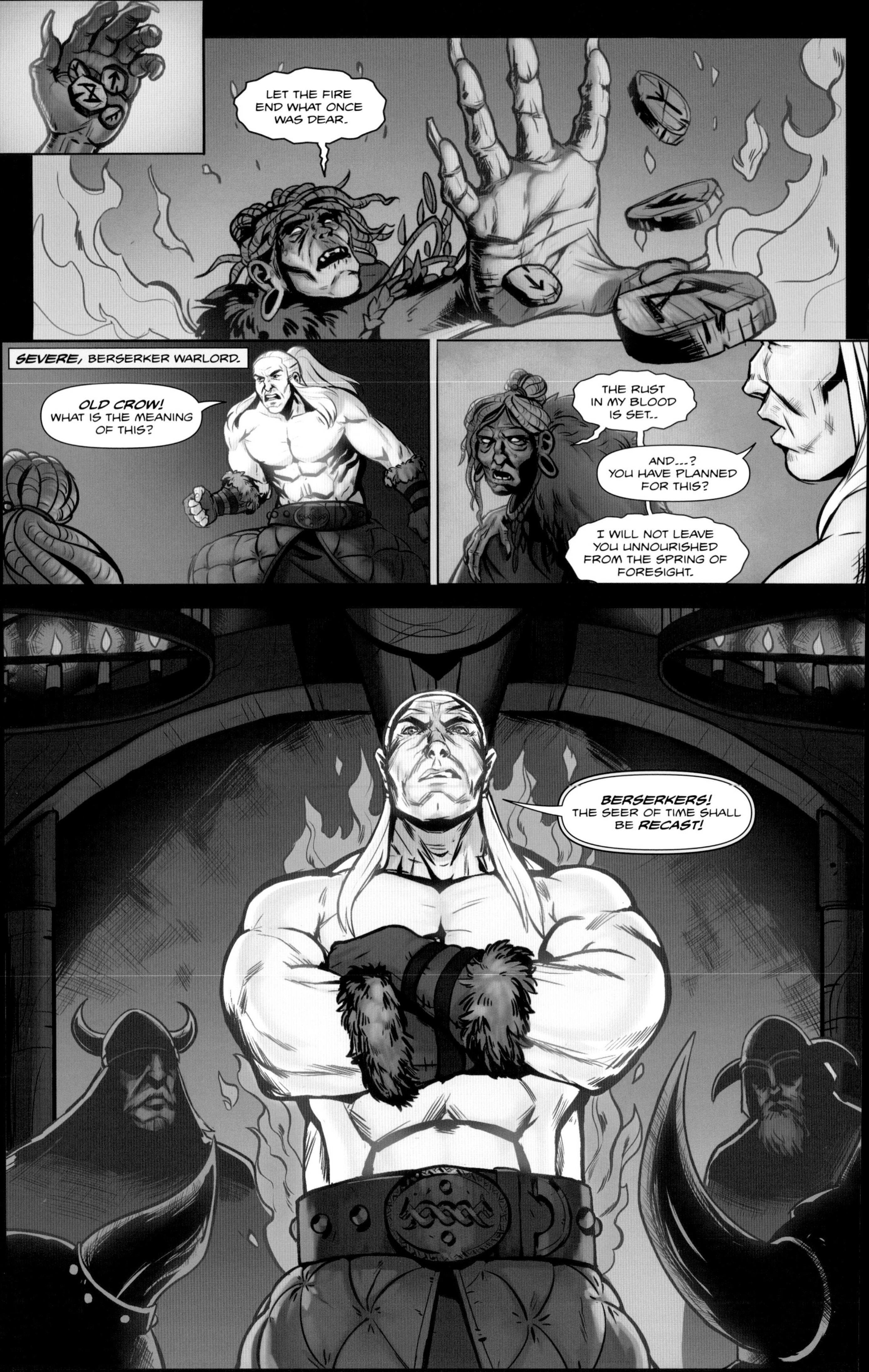
LET THE FIRE END WHAT ONCE WAS DEAR.
SEVERE, BERSERKER WARLORD.
OLD CROW! WHAT IS THE MEANING OF THIS?
THE RUST IN MY BLOOD IS SET..
AND...? YOU HAVE PLANNED FOR THIS?
I WILL NOT LEAVE YOU UNNOURISHED FROM THE SPRING OF FORESIGHT.
BERSERKERS! THE SEER OF TIME SHALL BE RECAST!

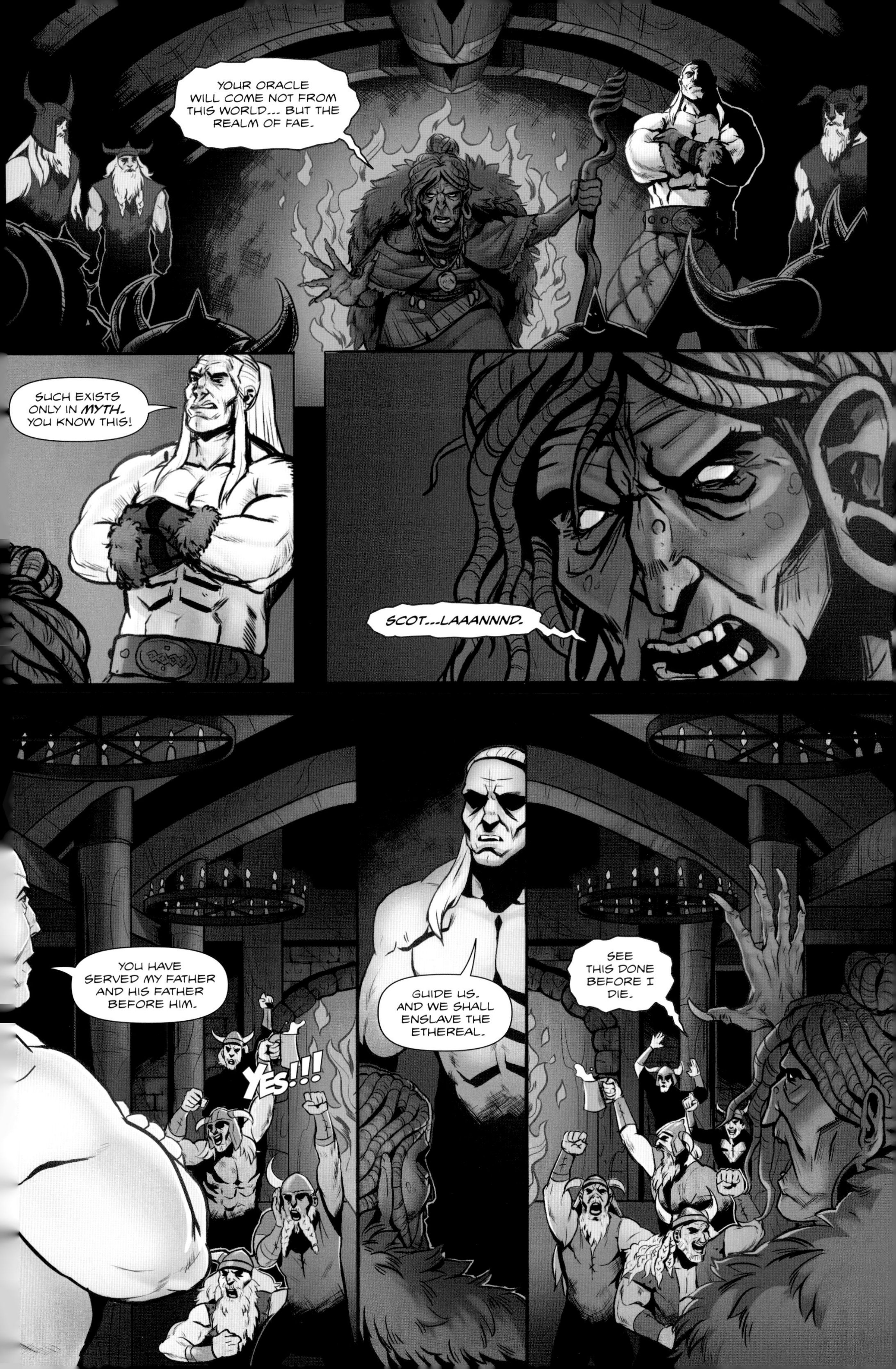
YOUR ORACLE WILL COME NOT FROM THIS WORLD... BUT THE REALM OF FAE.
SUCH EXISTS ONLY IN MYTH. YOU KNOW THIS!
SCOT...LAAANNND.
YOU HAVE SERVED MY FATHER AND HIS FATHER BEFORE HIM.
YES!!!
GUIDE US. AND WE SHALL ENSLAVE THE ETHEREAL.
SEE THIS DONE BEFORE I DIE.

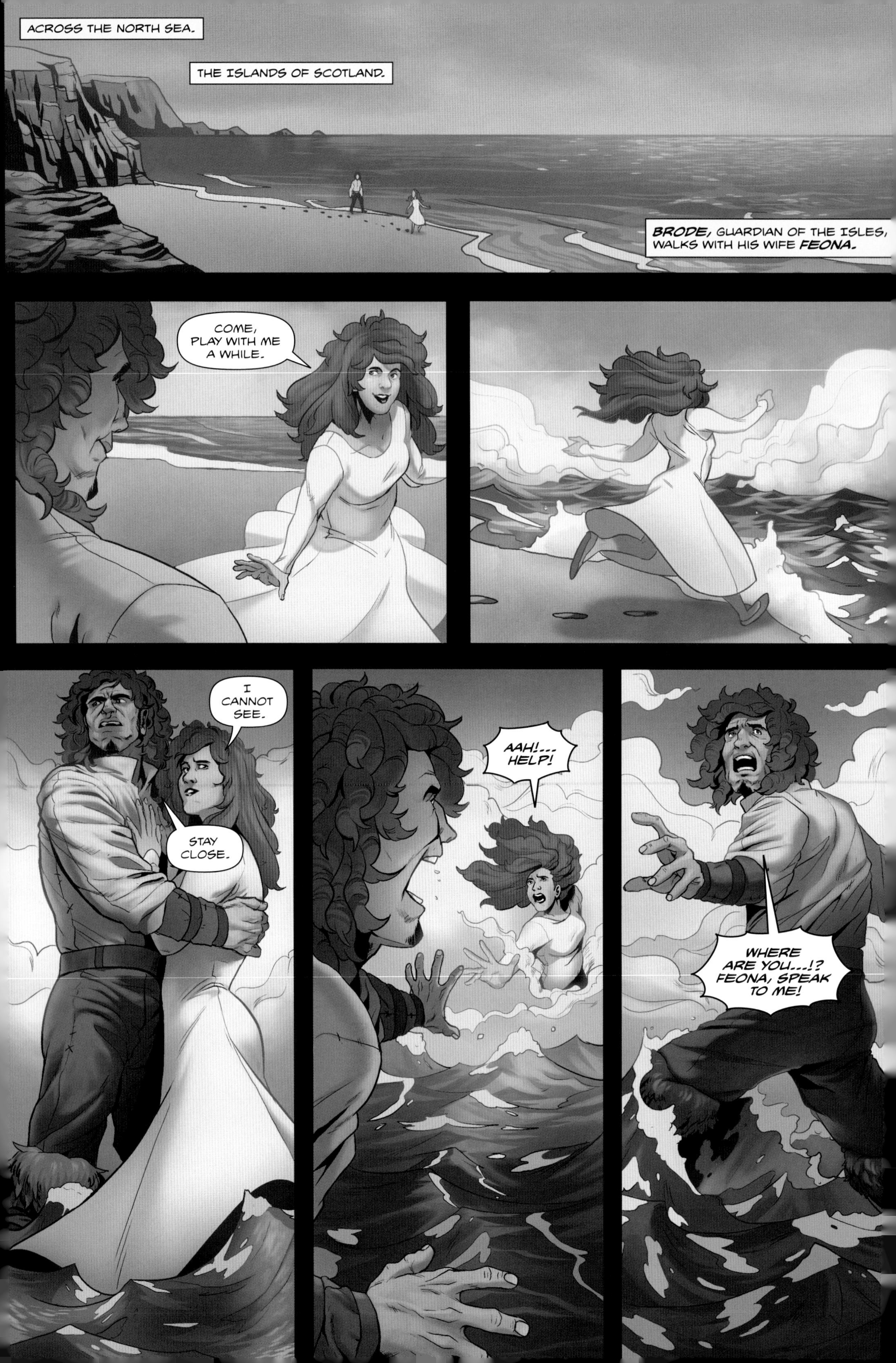
ACROSS THE NORTH SEA.
THE ISLANDS OF SCOTLAND.
BRODE, GUARDIAN OF THE ISLES, WALKS WITH HIS WIFE FEONA.
COME, PLAY WITH ME A WHILE.
I CANNOT SEE.
STAY CLOSE.
AAH!... HELP!
WHERE ARE YOU...!? FEONA, SPEAK TO ME!

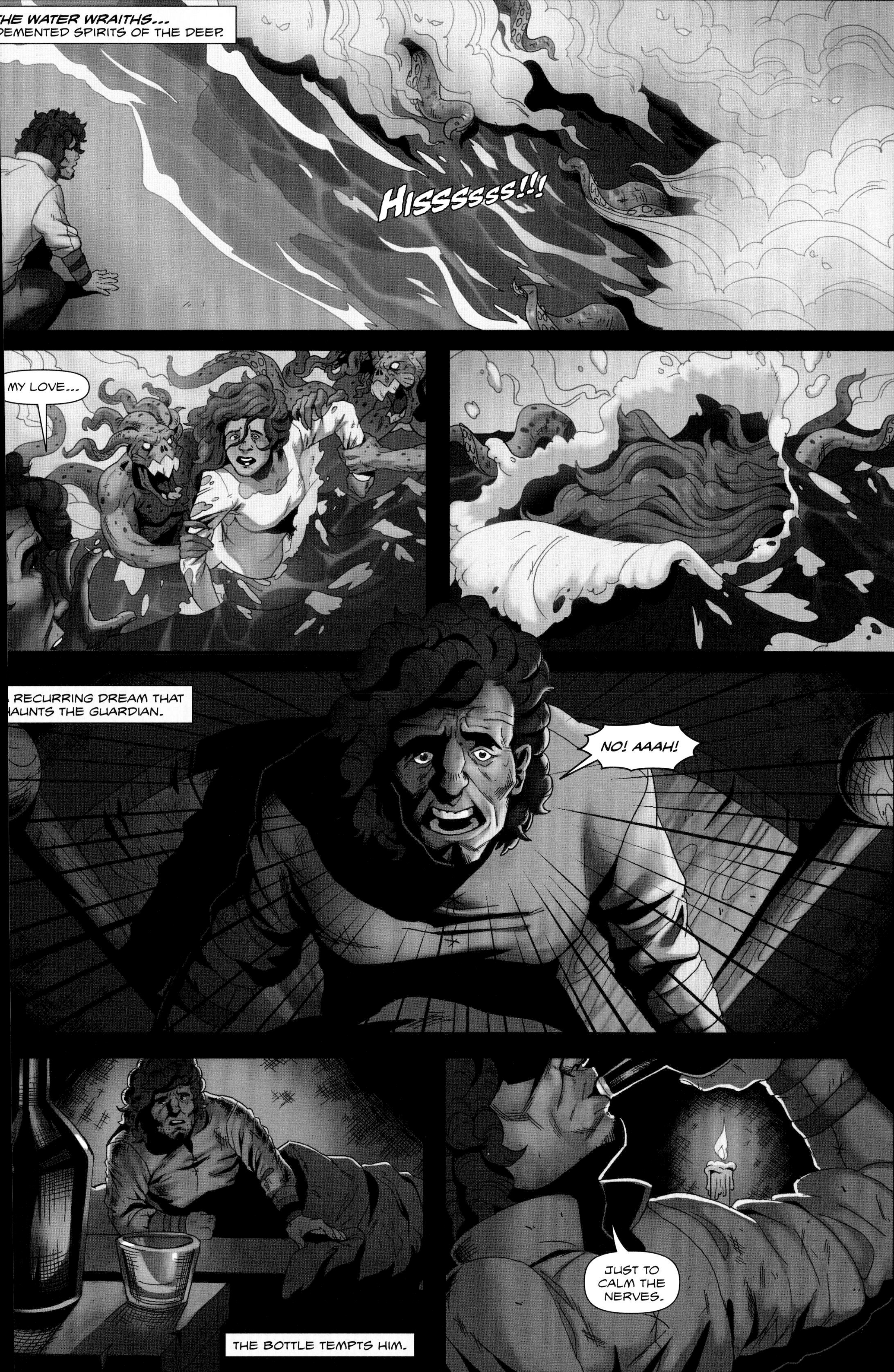
THE WATER WRAITHS...
DEMENTED SPIRITS OF THE DEEP.
HISSSSSS!!!
MY LOVE...
A RECURRING DREAM THAT HAUNTS THE GUARDIAN.
NO! AAAH!
THE BOTTLE TEMPTS HIM.
JUST TO CALM THE NERVES.

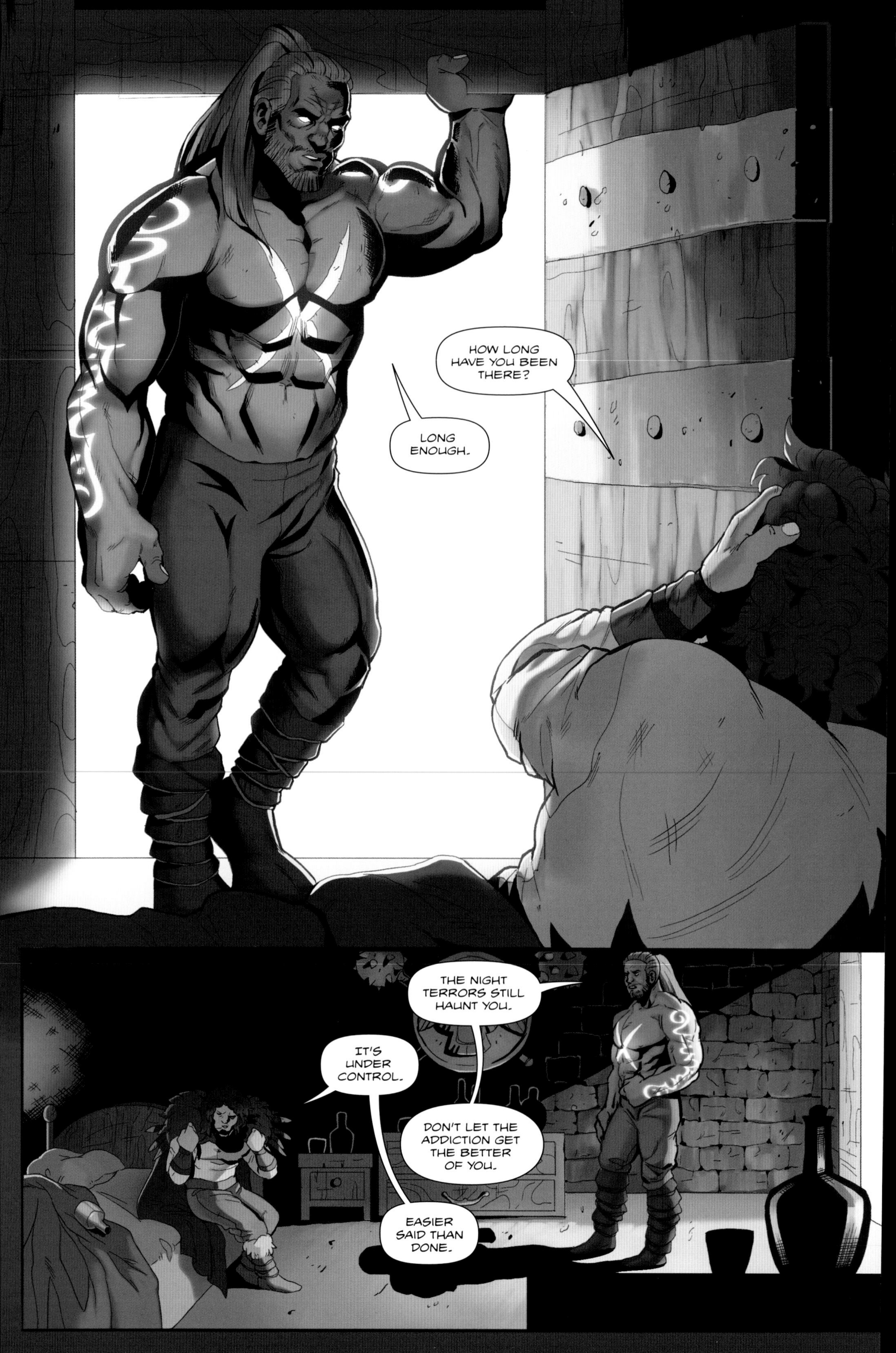
HOW LONG HAVE YOU BEEN THERE?
LONG ENOUGH.
THE NIGHT TERRORS STILL HAUNT YOU.
IT'S UNDER CONTROL.
DON'T LET THE ADDICTION GET THE BETTER OF YOU.
EASIER SAID THAN DONE.

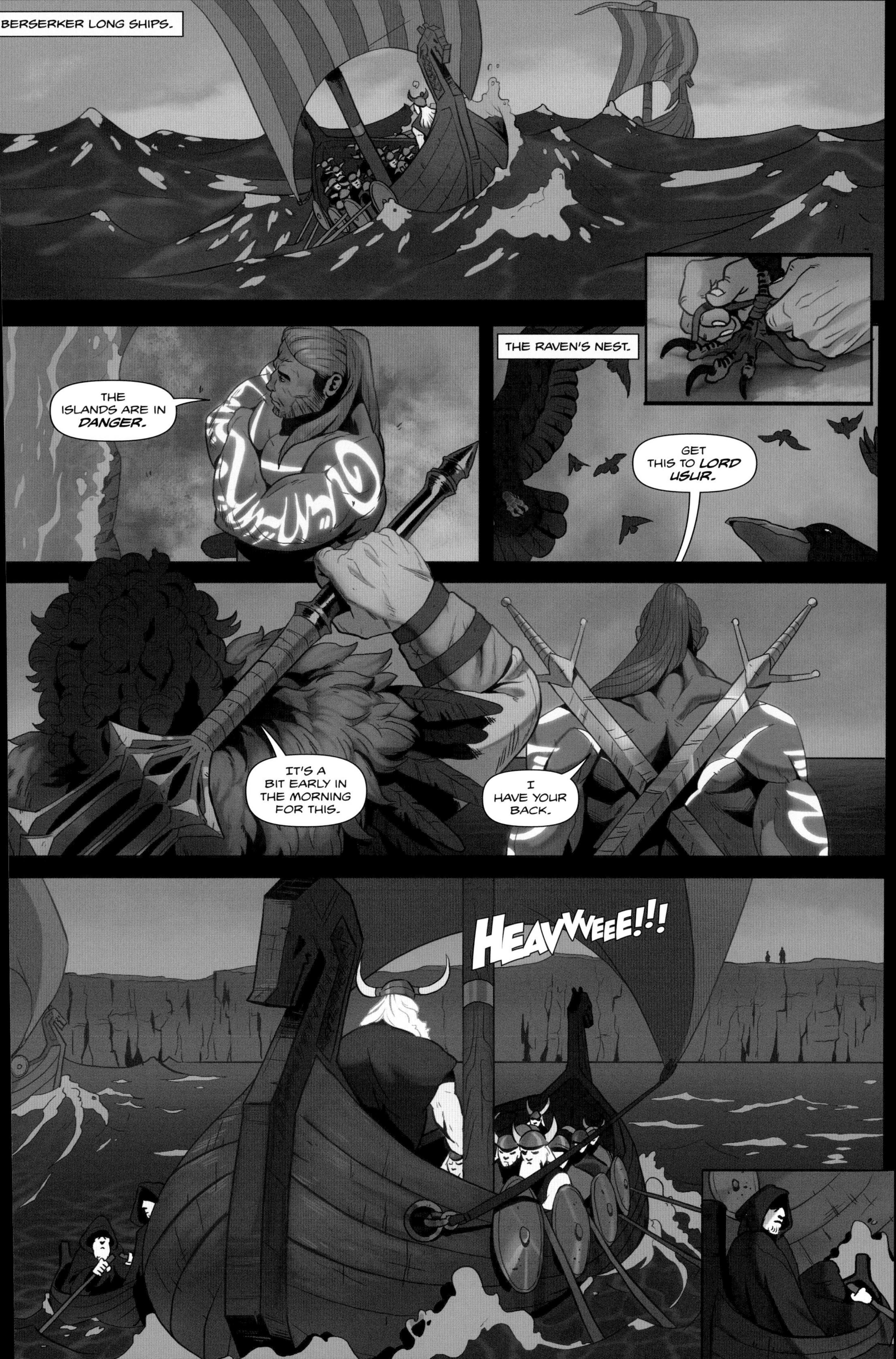
BERSERKER LONG SHIPS.
THE ISLANDS ARE IN DANGER.
THE RAVEN'S NEST.
GET THIS TO LORD USUR.
IT'S A BIT EARLY IN THE MORNING FOR THIS.
I HAVE YOUR BACK.
HEAVVVEEE!!!

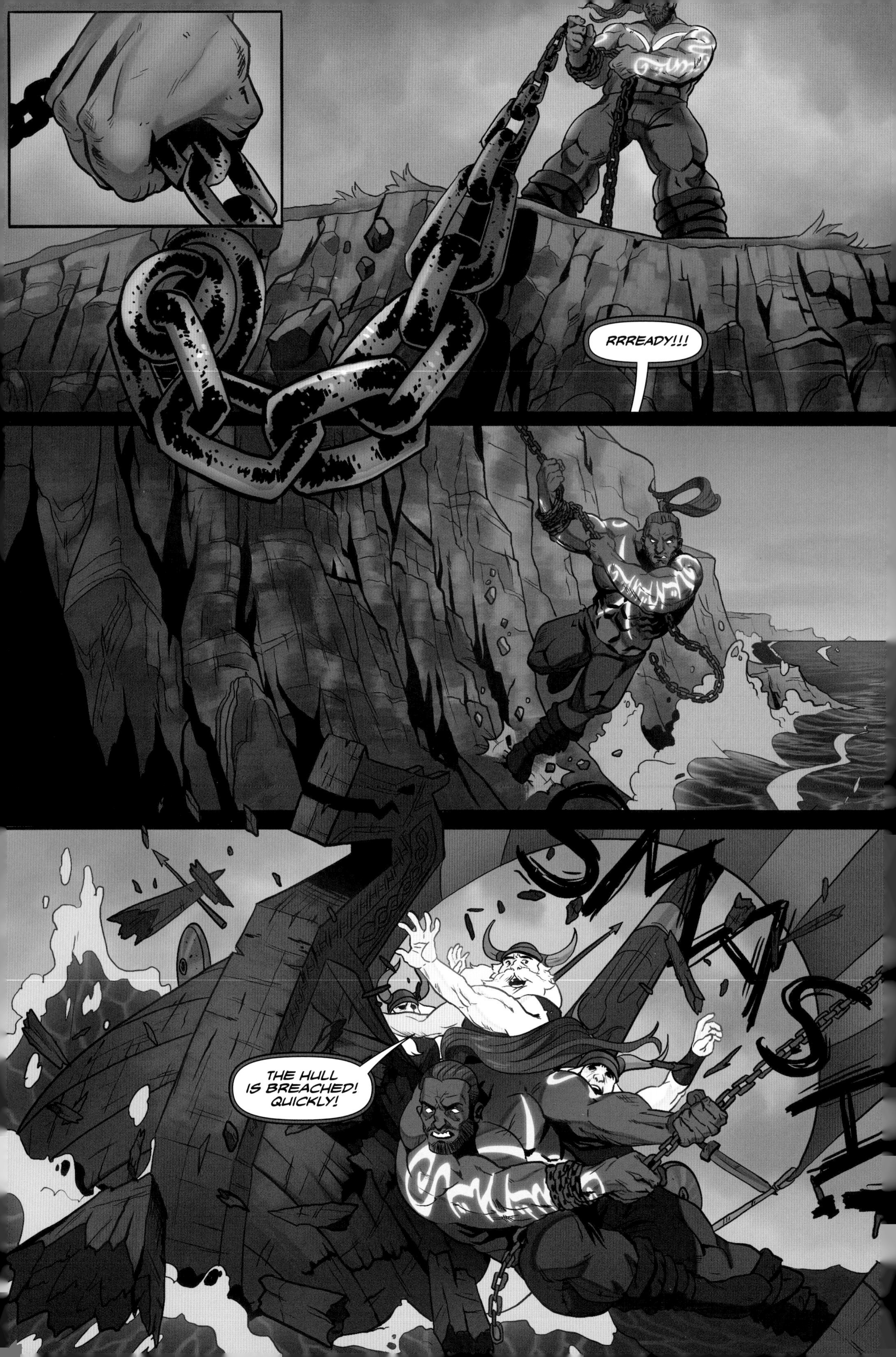
RRREADY!!!
SMASH
THE HULL IS BREACHED! QUICKLY!

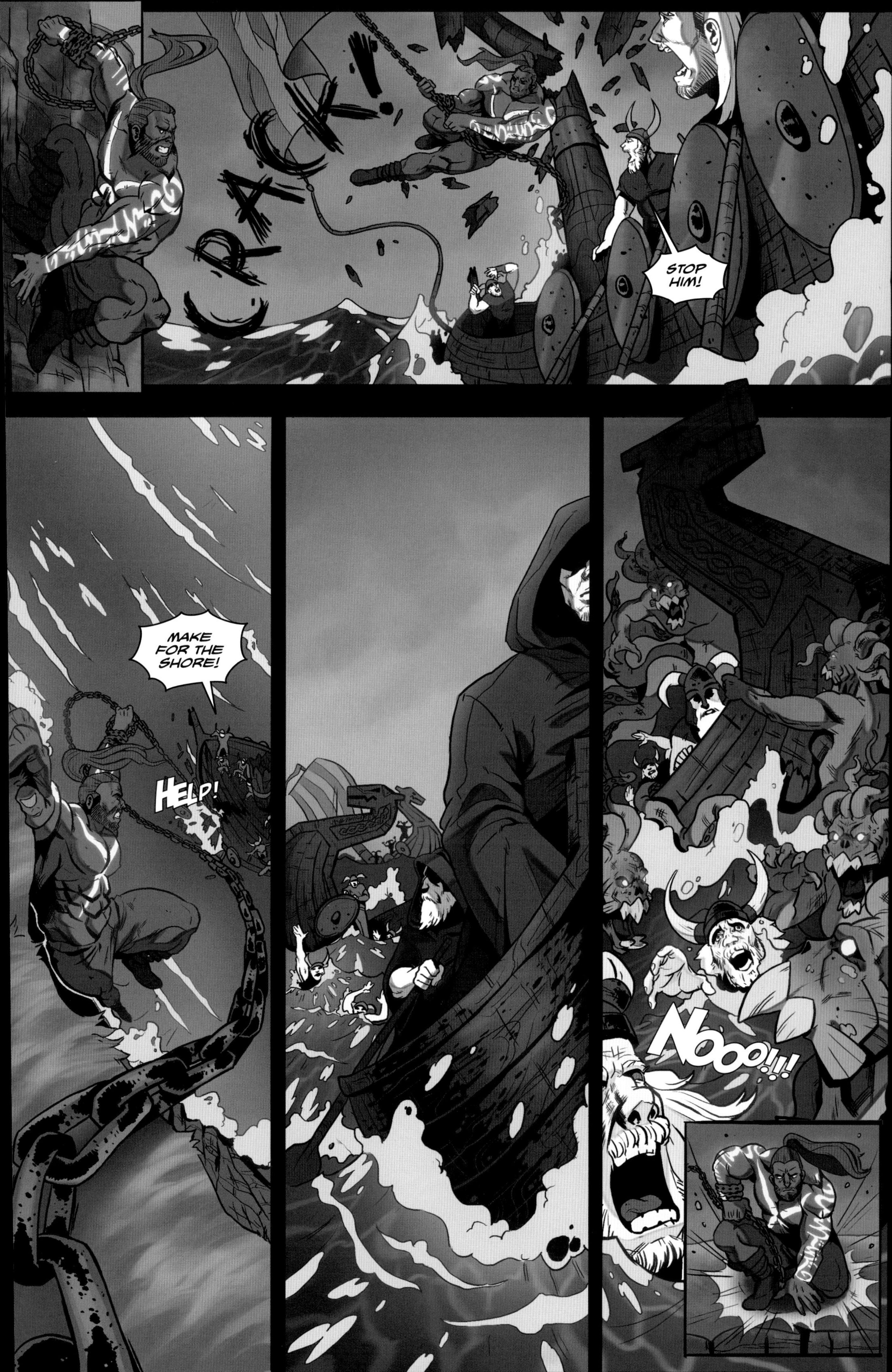
CRACK!
STOP HIM!
MAKE FOR THE SHORE!
HELP!
NOOO!!!

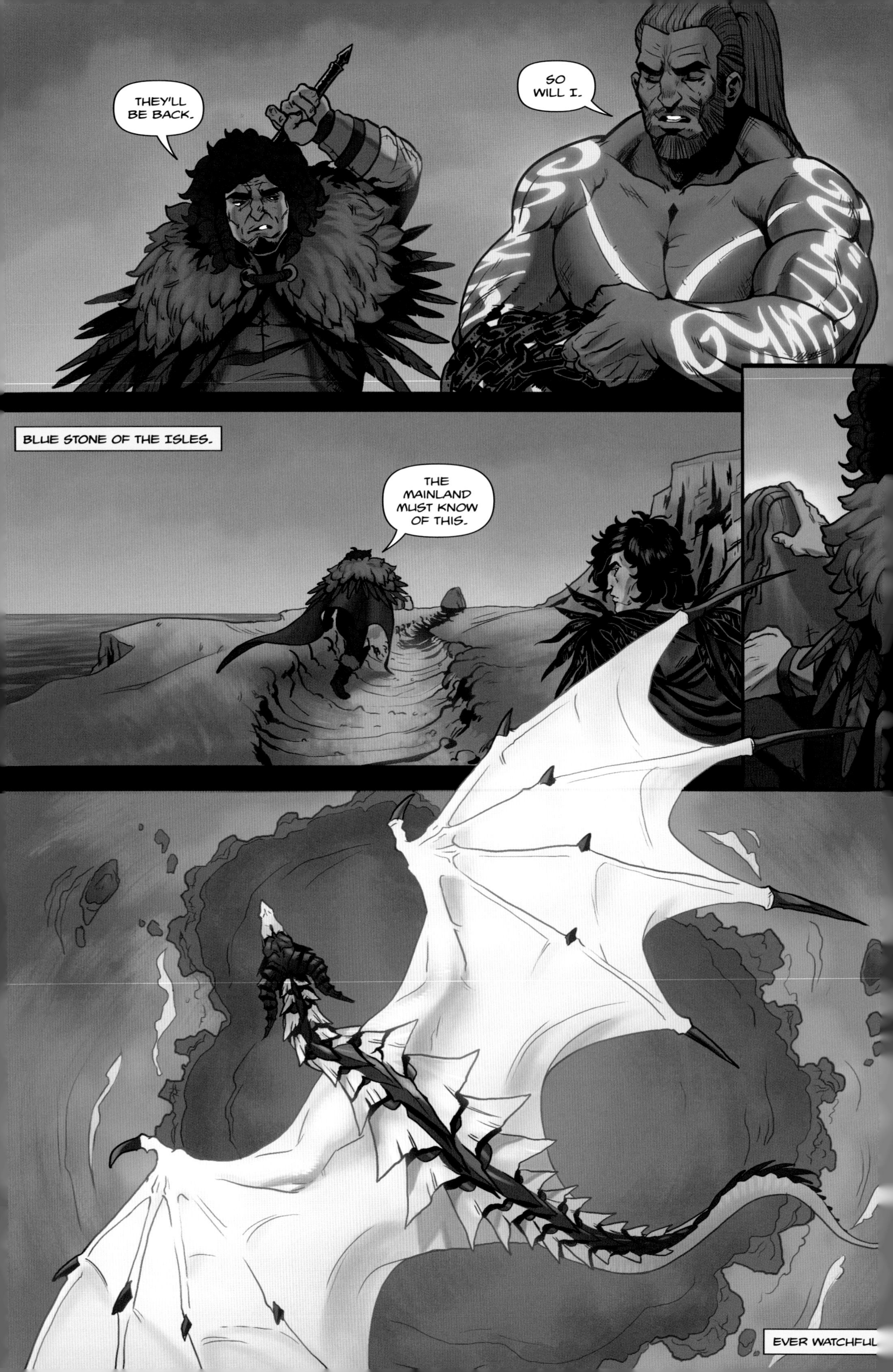
THEY'LL BE BACK.
SO WILL I.
BLUE STONE OF THE ISLES.
THE MAINLAND MUST KNOW OF THIS.
EVER WATCHFUL

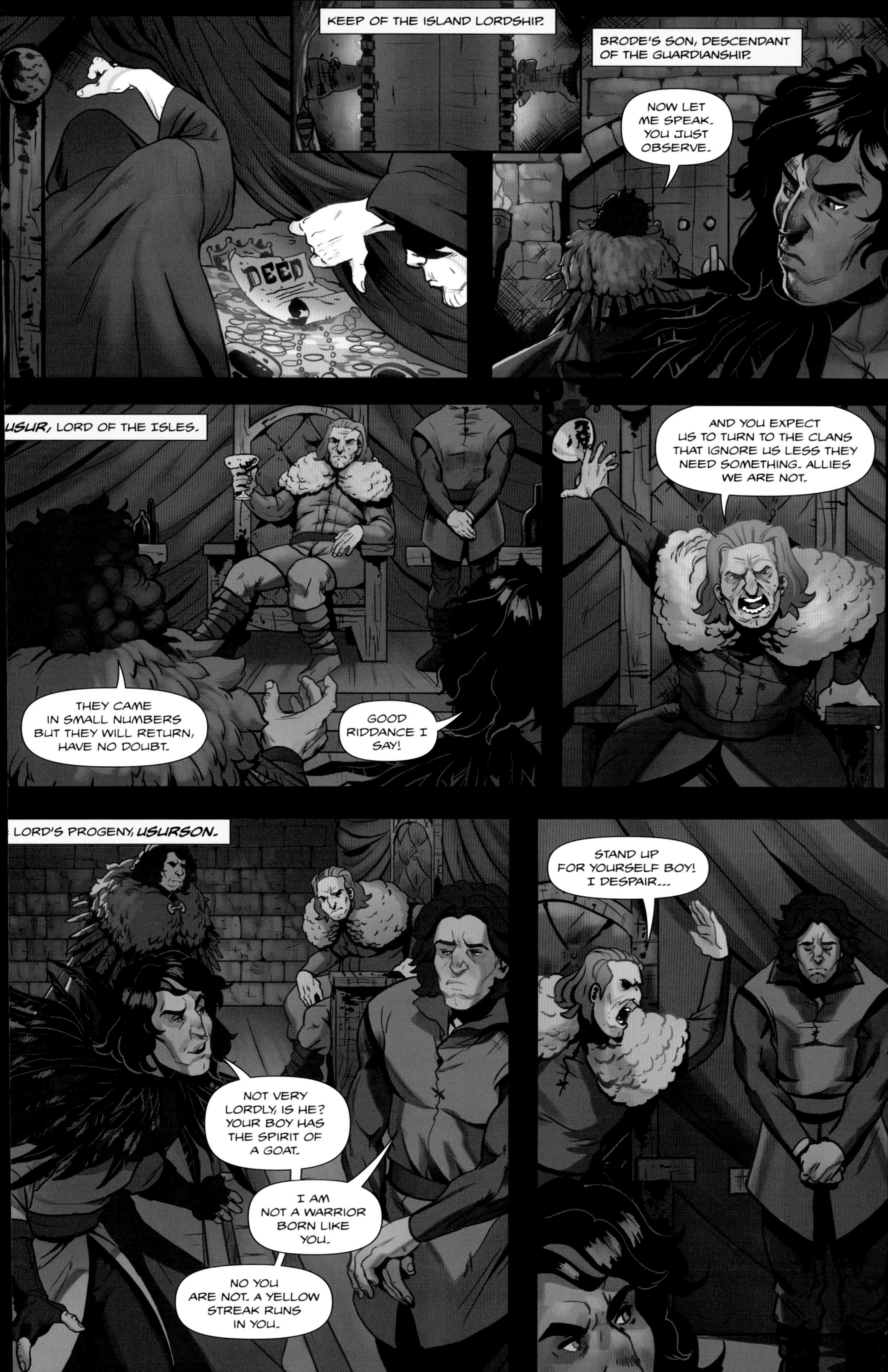
KEEP OF THE ISLAND LORDSHIP.
BRODE'S SON, DESCENDANT OF THE GUARDIANSHIP.
NOW LET ME SPEAK. YOU JUST OBSERVE.
USUR, LORD OF THE ISLES.
THEY CAME IN SMALL NUMBERS BUT THEY WILL RETURN, HAVE NO DOUBT.
GOOD RIDDANCE I SAY!
AND YOU EXPECT US TO TURN TO THE CLANS THAT IGNORE US LESS THEY NEED SOMETHING. ALLIES WE ARE NOT.
LORD'S PROGENY, USURSON.
NOT VERY LORDLY, IS HE? YOUR BOY HAS THE SPIRIT OF A GOAT.
I AM NOT A WARRIOR BORN LIKE YOU.
NO YOU ARE NOT. A YELLOW STREAK RUNS IN YOU.
STAND UP FOR YOURSELF BOY! I DESPAIR...

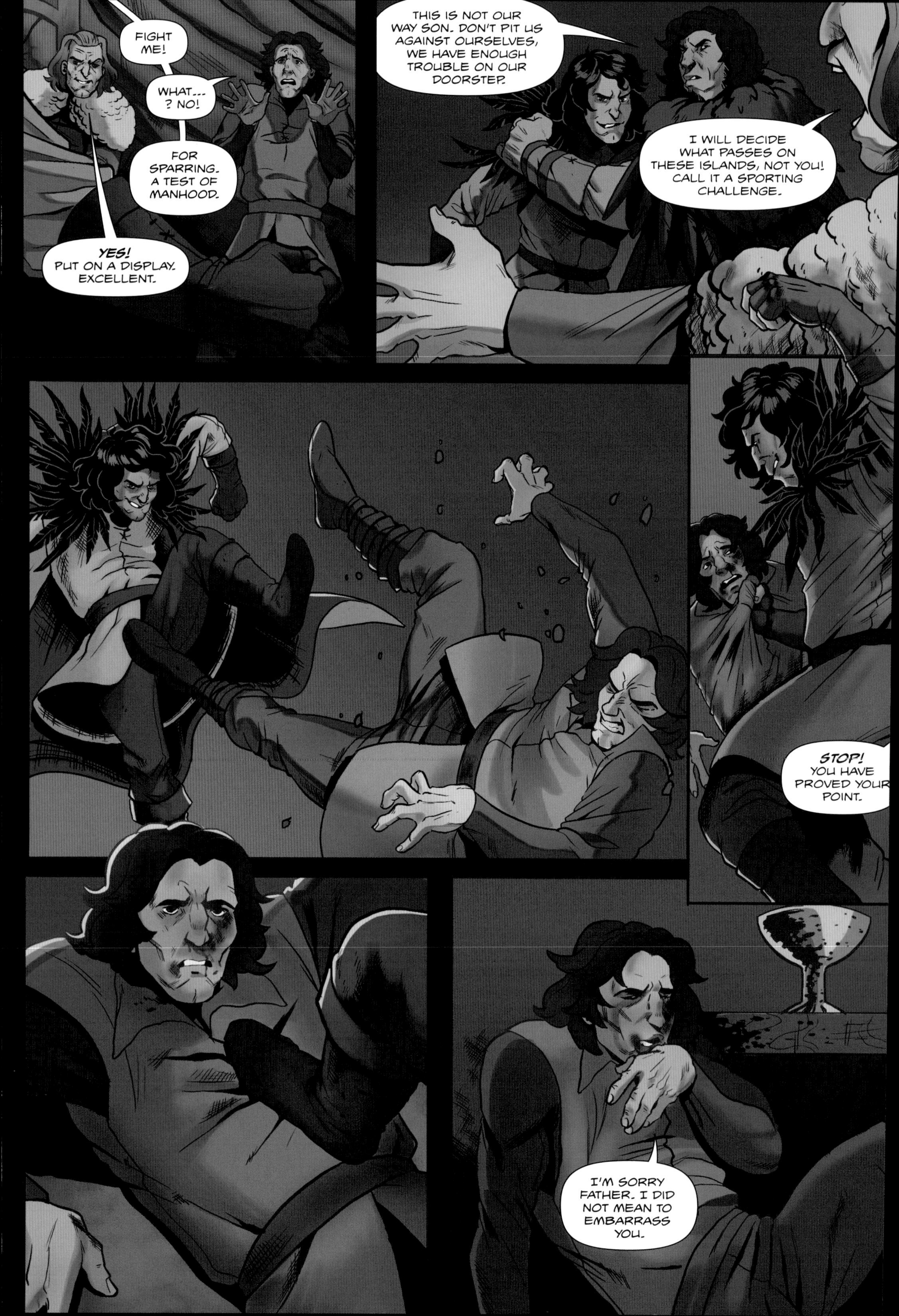
FIGHT ME!
WHAT... ? NO!
FOR SPARRING. A TEST OF MANHOOD.
YES! PUT ON A DISPLAY. EXCELLENT.
THIS IS NOT OUR WAY SON. DON'T PIT US AGAINST OURSELVES, WE HAVE ENOUGH TROUBLE ON OUR DOORSTEP.
I WILL DECIDE WHAT PASSES ON THESE ISLANDS, NOT YOU! CALL IT A SPORTING CHALLENGE.
STOP! YOU HAVE PROVED YOUR POINT.
I'M SORRY FATHER. I DID NOT MEAN TO EMBARRASS YOU.

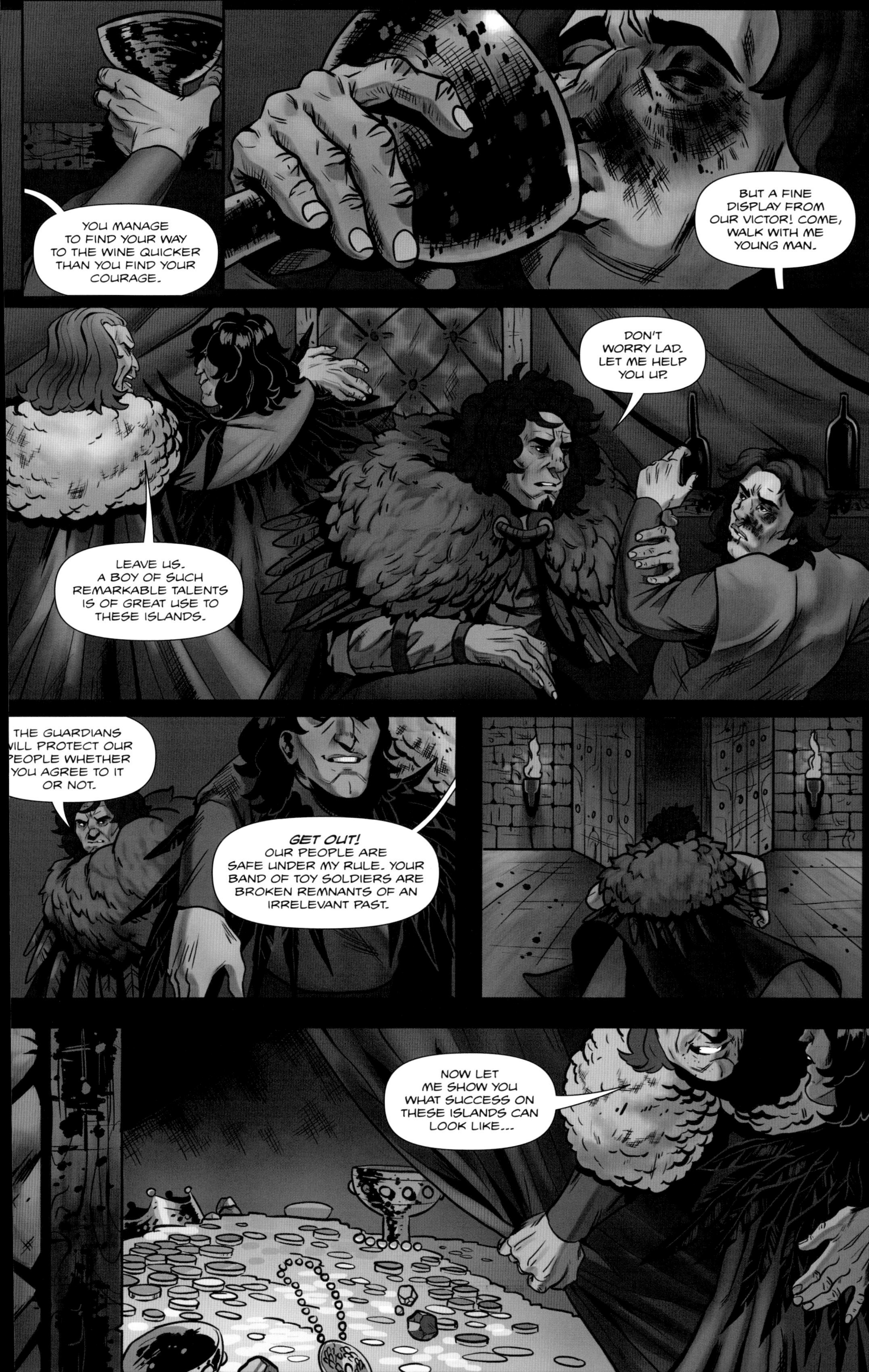
YOU MANAGE TO FIND YOUR WAY TO THE WINE QUICKER THAN YOU FIND YOUR COURAGE.
BUT A FINE DISPLAY FROM OUR VICTOR! COME, WALK WITH ME YOUNG MAN.
LEAVE US. A BOY OF SUCH REMARKABLE TALENTS IS OF GREAT USE TO THESE ISLANDS.
DON'T WORRY LAD. LET ME HELP YOU UP.
THE GUARDIANS WILL PROTECT OUR PEOPLE WHETHER YOU AGREE TO IT OR NOT.
GET OUT! OUR PEOPLE ARE SAFE UNDER MY RULE. YOUR BAND OF TOY SOLDIERS ARE BROKEN REMNANTS OF AN IRRELEVANT PAST.
NOW LET ME SHOW YOU WHAT SUCCESS ON THESE ISLANDS CAN LOOK LIKE...

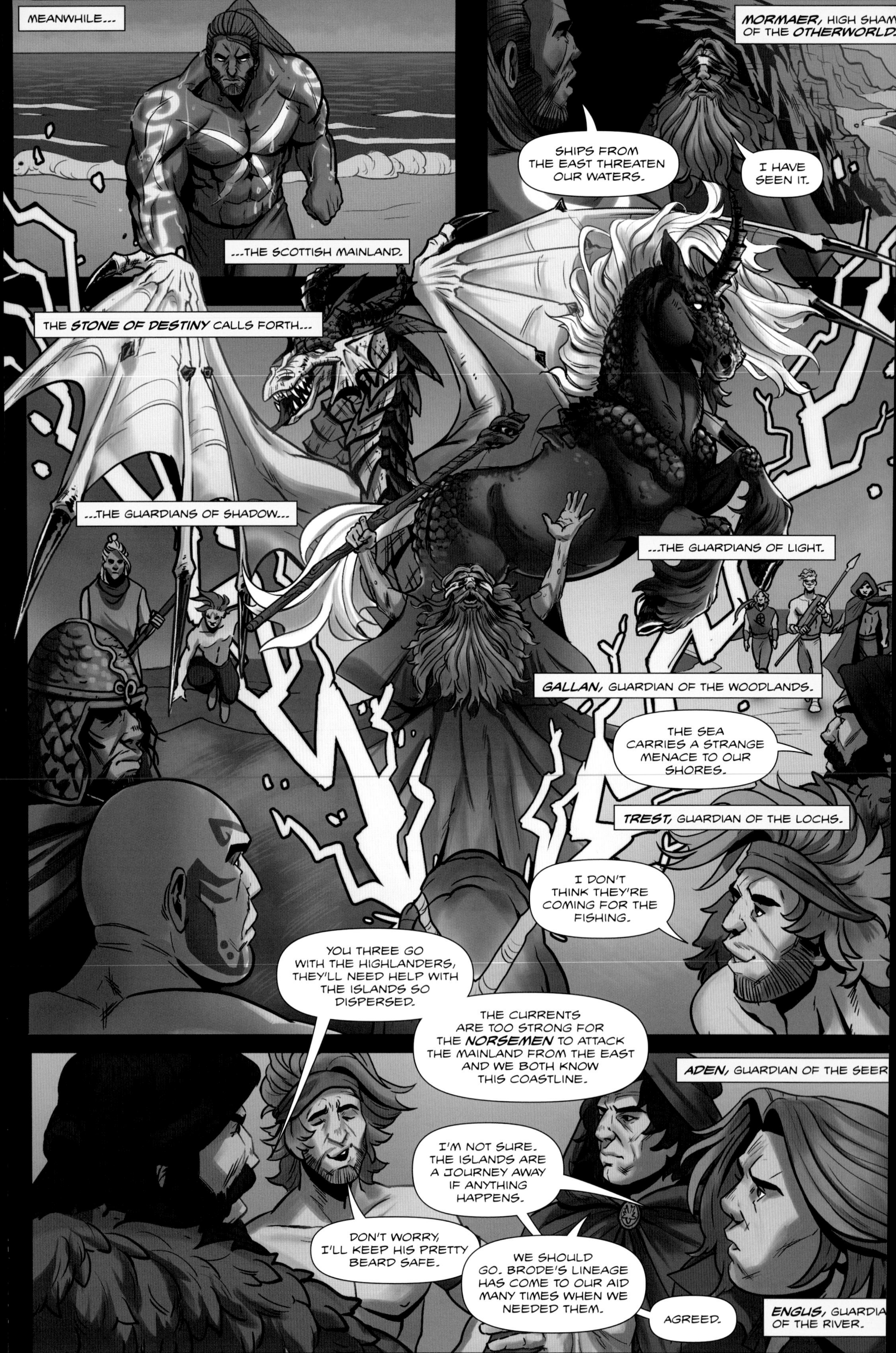
MEANWHILE...
...THE SCOTTISH MAINLAND.
MORMAER, HIGH SHAM
OF THE OTHERWORLD.
SHIPS FROM THE EAST THREATEN OUR WATERS.
I HAVE SEEN IT.
THE STONE OF DESTINY CALLS FORTH...
...THE GUARDIANS OF SHADOW...
...THE GUARDIANS OF LIGHT.
GALLAN, GUARDIAN OF THE WOODLANDS.
THE SEA CARRIES A STRANGE MENACE TO OUR SHORES.
TREST, GUARDIAN OF THE LOCHS.
I DON'T THINK THEY'RE COMING FOR THE FISHING.
YOU THREE GO WITH THE HIGHLANDERS, THEY'LL NEED HELP WITH THE ISLANDS SO DISPERSED.
THE CURRENTS ARE TOO STRONG FOR THE NORSEMEN TO ATTACK THE MAINLAND FROM THE EAST AND WE BOTH KNOW THIS COASTLINE.
ADEN, GUARDIAN OF THE SEER
I'M NOT SURE. THE ISLANDS ARE A JOURNEY AWAY IF ANYTHING HAPPENS.
DON'T WORRY, I'LL KEEP HIS PRETTY BEARD SAFE.
WE SHOULD GO. BRODE'S LINEAGE HAS COME TO OUR AID MANY TIMES WHEN WE NEEDED THEM.
AGREED.
ENGUS, GUARDIA
OF THE RIVER.

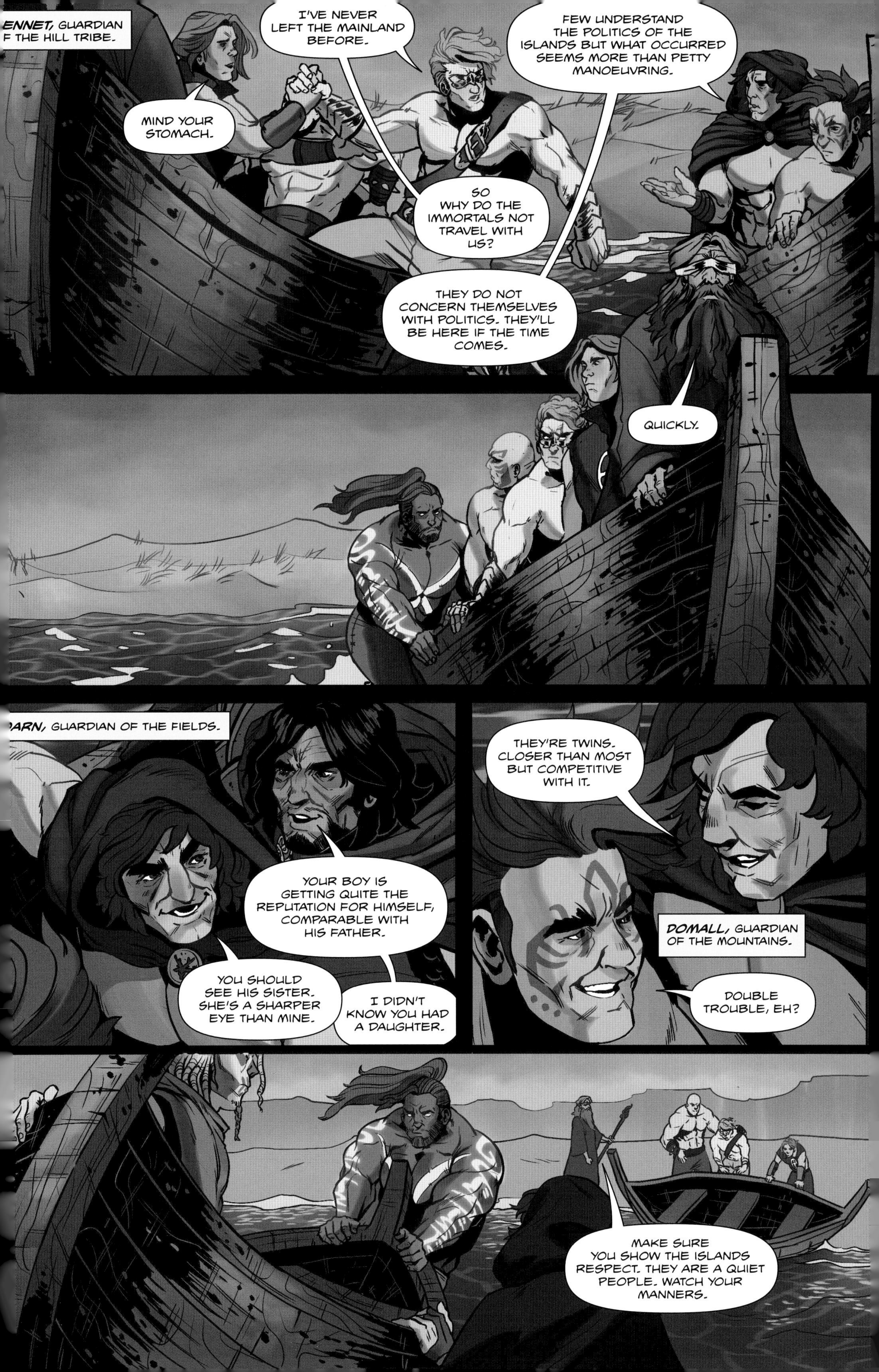
ENNET, GUARDIAN
F THE HILL TRIBE.
I'VE NEVER LEFT THE MAINLAND BEFORE.
MIND YOUR STOMACH.
FEW UNDERSTAND THE POLITICS OF THE ISLANDS BUT WHAT OCCURRED SEEMS MORE THAN PETTY MANOEUVRING.
SO WHY DO THE IMMORTALS NOT TRAVEL WITH US?
THEY DO NOT CONCERN THEMSELVES WITH POLITICS. THEY'LL BE HERE IF THE TIME COMES.
QUICKLY.
ARN, GUARDIAN OF THE FIELDS.
YOUR BOY IS GETTING QUITE THE REPUTATION FOR HIMSELF, COMPARABLE WITH HIS FATHER.
YOU SHOULD SEE HIS SISTER. SHE'S A SHARPER EYE THAN MINE.
I DIDN'T KNOW YOU HAD A DAUGHTER.
THEY'RE TWINS. CLOSER THAN MOST BUT COMPETITIVE WITH IT.
DOMALL, GUARDIAN OF THE MOUNTAINS.
DOUBLE TROUBLE, EH?
MAKE SURE YOU SHOW THE ISLANDS RESPECT. THEY ARE A QUIET PEOPLE. WATCH YOUR MANNERS.

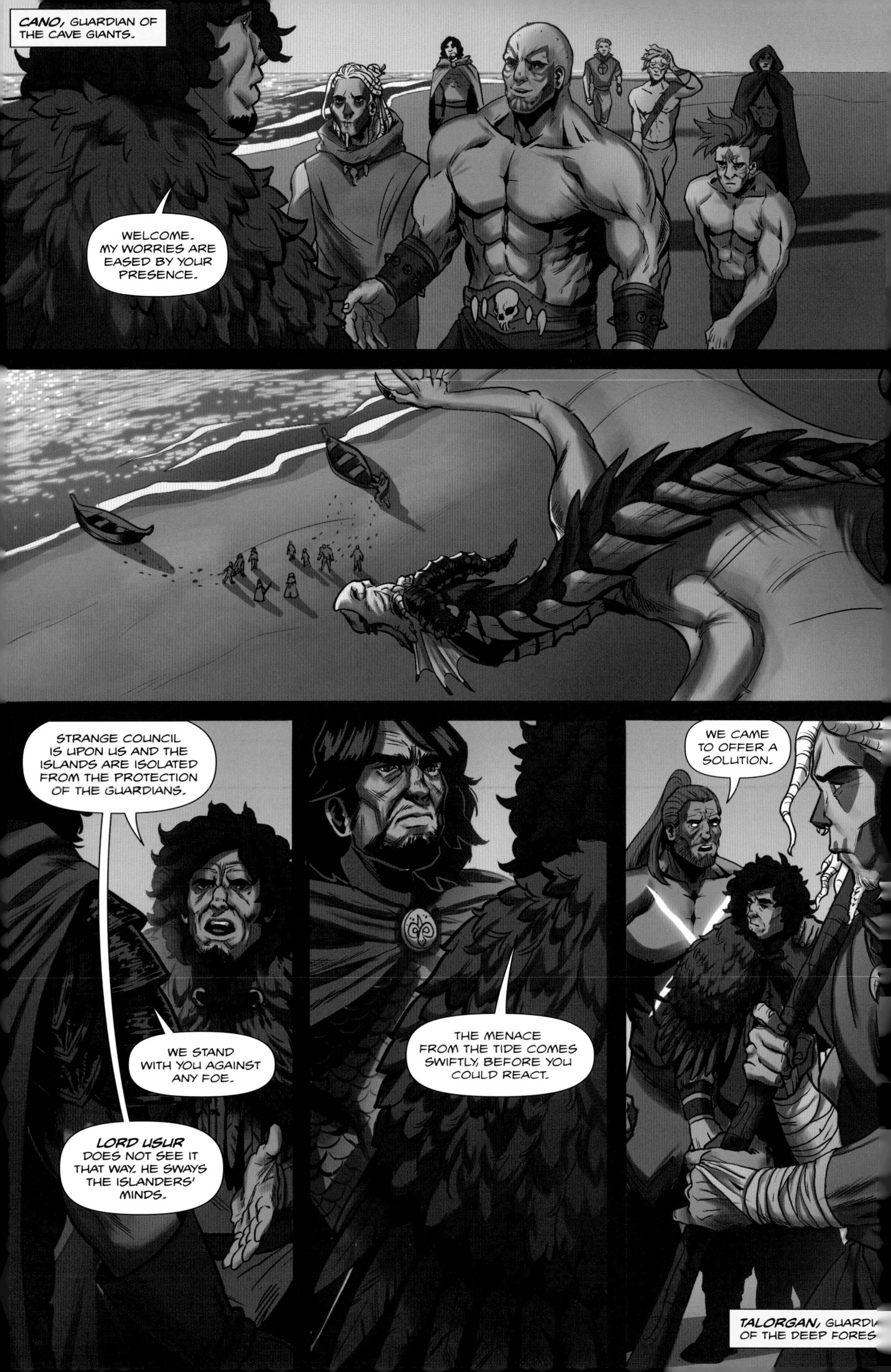
CANO, GUARDIAN OF THE CAVE GIANTS.
WELCOME. MY WORRIES ARE EASED BY YOUR PRESENCE.
STRANGE COUNCIL IS UPON US AND THE ISLANDS ARE ISOLATED FROM THE PROTECTION OF THE GUARDIANS.
LORD USUR DOES NOT SEE IT THAT WAY. HE SWAYS THE ISLANDERS' MINDS.
WE STAND WITH YOU AGAINST ANY FOE.
THE MENACE FROM THE TIDE COMES SWIFTLY, BEFORE YOU COULD REACT.
WE CAME TO OFFER A SOLUTION.
TALORGAN, GUARDI
OF THE DEEP FORES

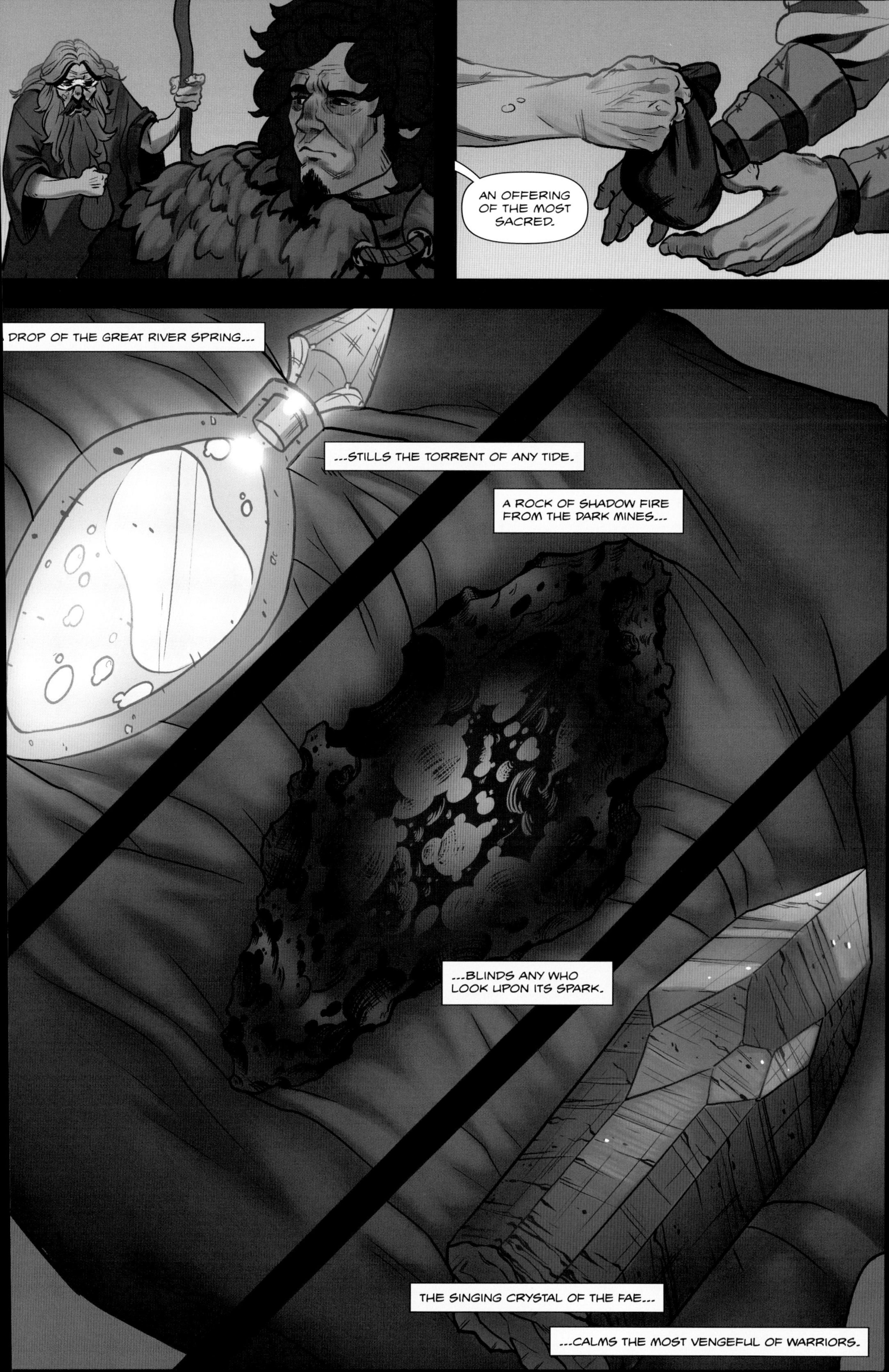
AN OFFERING OF THE MOST SACRED.
A DROP OF THE GREAT RIVER SPRING...
...STILLS THE TORRENT OF ANY TIDE.
A ROCK OF SHADOW FIRE FROM THE DARK MINES...
...BLINDS ANY WHO LOOK UPON ITS SPARK.
THE SINGING CRYSTAL OF THE FAE...
...CALMS THE MOST VENGEFUL OF WARRIORS.

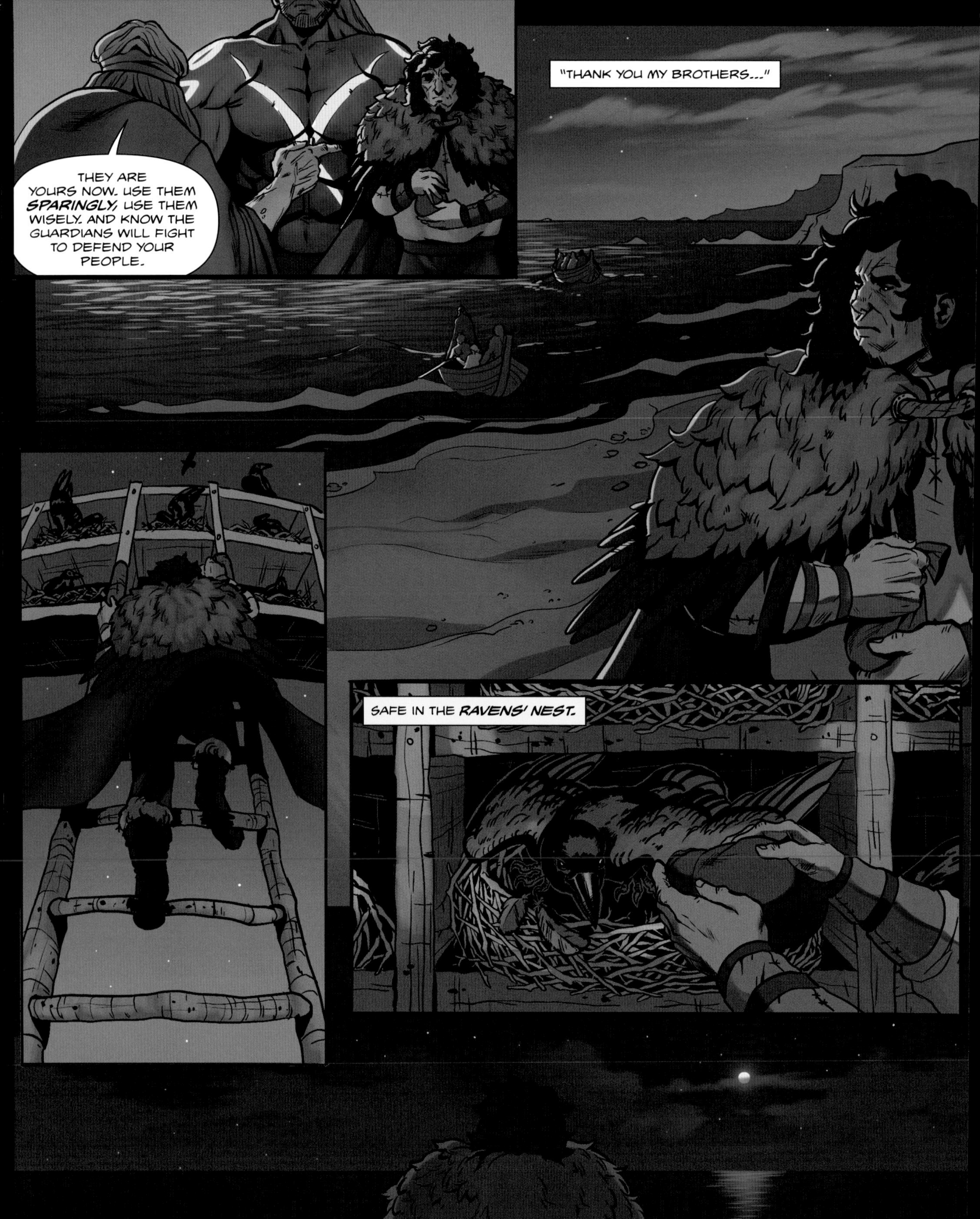
THEY ARE YOURS NOW. USE THEM SPARINGLY, USE THEM WISELY. AND KNOW THE GUARDIANS WILL FIGHT TO DEFEND YOUR PEOPLE.
"THANK YOU MY BROTHERS..."
SAFE IN THE RAVENS' NEST.

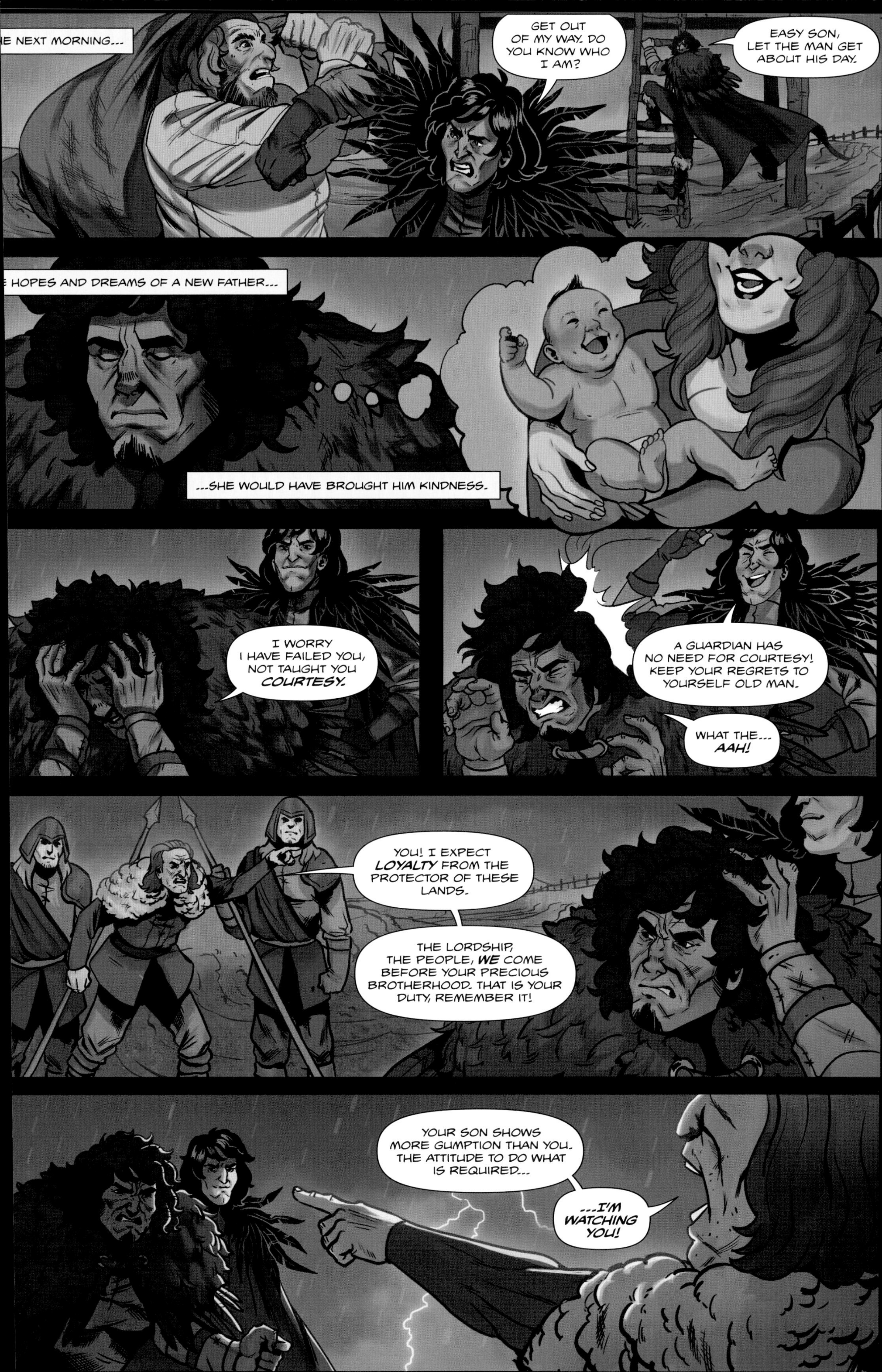
HE NEXT MORNING...
GET OUT OF MY WAY. DO YOU KNOW WHO I AM?
EASY SON, LET THE MAN GET ABOUT HIS DAY.
E HOPES AND DREAMS OF A NEW FATHER...
...SHE WOULD HAVE BROUGHT HIM KINDNESS.
I WORRY I HAVE FAILED YOU, NOT TAUGHT YOU COURTESY.
A GUARDIAN HAS NO NEED FOR COURTESY! KEEP YOUR REGRETS TO YOURSELF OLD MAN.
WHAT THE... AAH!
YOU! I EXPECT LOYALTY FROM THE PROTECTOR OF THESE LANDS.
THE LORDSHIP, THE PEOPLE, WE COME BEFORE YOUR PRECIOUS BROTHERHOOD. THAT IS YOUR DUTY, REMEMBER IT!
YOUR SON SHOWS MORE GUMPTION THAN YOU. THE ATTITUDE TO DO WHAT IS REQUIRED...
...I'M WATCHING YOU!

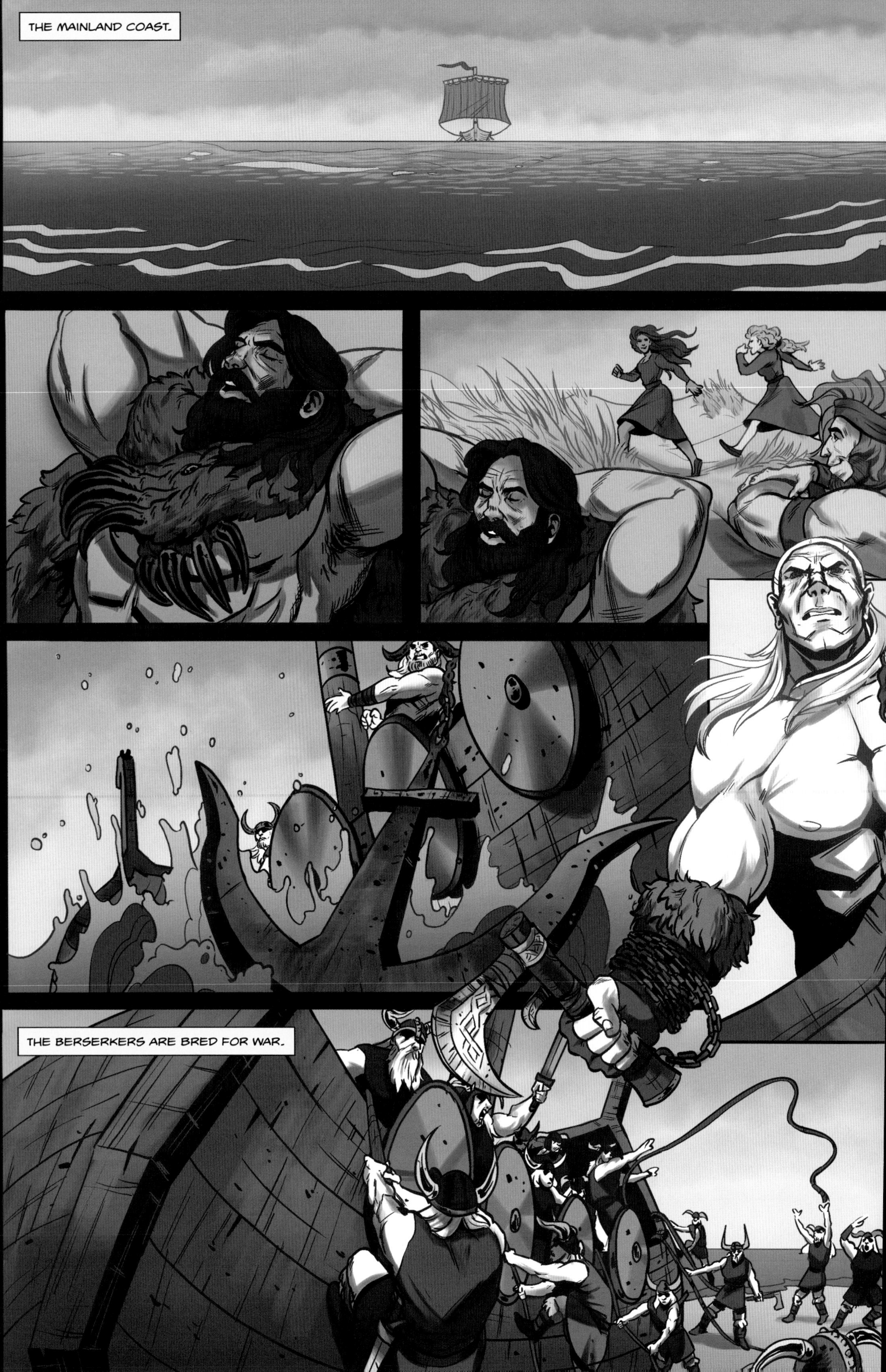
THE MAINLAND COAST.
THE BERSERKERS ARE BRED FOR WAR.

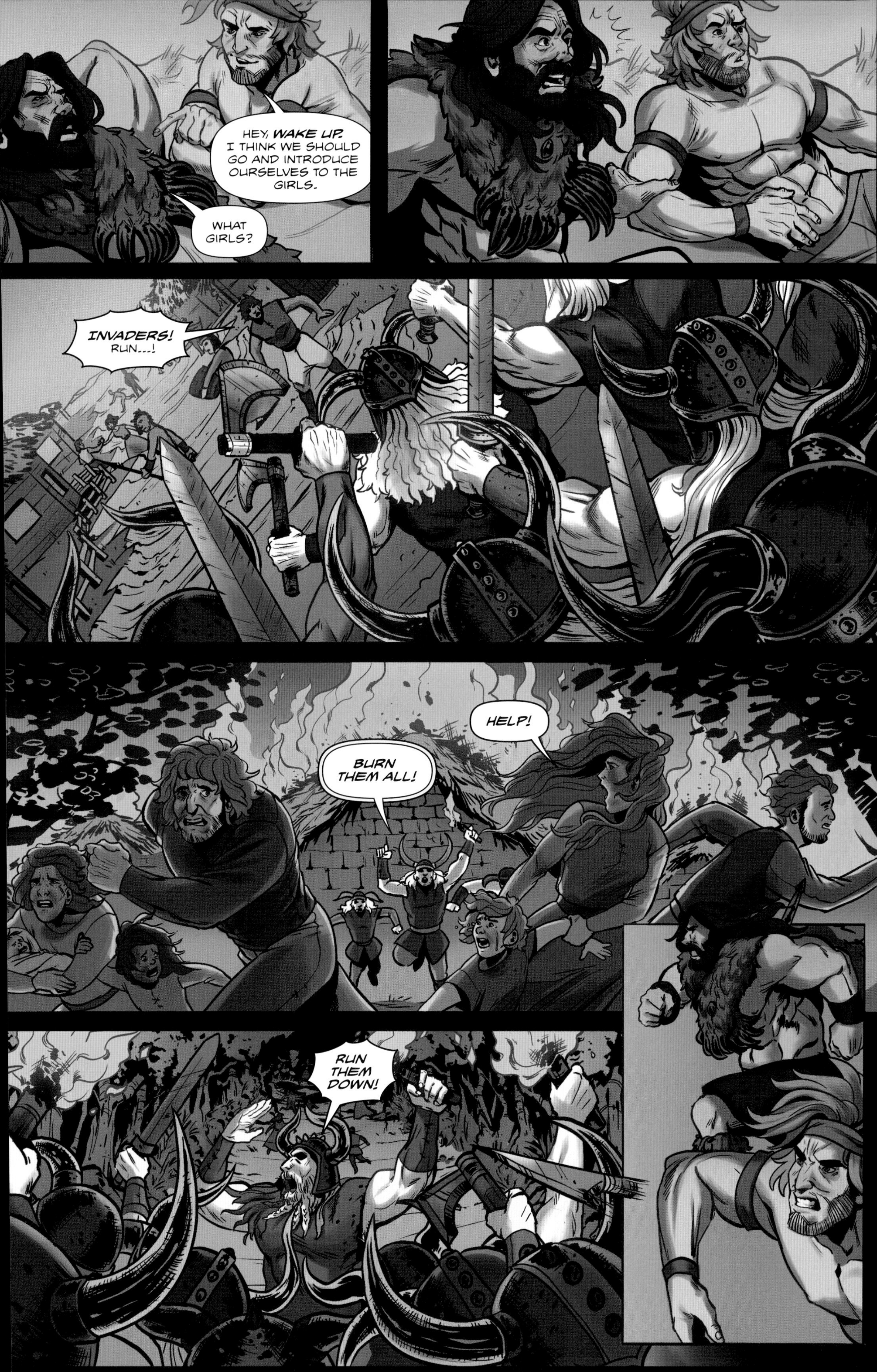
HEY, WAKE UP. I THINK WE SHOULD GO AND INTRODUCE OURSELVES TO THE GIRLS.
WHAT GIRLS?
INVADERS! RUN...!
HELP!
BURN THEM ALL!
RUN THEM DOWN!

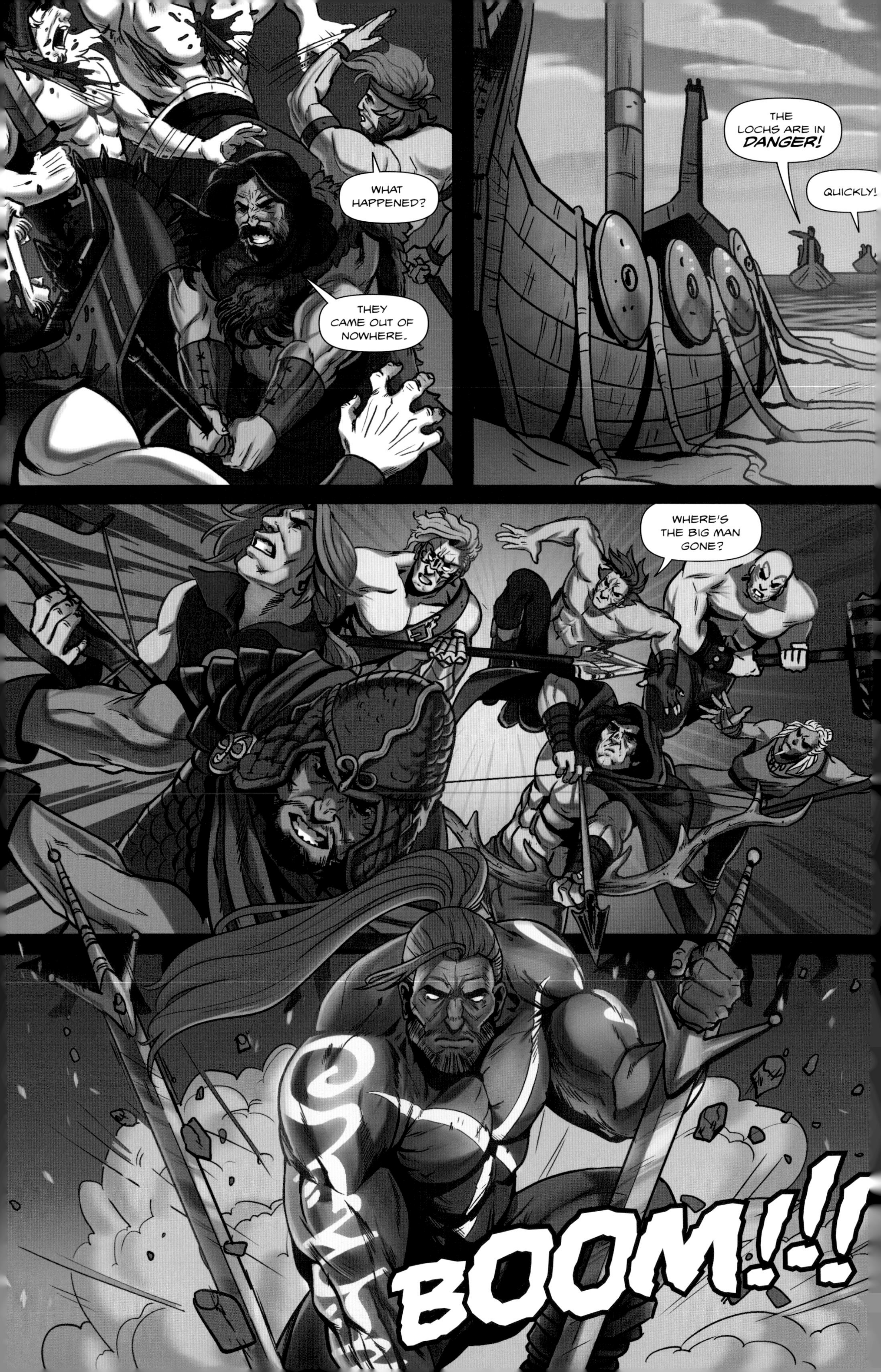
WHAT HAPPENED?
THEY CAME OUT OF NOWHERE.
THE LOCHS ARE IN DANGER!
QUICKLY!
WHERE'S THE BIG MAN GONE?
BOOM!!!

Chapter Two

Script: John Ferguson
Art: Lydia Praamsma
Colours: Kasey Schiavone
Letters: Phillip Vaughan
Editor: Clare Ferguson

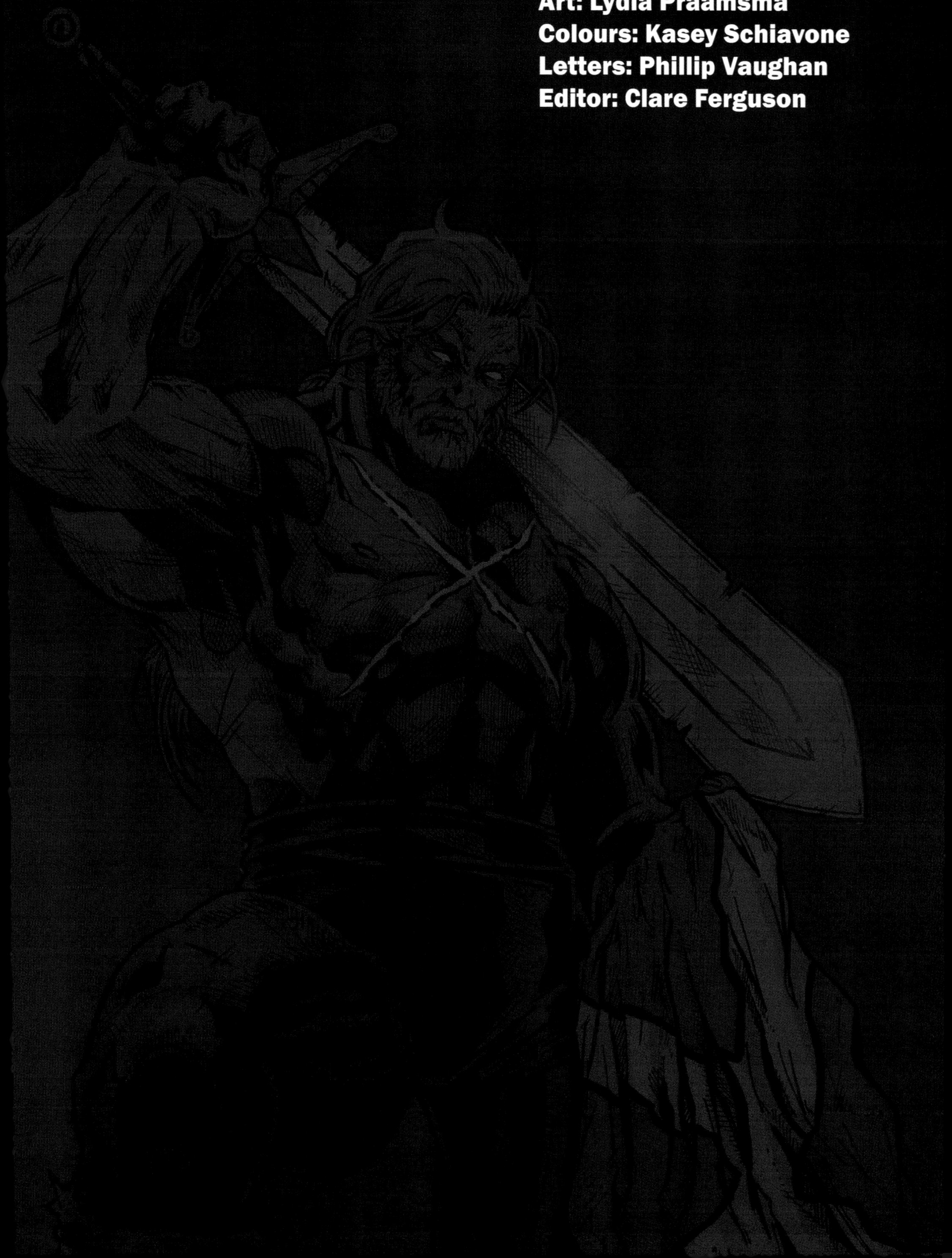

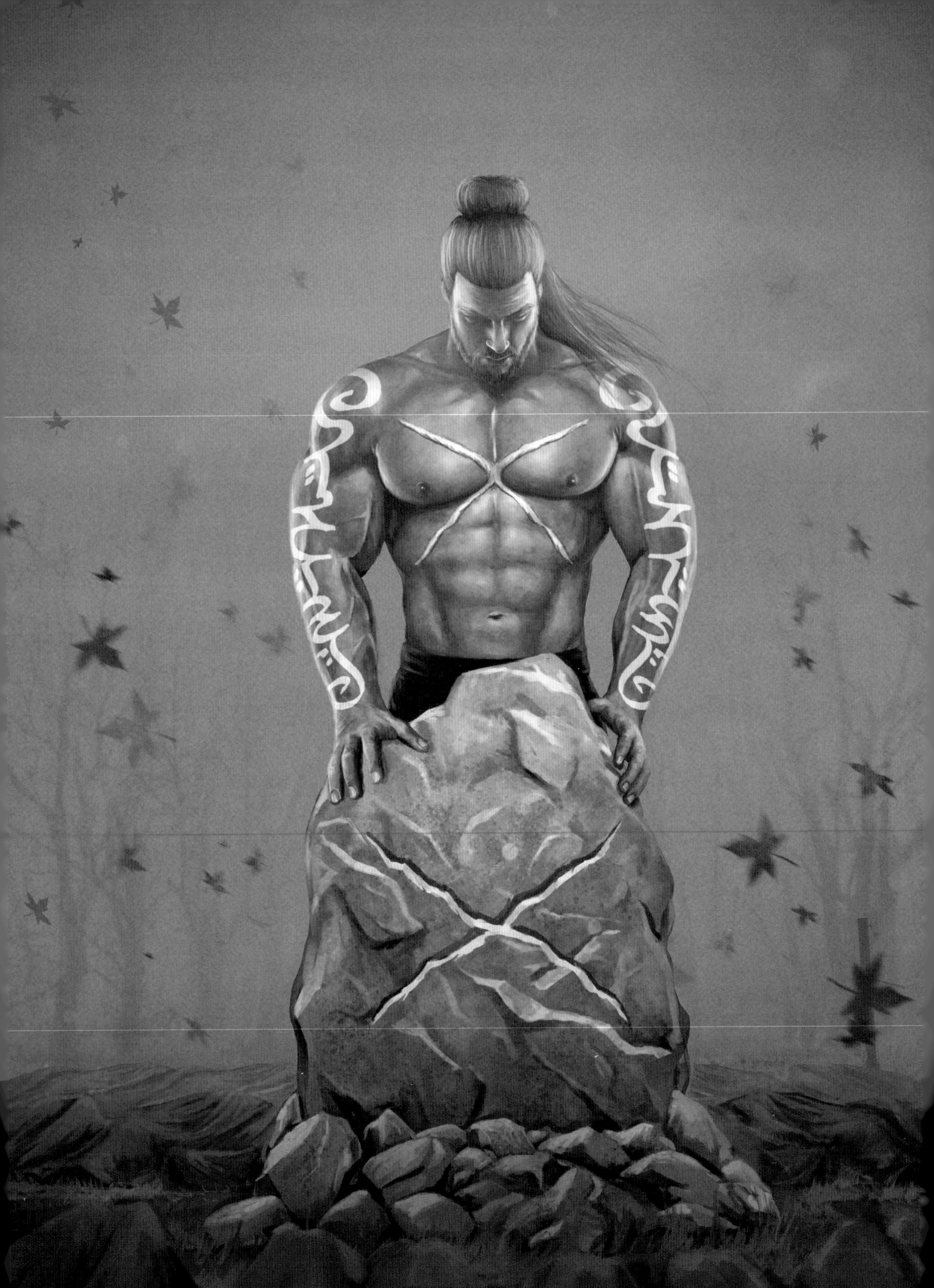

CHAPTER 2

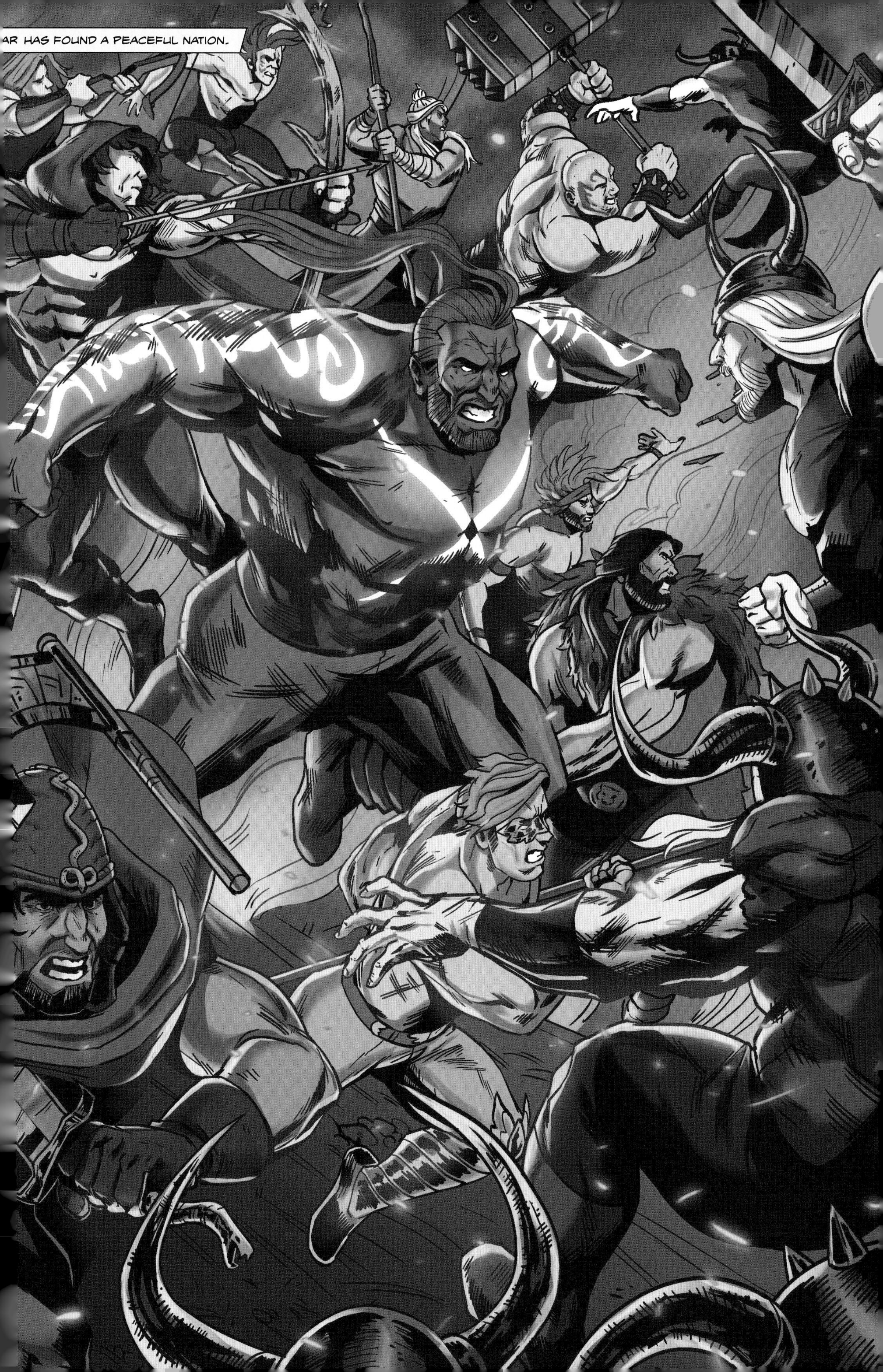
AR HAS FOUND A PEACEFUL NATION.

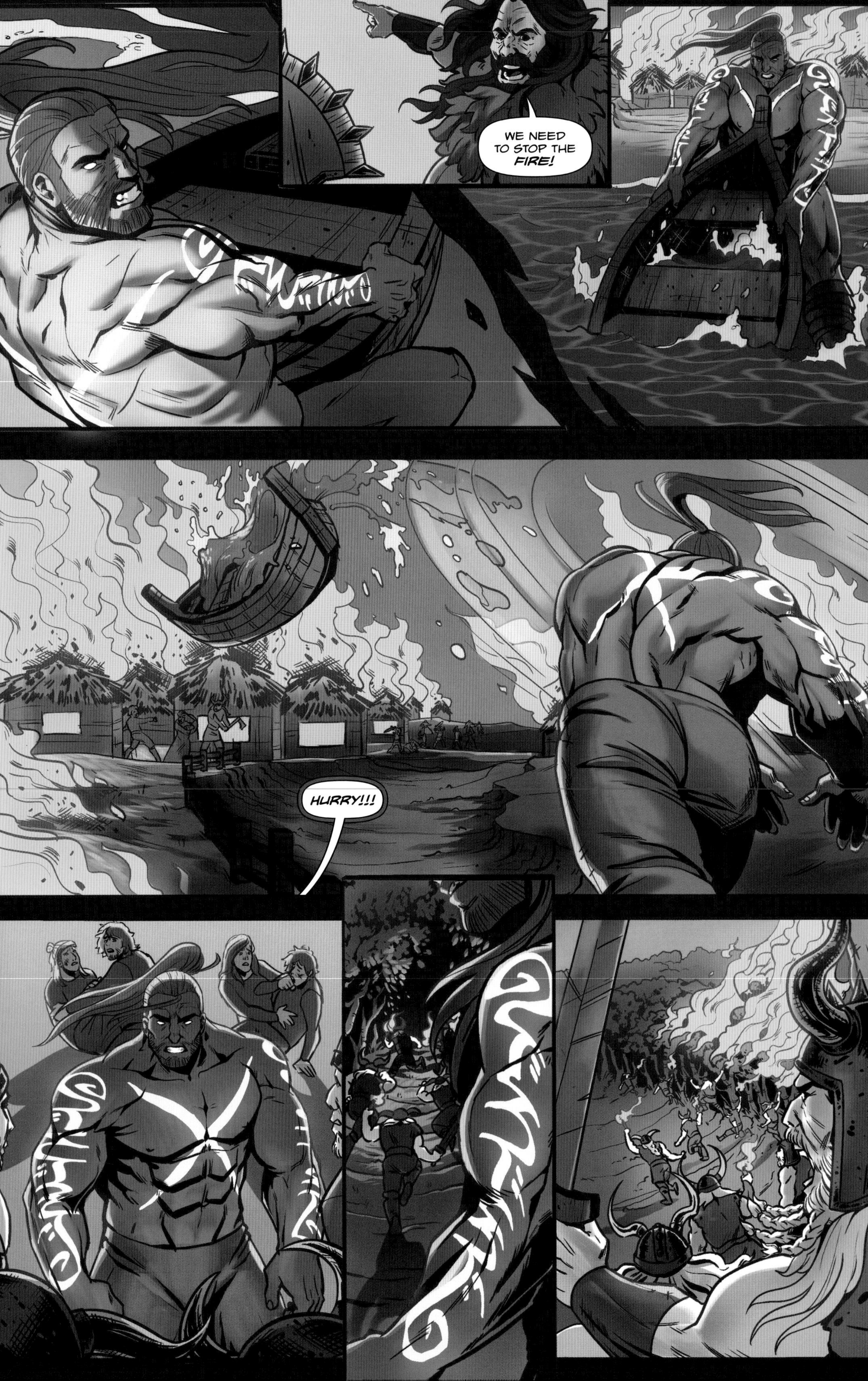
WE NEED TO STOP THE FIRE!
HURRY!!!

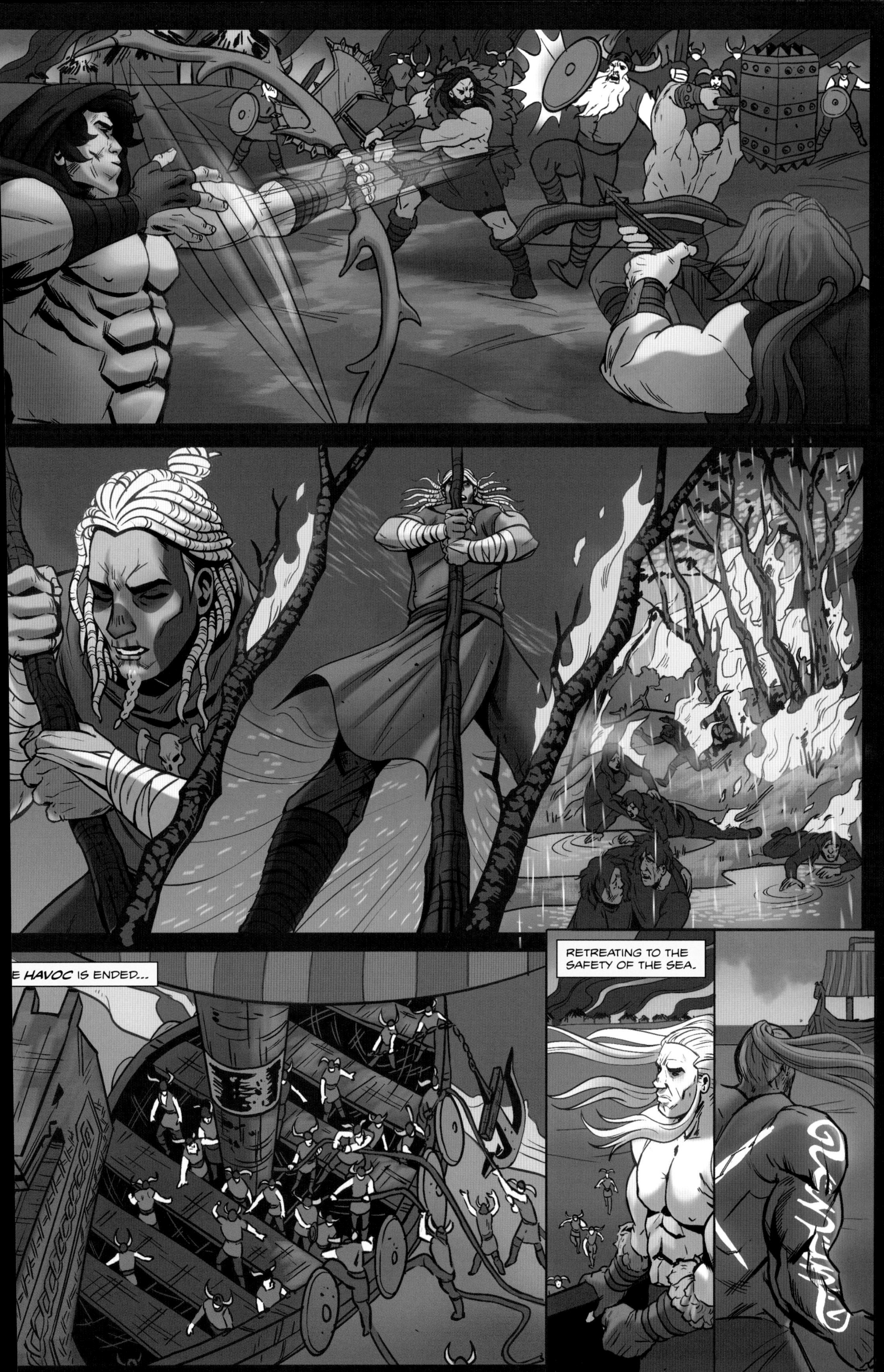
E HAVOC IS ENDED...
RETREATING TO THE SAFETY OF THE SEA.

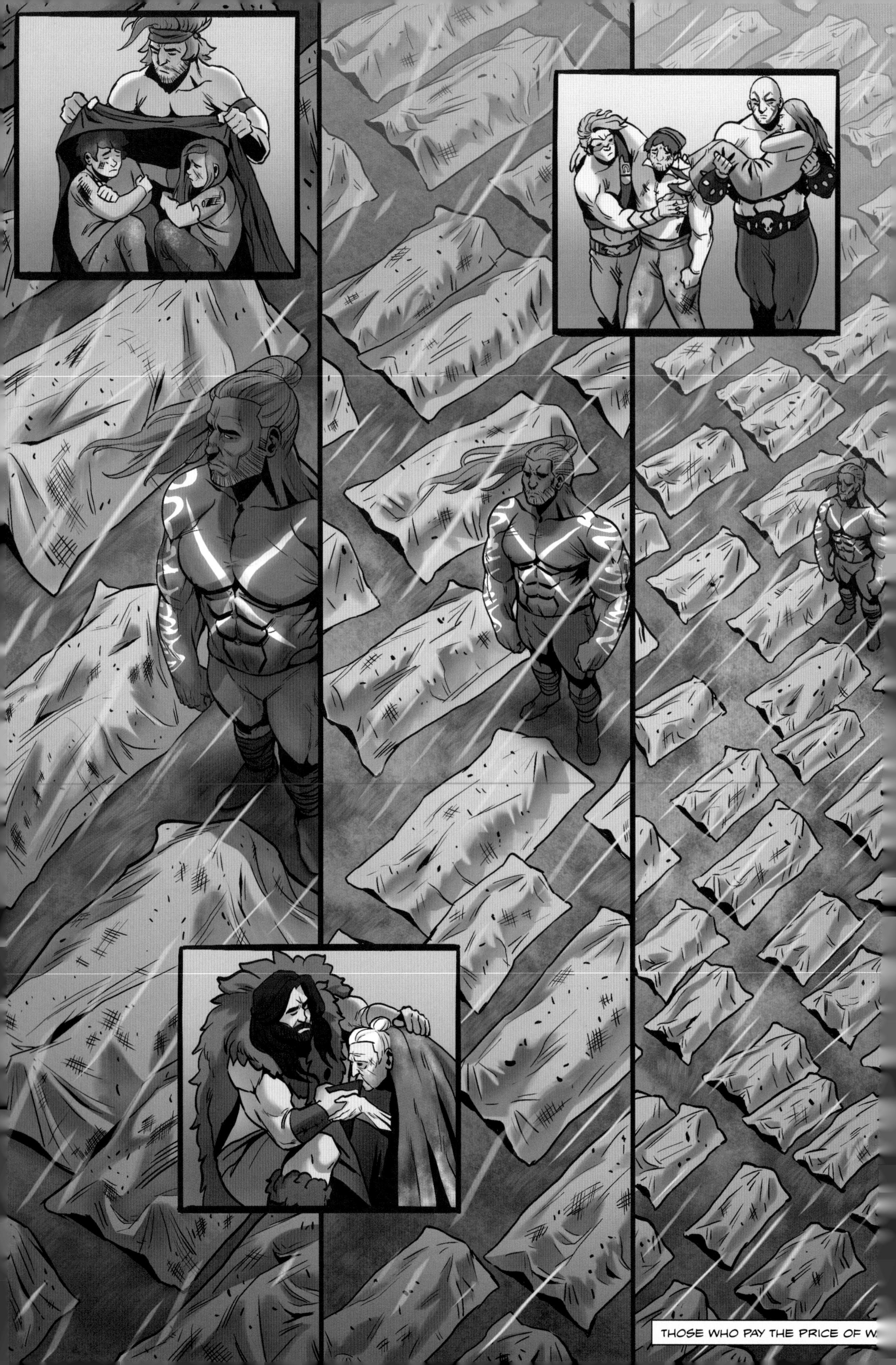
THOSE WHO PAY THE PRICE OF W

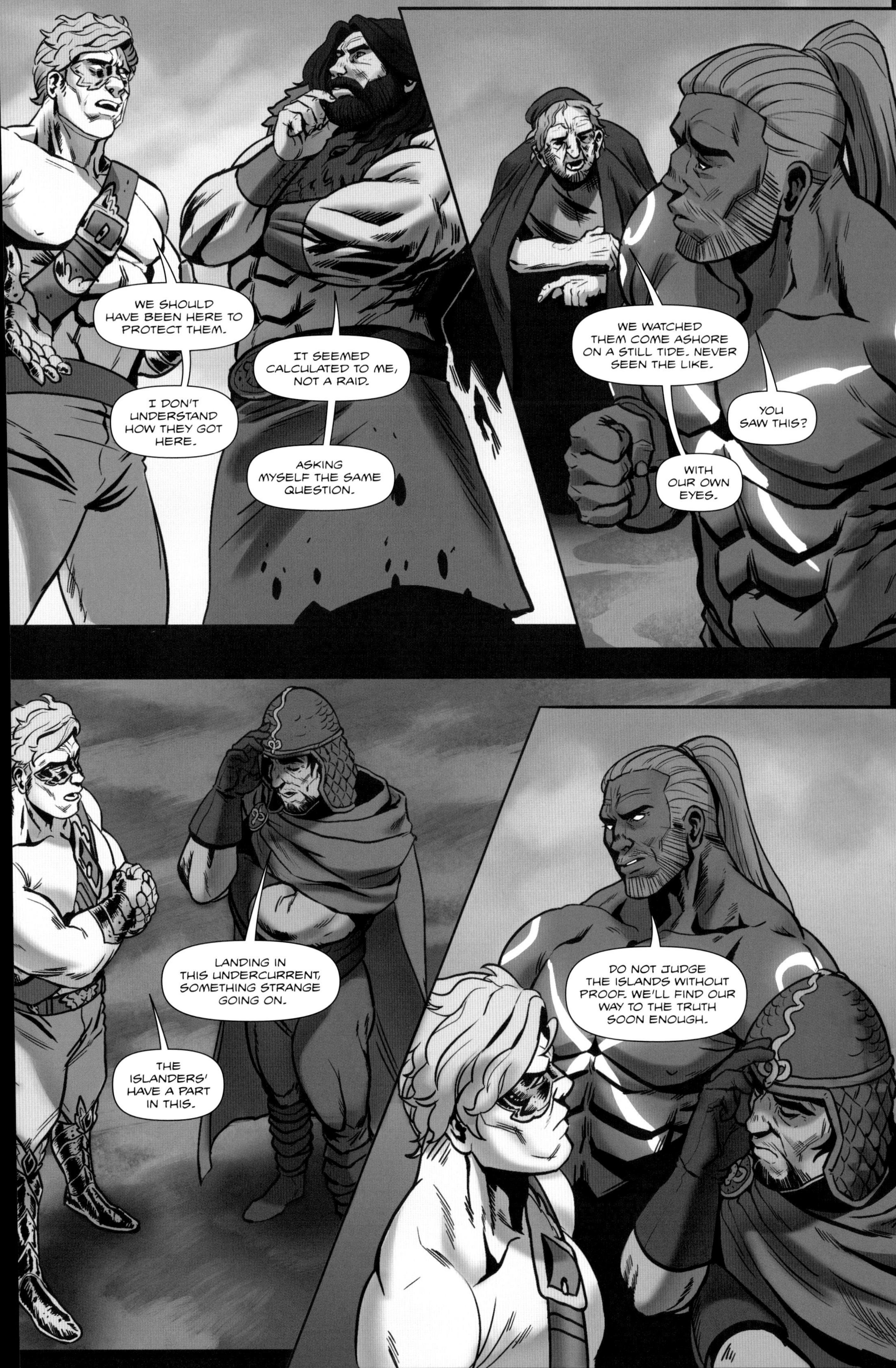
WE SHOULD HAVE BEEN HERE TO PROTECT THEM.
I DON'T UNDERSTAND HOW THEY GOT HERE.
IT SEEMED CALCULATED TO ME, NOT A RAID.
ASKING MYSELF THE SAME QUESTION.
WE WATCHED THEM COME ASHORE ON A STILL TIDE. NEVER SEEN THE LIKE.
YOU SAW THIS?
WITH OUR OWN EYES.
LANDING IN THIS UNDERCURRENT, SOMETHING STRANGE GOING ON.
THE ISLANDERS' HAVE A PART IN THIS.
DO NOT JUDGE THE ISLANDS WITHOUT PROOF. WE'LL FIND OUR WAY TO THE TRUTH SOON ENOUGH.

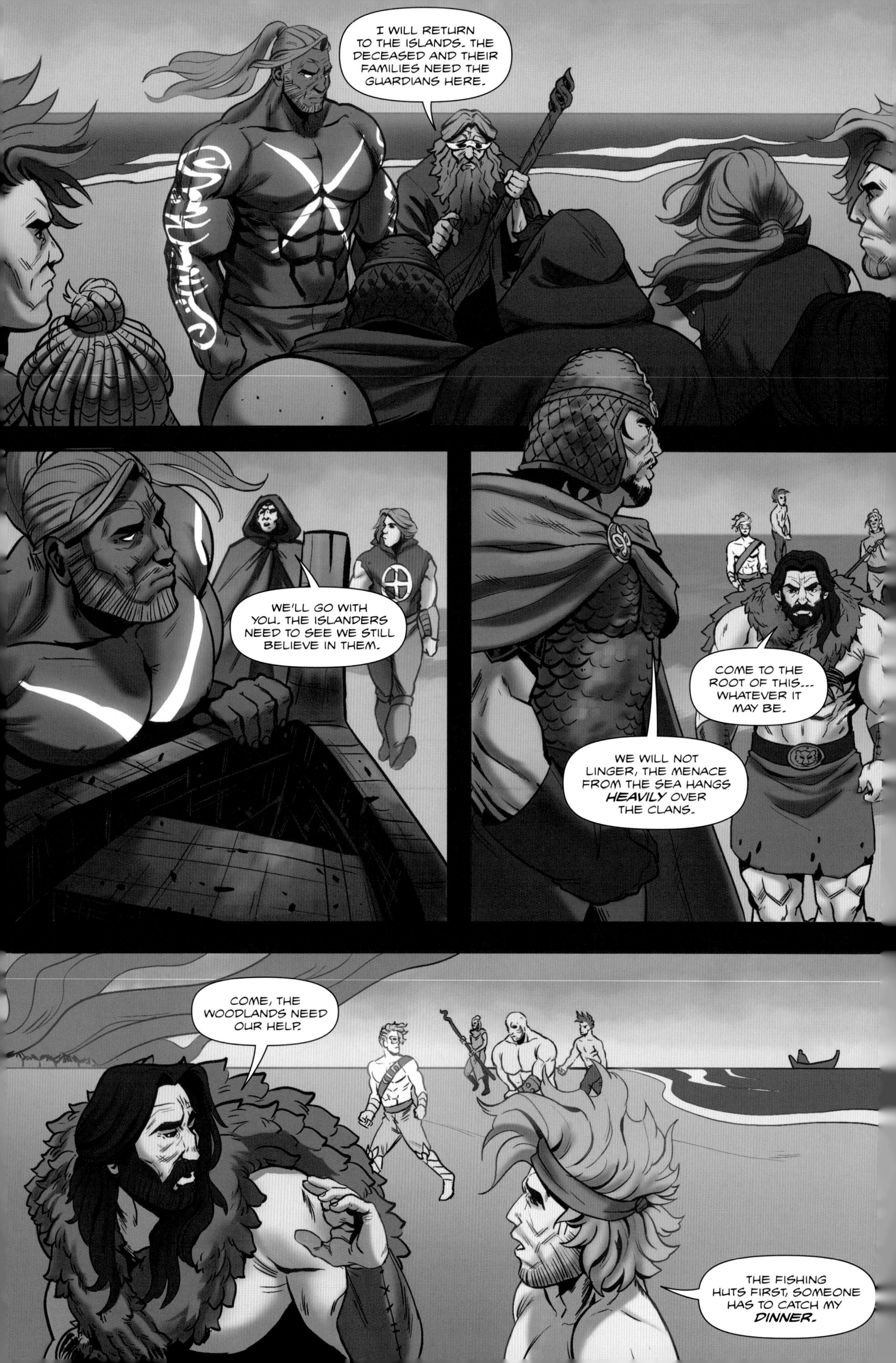
I WILL RETURN TO THE ISLANDS. THE DECEASED AND THEIR FAMILIES NEED THE GUARDIANS HERE.
WE'LL GO WITH YOU. THE ISLANDERS NEED TO SEE WE STILL BELIEVE IN THEM.
COME TO THE ROOT OF THIS... WHATEVER IT MAY BE.
WE WILL NOT LINGER, THE MENACE FROM THE SEA HANGS *HEAVILY* OVER THE CLANS.
COME, THE WOODLANDS NEED OUR HELP.
THE FISHING HUTS FIRST, SOMEONE HAS TO CATCH MY *DINNER.*

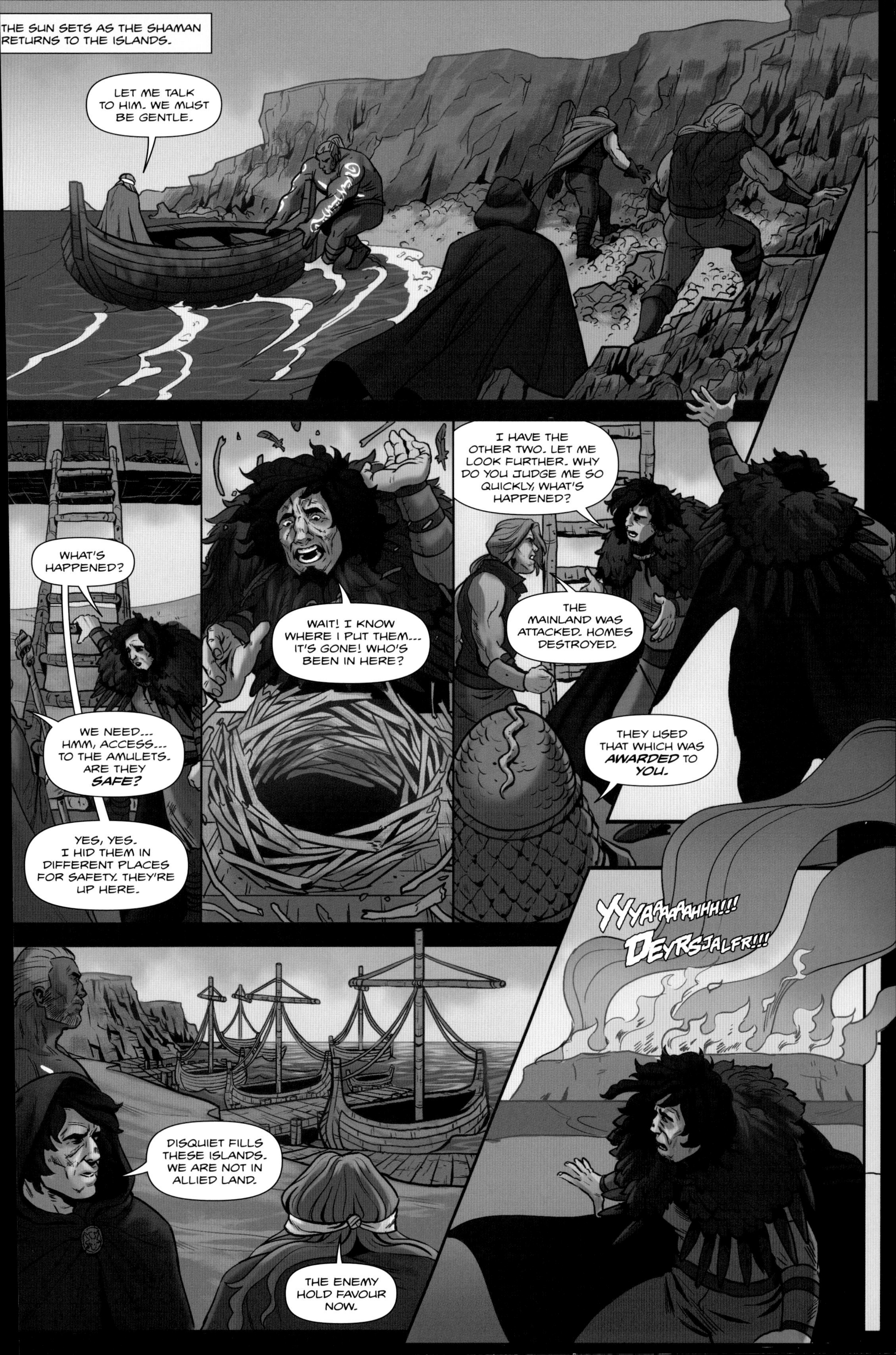
THE SUN SETS AS THE SHAMAN RETURNS TO THE ISLANDS.
LET ME TALK TO HIM. WE MUST BE GENTLE.
WHAT'S HAPPENED?
WE NEED... HMM, ACCESS... TO THE AMULETS. ARE THEY *SAFE?*
YES, YES. I HID THEM IN DIFFERENT PLACES FOR SAFETY. THEY'RE UP HERE.
WAIT! I KNOW WHERE I PUT THEM... IT'S GONE! WHO'S BEEN IN HERE?
I HAVE THE OTHER TWO. LET ME LOOK FURTHER. WHY DO YOU JUDGE ME SO QUICKLY, WHAT'S HAPPENED?
THE MAINLAND WAS ATTACKED. HOMES DESTROYED.
THEY USED THAT WHICH WAS *AWARDED* TO *YOU.*
YYYAAAAAHHH!!!
DEYRSJALFR!!!
DISQUIET FILLS THESE ISLANDS. WE ARE NOT IN ALLIED LAND.
THE ENEMY HOLD FAVOUR NOW.

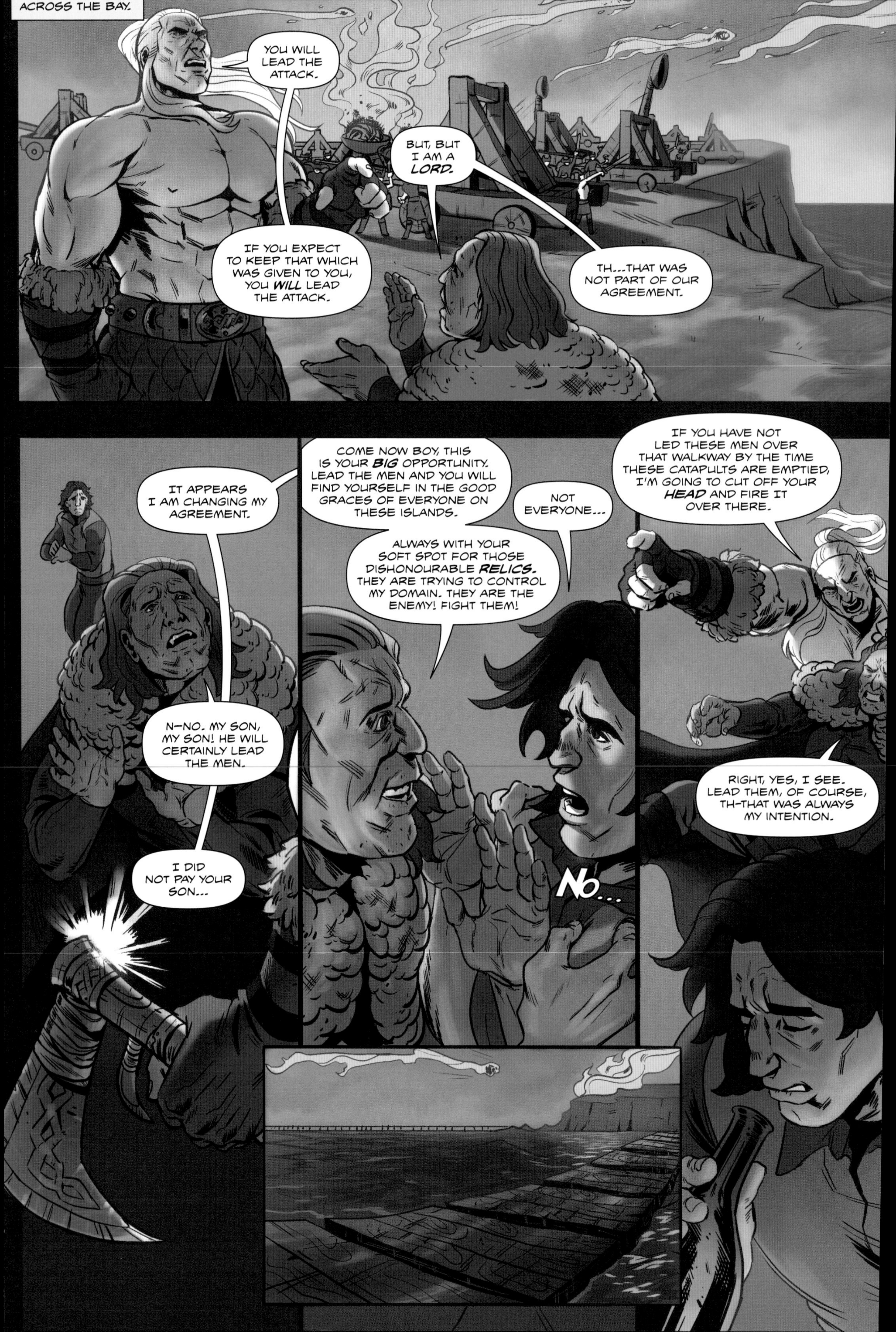
ACROSS THE BAY.
YOU WILL LEAD THE ATTACK.
BUT, BUT I AM A LORD.
IF YOU EXPECT TO KEEP THAT WHICH WAS GIVEN TO YOU, YOU WILL LEAD THE ATTACK.
TH...THAT WAS NOT PART OF OUR AGREEMENT.
IT APPEARS I AM CHANGING MY AGREEMENT.
N-NO. MY SON, MY SON! HE WILL CERTAINLY LEAD THE MEN.
I DID NOT PAY YOUR SON...
COME NOW BOY, THIS IS YOUR BIG OPPORTUNITY. LEAD THE MEN AND YOU WILL FIND YOURSELF IN THE GOOD GRACES OF EVERYONE ON THESE ISLANDS.
NOT EVERYONE...
ALWAYS WITH YOUR SOFT SPOT FOR THOSE DISHONOURABLE RELICS. THEY ARE TRYING TO CONTROL MY DOMAIN. THEY ARE THE ENEMY! FIGHT THEM!
NO...
IF YOU HAVE NOT LED THESE MEN OVER THAT WALKWAY BY THE TIME THESE CATAPULTS ARE EMPTIED, I'M GOING TO CUT OFF YOUR HEAD AND FIRE IT OVER THERE.
RIGHT, YES, I SEE. LEAD THEM, OF COURSE, TH-THAT WAS ALWAYS MY INTENTION.

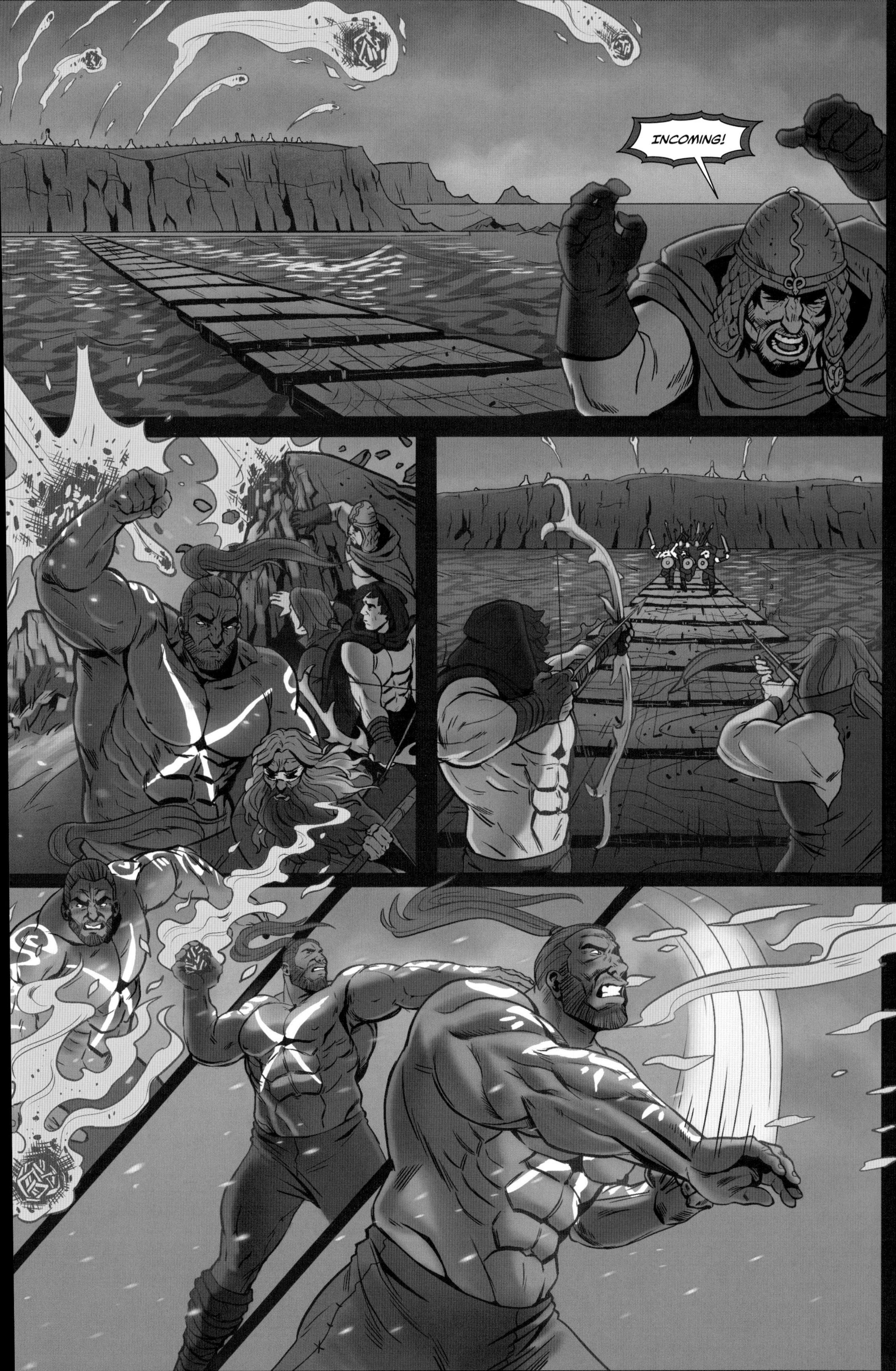
INCOMING!

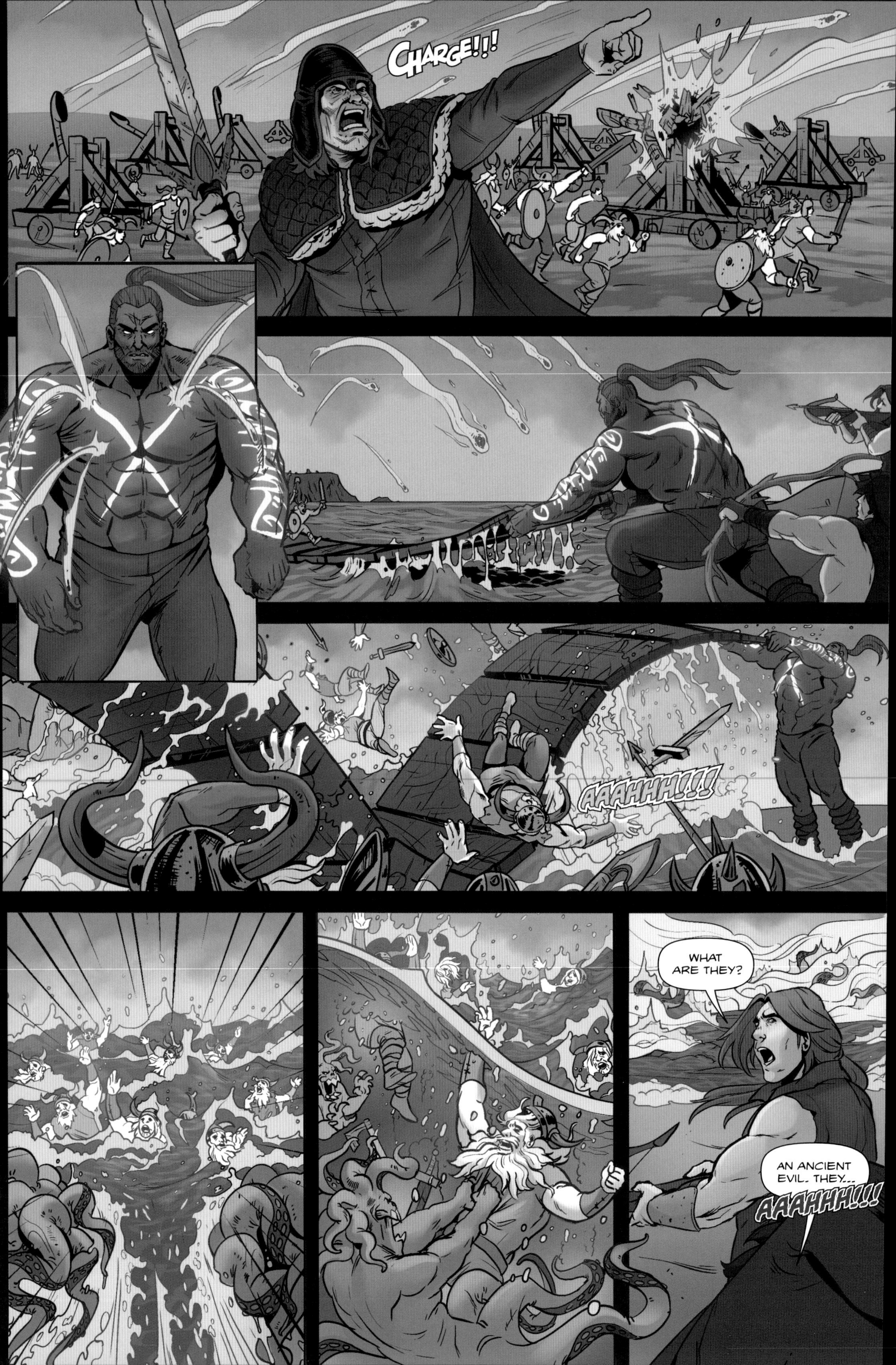
CHARGE!!!
AAAHHH!!!
WHAT ARE THEY?
AN ANCIENT EVIL. THEY...
AAAHHH!!!

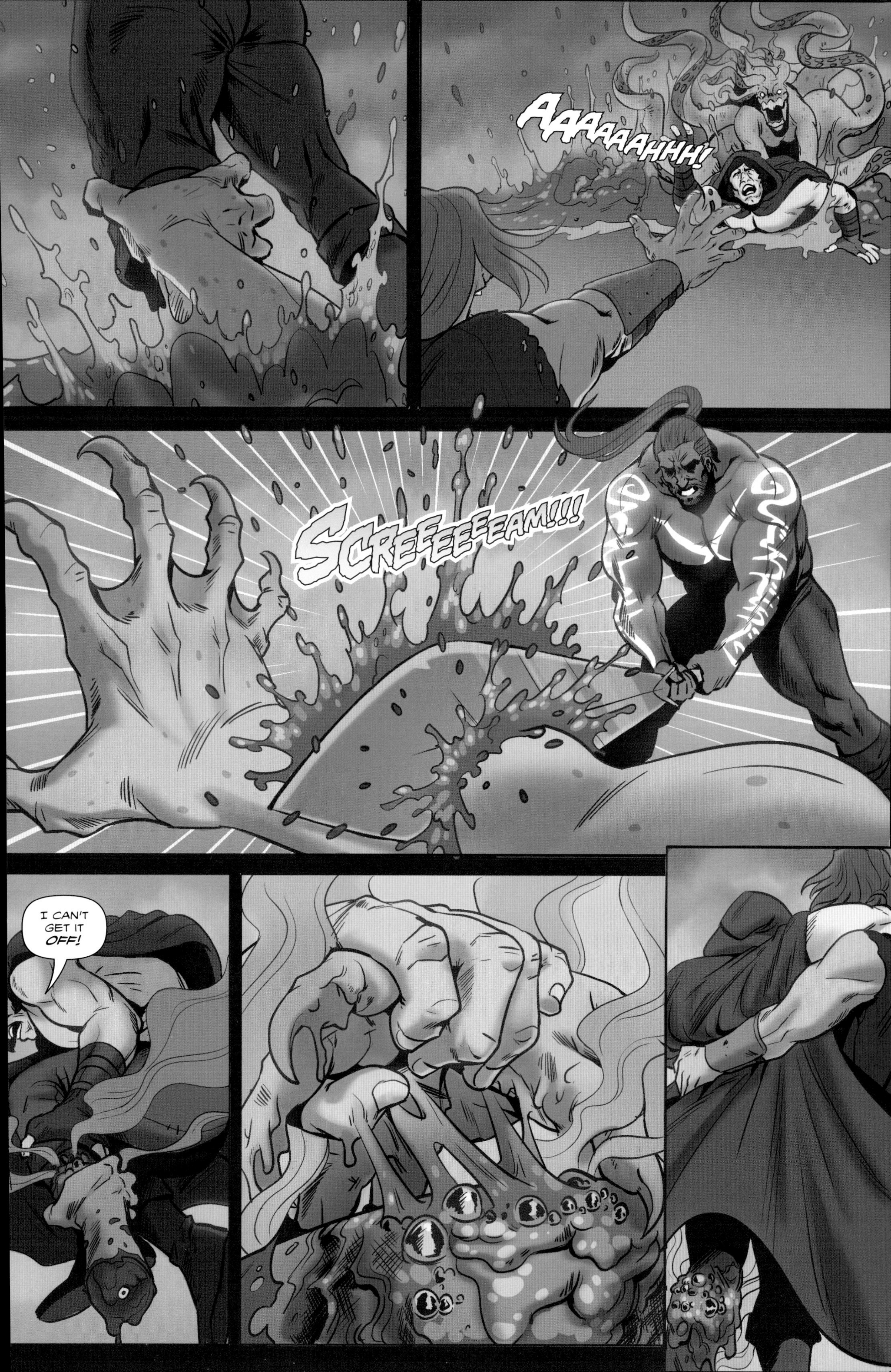
AAAAAAHHH!
SCREEEEEEEAM!!!
I CAN'T GET IT OFF!

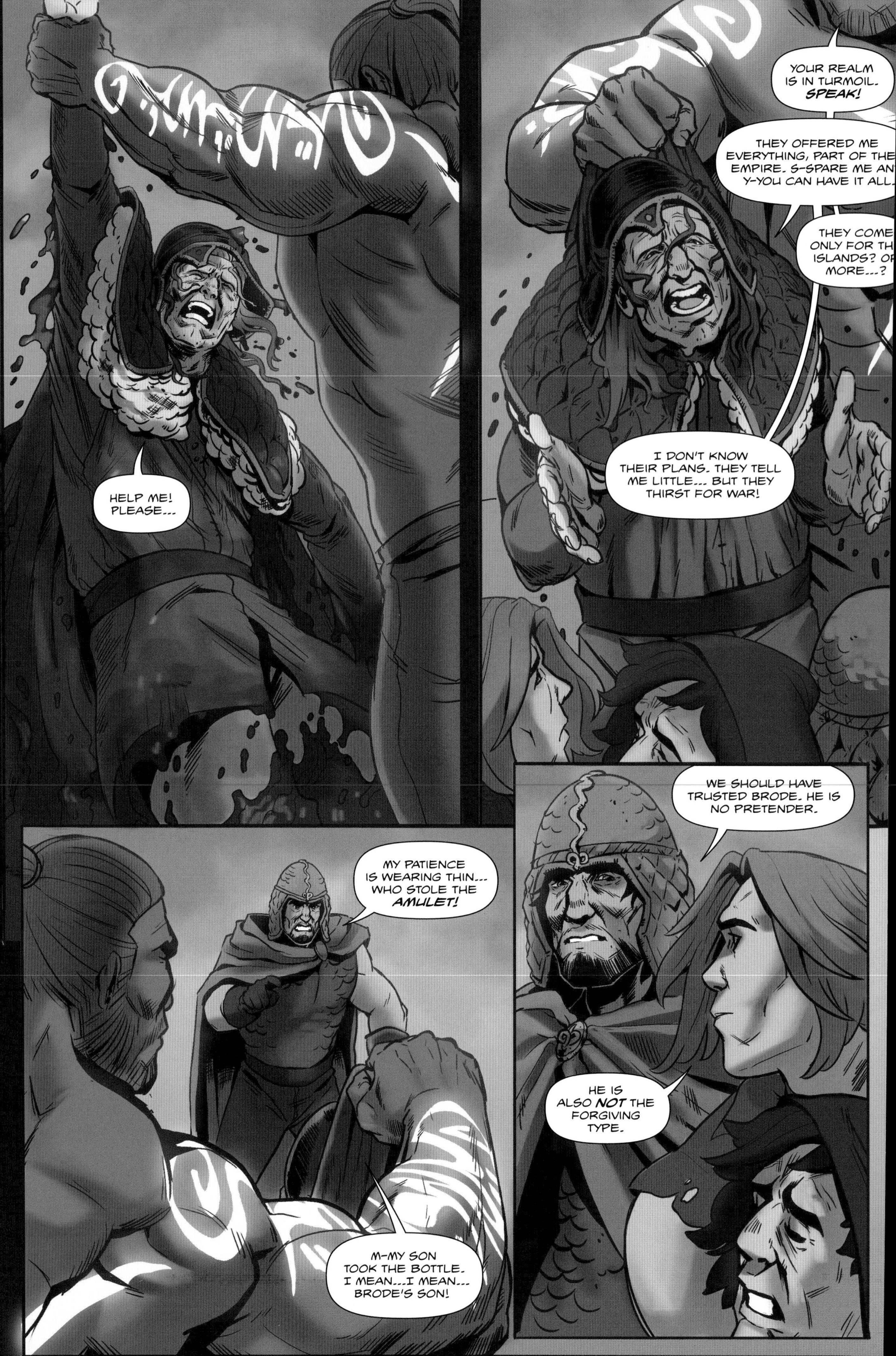
HELP ME! PLEASE...
YOUR REALM IS IN TURMOIL. SPEAK!
THEY OFFERED ME EVERYTHING, PART OF THE EMPIRE. S-SPARE ME AN Y-YOU CAN HAVE IT ALL.
THEY COME ONLY FOR TH ISLANDS? O MORE...?
I DON'T KNOW THEIR PLANS. THEY TELL ME LITTLE... BUT THEY THIRST FOR WAR!
MY PATIENCE IS WEARING THIN... WHO STOLE THE AMULET!
M-MY SON TOOK THE BOTTLE. I MEAN...I MEAN... BRODE'S SON!
WE SHOULD HAVE TRUSTED BRODE. HE IS NO PRETENDER.
HE IS ALSO NOT THE FORGIVING TYPE.

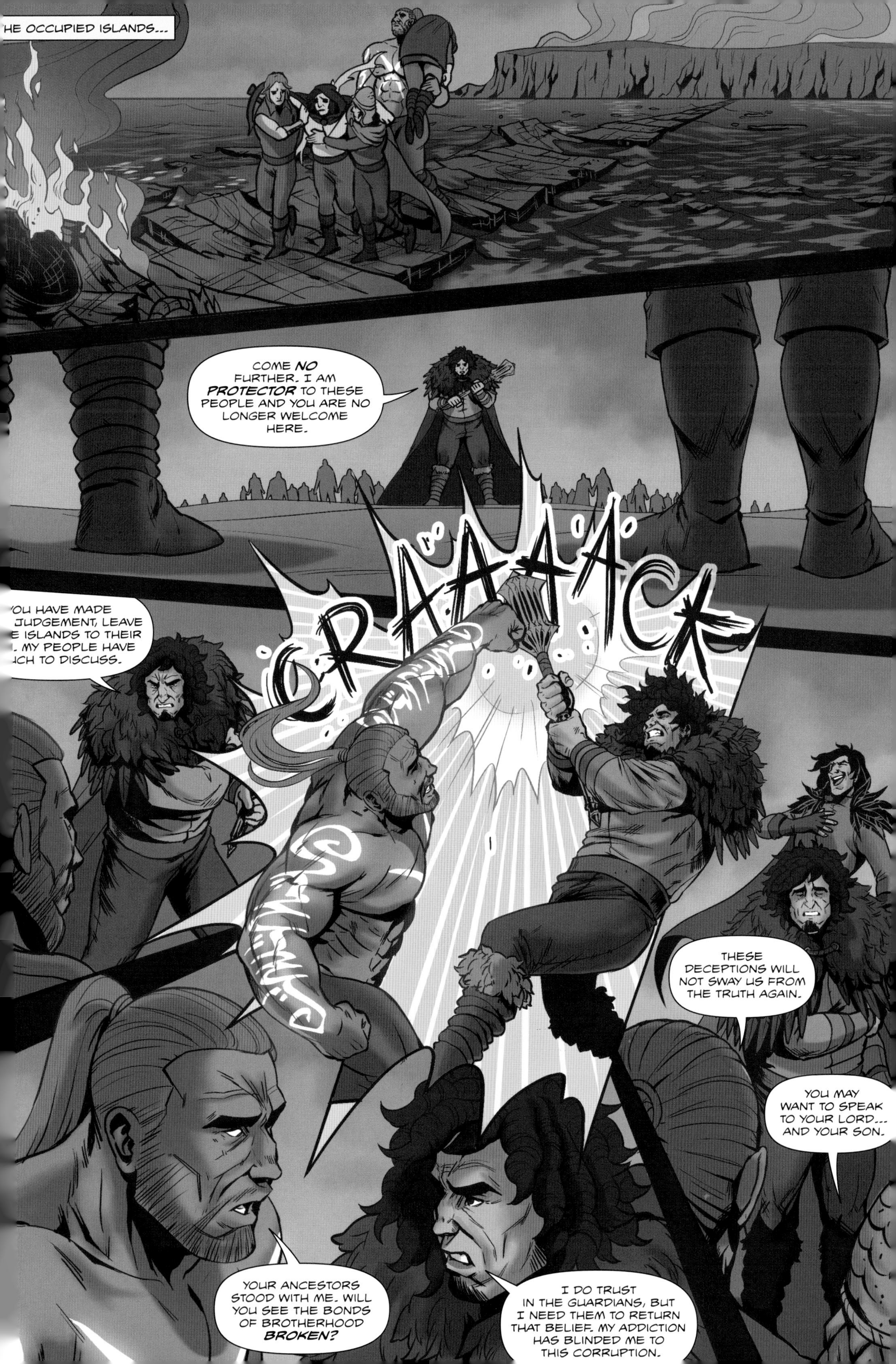
HE OCCUPIED ISLANDS...
COME NO FURTHER. I AM PROTECTOR TO THESE PEOPLE AND YOU ARE NO LONGER WELCOME HERE.
CRAAAACK
OU HAVE MADE JUDGEMENT, LEAVE E ISLANDS TO THEIR . MY PEOPLE HAVE CH TO DISCUSS.
THESE DECEPTIONS WILL NOT SWAY US FROM THE TRUTH AGAIN.
YOU MAY WANT TO SPEAK TO YOUR LORD... AND YOUR SON.
YOUR ANCESTORS STOOD WITH ME. WILL YOU SEE THE BONDS OF BROTHERHOOD BROKEN?
I DO TRUST IN THE GUARDIANS, BUT I NEED THEM TO RETURN THAT BELIEF. MY ADDICTION HAS BLINDED ME TO THIS CORRUPTION.

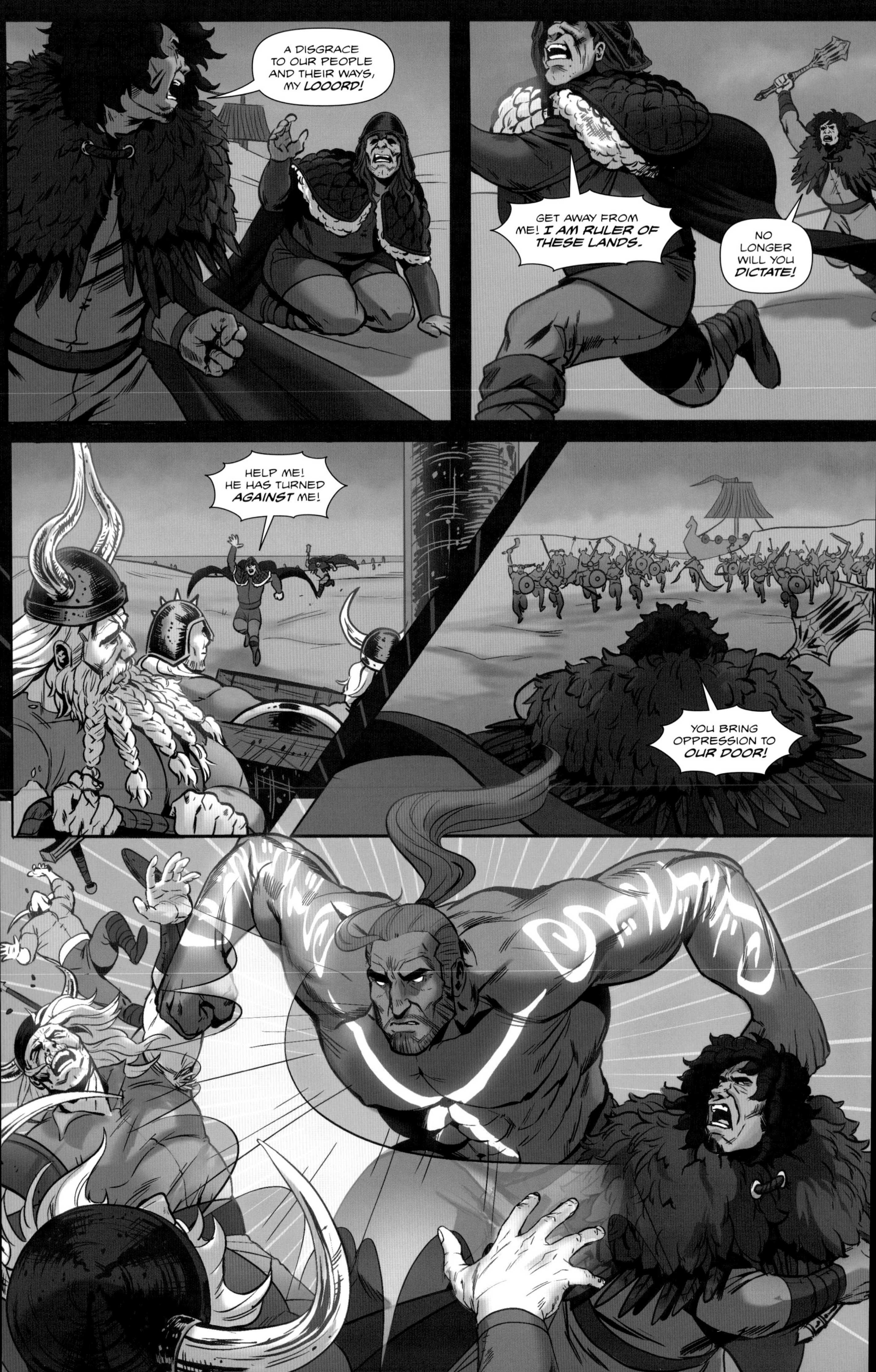
A DISGRACE TO OUR PEOPLE AND THEIR WAYS, MY LOOORD!
GET AWAY FROM ME! I AM RULER OF THESE LANDS.
NO LONGER WILL YOU DICTATE!
HELP ME! HE HAS TURNED AGAINST ME!
YOU BRING OPPRESSION TO OUR DOOR!

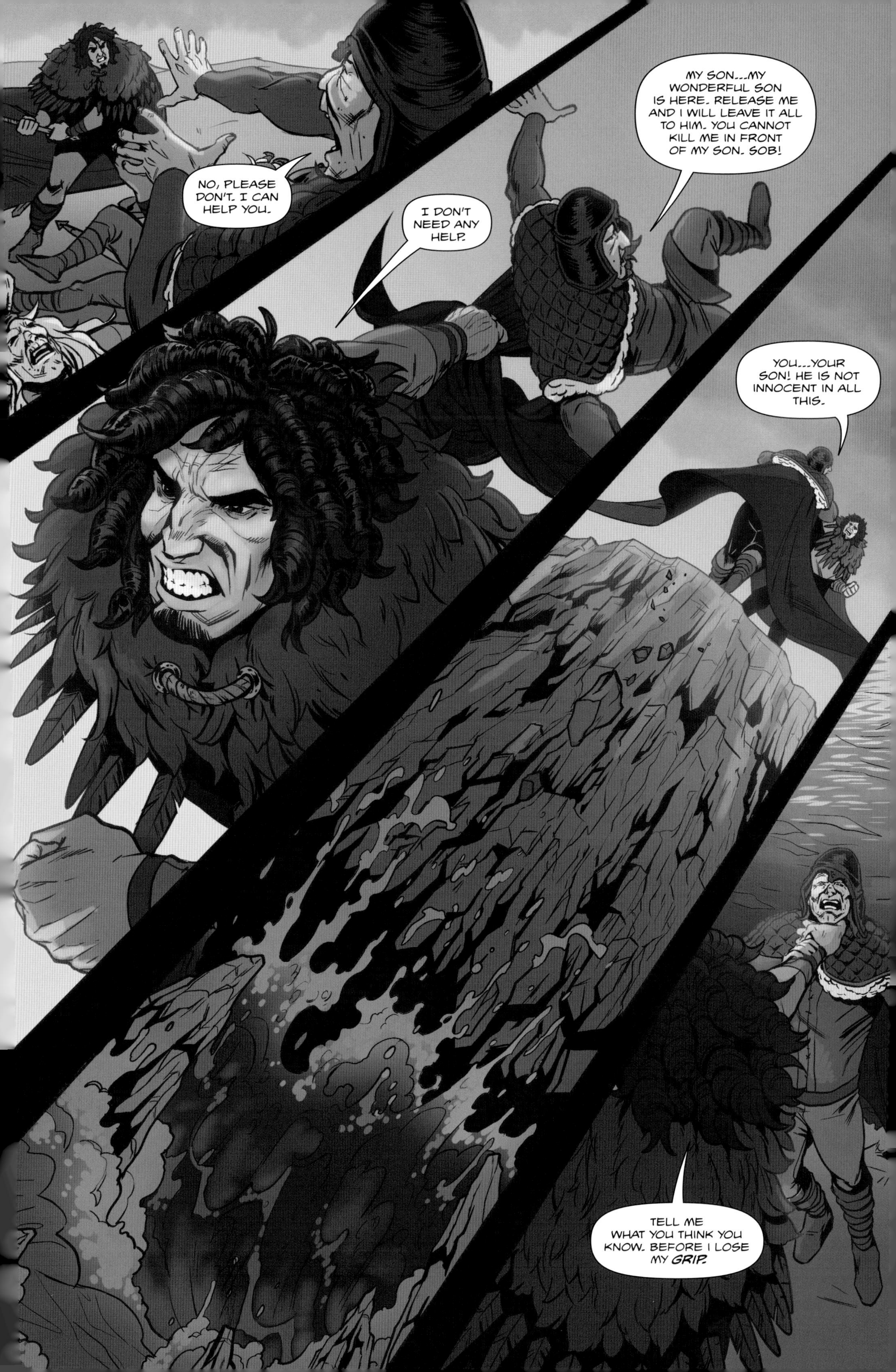
NO, PLEASE DON'T. I CAN HELP YOU.
I DON'T NEED ANY HELP.
MY SON...MY WONDERFUL SON IS HERE. RELEASE ME AND I WILL LEAVE IT ALL TO HIM. YOU CANNOT KILL ME IN FRONT OF MY SON. SOB!
YOU...YOUR SON! HE IS NOT INNOCENT IN ALL THIS.
TELL ME WHAT YOU THINK YOU KNOW. BEFORE I LOSE MY GRIP.

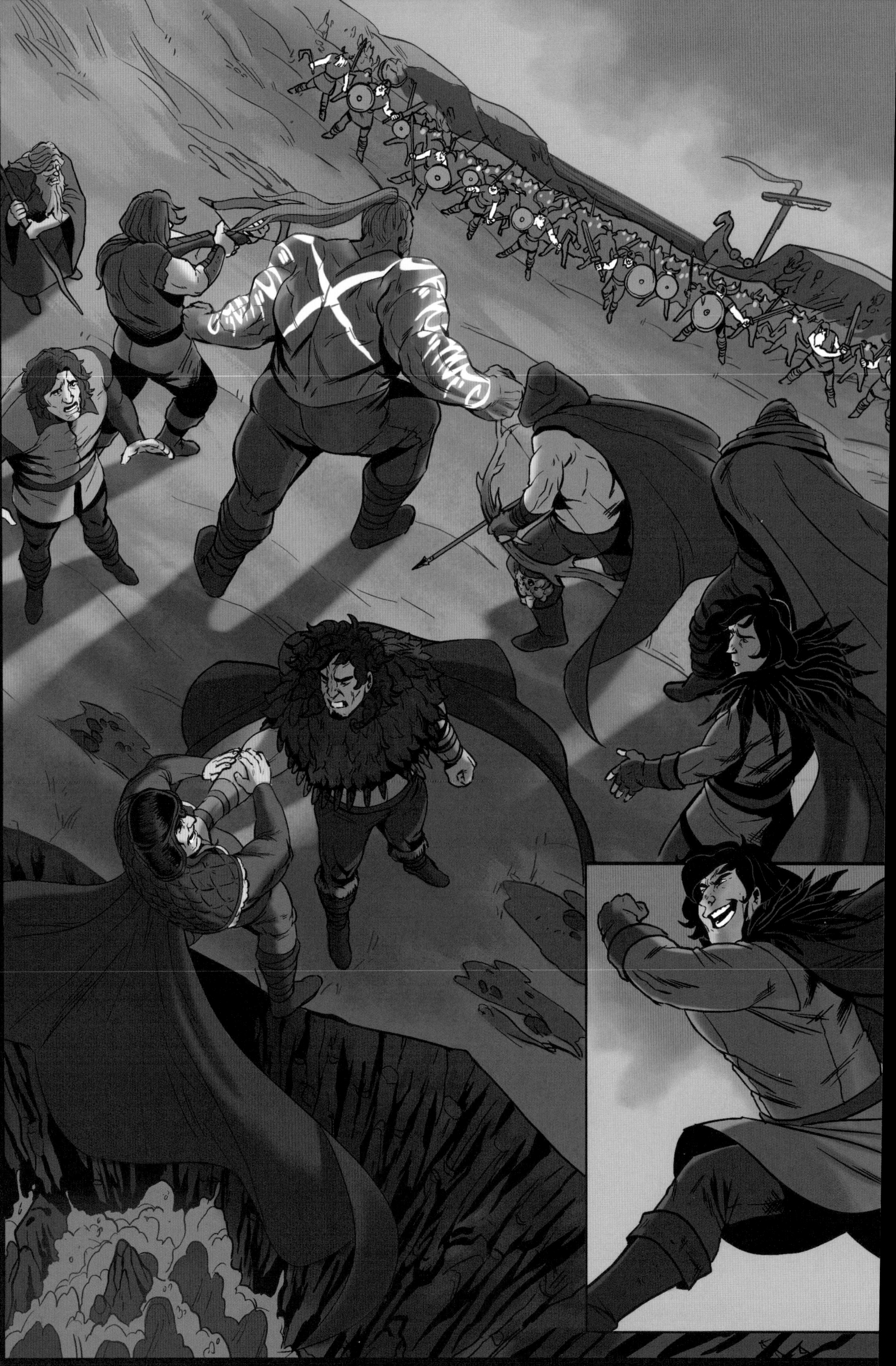

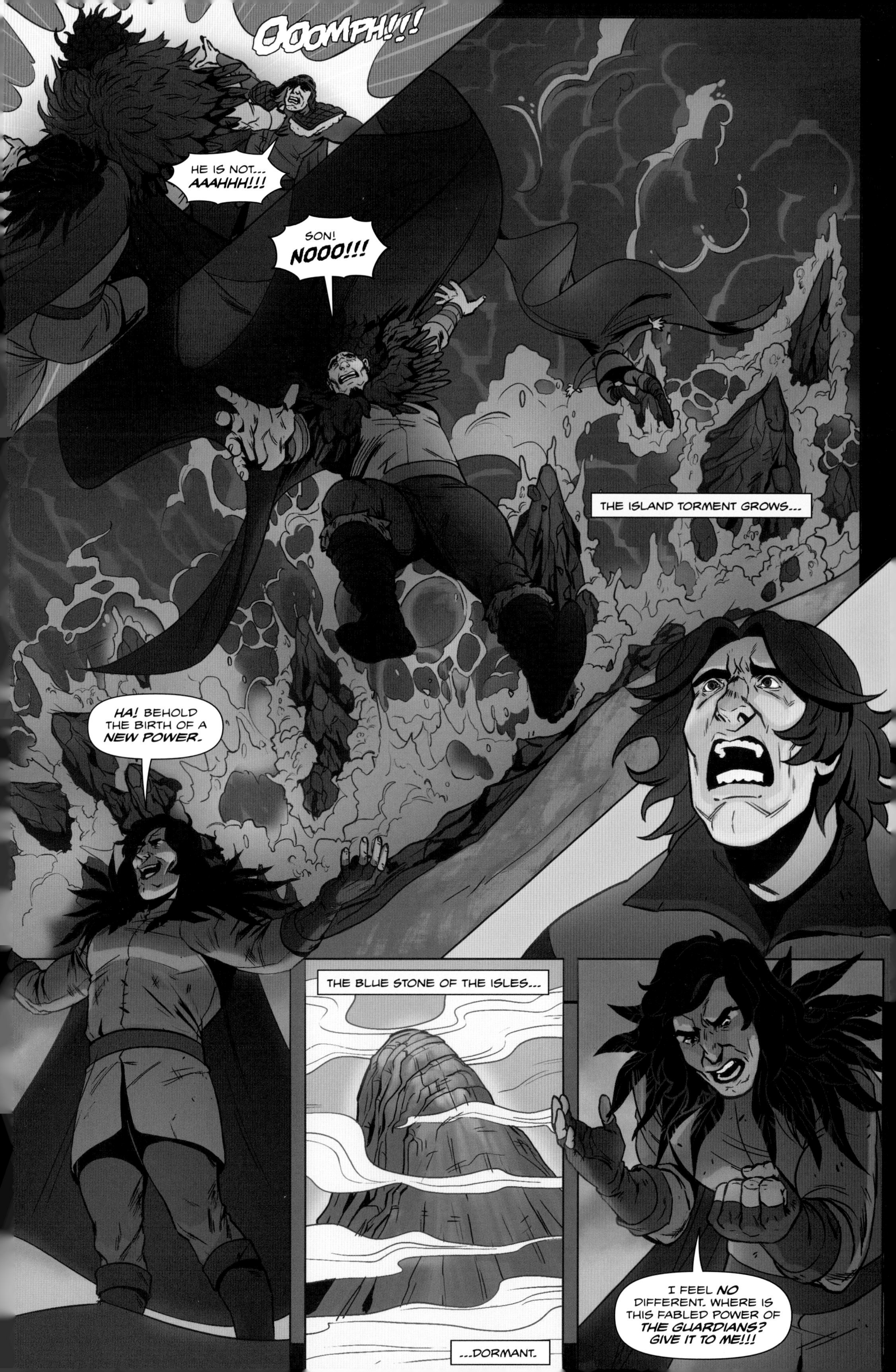
OOOMPH!!!
HE IS NOT... AAAHHH!!!
SON! NOOO!!!
THE ISLAND TORMENT GROWS...
HA! BEHOLD THE BIRTH OF A NEW POWER.
THE BLUE STONE OF THE ISLES...
...DORMANT.
I FEEL NO DIFFERENT. WHERE IS THIS FABLED POWER OF THE GUARDIANS? GIVE IT TO ME!!!

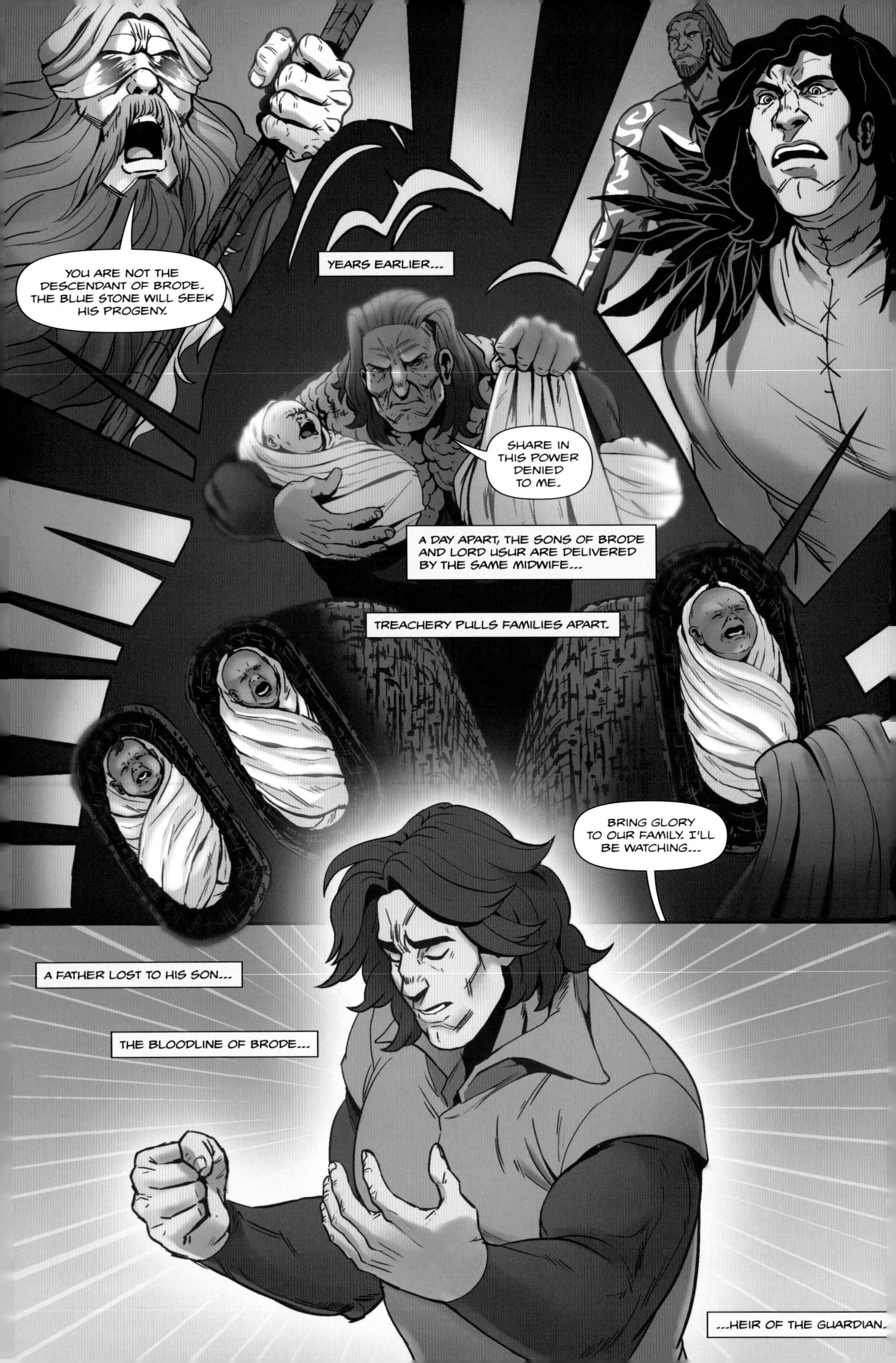
YOU ARE NOT THE DESCENDANT OF BRODE. THE BLUE STONE WILL SEEK HIS PROGENY.
YEARS EARLIER...
SHARE IN THIS POWER DENIED TO ME.
A DAY APART, THE SONS OF BRODE AND LORD USUR ARE DELIVERED BY THE SAME MIDWIFE...
TREACHERY PULLS FAMILIES APART.
BRING GLORY TO OUR FAMILY. I'LL BE WATCHING...
A FATHER LOST TO HIS SON...
THE BLOODLINE OF BRODE...
...HEIR OF THE GUARDIAN.

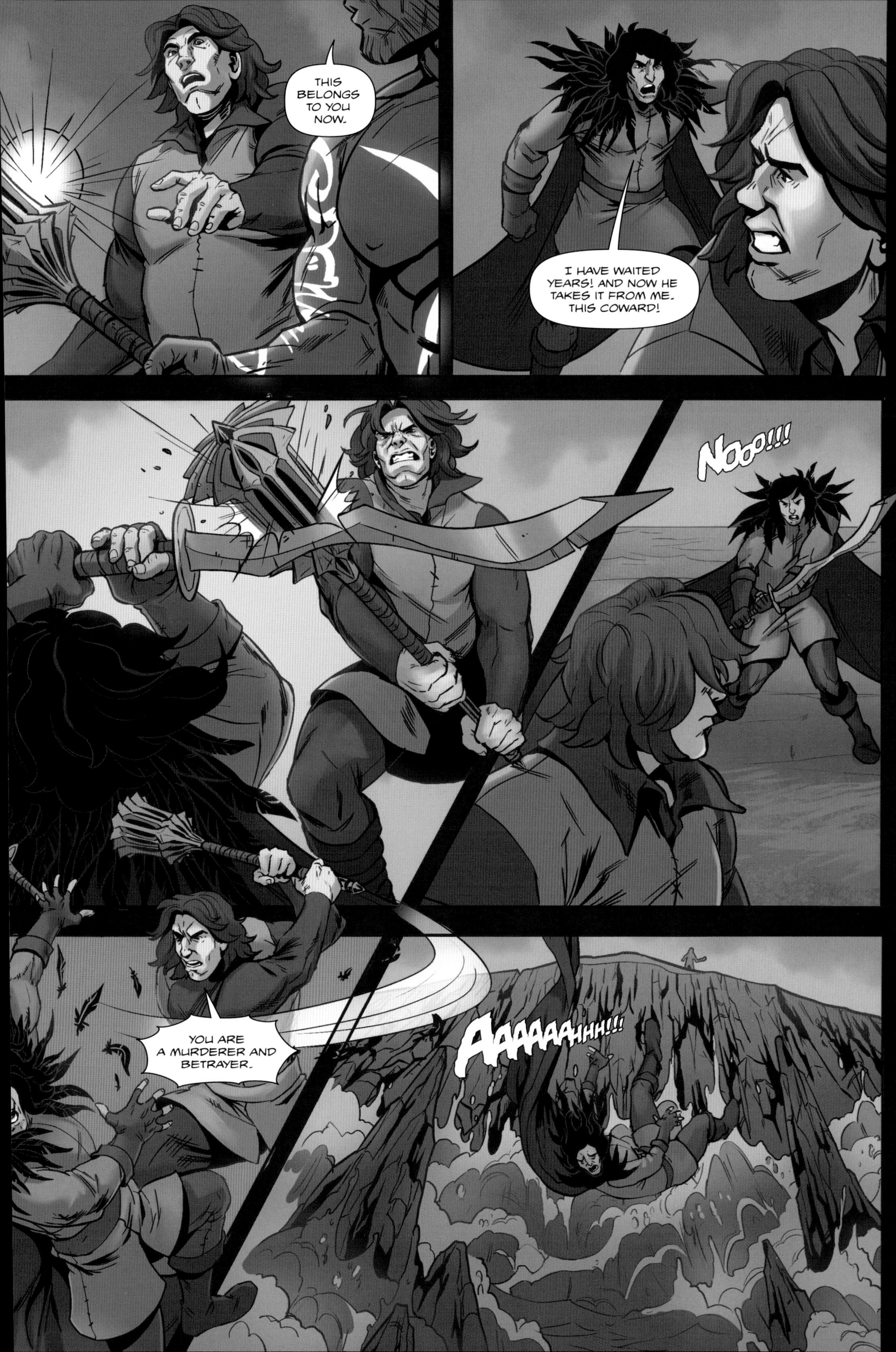
THIS BELONGS TO YOU NOW.
I HAVE WAITED YEARS! AND NOW HE TAKES IT FROM ME. THIS COWARD!
NOoo!!!
YOU ARE A MURDERER AND BETRAYER.
AAAAAAHHH!!!

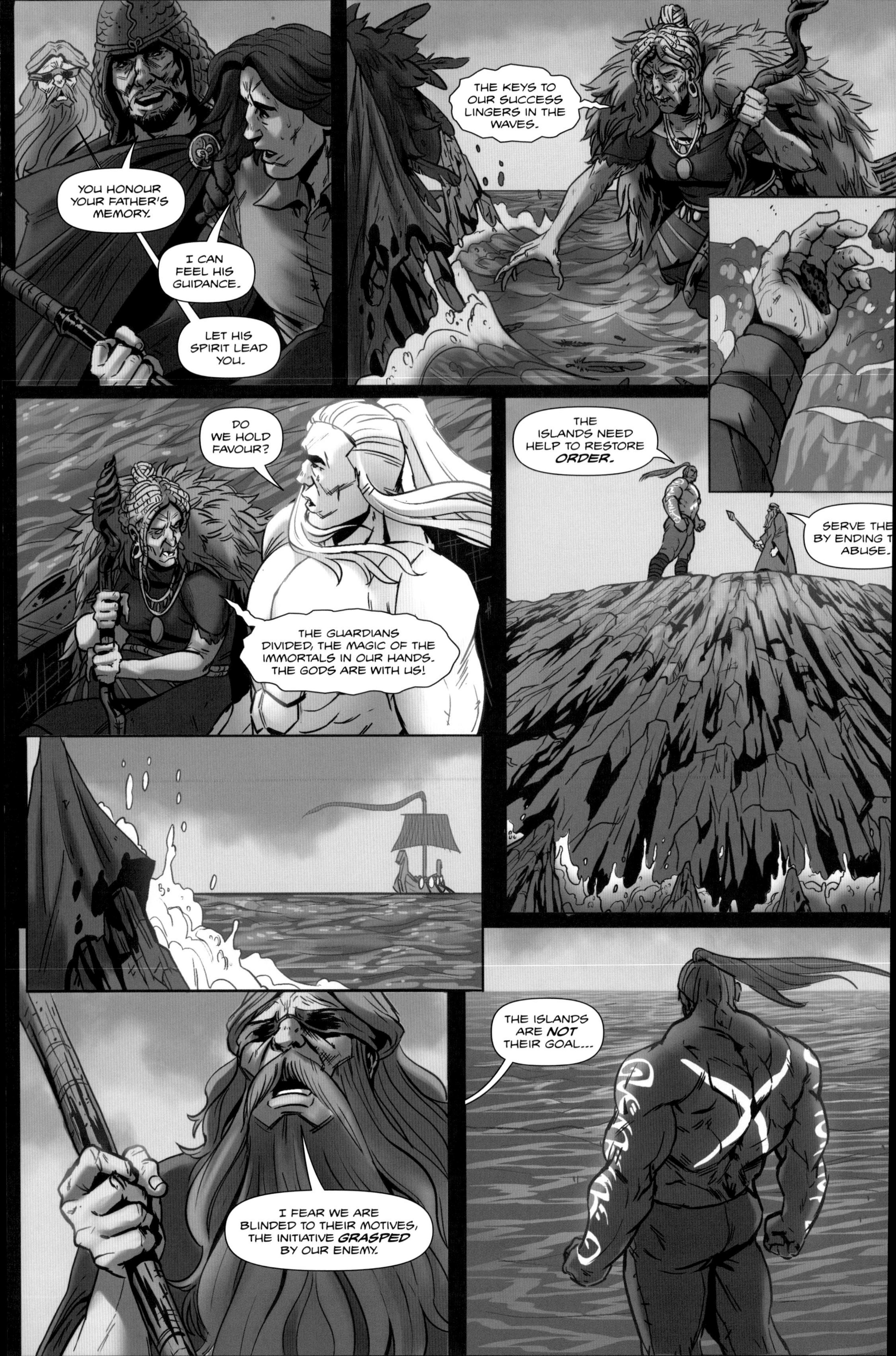

YOU HONOUR YOUR FATHER'S MEMORY.
I CAN FEEL HIS GUIDANCE.
LET HIS SPIRIT LEAD YOU.
THE KEYS TO OUR SUCCESS LINGERS IN THE WAVES.
DO WE HOLD FAVOUR?
THE GUARDIANS DIVIDED, THE MAGIC OF THE IMMORTALS IN OUR HANDS. THE GODS ARE WITH US!
THE ISLANDS NEED HELP TO RESTORE *ORDER.*
SERVE THE
BY ENDING T
ABUSE.
THE ISLANDS ARE *NOT* THEIR GOAL...
I FEAR WE ARE BLINDED TO THEIR MOTIVES, THE INITIATIVE *GRASPED* BY OUR ENEMY.

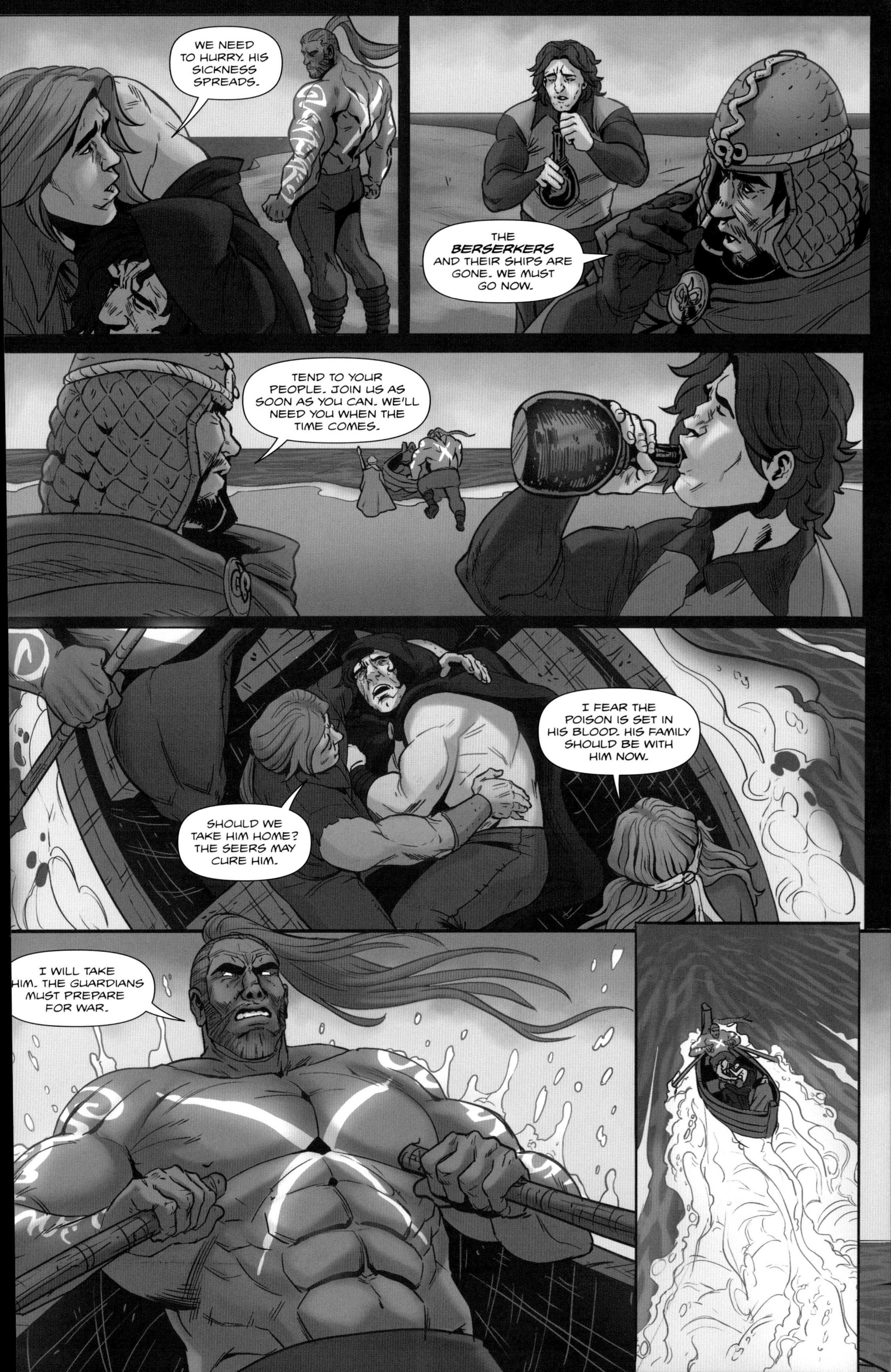

WE NEED TO HURRY. HIS SICKNESS SPREADS.
THE *BERSERKERS* AND THEIR SHIPS ARE GONE. WE MUST GO NOW.
TEND TO YOUR PEOPLE. JOIN US AS SOON AS YOU CAN. WE'LL NEED YOU WHEN THE TIME COMES.
SHOULD WE TAKE HIM HOME? THE SEERS MAY CURE HIM.
I FEAR THE POISON IS SET IN HIS BLOOD. HIS FAMILY SHOULD BE WITH HIM NOW.
I WILL TAKE HIM. THE GUARDIANS MUST PREPARE FOR WAR.

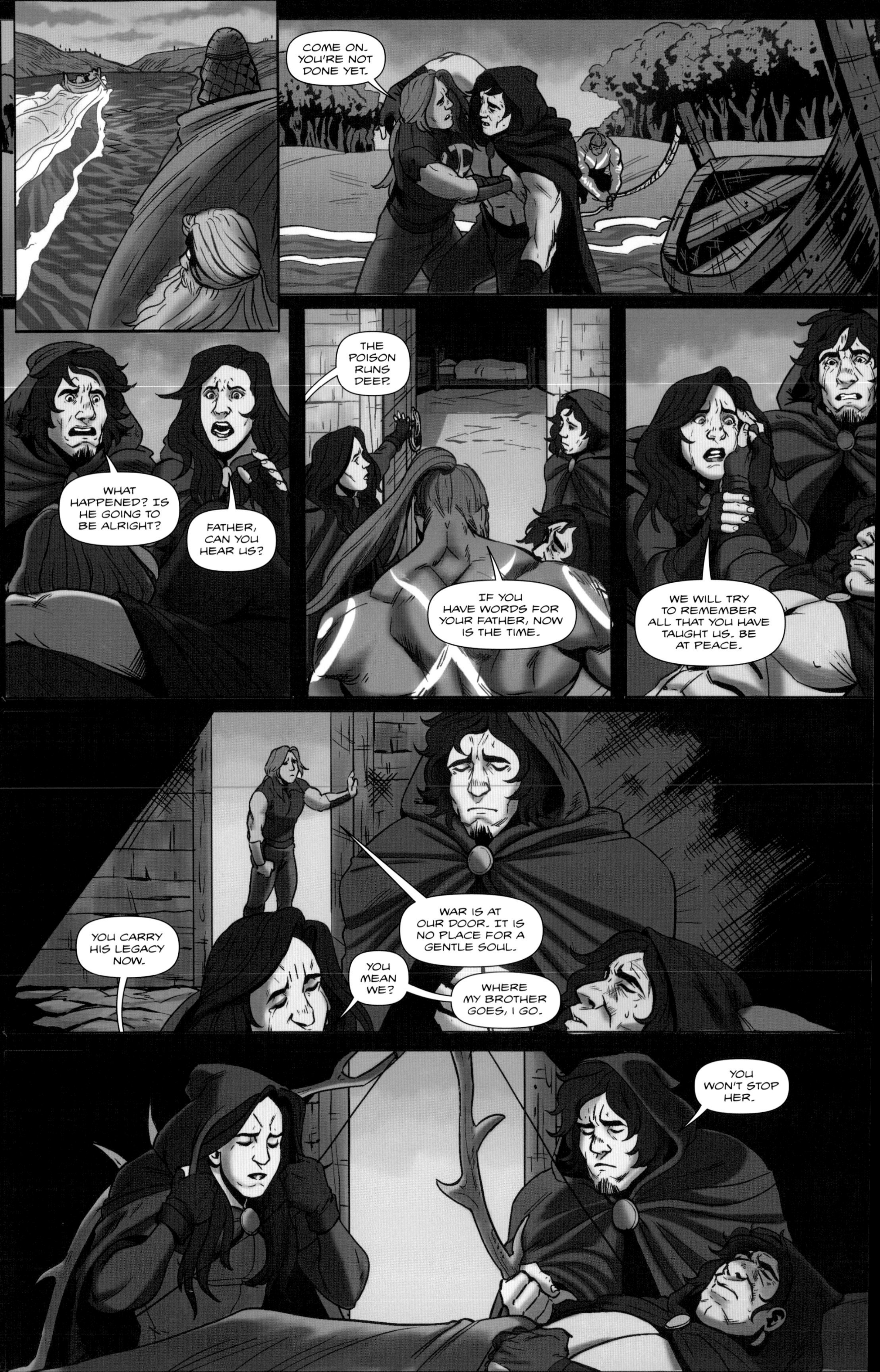
COME ON. YOU'RE NOT DONE YET.
WHAT HAPPENED? IS HE GOING TO BE ALRIGHT?
FATHER, CAN YOU HEAR US?
THE POISON RUNS DEEP.
IF YOU HAVE WORDS FOR YOUR FATHER, NOW IS THE TIME.
WE WILL TRY TO REMEMBER ALL THAT YOU HAVE TAUGHT US. BE AT PEACE.
WAR IS AT OUR DOOR. IT IS NO PLACE FOR A GENTLE SOUL.
YOU CARRY HIS LEGACY NOW.
YOU MEAN WE?
WHERE MY BROTHER GOES, I GO.
YOU WON'T STOP HER.

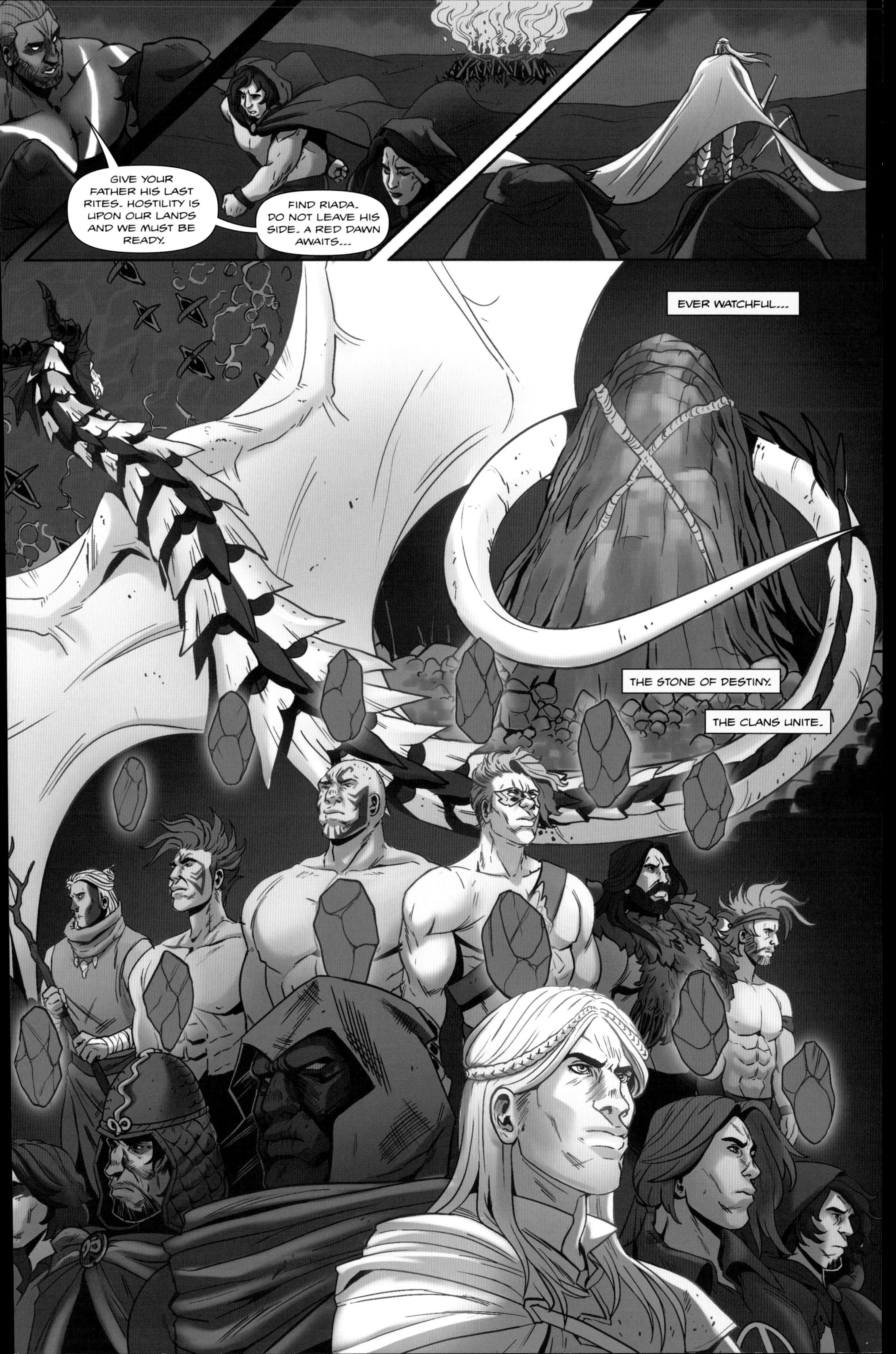
GIVE YOUR FATHER HIS LAST RITES. HOSTILITY IS UPON OUR LANDS AND WE MUST BE READY.
FIND RIADA. DO NOT LEAVE HIS SIDE. A RED DAWN AWAITS...
EVER WATCHFUL...
THE STONE OF DESTINY.
THE CLANS UNITE.

Chapter Three

Script: John Ferguson
Art: Alvaro Feliu Gutierrez
Colours: Lauren Knight
Letters: Phillip Vaughan
Editor: Clare Ferguson

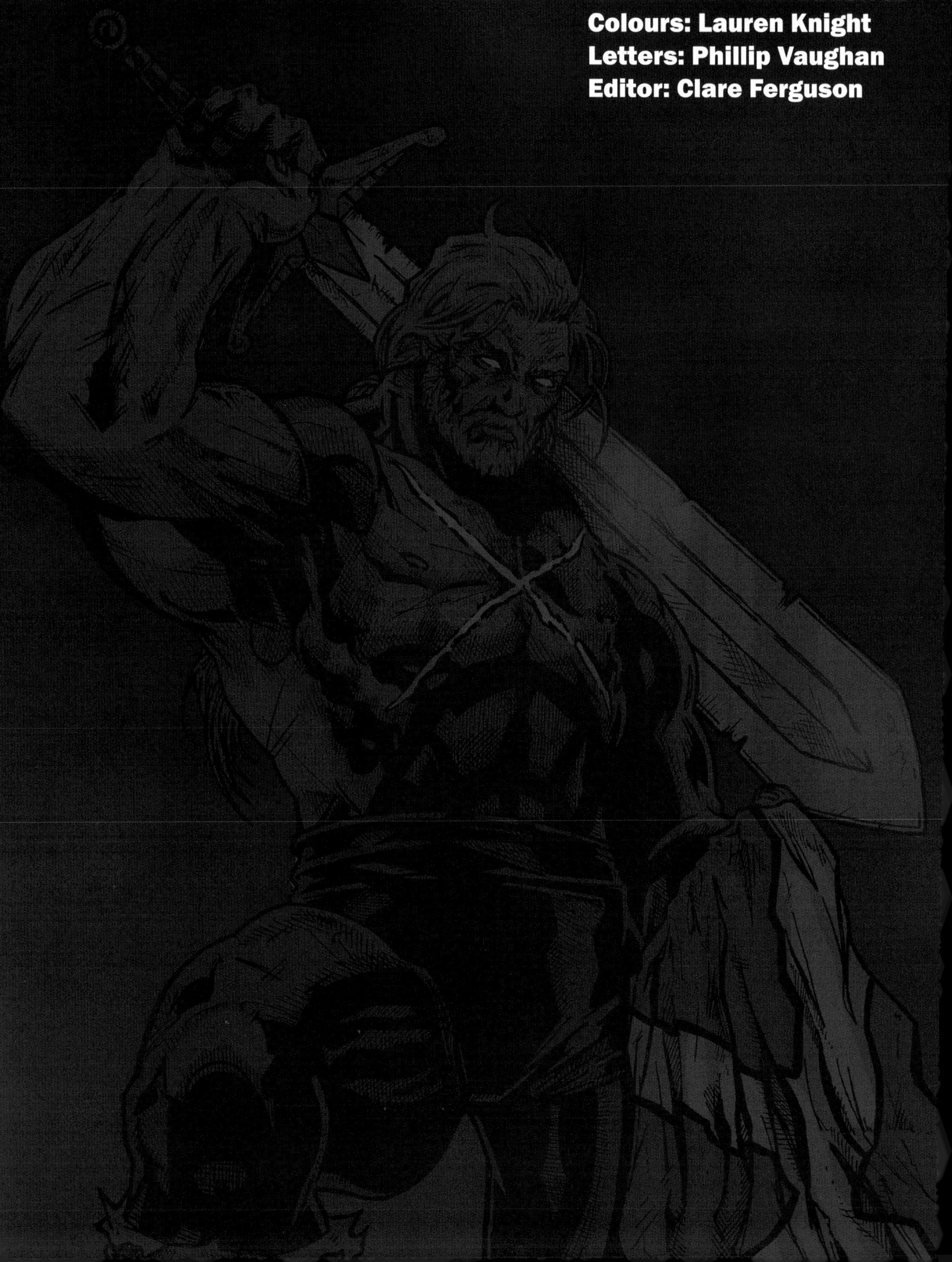

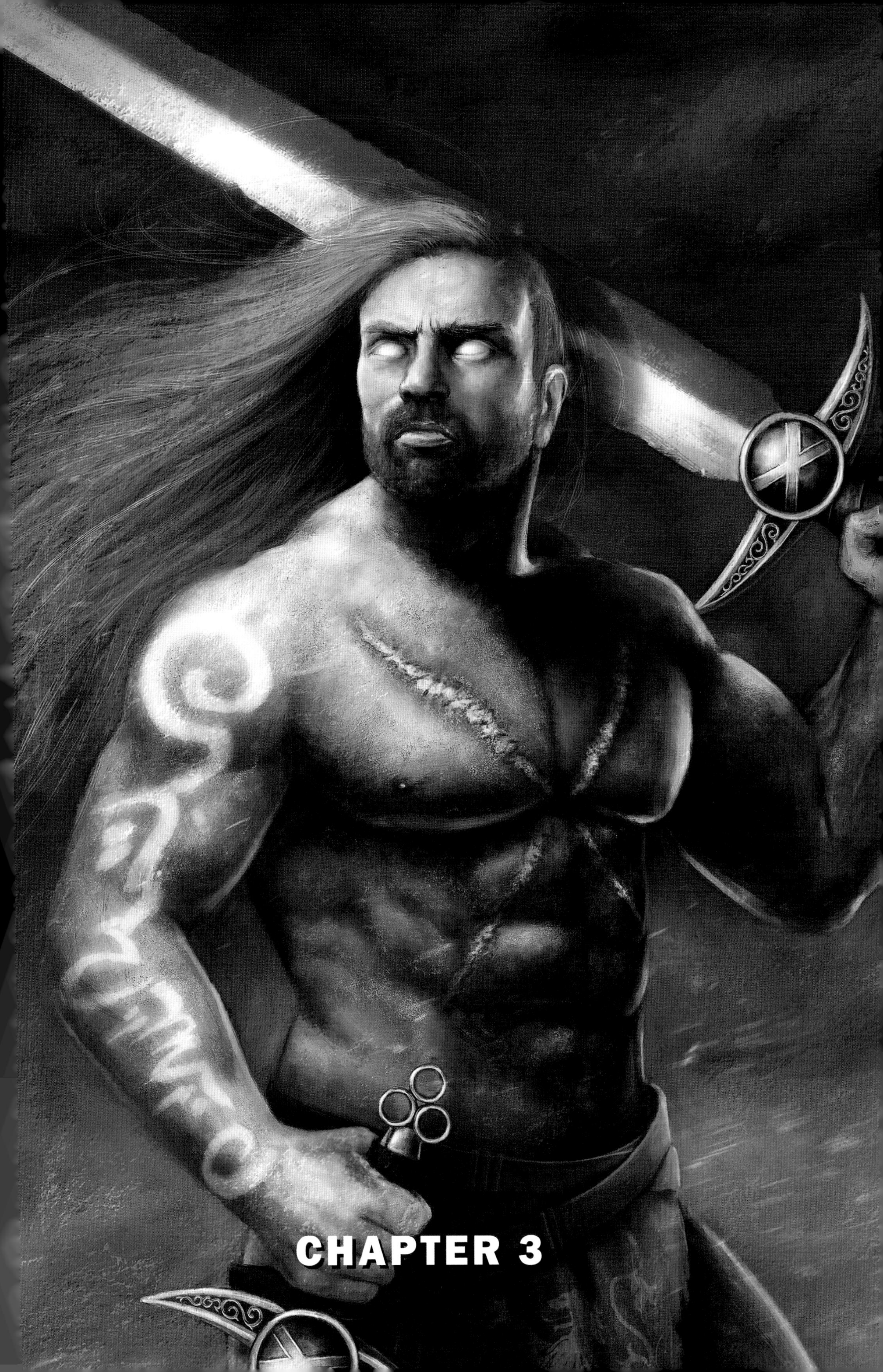

CHAPTER 3

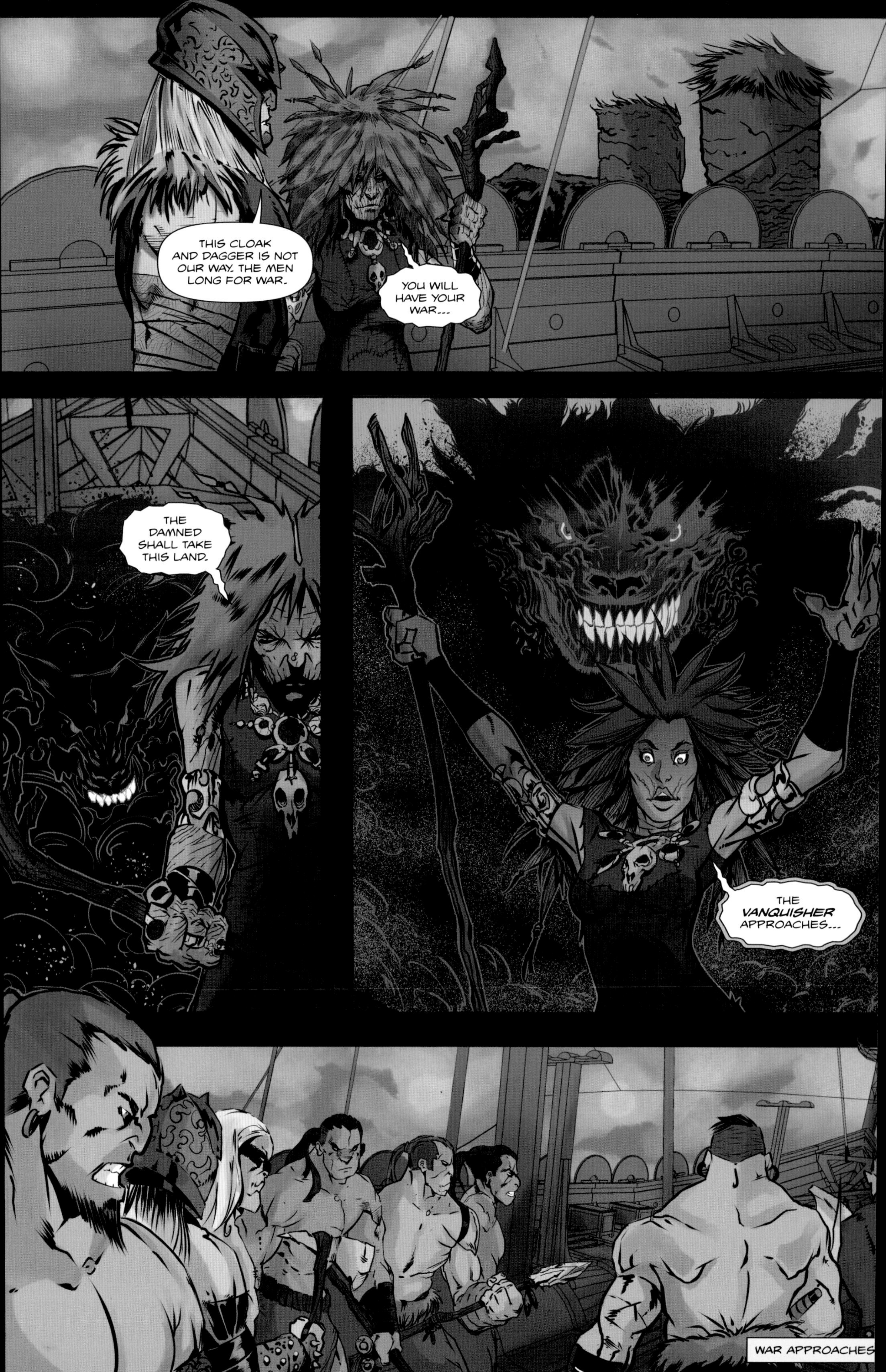
THIS CLOAK AND DAGGER IS NOT OUR WAY. THE MEN LONG FOR WAR.
YOU WILL HAVE YOUR WAR...
THE DAMNED SHALL TAKE THIS LAND.
THE VANQUISHER APPROACHES...
WAR APPROACHES

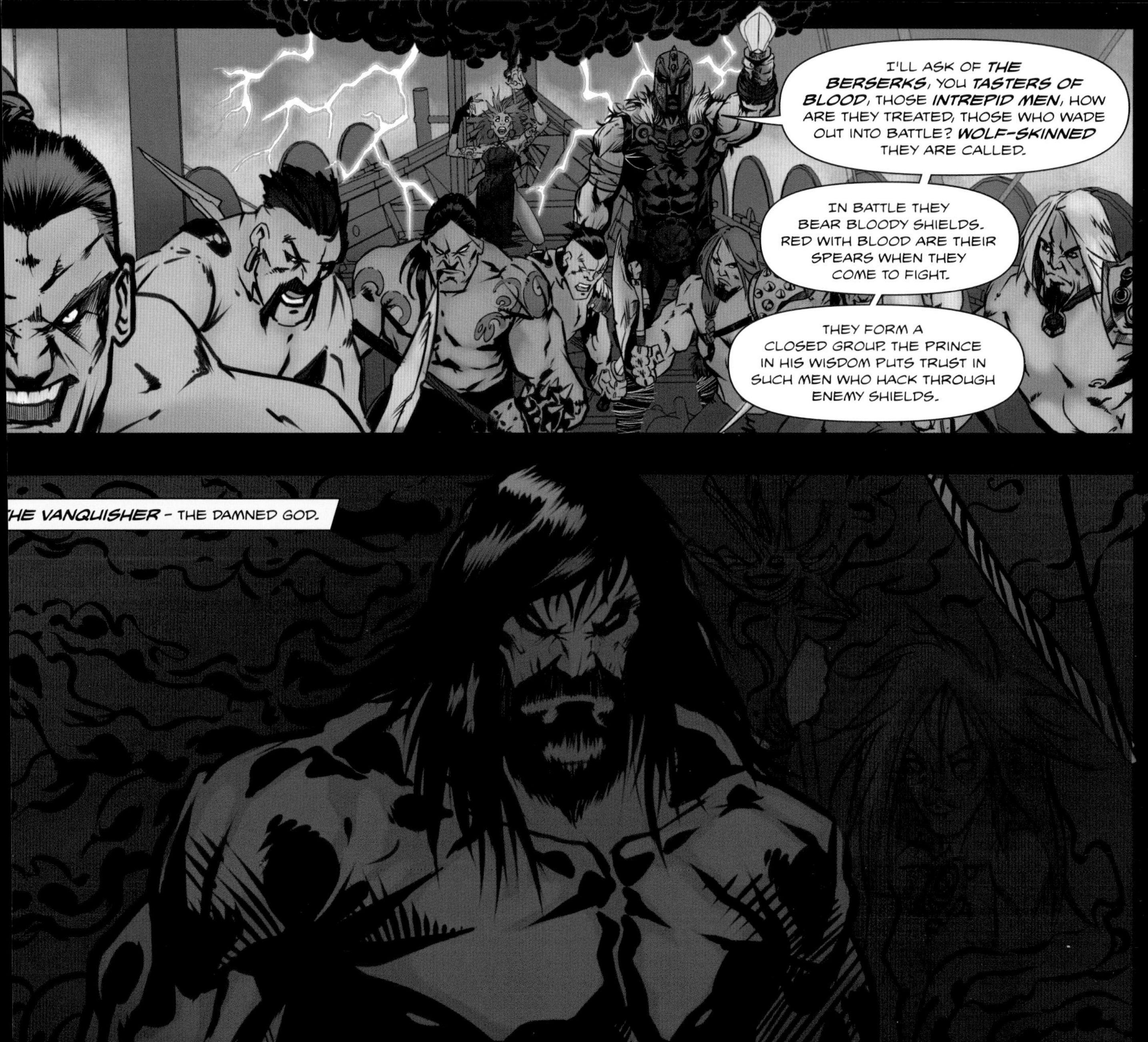
I'LL ASK OF THE BERSERKS, YOU TASTERS OF BLOOD, THOSE INTREPID MEN, HOW ARE THEY TREATED, THOSE WHO WADE OUT INTO BATTLE? WOLF-SKINNED THEY ARE CALLED.
IN BATTLE THEY BEAR BLOODY SHIELDS. RED WITH BLOOD ARE THEIR SPEARS WHEN THEY COME TO FIGHT.
THEY FORM A CLOSED GROUP. THE PRINCE IN HIS WISDOM PUTS TRUST IN SUCH MEN WHO HACK THROUGH ENEMY SHIELDS.
HE VANQUISHER - THE DAMNED GOD.

EVER WATCHFUL....

THE SHIPS CIRCLE THE COASTLINE, WAITING...

WHATEVER THEY BRING, WE ARE READY.

THEY BRING *DEATH*...

WATCH OVER HIM.

THE FIELD OF BATTLE IS SET. ITS PIECES MOVE INTO PLAC

ELFLAME, THE ETHEREAL REALM.

EILYS, THE ORACLE, BEFORE THE STATUE OF THE GODDESS *ARWEN.*

I AM CALLED TO THE MORTAL WORLD.

THE PROPHECY OF ARWEN PLEADS CAUTION.

RIADA, GUARDIAN OF THE FAE.

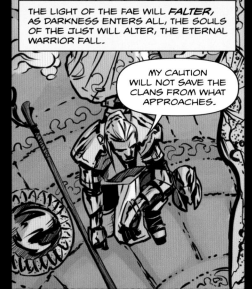

THE LIGHT OF THE FAE WILL *FALTER,* AS DARKNESS ENTERS ALL, THE SOULS OF THE JUST WILL ALTER, THE ETERNAL WARRIOR FALL.

MY CAUTION WILL NOT SAVE THE CLANS FROM WHAT APPROACHES.

INO, THE STONE FOOTPR *LAND OF THE SEERS.*

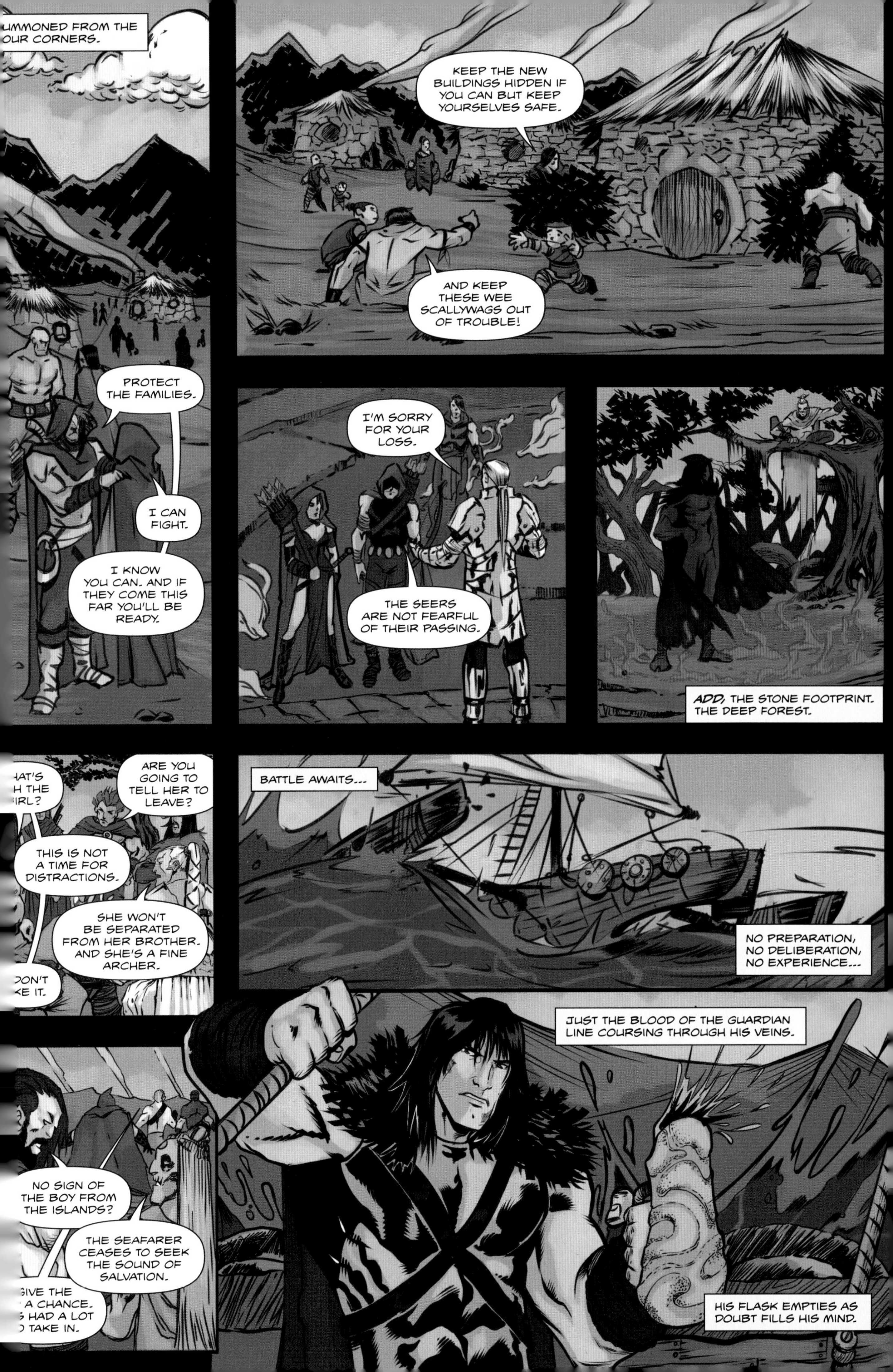
UMMONED FROM THE
OUR CORNERS.
KEEP THE NEW BUILDINGS HIDDEN IF YOU CAN BUT KEEP YOURSELVES SAFE.
AND KEEP THESE WEE SCALLYWAGS OUT OF TROUBLE!
PROTECT THE FAMILIES.
I CAN FIGHT.
I KNOW YOU CAN. AND IF THEY COME THIS FAR YOU'LL BE READY.
I'M SORRY FOR YOUR LOSS.
THE SEERS ARE NOT FEARFUL OF THEIR PASSING.
ADD, THE STONE FOOTPRINT. THE DEEP FOREST.
HAT'S H THE IRL?
ARE YOU GOING TO TELL HER TO LEAVE?
THIS IS NOT A TIME FOR DISTRACTIONS.
SHE WON'T BE SEPARATED FROM HER BROTHER. AND SHE'S A FINE ARCHER.
DON'T KE IT.
BATTLE AWAITS...
NO PREPARATION, NO DELIBERATION, NO EXPERIENCE...
JUST THE BLOOD OF THE GUARDIAN LINE COURSING THROUGH HIS VEINS.
NO SIGN OF THE BOY FROM THE ISLANDS?
THE SEAFARER CEASES TO SEEK THE SOUND OF SALVATION.
GIVE THE A CHANCE. HAD A LOT TAKE IN.
HIS FLASK EMPTIES AS DOUBT FILLS HIS MIND.

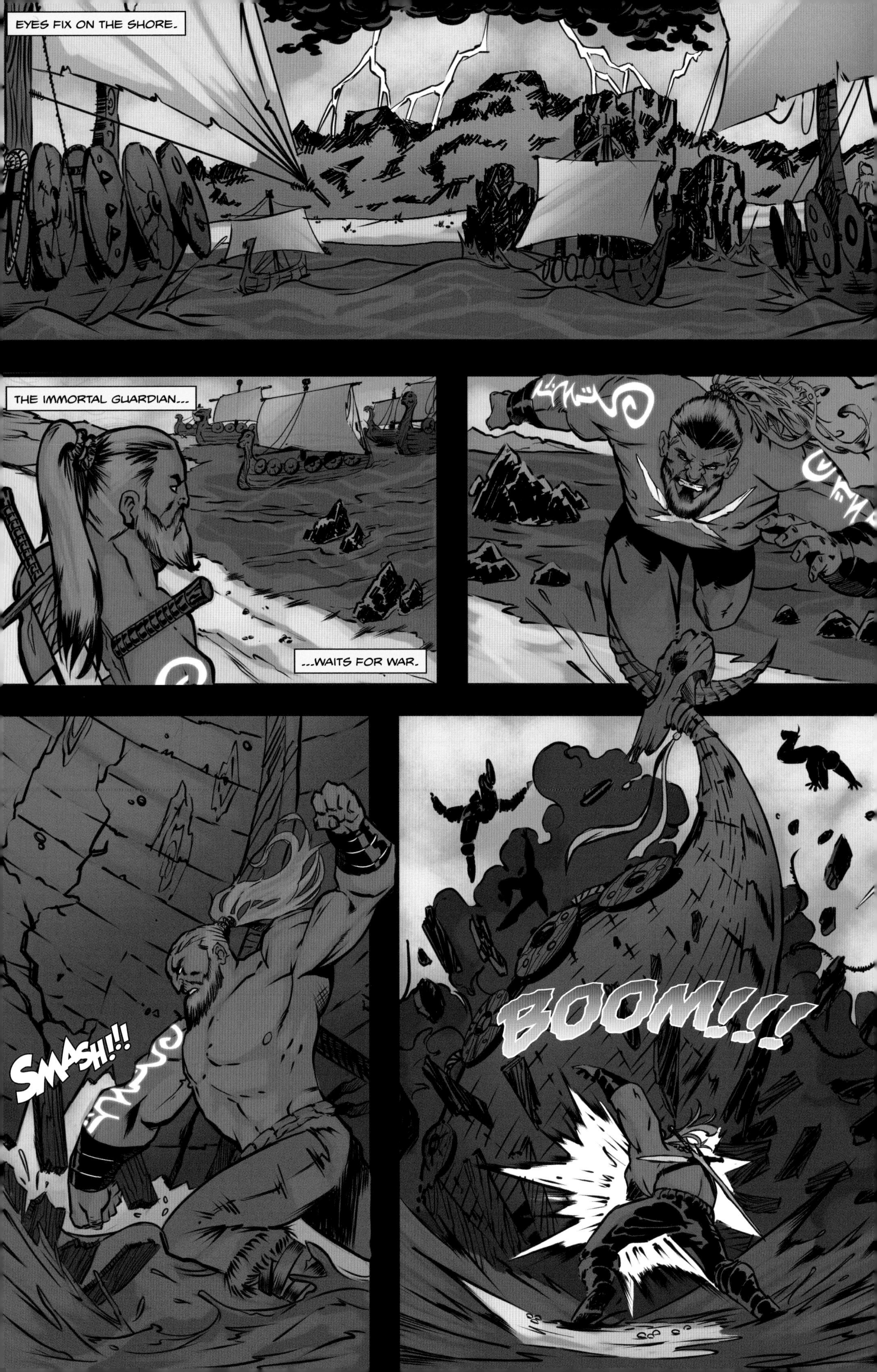
EYES FIX ON THE SHORE.
THE IMMORTAL GUARDIAN...
...WAITS FOR WAR.
SMASH!!!
BOOM!!!

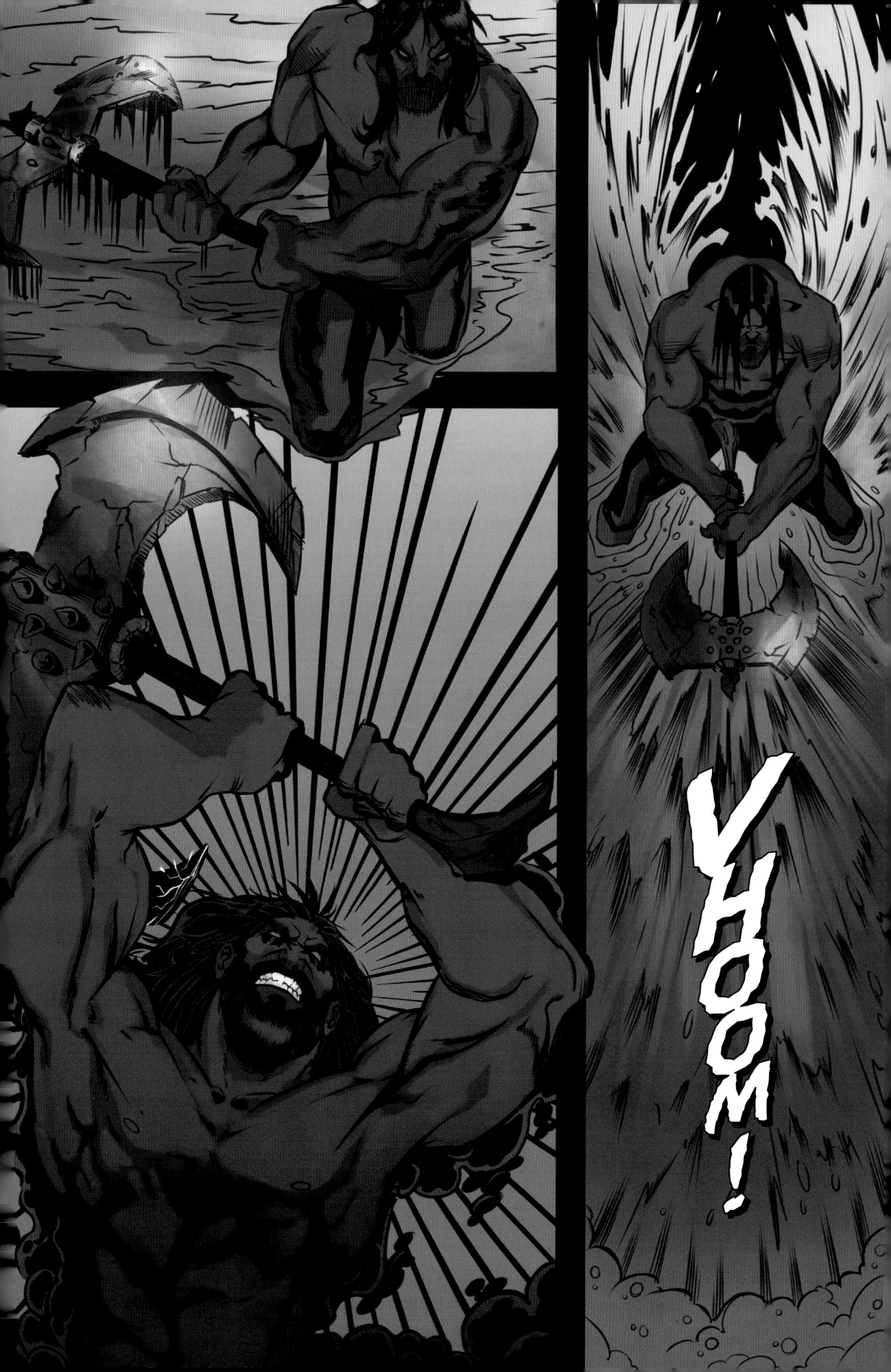
VHOOM!

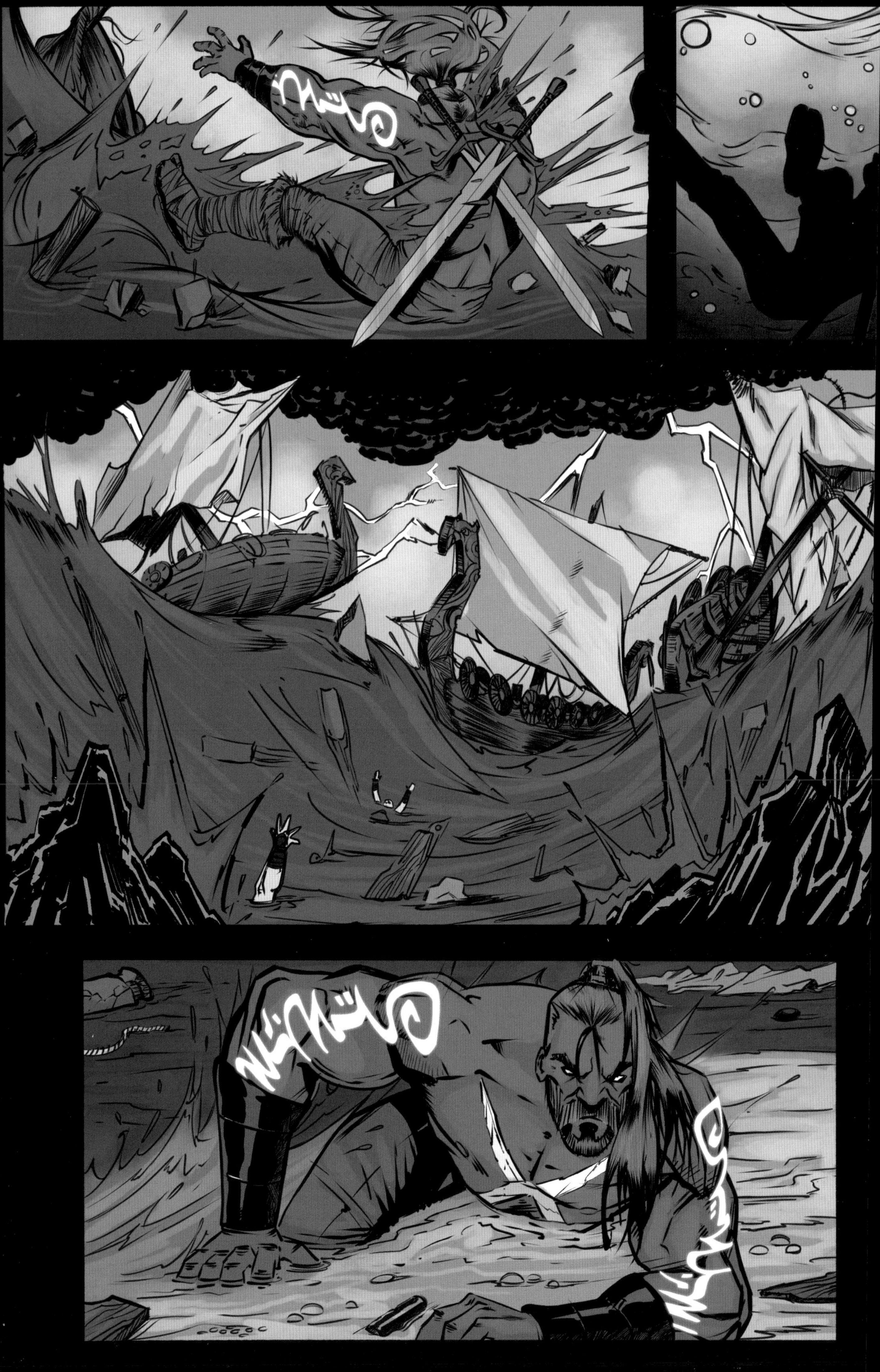

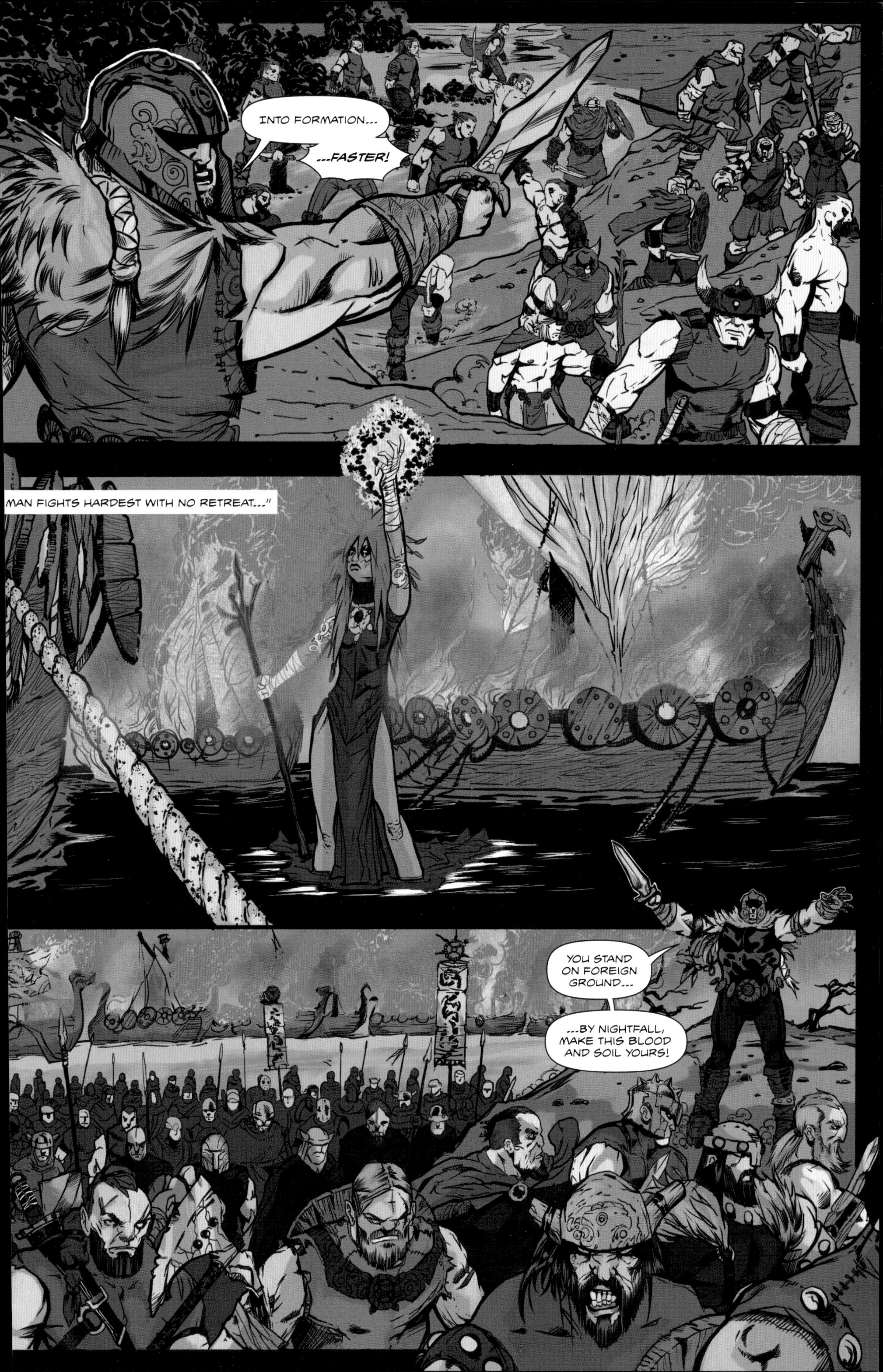
INTO FORMATION...
...FASTER!
MAN FIGHTS HARDEST WITH NO RETREAT..."
YOU STAND ON FOREIGN GROUND...
...BY NIGHTFALL, MAKE THIS BLOOD AND SOIL YOURS!

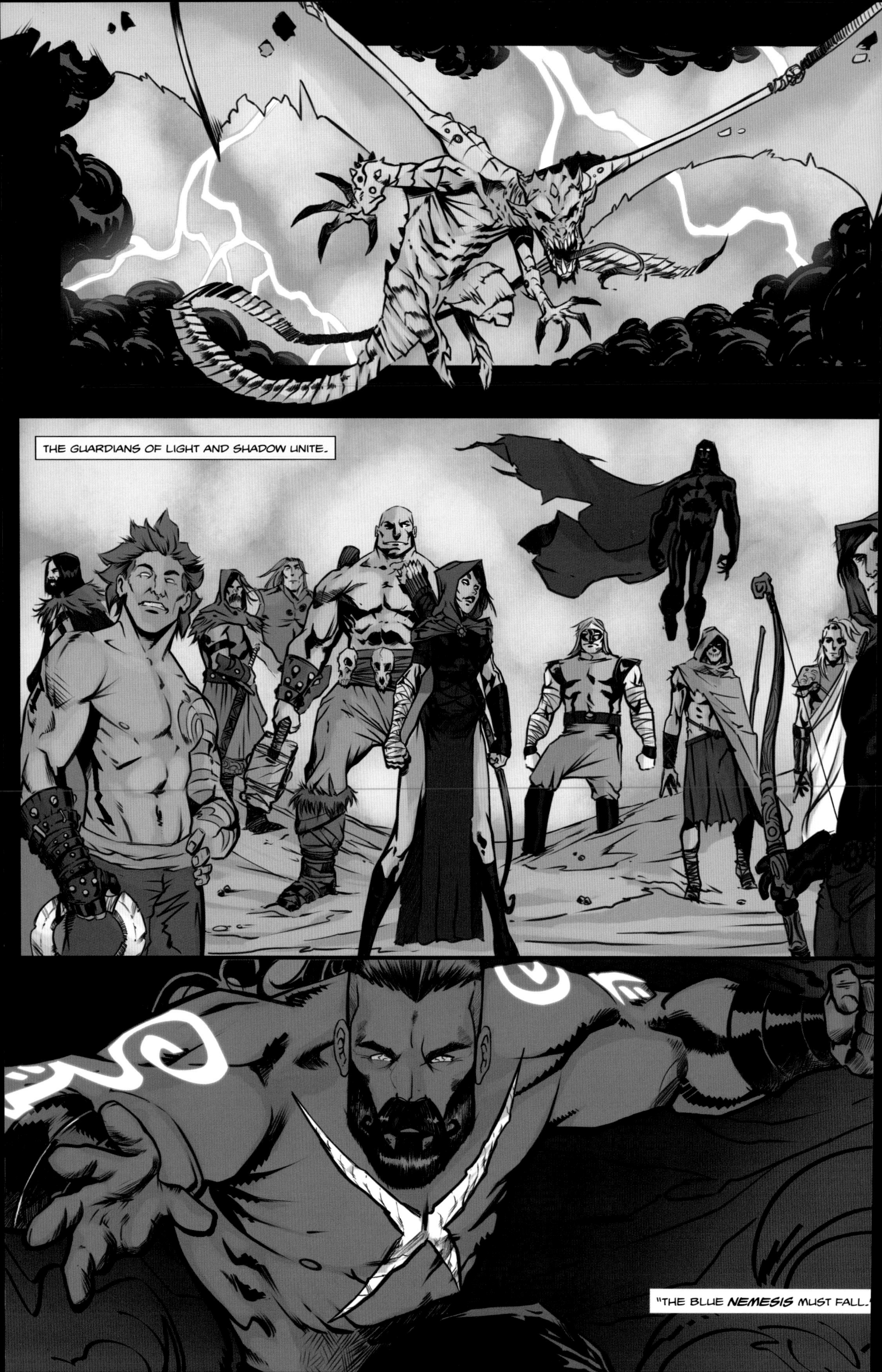
THE GUARDIANS OF LIGHT AND SHADOW UNITE.
"THE BLUE NEMESIS MUST FALL.

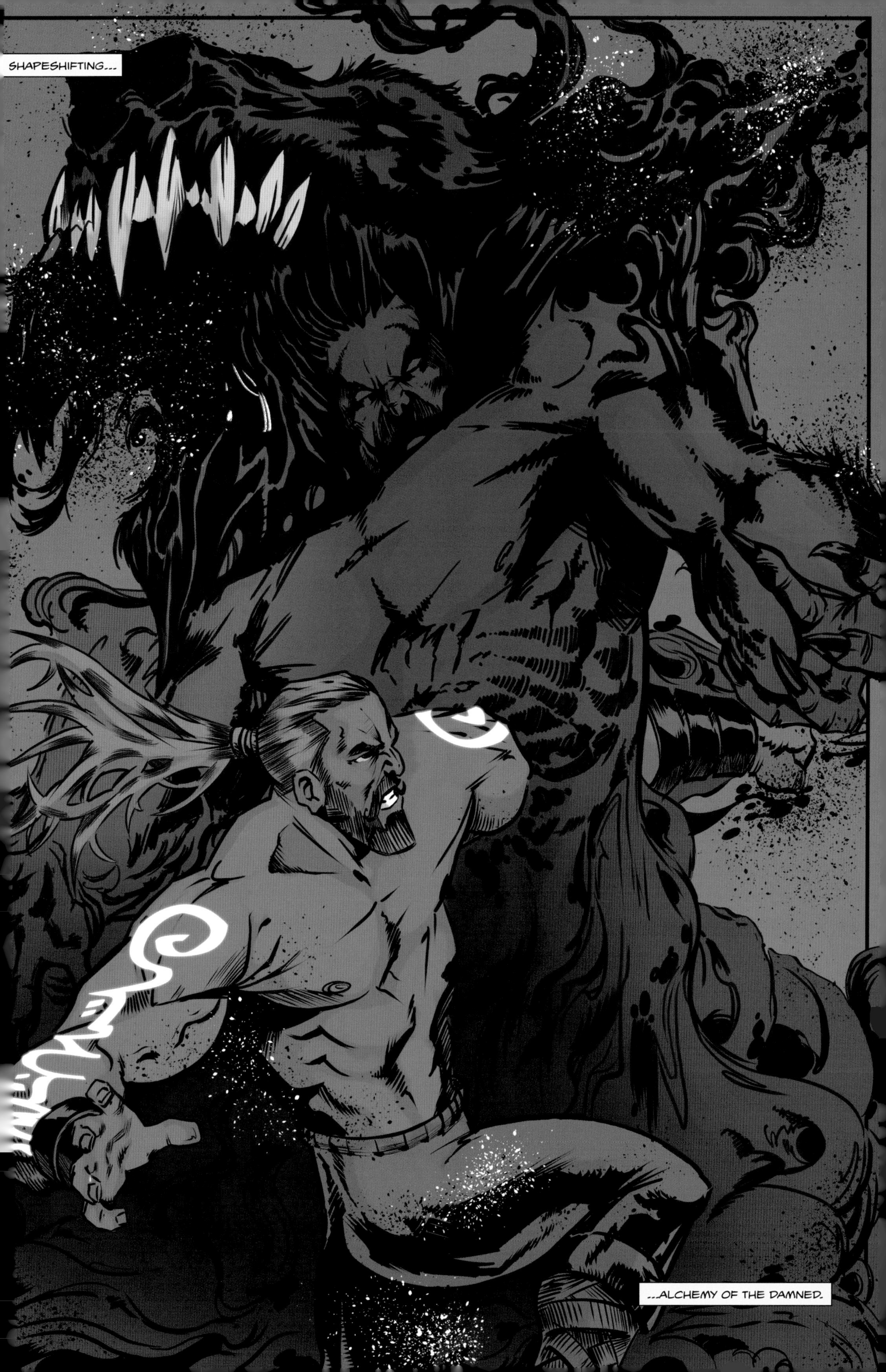

SHAPESHIFTING...
...ALCHEMY OF THE DAMNED.

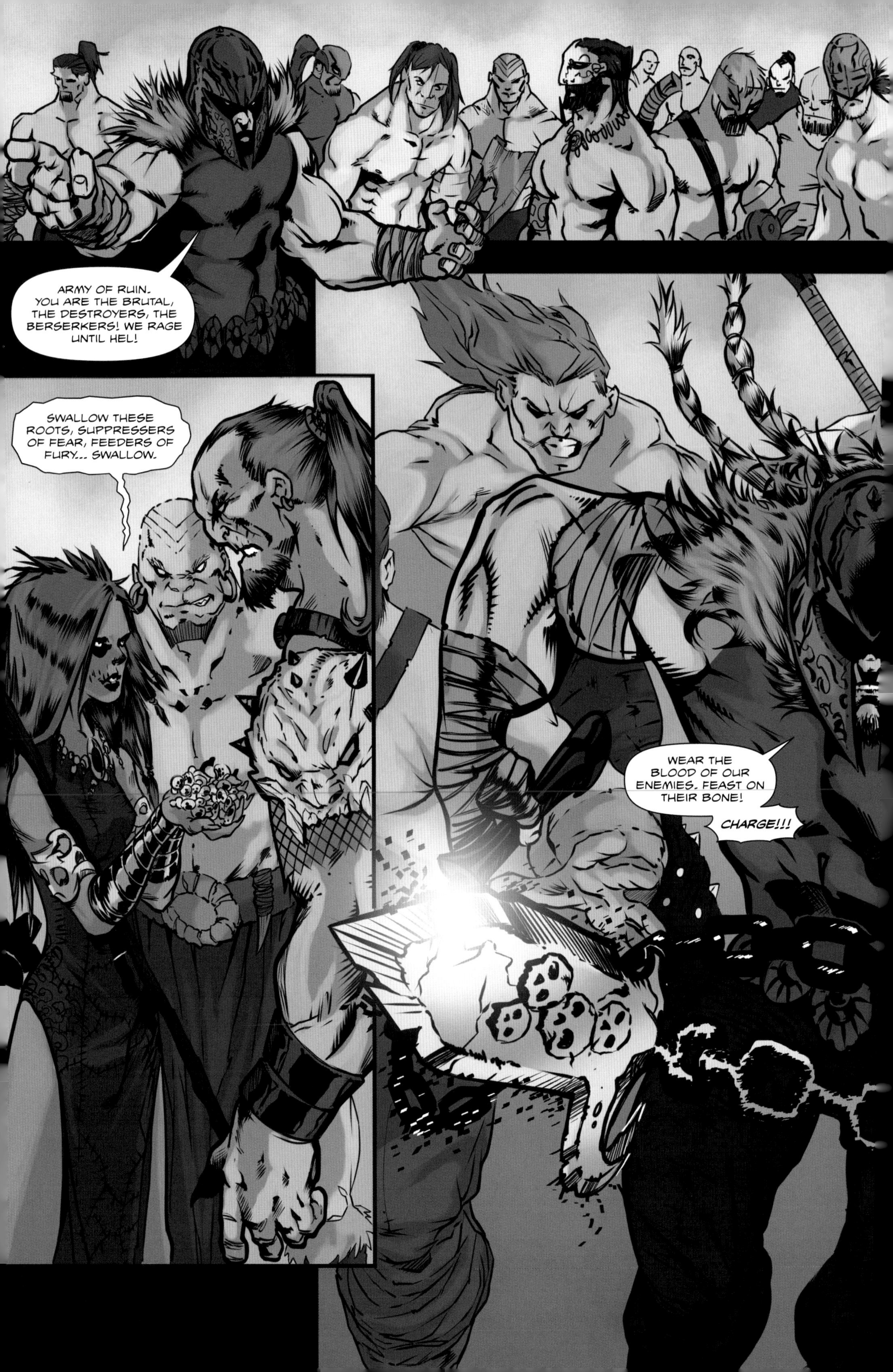
ARMY OF RUIN. YOU ARE THE BRUTAL, THE DESTROYERS, THE BERSERKERS! WE RAGE UNTIL HEL!
SWALLOW THESE ROOTS, SUPPRESSERS OF FEAR, FEEDERS OF FURY... SWALLOW.
WEAR THE BLOOD OF OUR ENEMIES. FEAST ON THEIR BONE!
CHARGE!!!

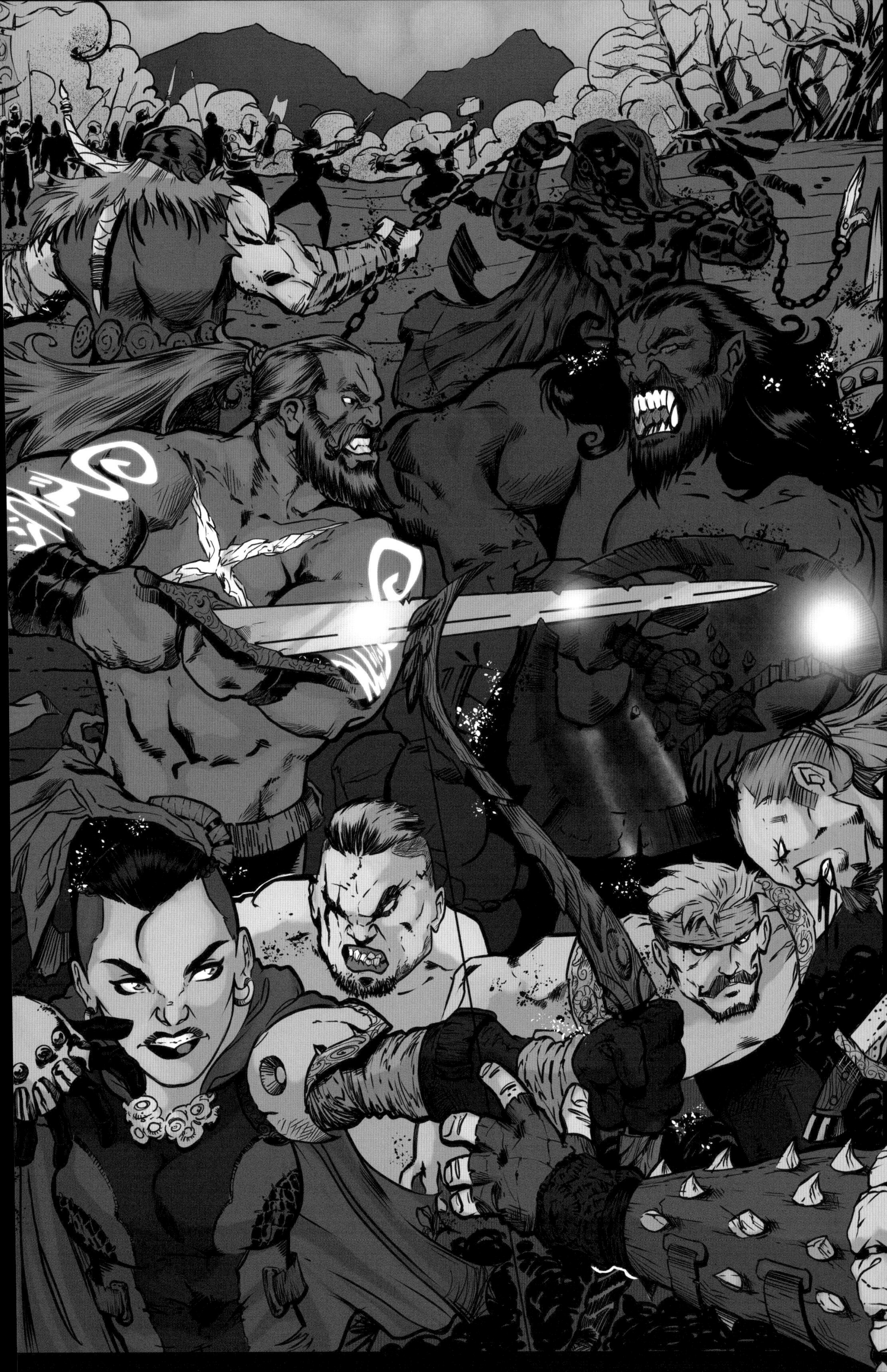

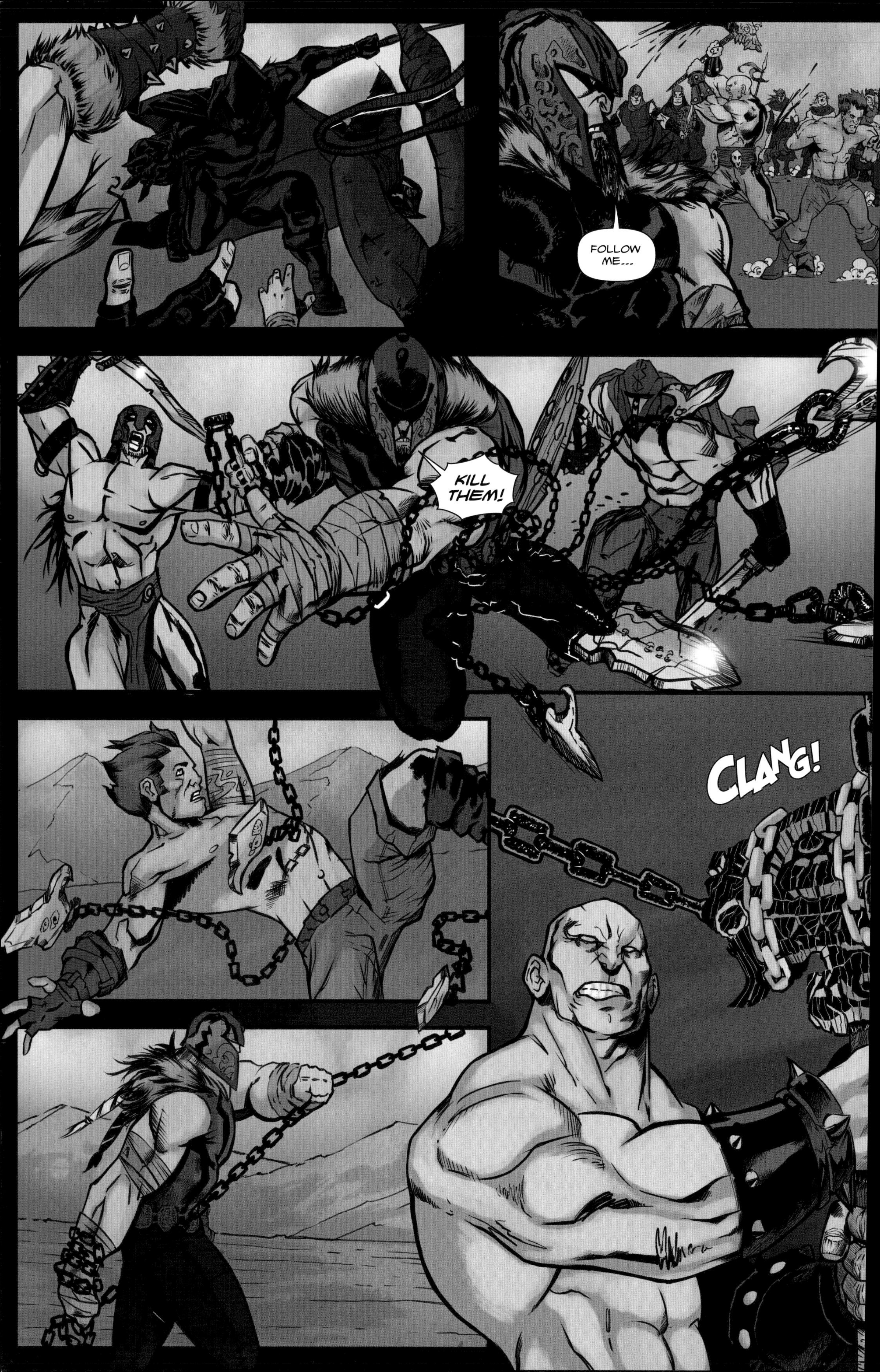
FOLLOW ME...
KILL THEM!
CLANG!

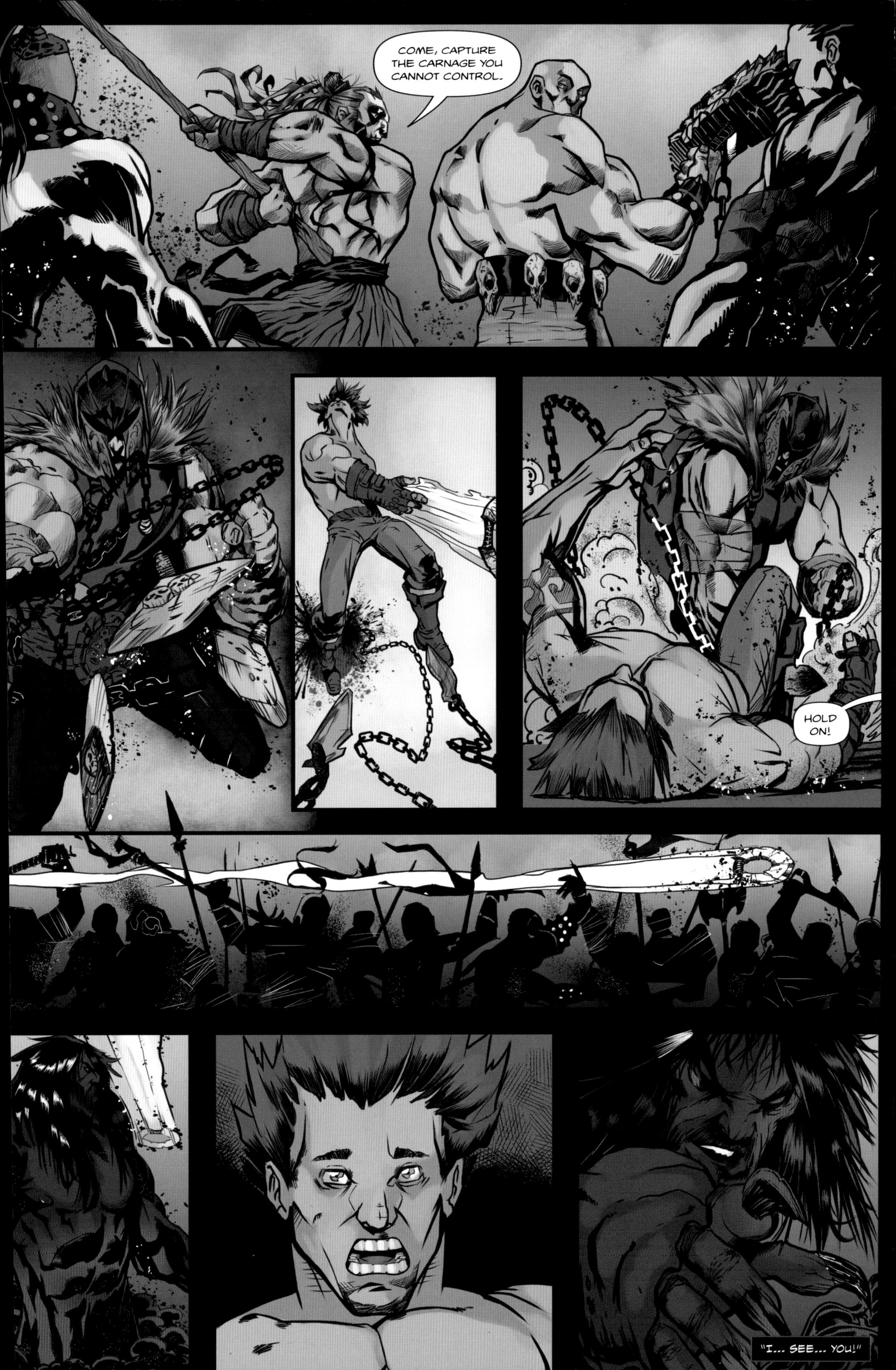
COME, CAPTURE THE CARNAGE YOU CANNOT CONTROL.
HOLD ON!
"I... SEE... YOU!"

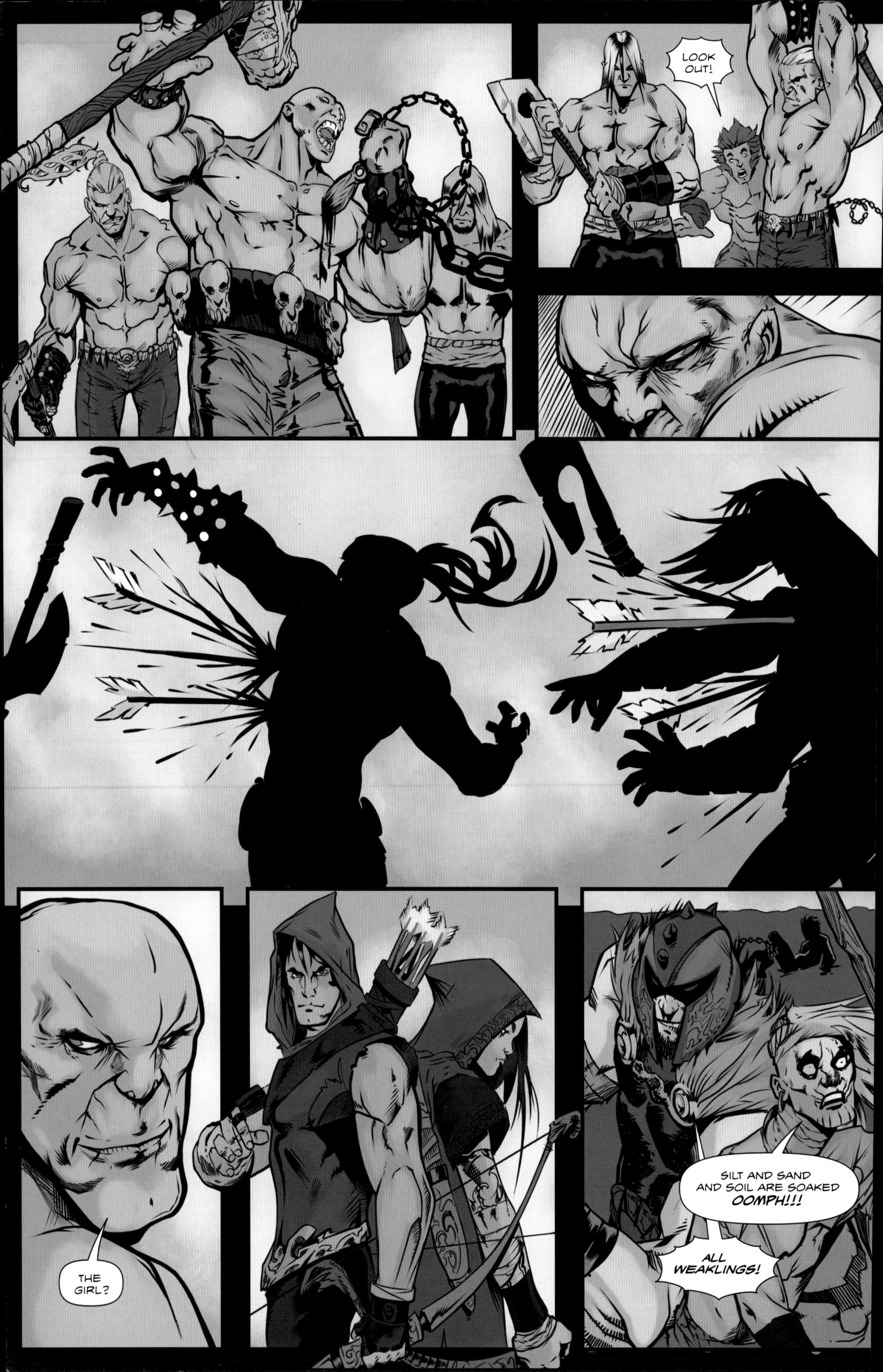
LOOK OUT!
THE GIRL?
SILT AND SAND AND SOIL ARE SOAKED OOMPH!!!
ALL WEAKLINGS!

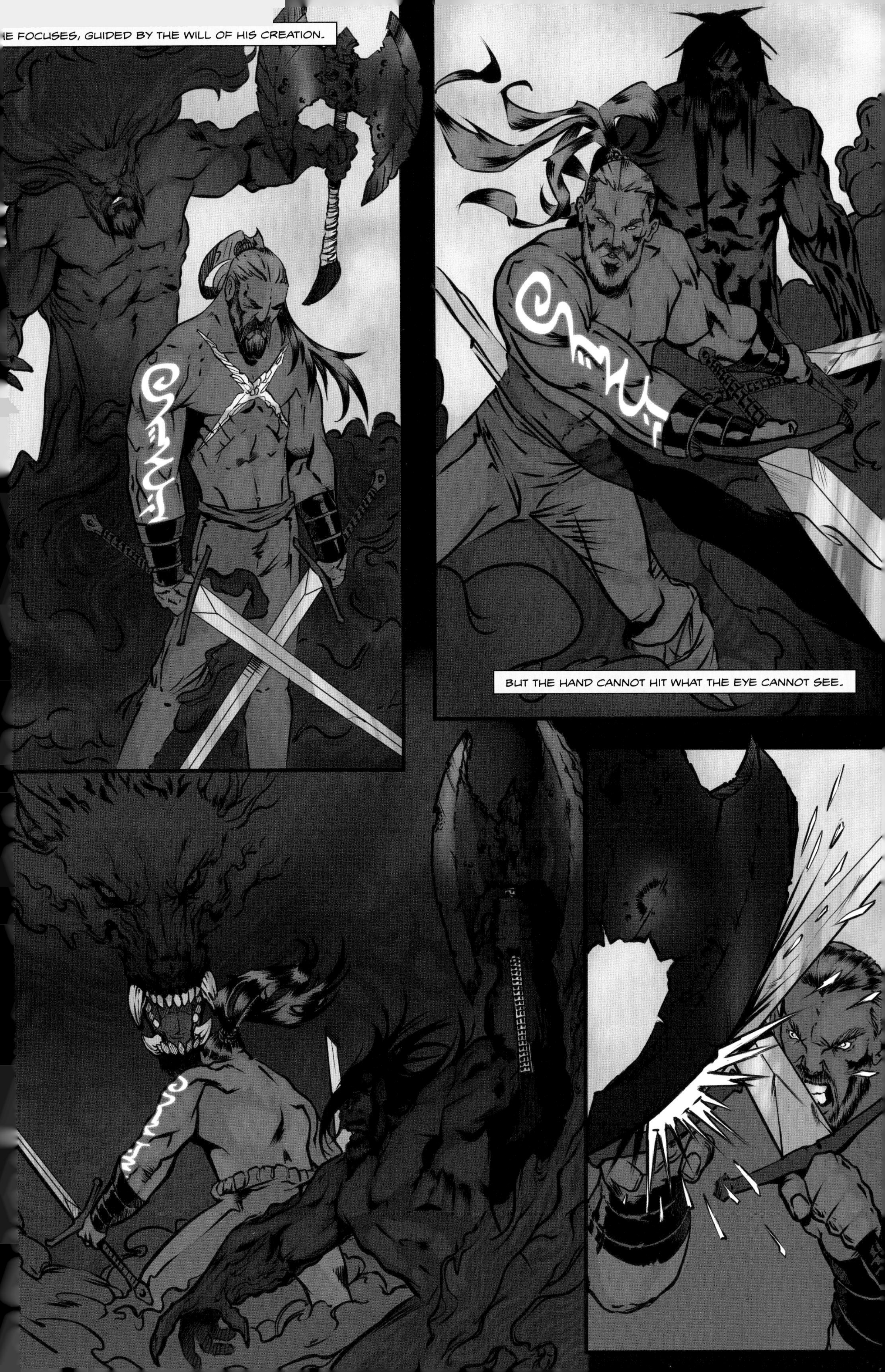

E FOCUSES, GUIDED BY THE WILL OF HIS CREATION.
BUT THE HAND CANNOT HIT WHAT THE EYE CANNOT SEE.

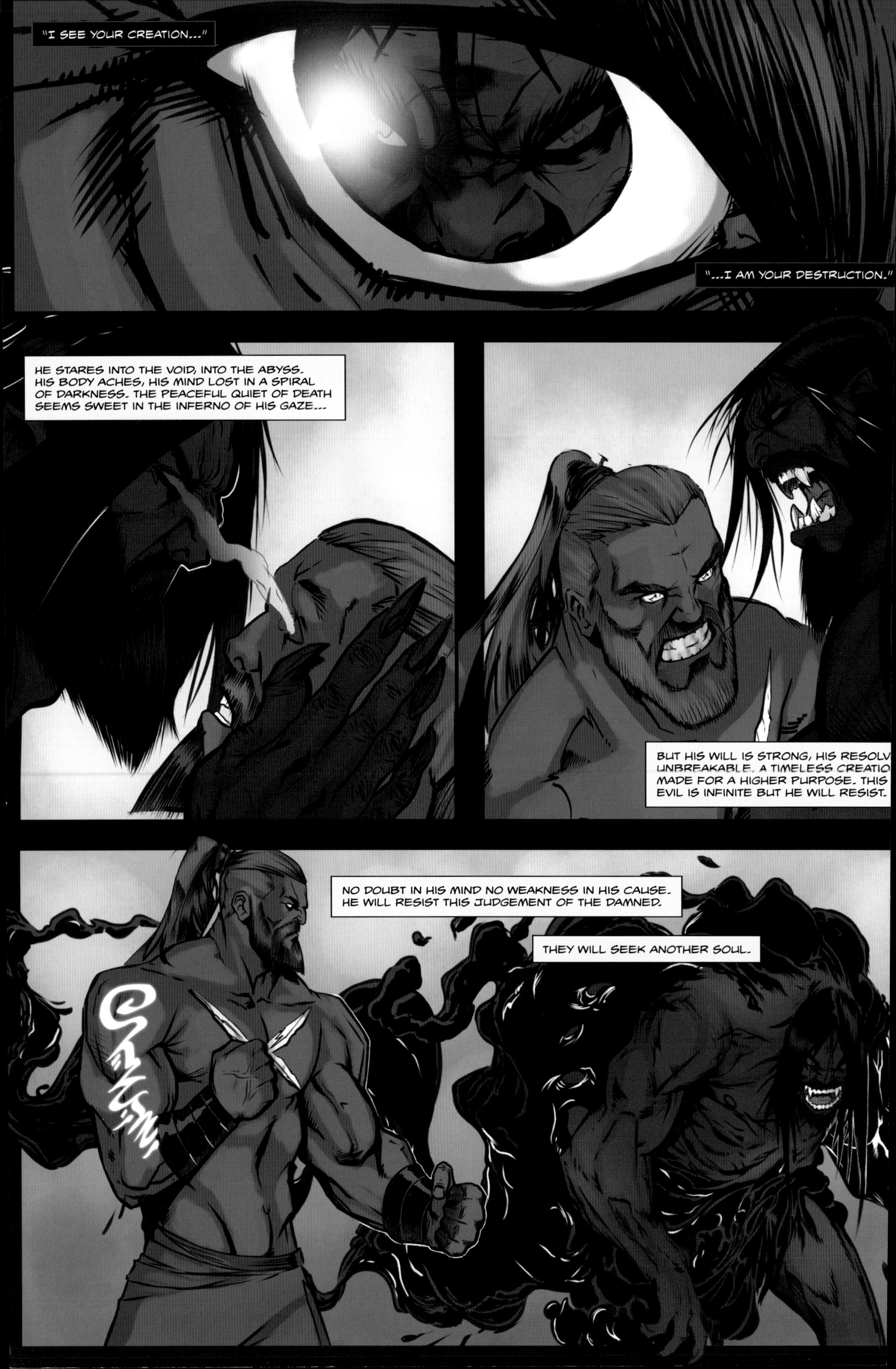
"I SEE YOUR CREATION..."
"...I AM YOUR DESTRUCTION."
HE STARES INTO THE VOID, INTO THE ABYSS. HIS BODY ACHES, HIS MIND LOST IN A SPIRAL OF DARKNESS. THE PEACEFUL QUIET OF DEATH SEEMS SWEET IN THE INFERNO OF HIS GAZE...
BUT HIS WILL IS STRONG, HIS RESOLV UNBREAKABLE. A TIMELESS CREATIO MADE FOR A HIGHER PURPOSE. THIS EVIL IS INFINITE BUT HE WILL RESIST.
NO DOUBT IN HIS MIND NO WEAKNESS IN HIS CAUSE. HE WILL RESIST THIS JUDGEMENT OF THE DAMNED.
THEY WILL SEEK ANOTHER SOUL.

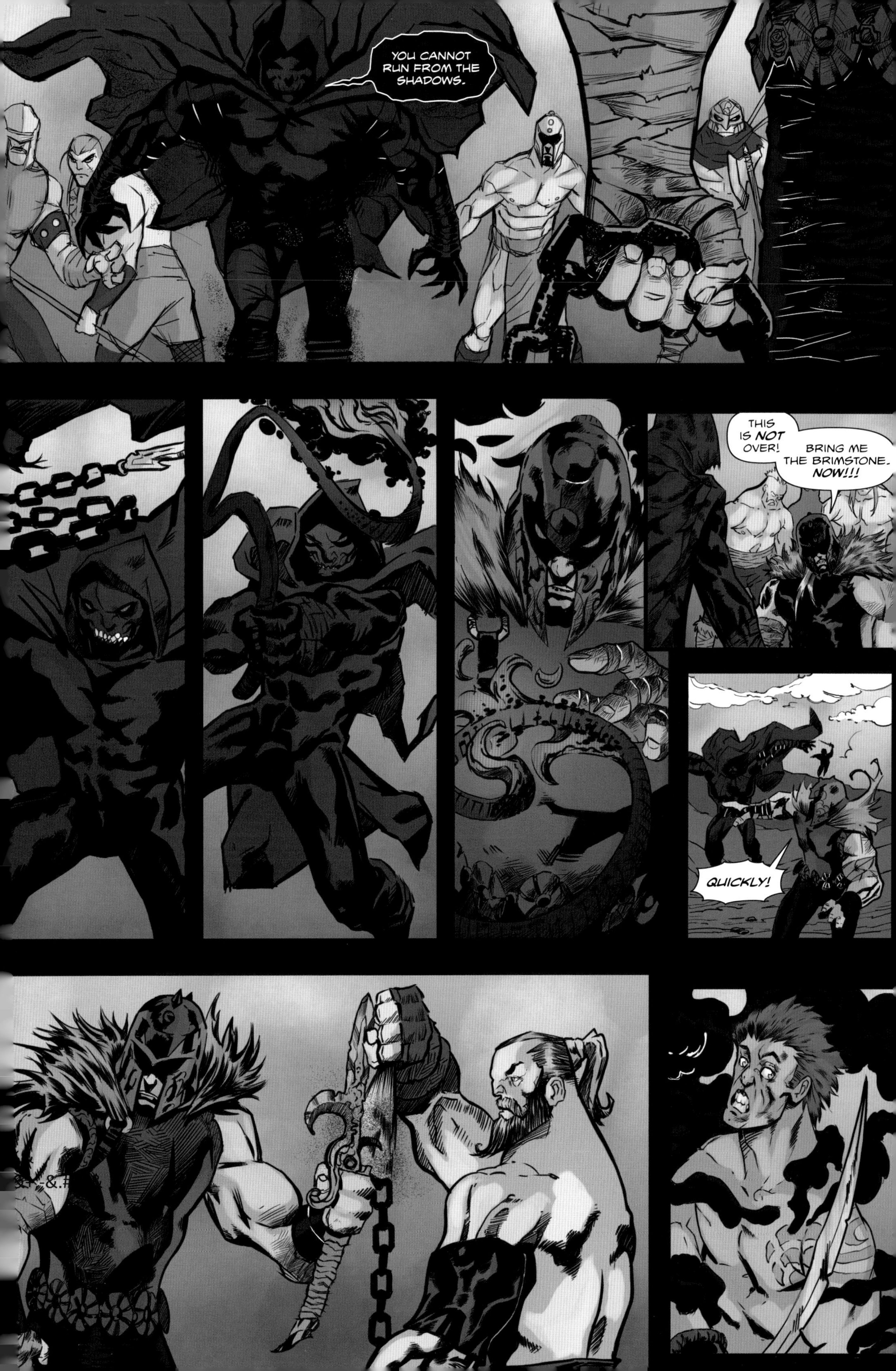
YOU CANNOT RUN FROM THE SHADOWS.
THIS IS ***NOT*** OVER!
BRING ME THE BRIMSTONE. ***NOW!!!***
QUICKLY!

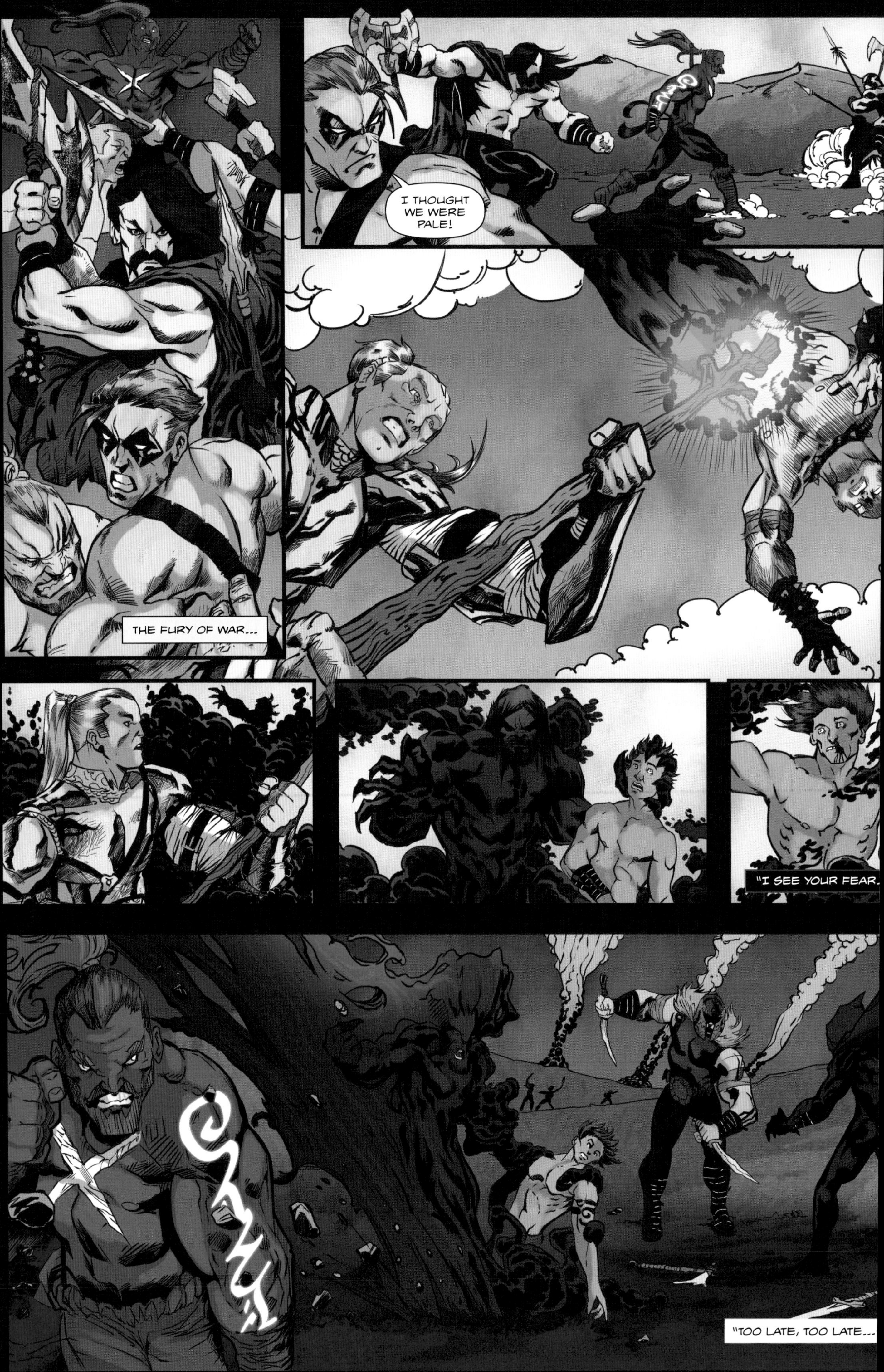
I THOUGHT WE WERE PALE!
THE FURY OF WAR...
"I SEE YOUR FEAR.
"TOO LATE, TOO LATE...

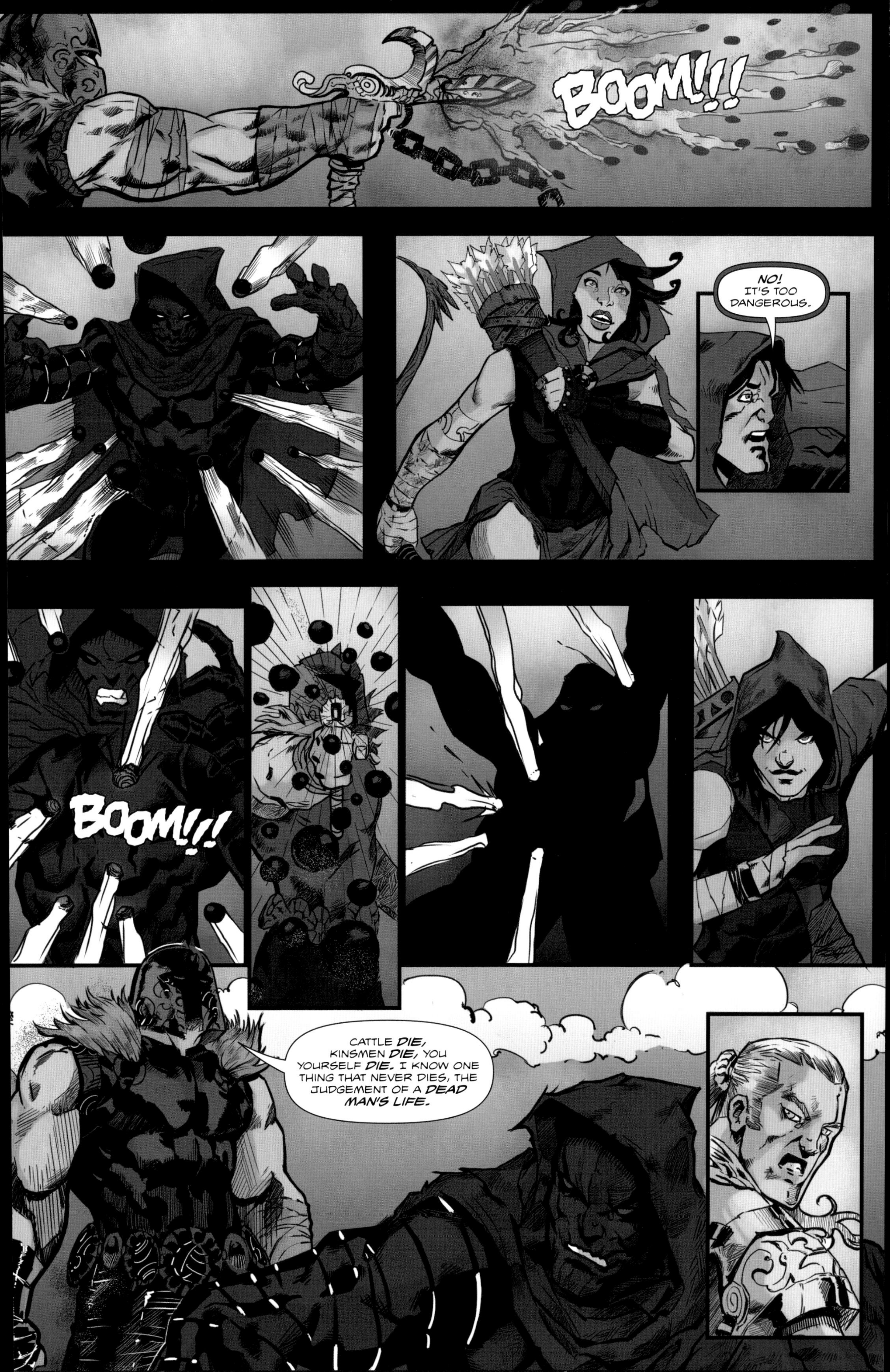
BOOM!!!
NO! IT'S TOO DANGEROUS.
BOOM!!!
CATTLE DIE, KINSMEN DIE, YOU YOURSELF DIE. I KNOW ONE THING THAT NEVER DIES, THE JUDGEMENT OF A DEAD MAN'S LIFE.

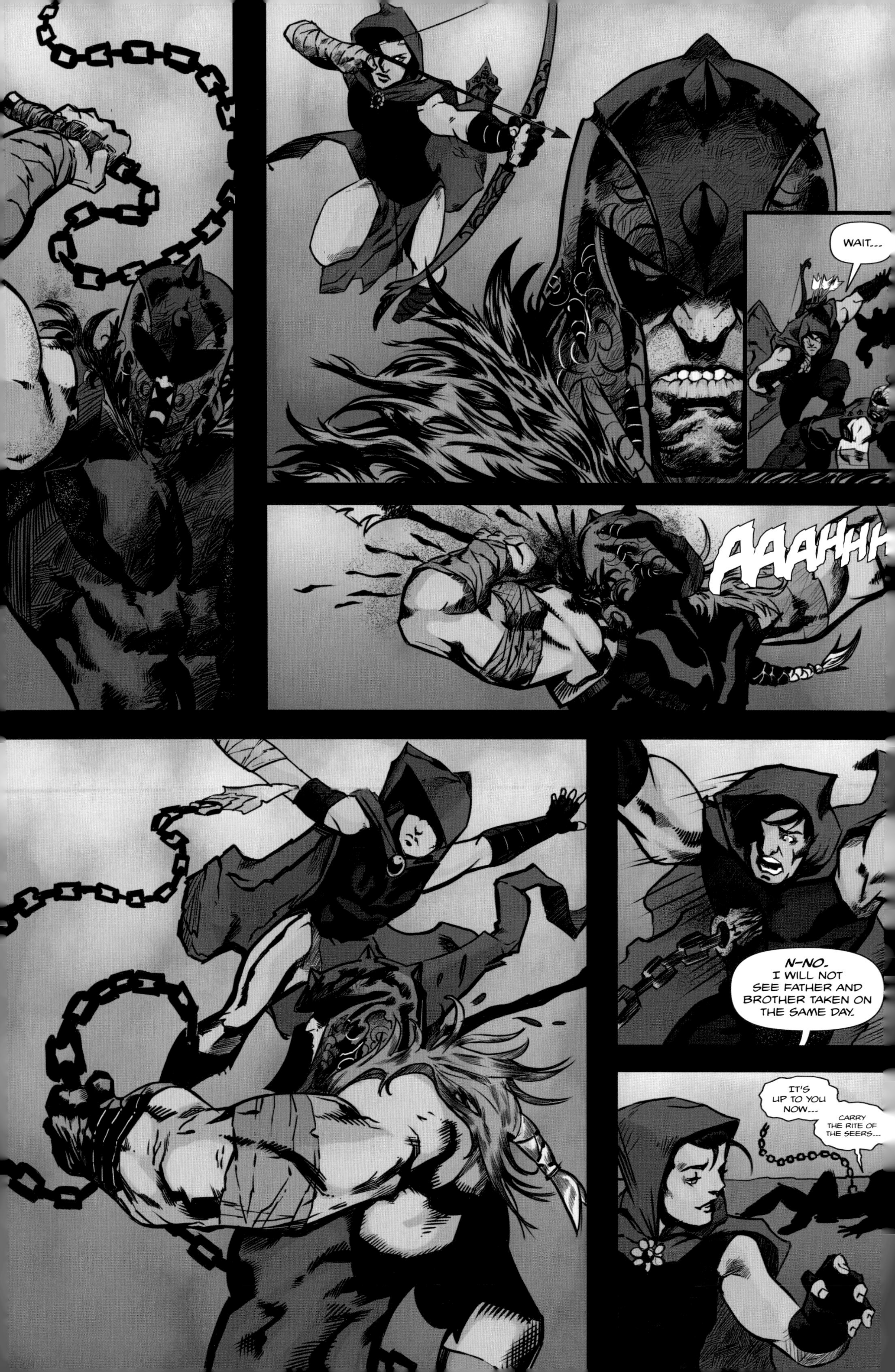
WAIT...
AAAHHH
N-NO. I WILL NOT SEE FATHER AND BROTHER TAKEN ON THE SAME DAY.
IT'S UP TO YOU NOW...
CARRY THE RITE OF THE SEERS...

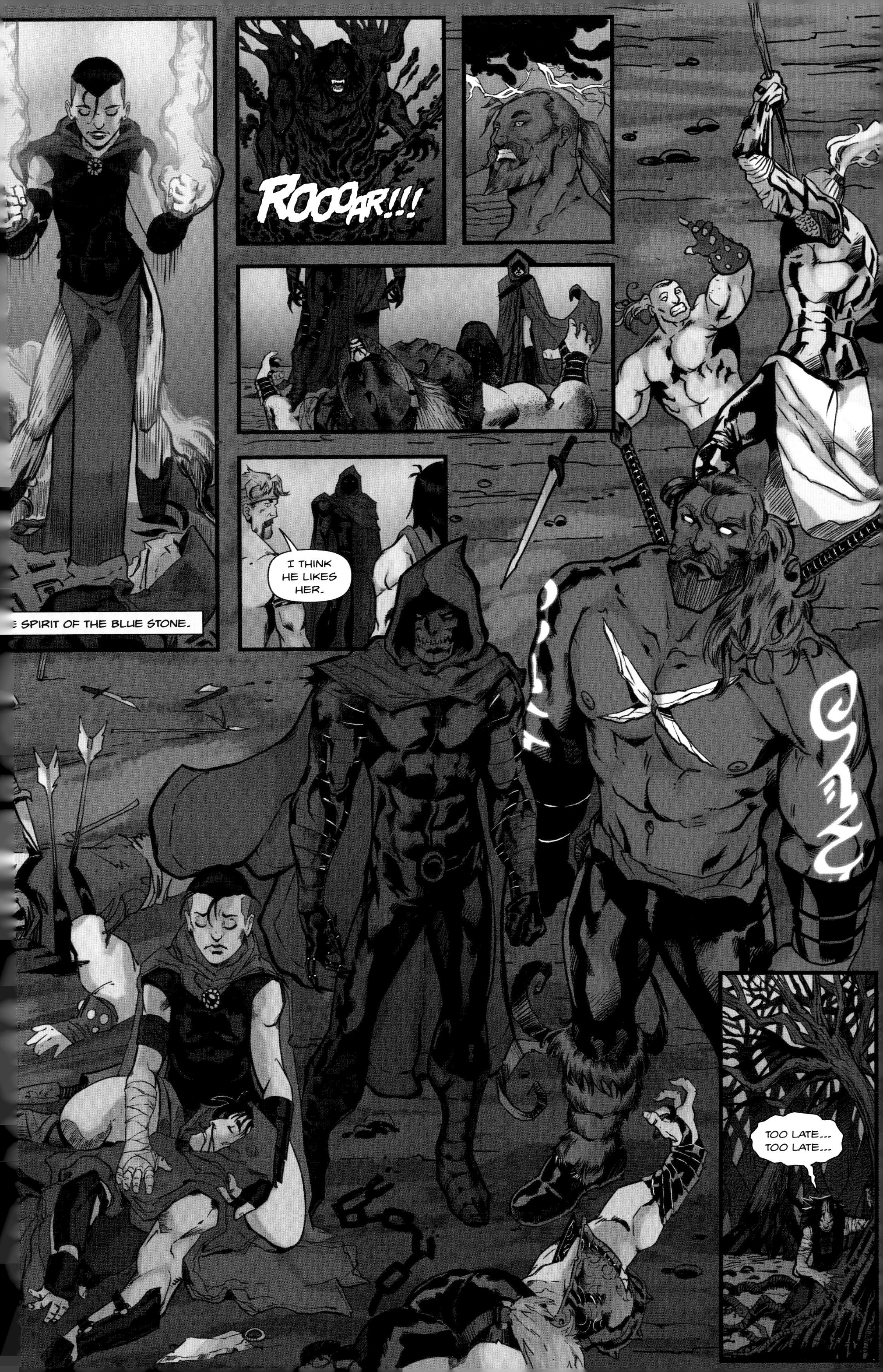
ROOOAR!!!
...E SPIRIT OF THE BLUE STONE.
I THINK HE LIKES HER.
TOO LATE... TOO LATE...

Chapter Four

Script: John Ferguson
Art: Toni Doya Heredia
Colours: Rebecca Horner
Letters: Phillip Vaughan
Editor: Clare Ferguson

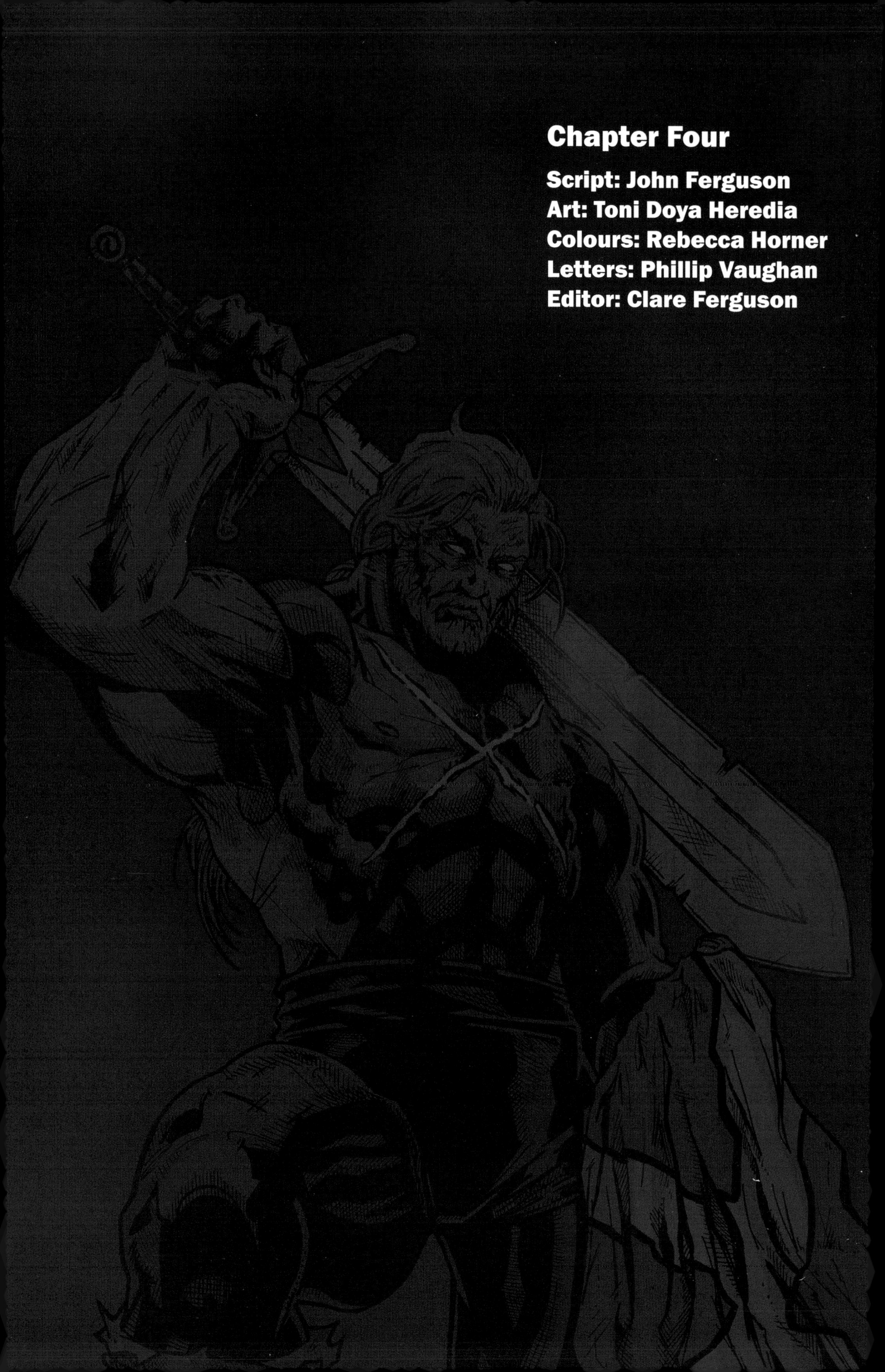

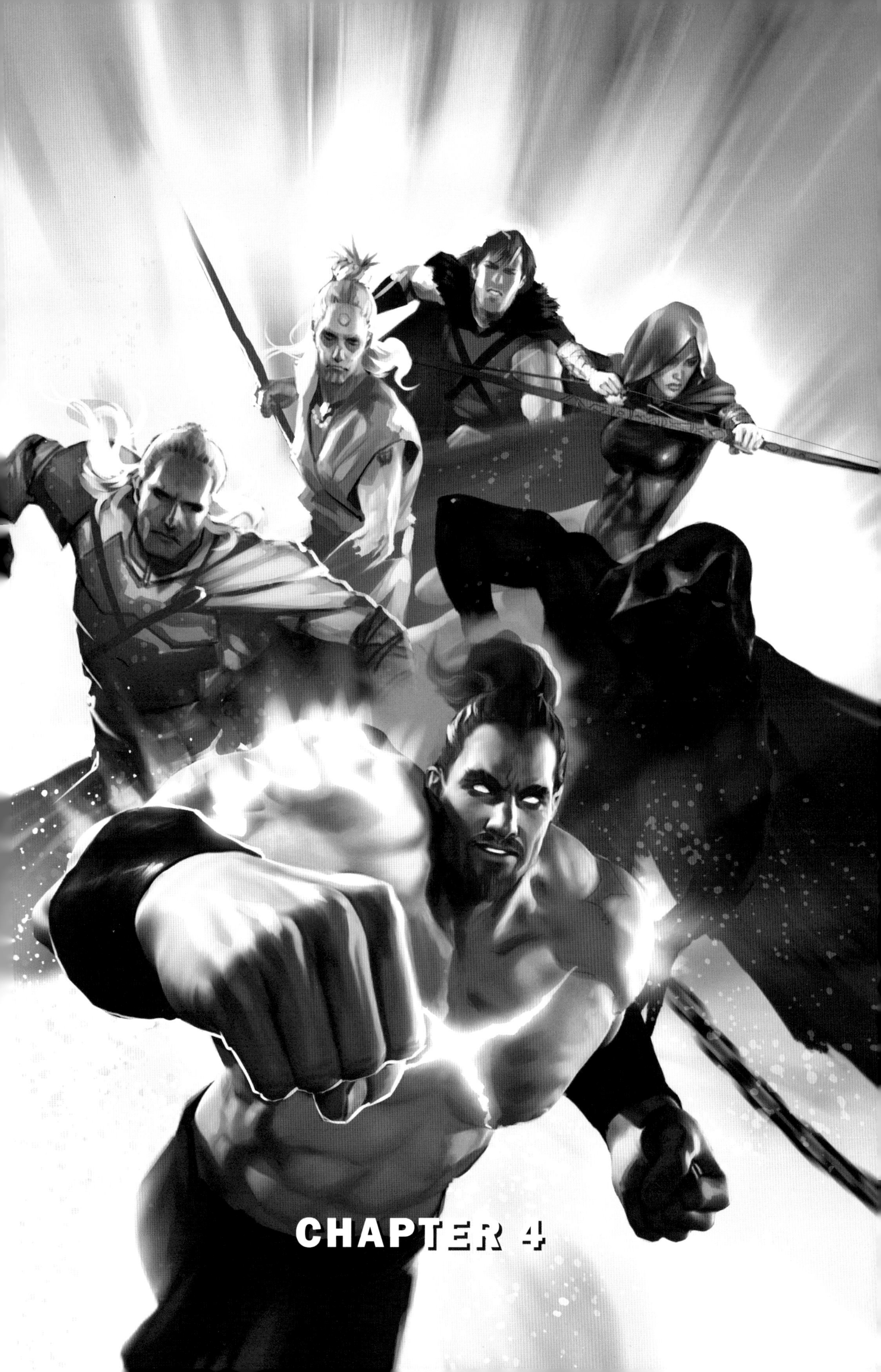
CHAPTER 4

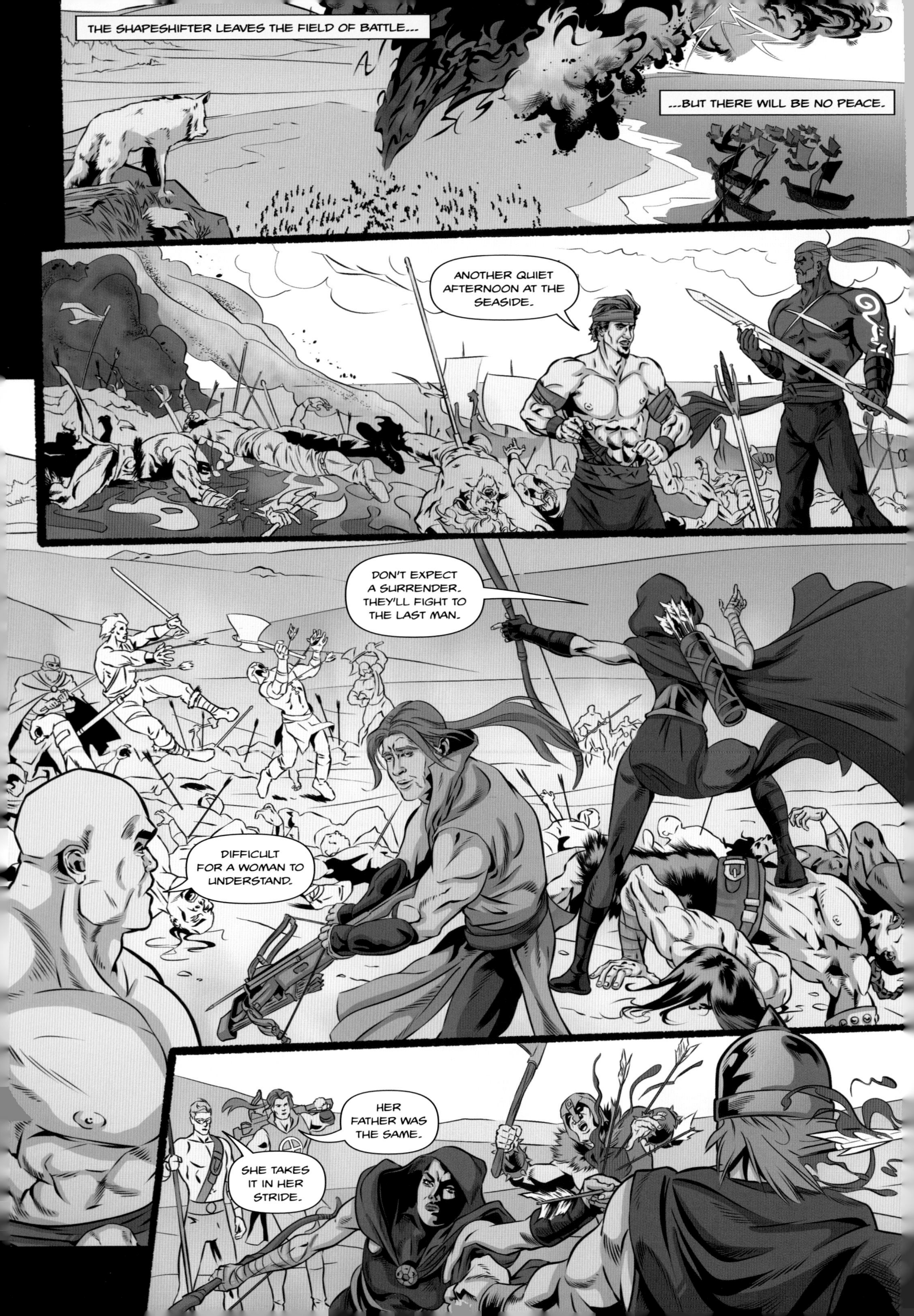
THE SHAPESHIFTER LEAVES THE FIELD OF BATTLE...
...BUT THERE WILL BE NO PEACE.
ANOTHER QUIET AFTERNOON AT THE SEASIDE.
DON'T EXPECT A SURRENDER. THEY'LL FIGHT TO THE LAST MAN.
DIFFICULT FOR A WOMAN TO UNDERSTAND.
HER FATHER WAS THE SAME.
SHE TAKES IT IN HER STRIDE.

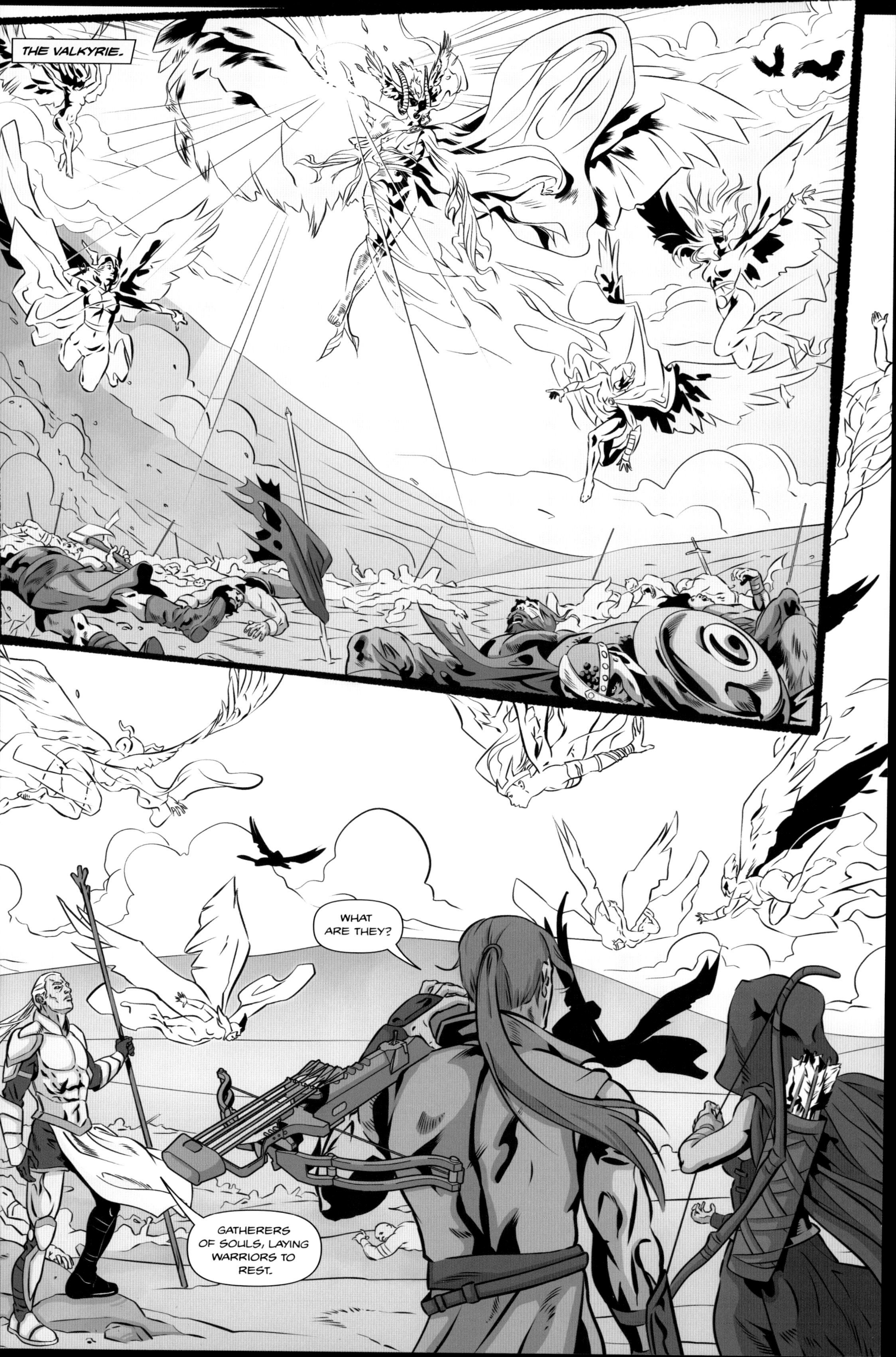
THE VALKYRIE.
WHAT ARE THEY?
GATHERERS OF SOULS, LAYING WARRIORS TO REST.

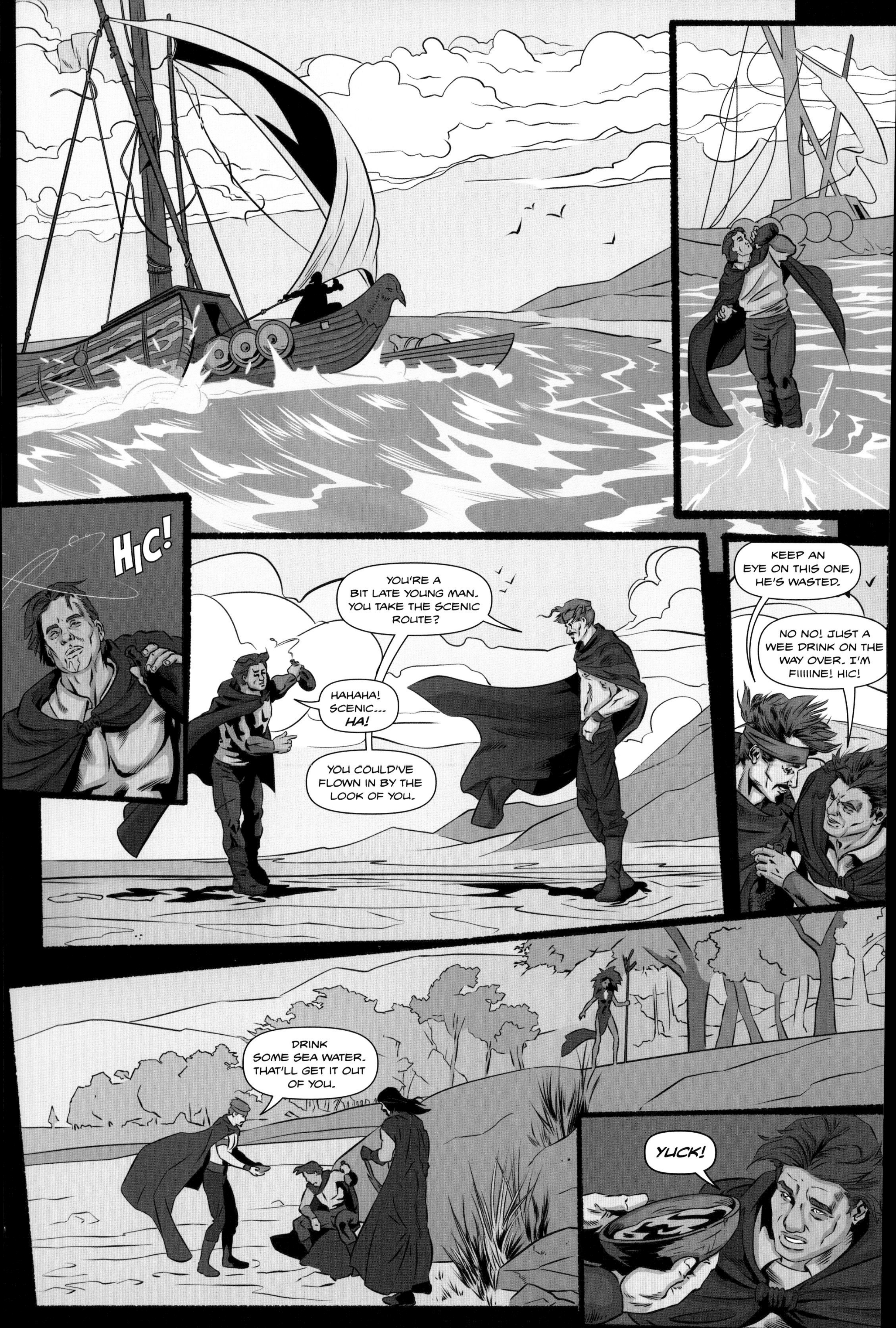
HIC!
YOU'RE A BIT LATE YOUNG MAN. YOU TAKE THE SCENIC ROUTE?
HAHAHA! SCENIC... HA!
YOU COULD'VE FLOWN IN BY THE LOOK OF YOU.
KEEP AN EYE ON THIS ONE, HE'S WASTED.
NO NO! JUST A WEE DRINK ON THE WAY OVER. I'M FIIIIINE! HIC!
DRINK SOME SEA WATER. THAT'LL GET IT OUT OF YOU.
YUCK!

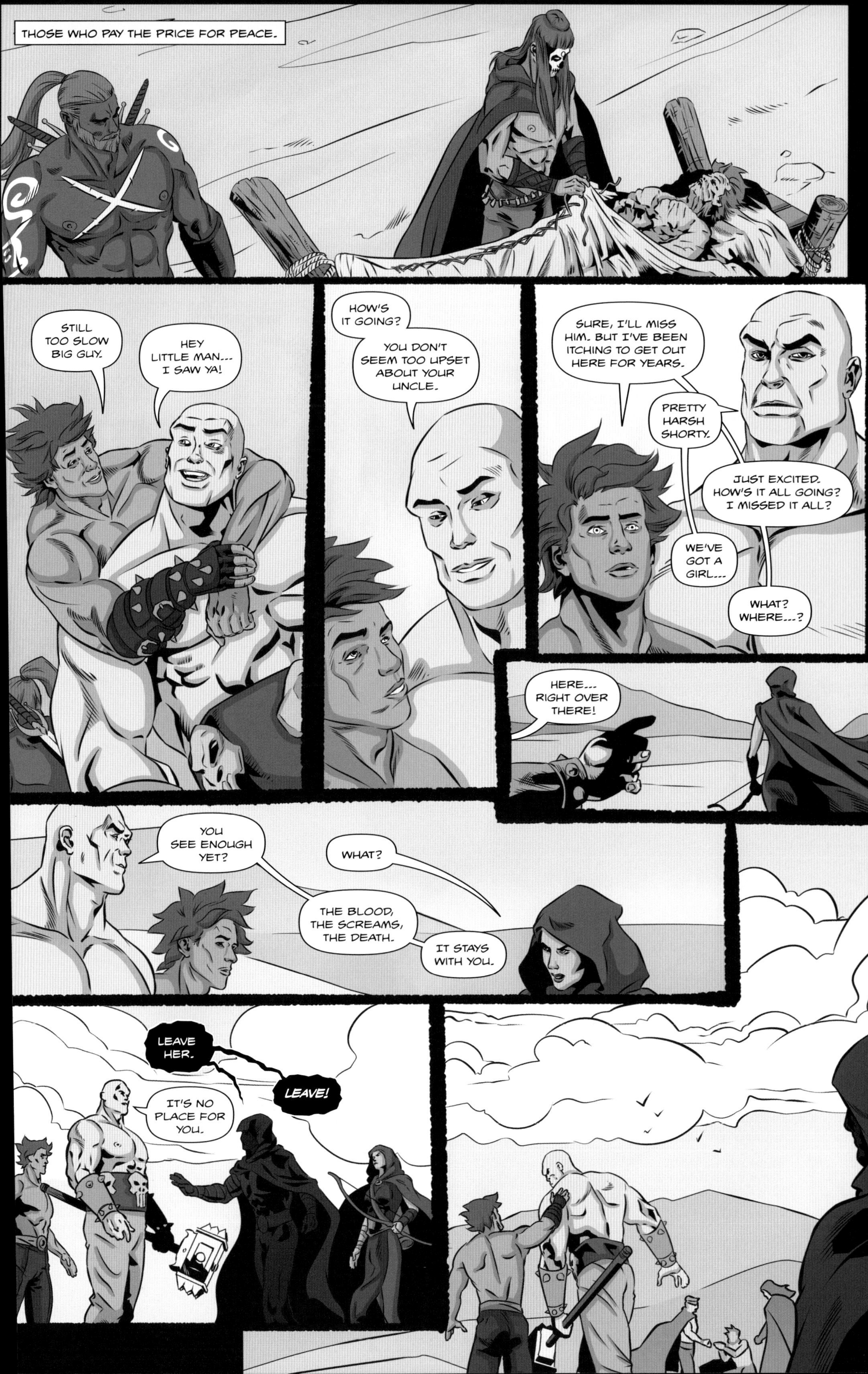
THOSE WHO PAY THE PRICE FOR PEACE.
STILL TOO SLOW BIG GUY.
HEY LITTLE MAN... I SAW YA!
HOW'S IT GOING?
YOU DON'T SEEM TOO UPSET ABOUT YOUR UNCLE.
SURE, I'LL MISS HIM. BUT I'VE BEEN ITCHING TO GET OUT HERE FOR YEARS.
PRETTY HARSH SHORTY.
JUST EXCITED. HOW'S IT ALL GOING? I MISSED IT ALL?
WE'VE GOT A GIRL...
WHAT? WHERE...?
HERE... RIGHT OVER THERE!
YOU SEE ENOUGH YET?
WHAT?
THE BLOOD, THE SCREAMS, THE DEATH.
IT STAYS WITH YOU.
LEAVE HER.
LEAVE!
IT'S NO PLACE FOR YOU.

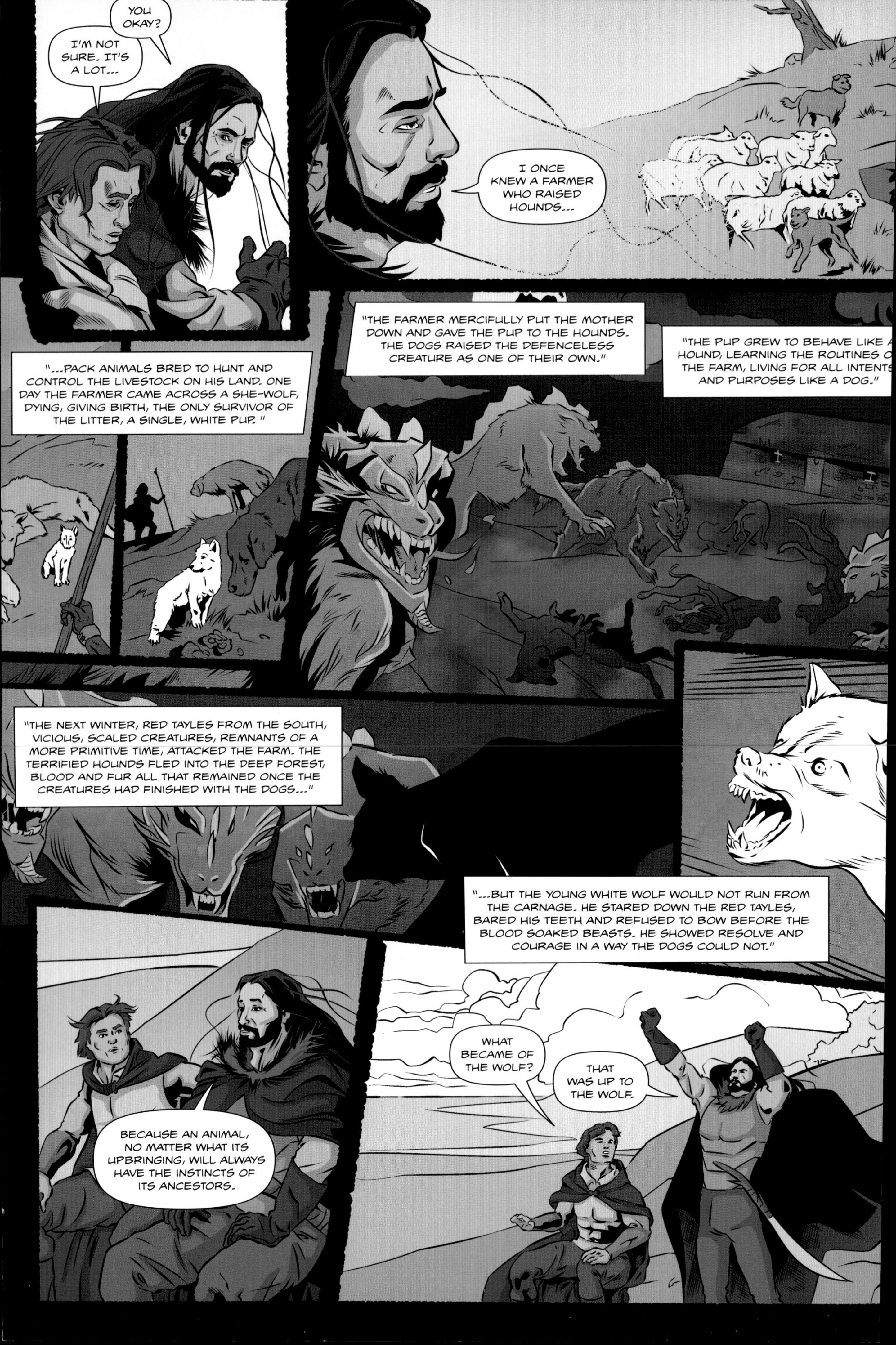

YOU OKAY?
I'M NOT SURE. IT'S A LOT...
I ONCE KNEW A FARMER WHO RAISED HOUNDS...
"...PACK ANIMALS BRED TO HUNT AND CONTROL THE LIVESTOCK ON HIS LAND. ONE DAY THE FARMER CAME ACROSS A SHE-WOLF, DYING, GIVING BIRTH, THE ONLY SURVIVOR OF THE LITTER, A SINGLE, WHITE PUP."
"THE FARMER MERCIFULLY PUT THE MOTHER DOWN AND GAVE THE PUP TO THE HOUNDS. THE DOGS RAISED THE DEFENCELESS CREATURE AS ONE OF THEIR OWN."
"THE PUP GREW TO BEHAVE LIKE A HOUND, LEARNING THE ROUTINES OF THE FARM, LIVING FOR ALL INTENTS AND PURPOSES LIKE A DOG."
"THE NEXT WINTER, RED TAYLES FROM THE SOUTH, VICIOUS, SCALED CREATURES, REMNANTS OF A MORE PRIMITIVE TIME, ATTACKED THE FARM. THE TERRIFIED HOUNDS FLED INTO THE DEEP FOREST, BLOOD AND FUR ALL THAT REMAINED ONCE THE CREATURES HAD FINISHED WITH THE DOGS..."
"...BUT THE YOUNG WHITE WOLF WOULD NOT RUN FROM THE CARNAGE. HE STARED DOWN THE RED TAYLES, BARED HIS TEETH AND REFUSED TO BOW BEFORE THE BLOOD SOAKED BEASTS. HE SHOWED RESOLVE AND COURAGE IN A WAY THE DOGS COULD NOT."
BECAUSE AN ANIMAL, NO MATTER WHAT ITS UPBRINGING, WILL ALWAYS HAVE THE INSTINCTS OF ITS ANCESTORS.
WHAT BECAME OF THE WOLF?
THAT WAS UP TO THE WOLF.

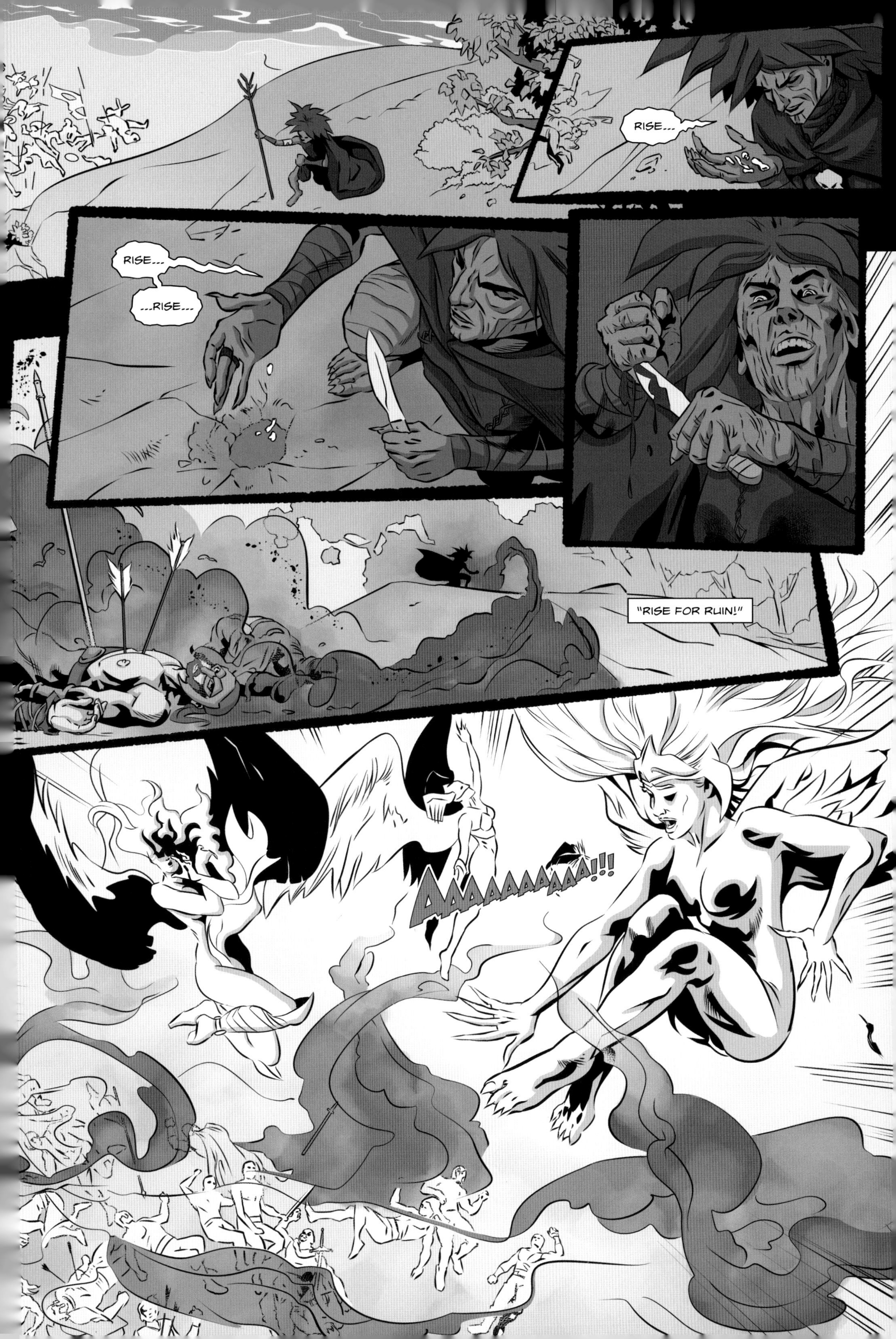
RISE...
RISE...
...RISE...
"RISE FOR RUIN!"
AAAAAAAAAA!!!

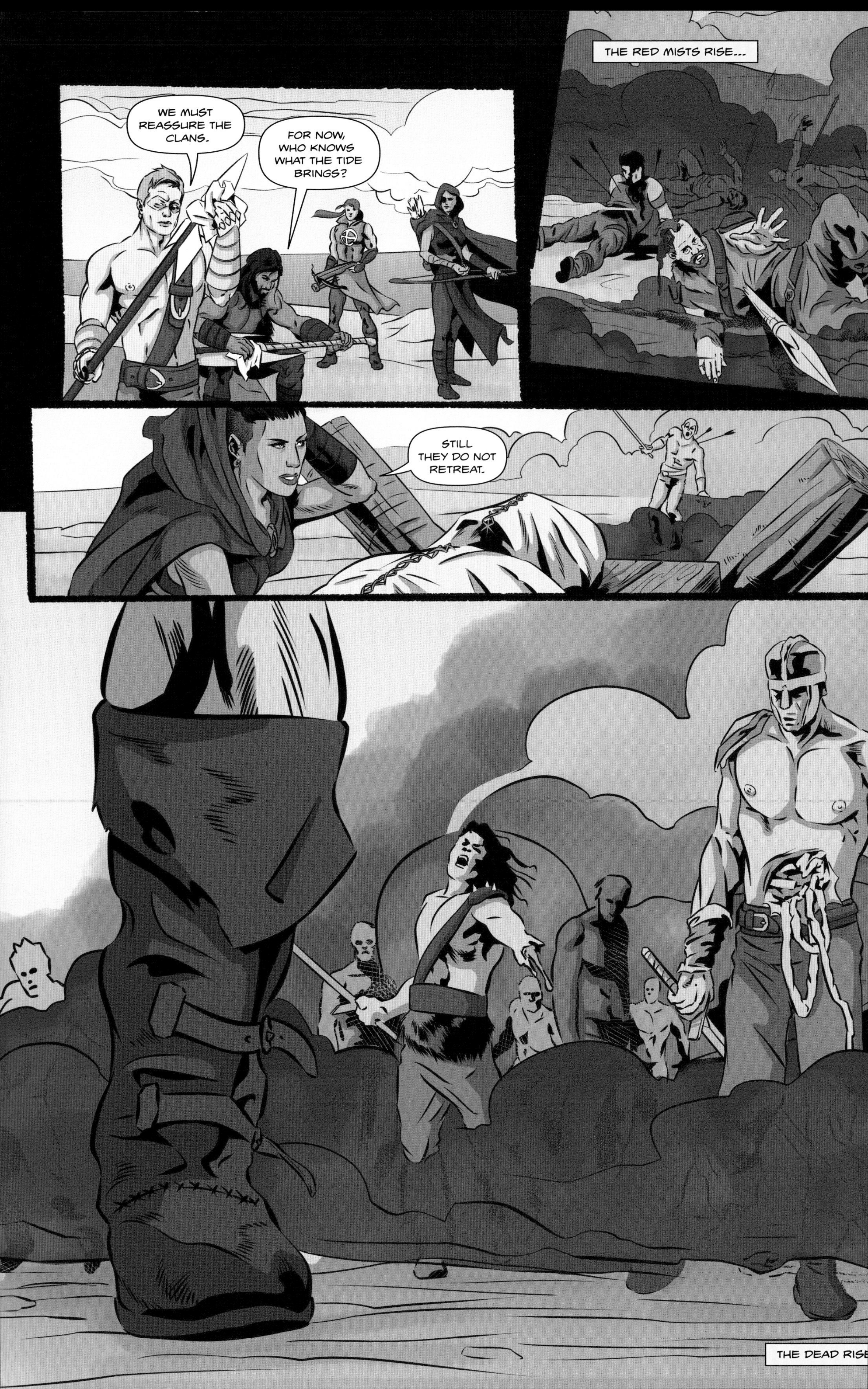
WE MUST REASSURE THE CLANS.
FOR NOW, WHO KNOWS WHAT THE TIDE BRINGS?
THE RED MISTS RISE...
STILL THEY DO NOT RETREAT.
THE DEAD RISE

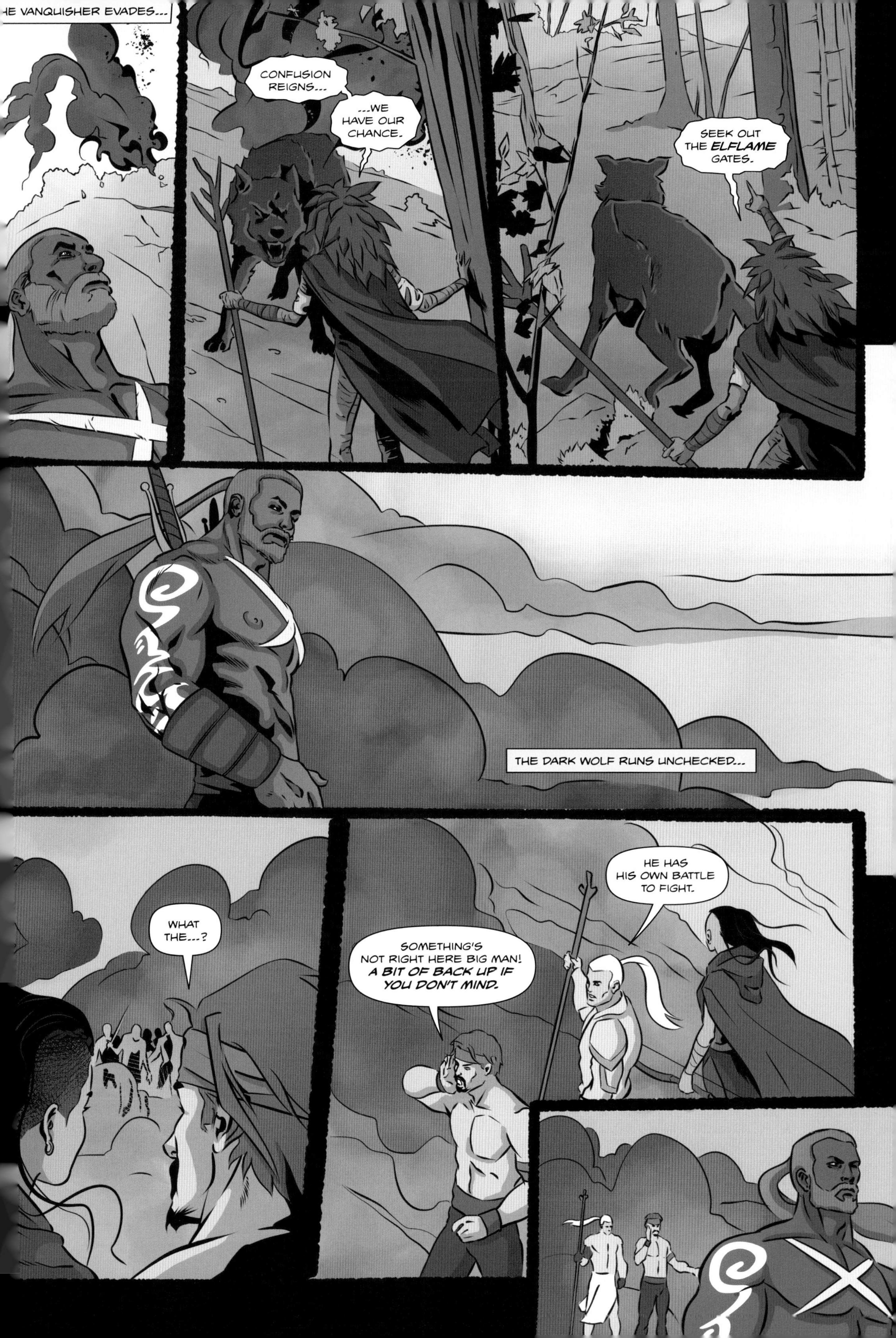
HE VANQUISHER EVADES...
CONFUSION REIGNS...
...WE HAVE OUR CHANCE.
SEEK OUT THE ELFLAME GATES.
THE DARK WOLF RUNS UNCHECKED...
WHAT THE...?
SOMETHING'S NOT RIGHT HERE BIG MAN! A BIT OF BACK UP IF YOU DON'T MIND.
HE HAS HIS OWN BATTLE TO FIGHT.

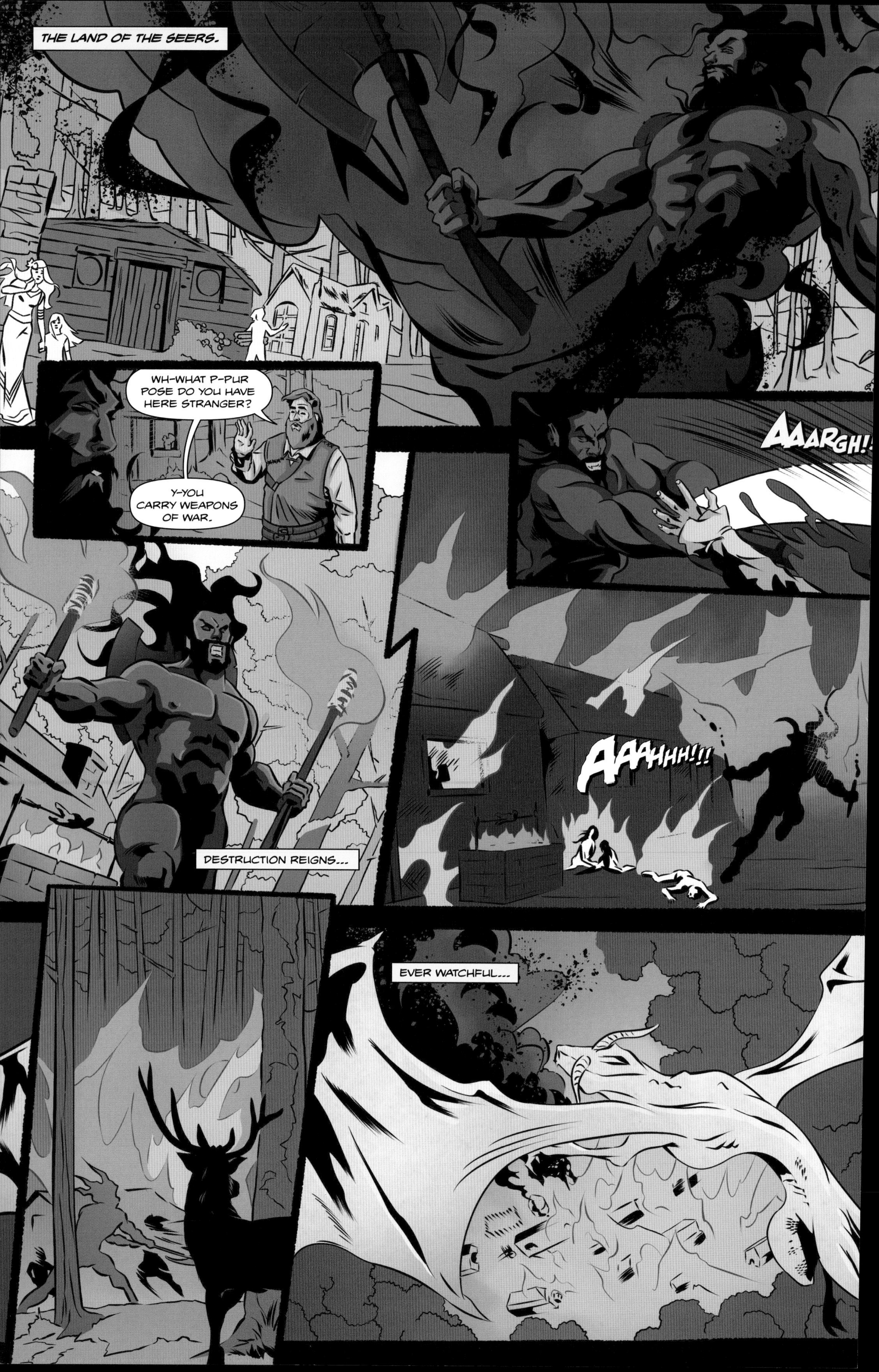
THE LAND OF THE SEERS.
WH-WHAT P-PUR POSE DO YOU HAVE HERE STRANGER?
Y-YOU CARRY WEAPONS OF WAR.
AAARGH!!
AAAHHH!!!
DESTRUCTION REIGNS...
EVER WATCHFUL...

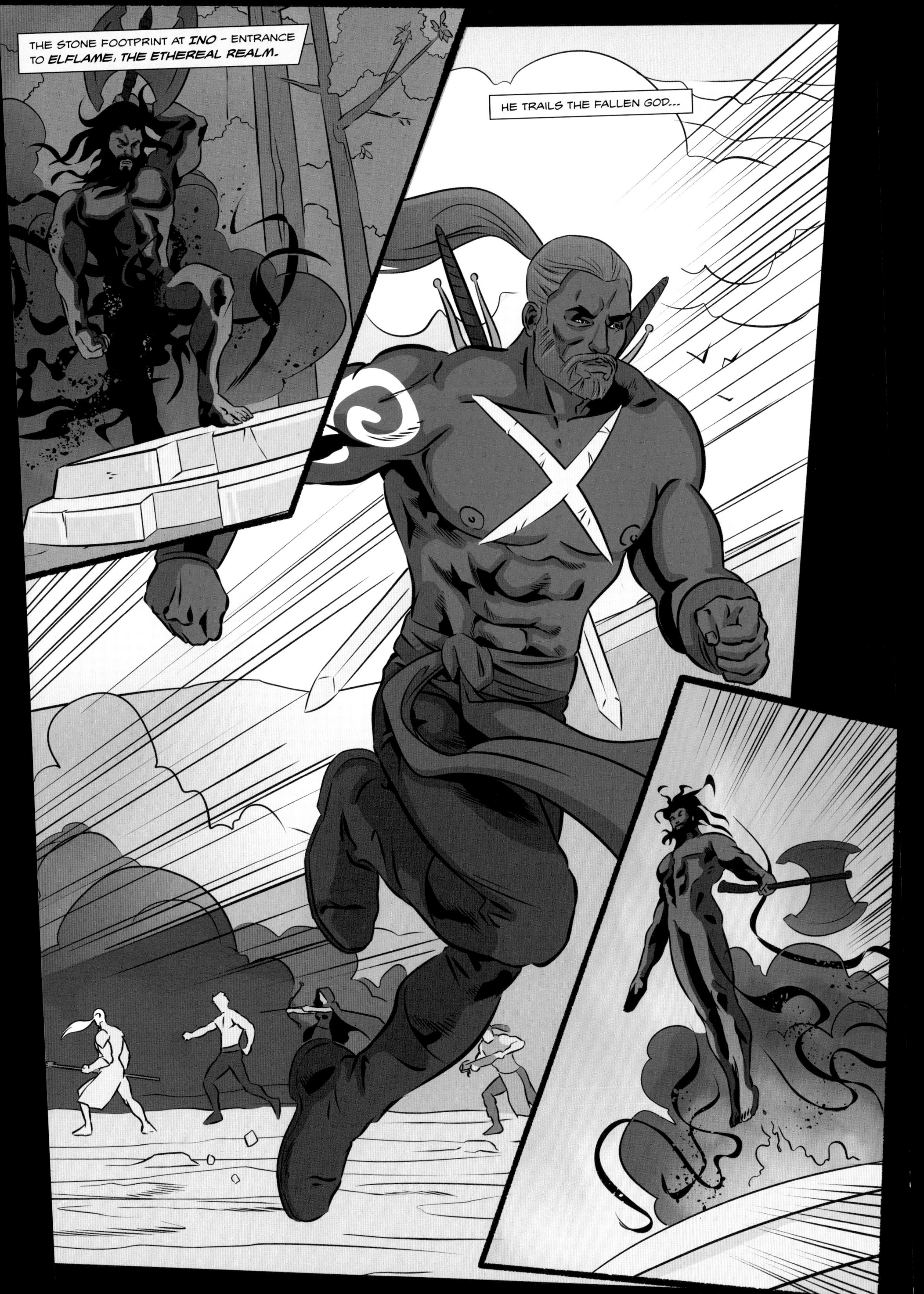
THE STONE FOOTPRINT AT INO - ENTRANCE TO ELFLAME, THE ETHEREAL REALM.
HE TRAILS THE FALLEN GOD...

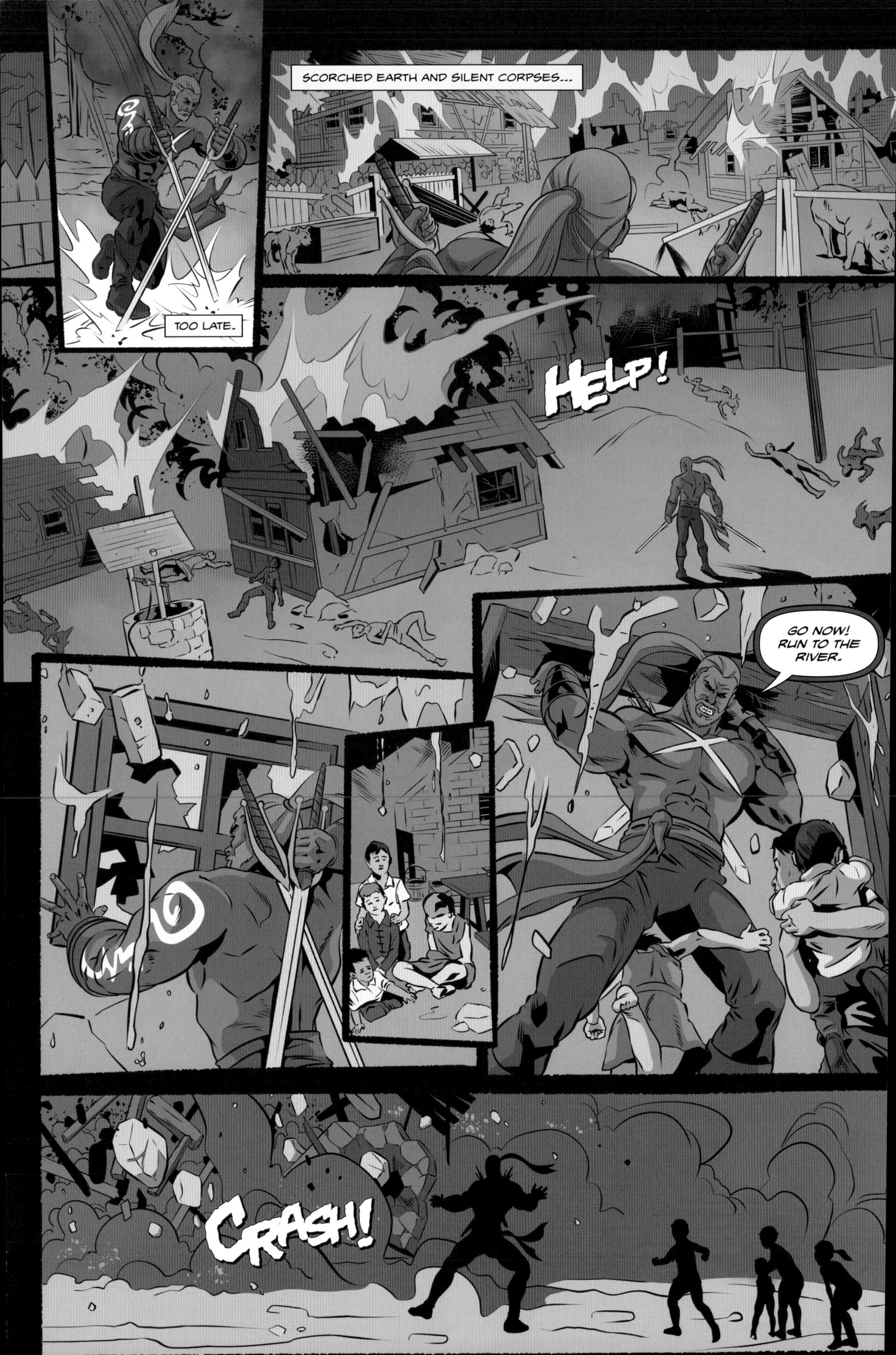
SCORCHED EARTH AND SILENT CORPSES...
TOO LATE.
HELP!
GO NOW! RUN TO THE RIVER.
CRASH!

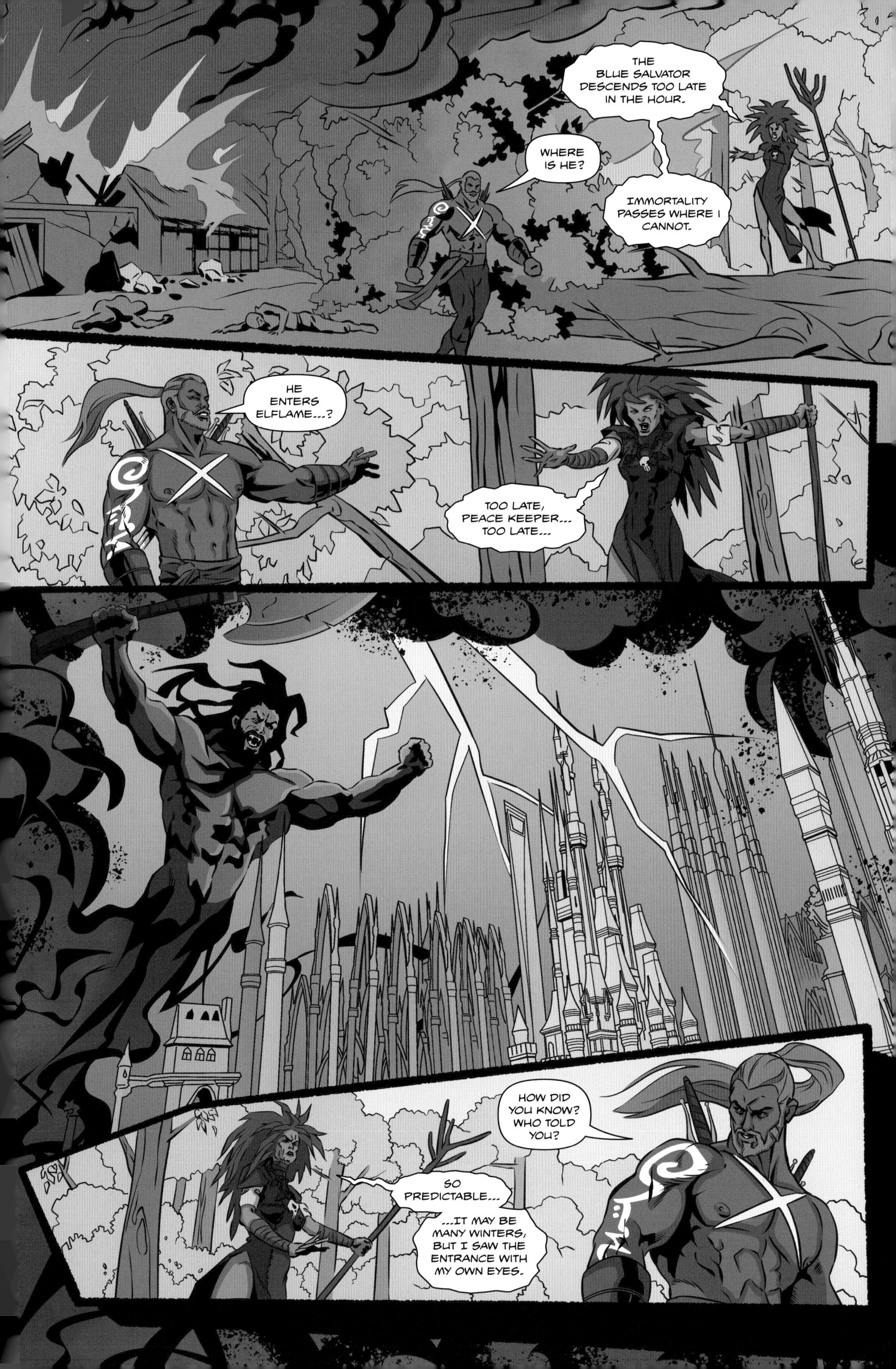
THE BLUE SALVATOR DESCENDS TOO LATE IN THE HOUR.
WHERE IS HE?
IMMORTALITY PASSES WHERE I CANNOT.
HE ENTERS ELFLAME...?
TOO LATE, PEACE KEEPER... TOO LATE...
HOW DID YOU KNOW? WHO TOLD YOU?
SO PREDICTABLE...
...IT MAY BE MANY WINTERS, BUT I SAW THE ENTRANCE WITH MY OWN EYES.

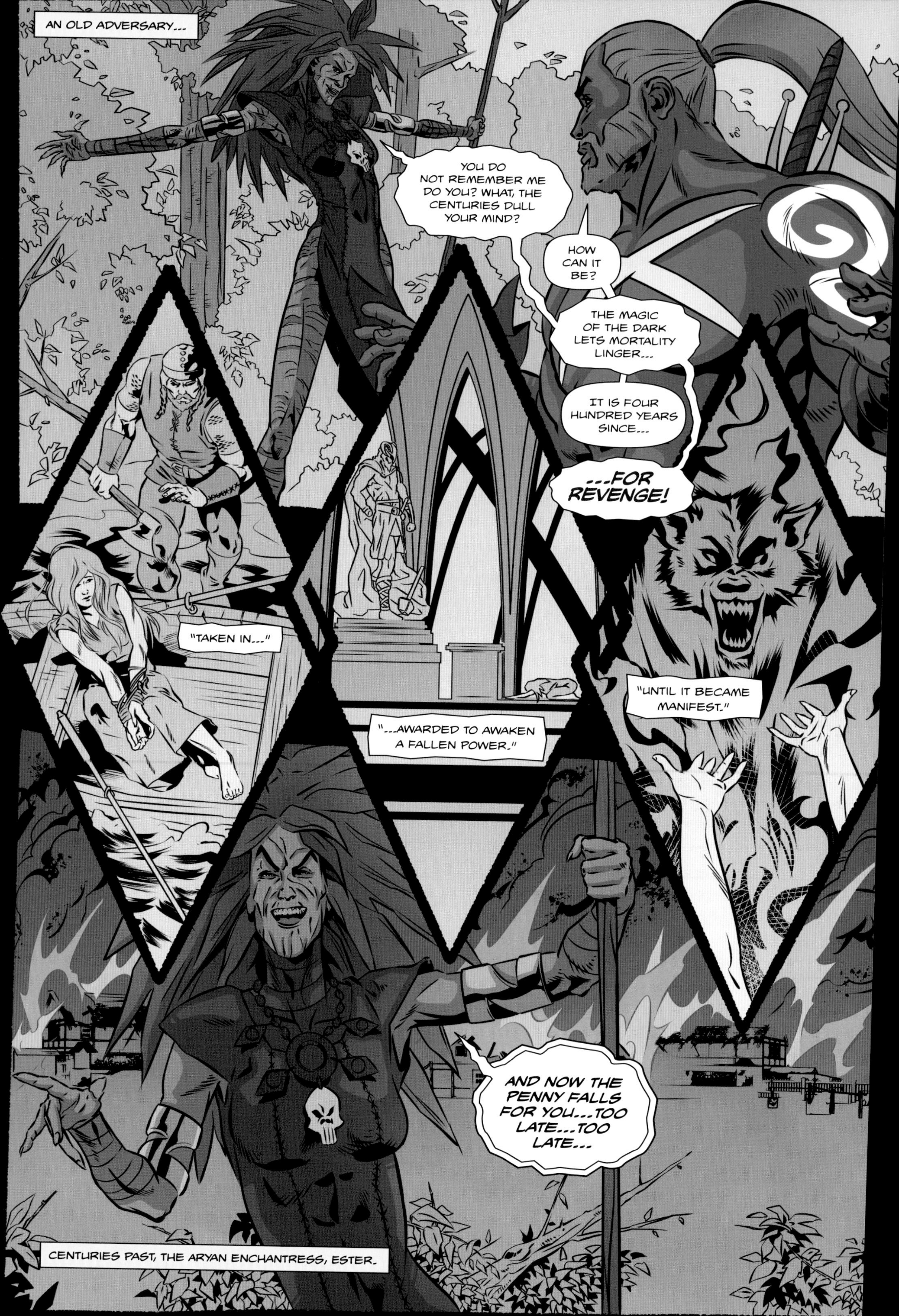

AN OLD ADVERSARY...
YOU DO NOT REMEMBER ME DO YOU? WHAT, THE CENTURIES DULL YOUR MIND?
HOW CAN IT BE?
THE MAGIC OF THE DARK LETS MORTALITY LINGER...
IT IS FOUR HUNDRED YEARS SINCE...
...FOR REVENGE!
"TAKEN IN..."
"...AWARDED TO AWAKEN A FALLEN POWER."
"UNTIL IT BECAME MANIFEST."
AND NOW THE PENNY FALLS FOR YOU...TOO LATE...TOO LATE...
CENTURIES PAST, THE ARYAN ENCHANTRESS, ESTER.

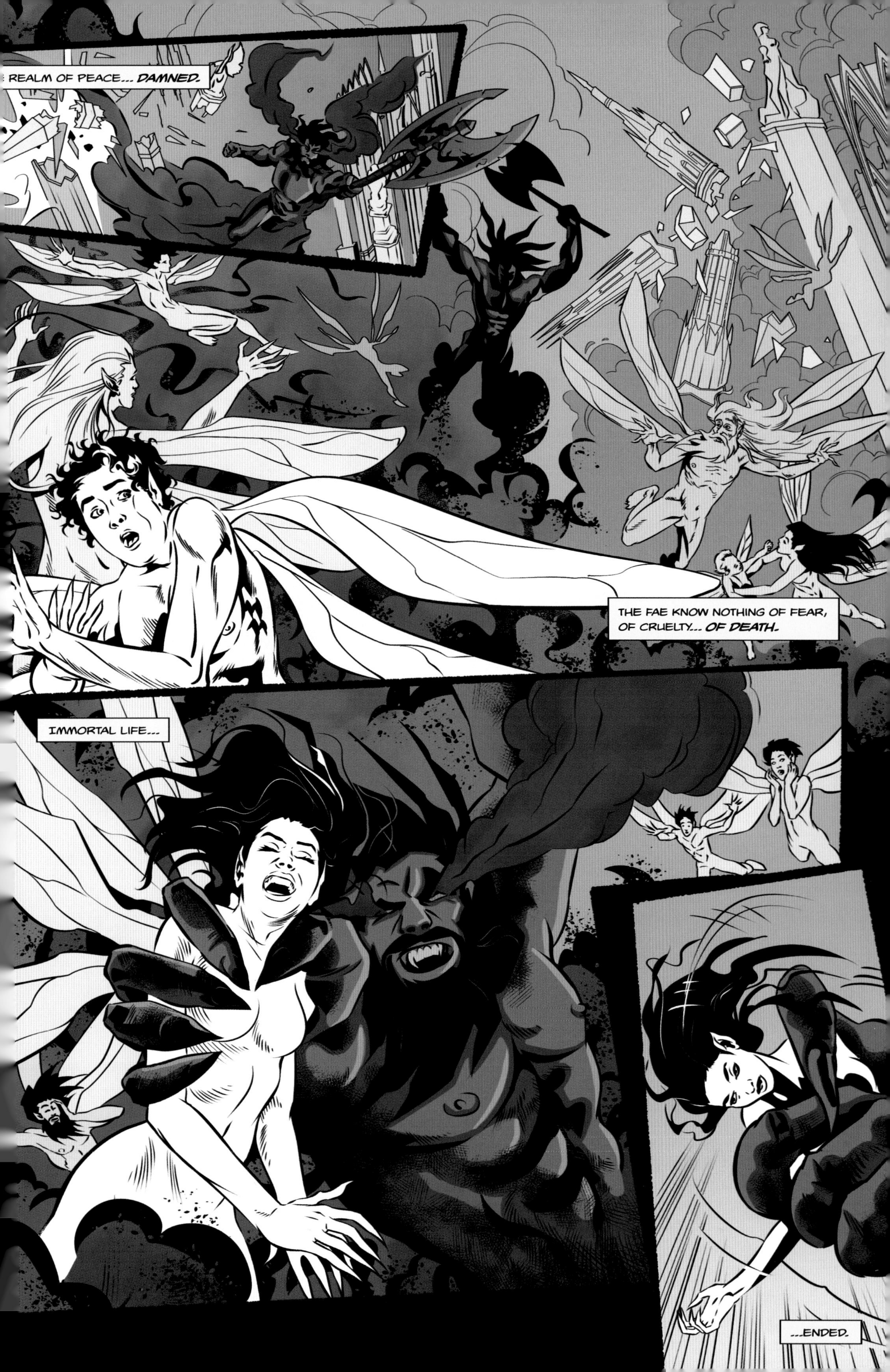
REALM OF PEACE... DAMNED.
THE FAE KNOW NOTHING OF FEAR, OF CRUELTY... OF DEATH.
IMMORTAL LIFE...
...ENDED.

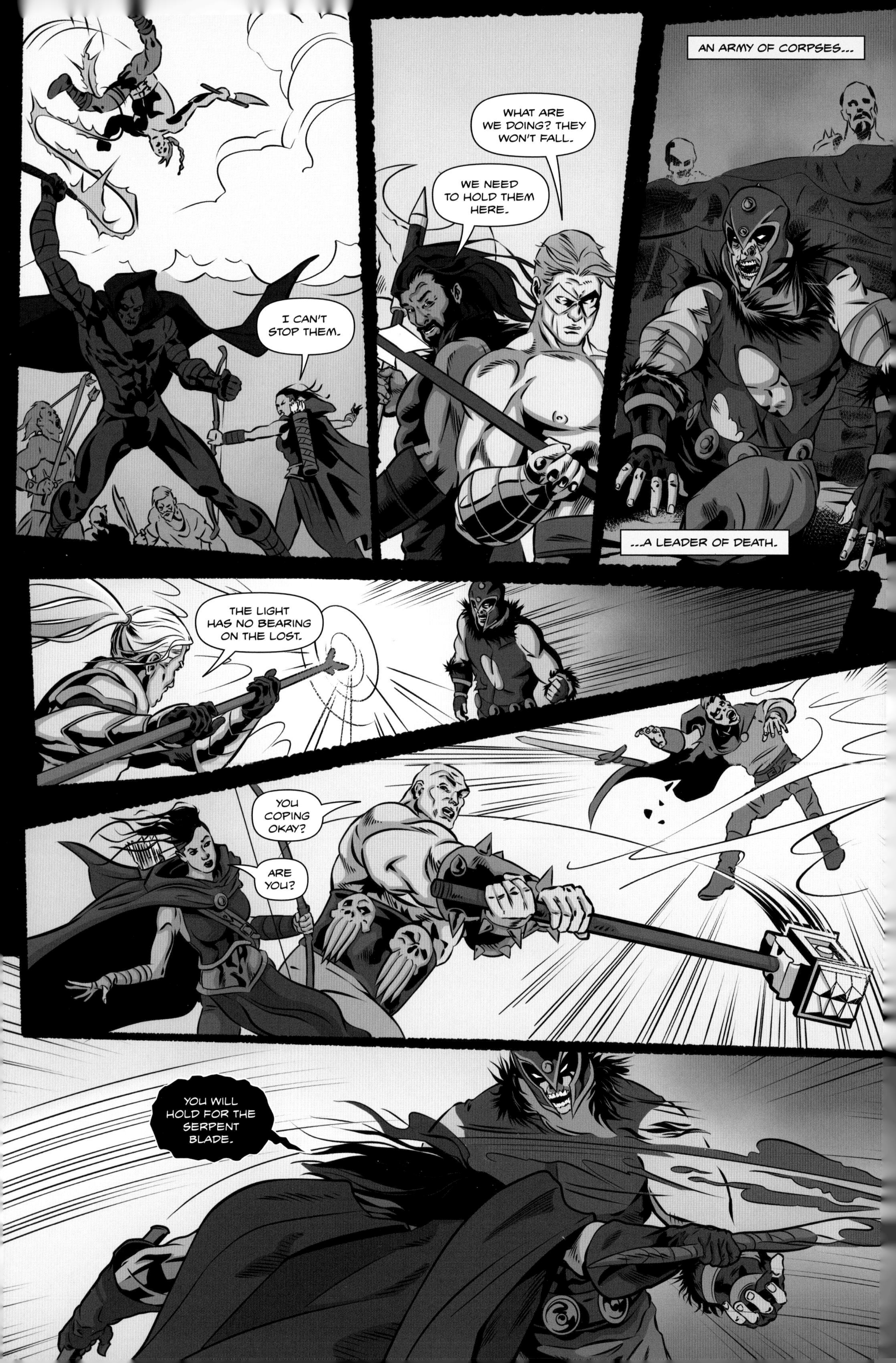
I CAN'T STOP THEM.
WHAT ARE WE DOING? THEY WON'T FALL.
WE NEED TO HOLD THEM HERE.
AN ARMY OF CORPSES...
...A LEADER OF DEATH.
THE LIGHT HAS NO BEARING ON THE LOST.
YOU COPING OKAY?
ARE YOU?
YOU WILL HOLD FOR THE SERPENT BLADE.

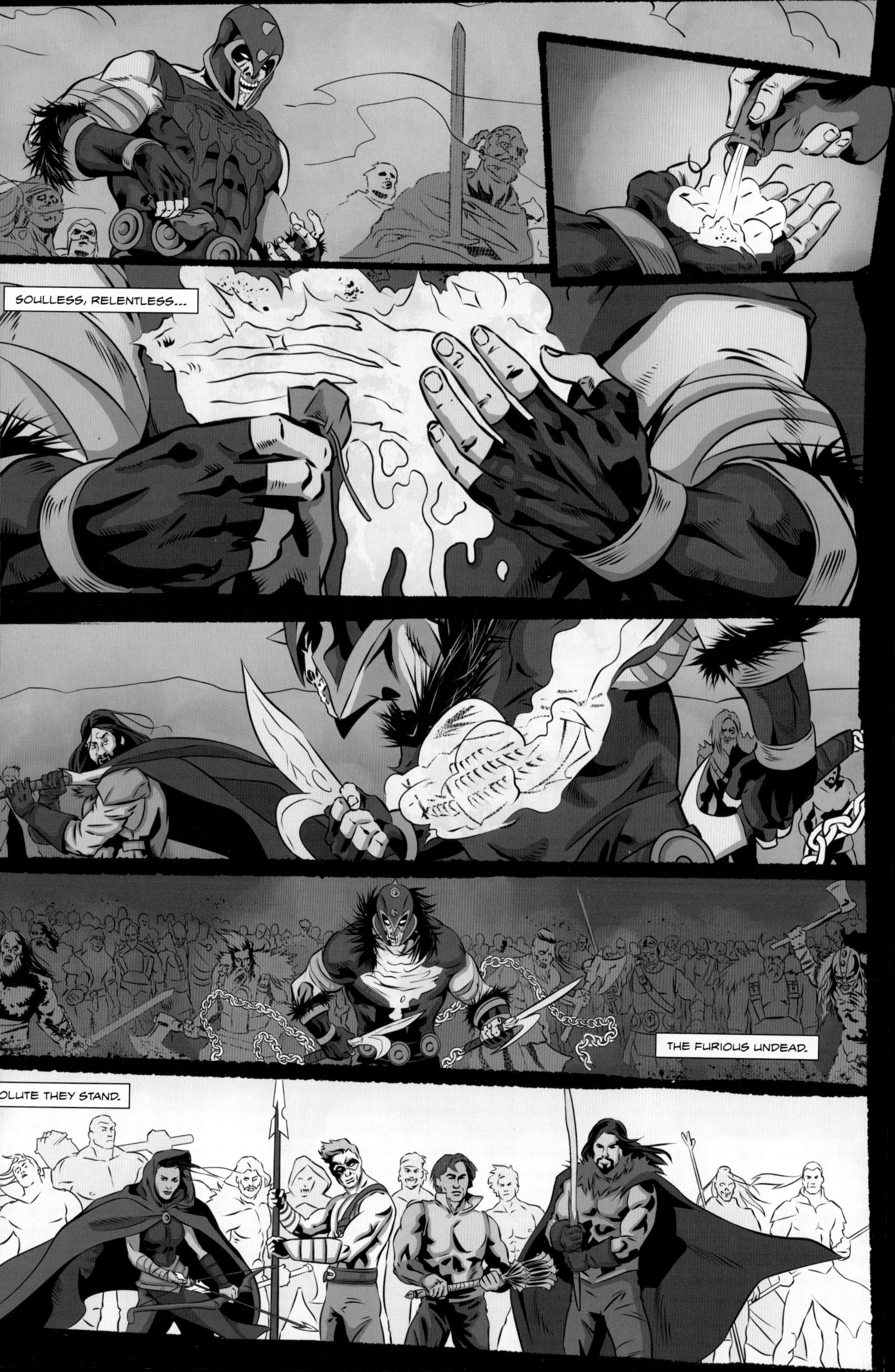
SOULLESS, RELENTLESS...
THE FURIOUS UNDEAD.
OLUTE THEY STAND.

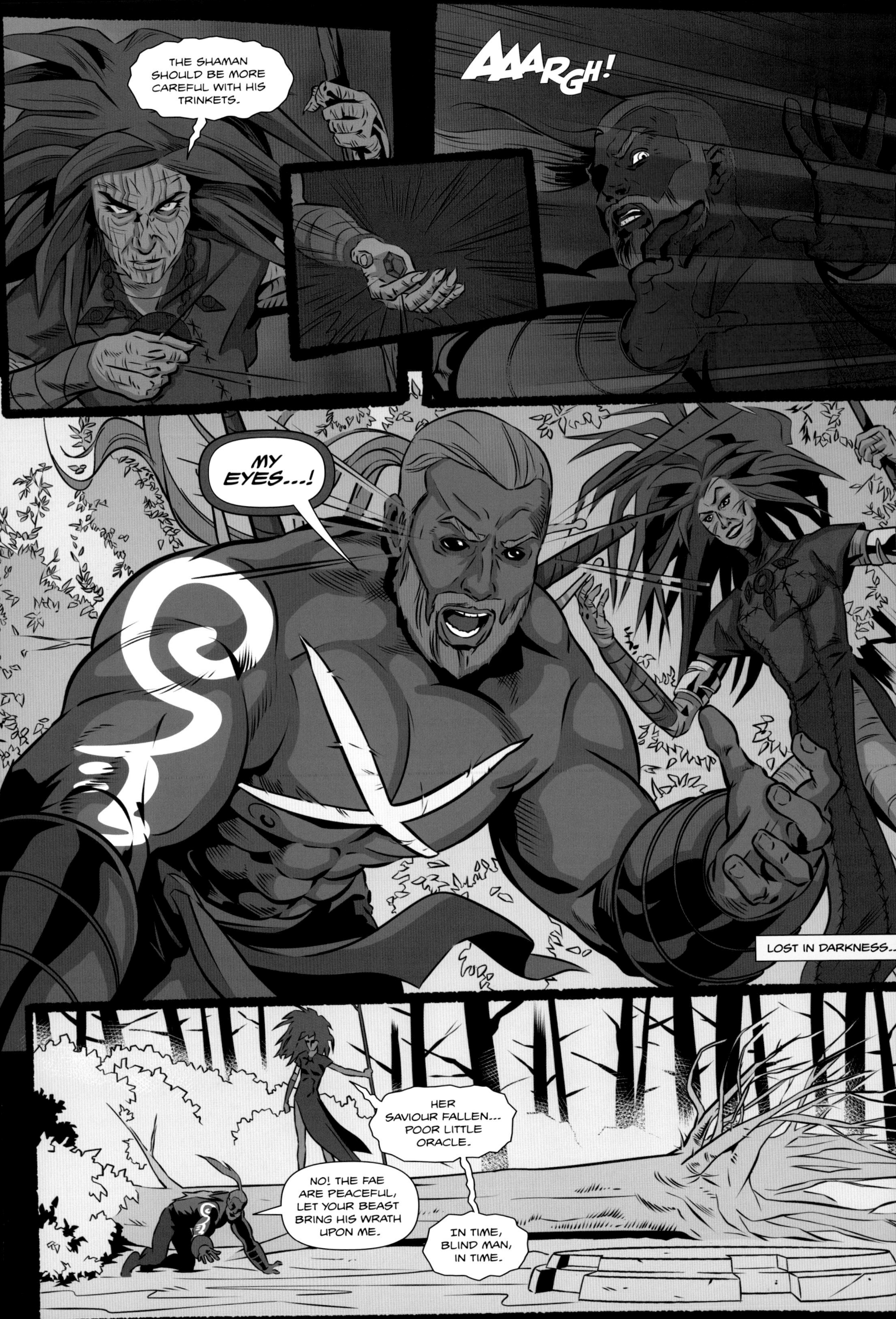

THE SHAMAN SHOULD BE MORE CAREFUL WITH HIS TRINKETS.
AAARGH!
MY EYES...!
LOST IN DARKNESS...
HER SAVIOUR FALLEN... POOR LITTLE ORACLE.
NO! THE FAE ARE PEACEFUL, LET YOUR BEAST BRING HIS WRATH UPON ME.
IN TIME, BLIND MAN, IN TIME.

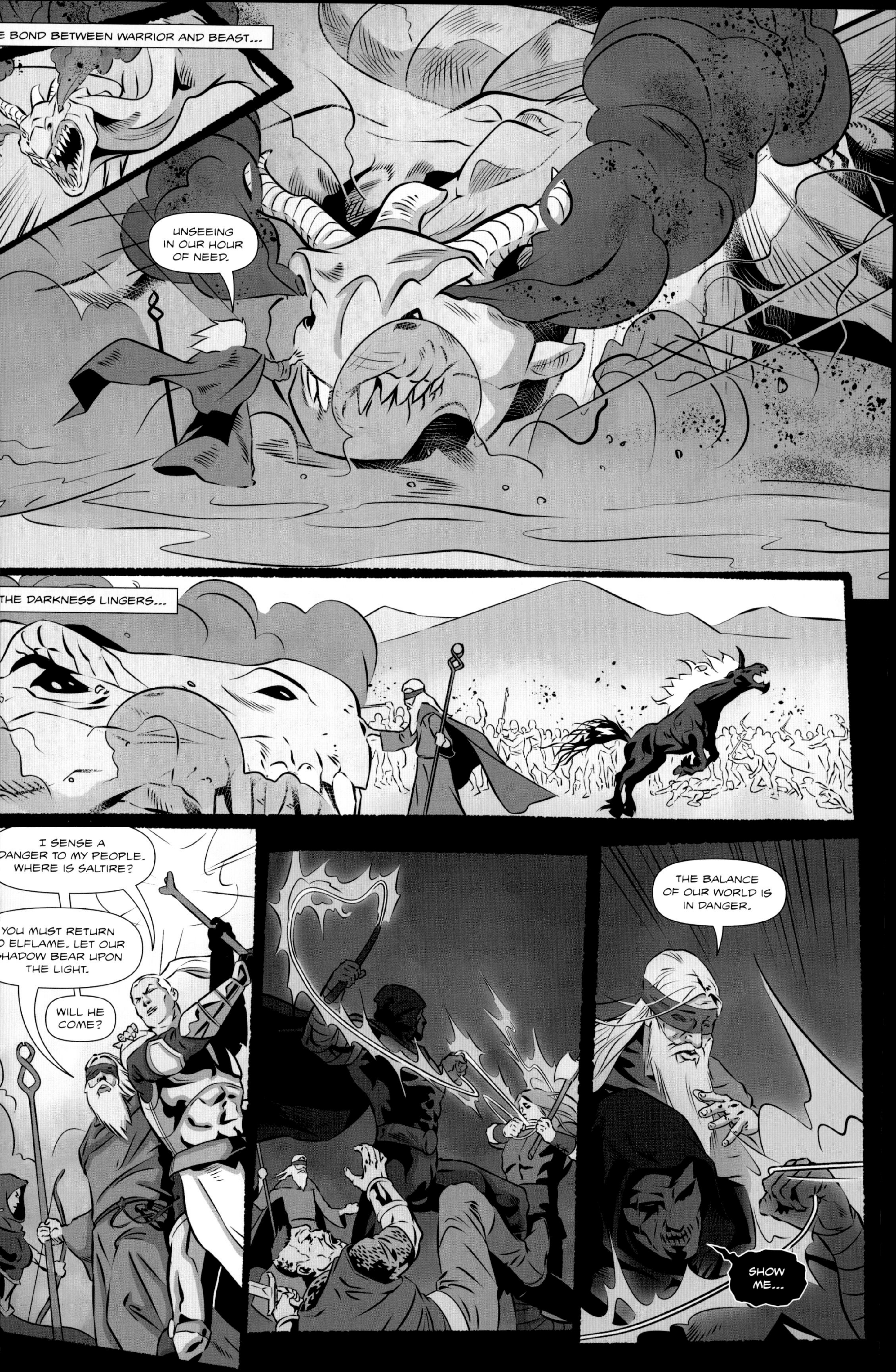
E BOND BETWEEN WARRIOR AND BEAST...
UNSEEING IN OUR HOUR OF NEED.
THE DARKNESS LINGERS...
I SENSE A DANGER TO MY PEOPLE. WHERE IS SALTIRE?
YOU MUST RETURN O ELFLAME. LET OUR HADOW BEAR UPON THE LIGHT.
WILL HE COME?
THE BALANCE OF OUR WORLD IS IN DANGER.
SHOW ME...

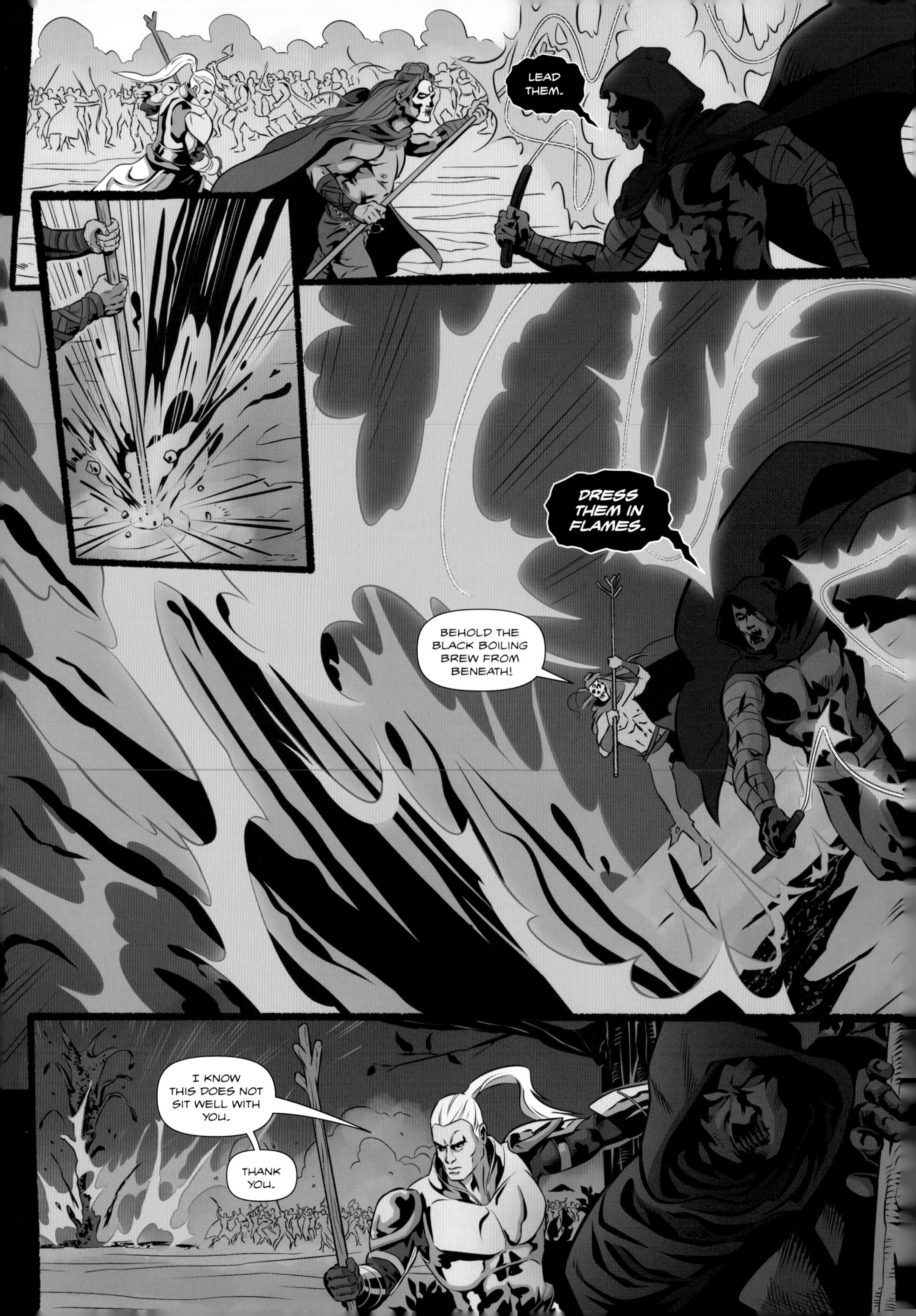
LEAD THEM.
DRESS THEM IN FLAMES.
BEHOLD THE BLACK BOILING BREW FROM BENEATH!
I KNOW THIS DOES NOT SIT WELL WITH YOU.
THANK YOU.

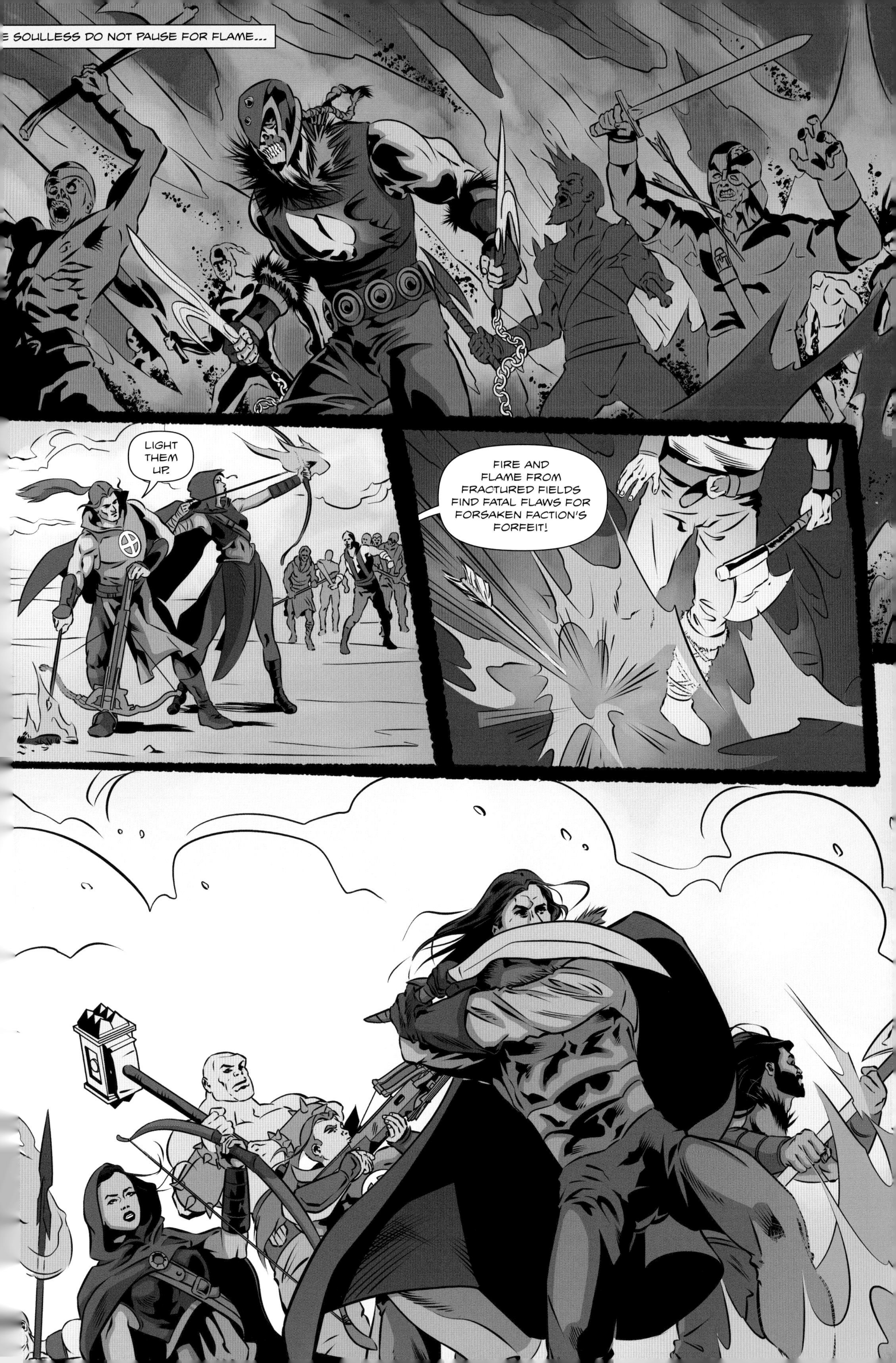
E SOULLESS DO NOT PAUSE FOR FLAME...
LIGHT THEM UP.
FIRE AND FLAME FROM FRACTURED FIELDS FIND FATAL FLAWS FOR FORSAKEN FACTION'S FORFEIT!

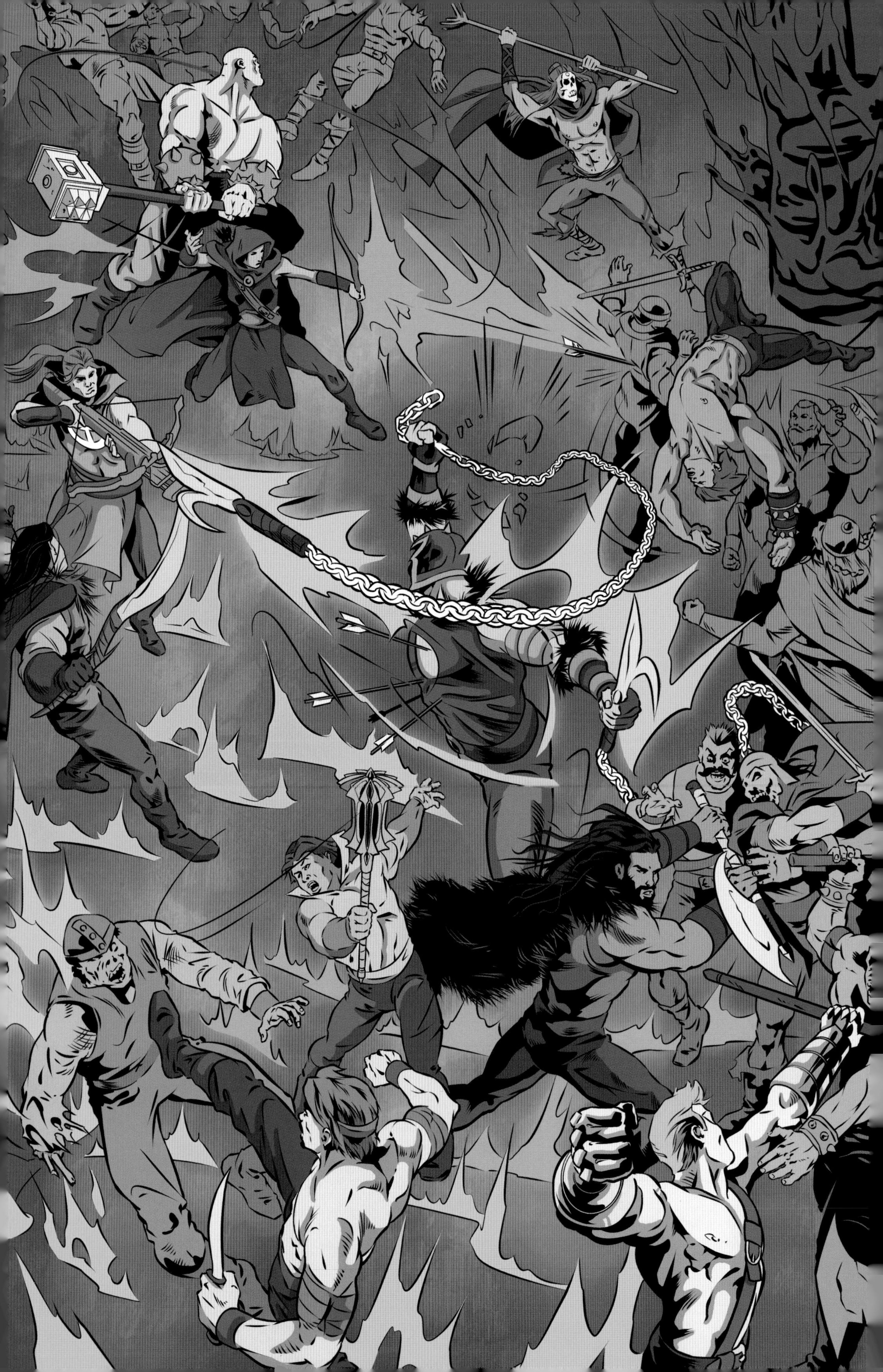

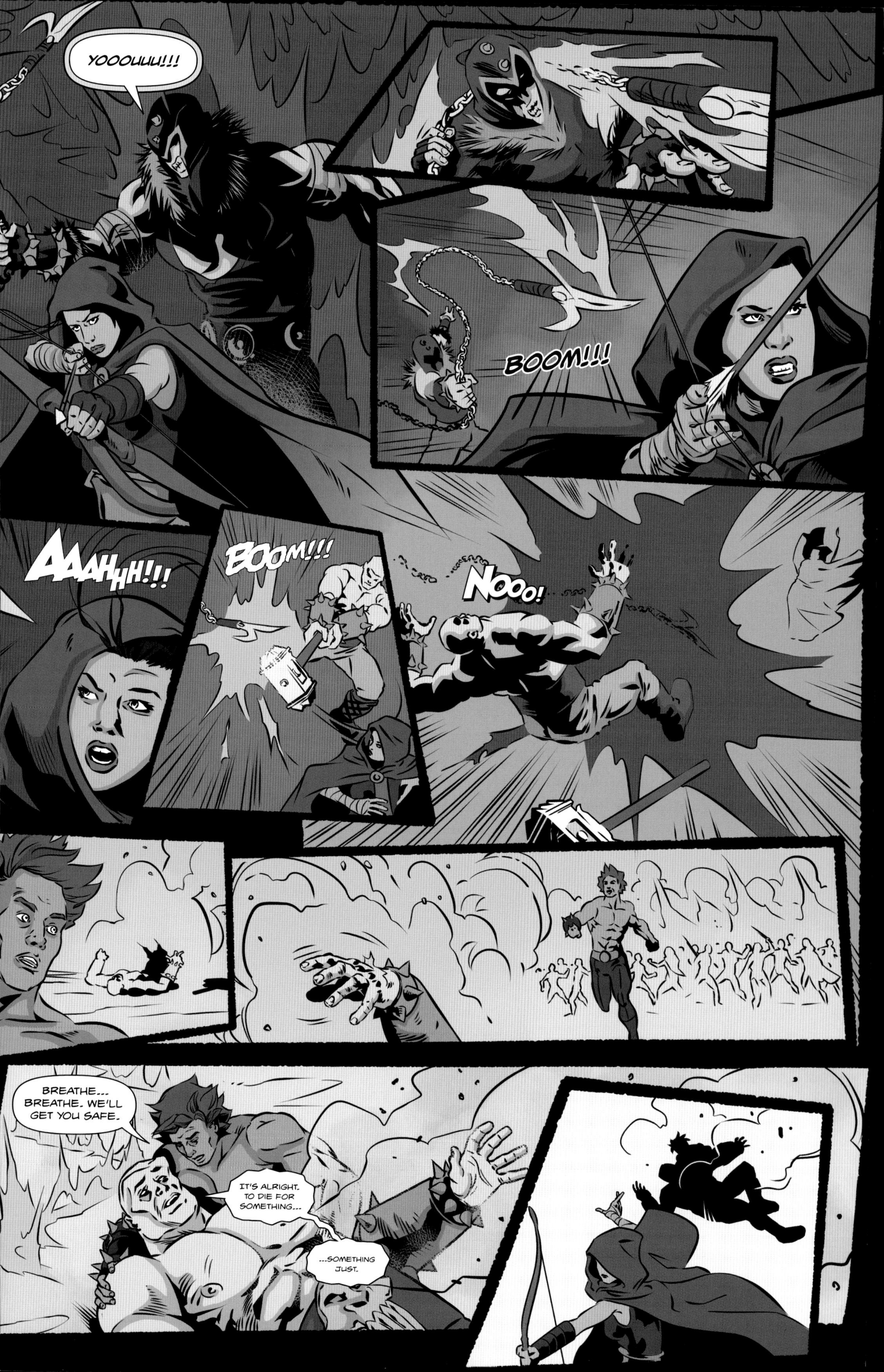
YOOOUUU!!!
BOOM!!!
AAAHHH!!!
BOOM!!!
NOOO!
BREATHE... BREATHE. WE'LL GET YOU SAFE.
IT'S ALRIGHT. TO DIE FOR SOMETHING...
...SOMETHING JUST.

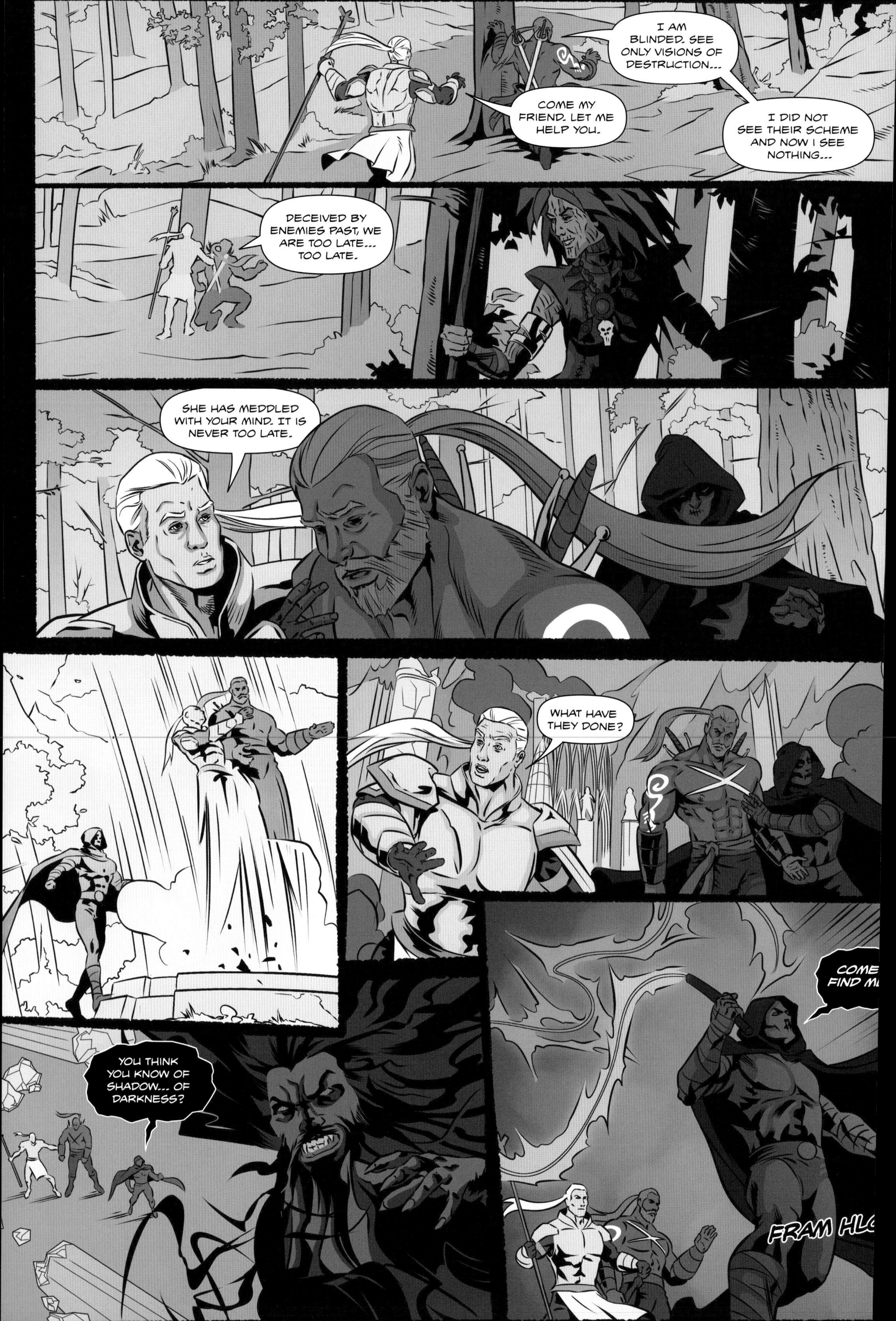
I AM BLINDED. SEE ONLY VISIONS OF DESTRUCTION...
COME MY FRIEND. LET ME HELP YOU.
I DID NOT SEE THEIR SCHEME AND NOW I SEE NOTHING...
DECEIVED BY ENEMIES PAST, WE ARE TOO LATE... TOO LATE.
SHE HAS MEDDLED WITH YOUR MIND. IT IS NEVER TOO LATE.
WHAT HAVE THEY DONE?
YOU THINK YOU KNOW OF SHADOW... OF DARKNESS?
COME
FIND

Chapter Five

Script: John Ferguson
Art: Toni Doya Heredia
Colours: Rebecca Horner
Letters: Phillip Vaughan
Editor: Clare Ferguson

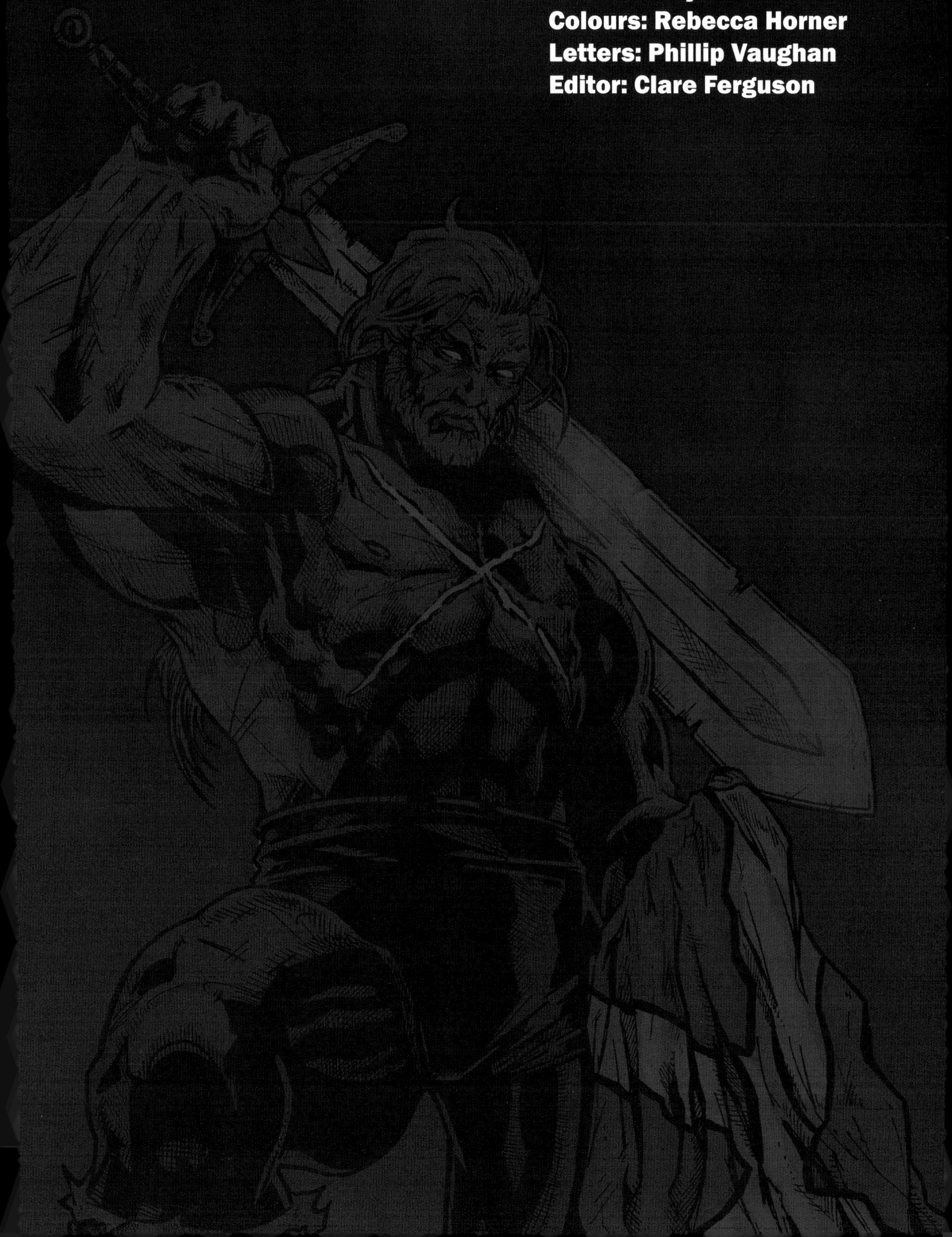

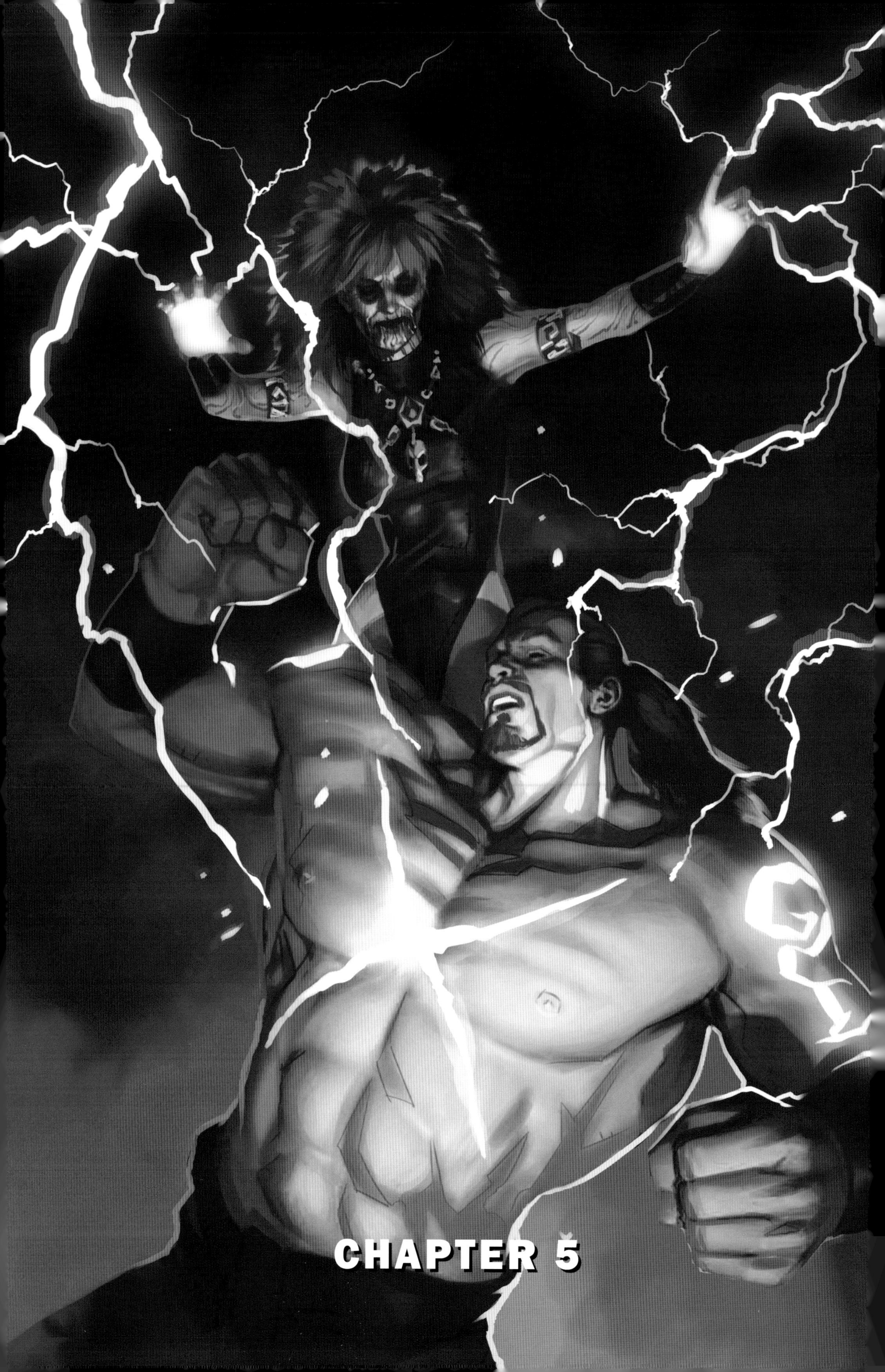
CHAPTER 5

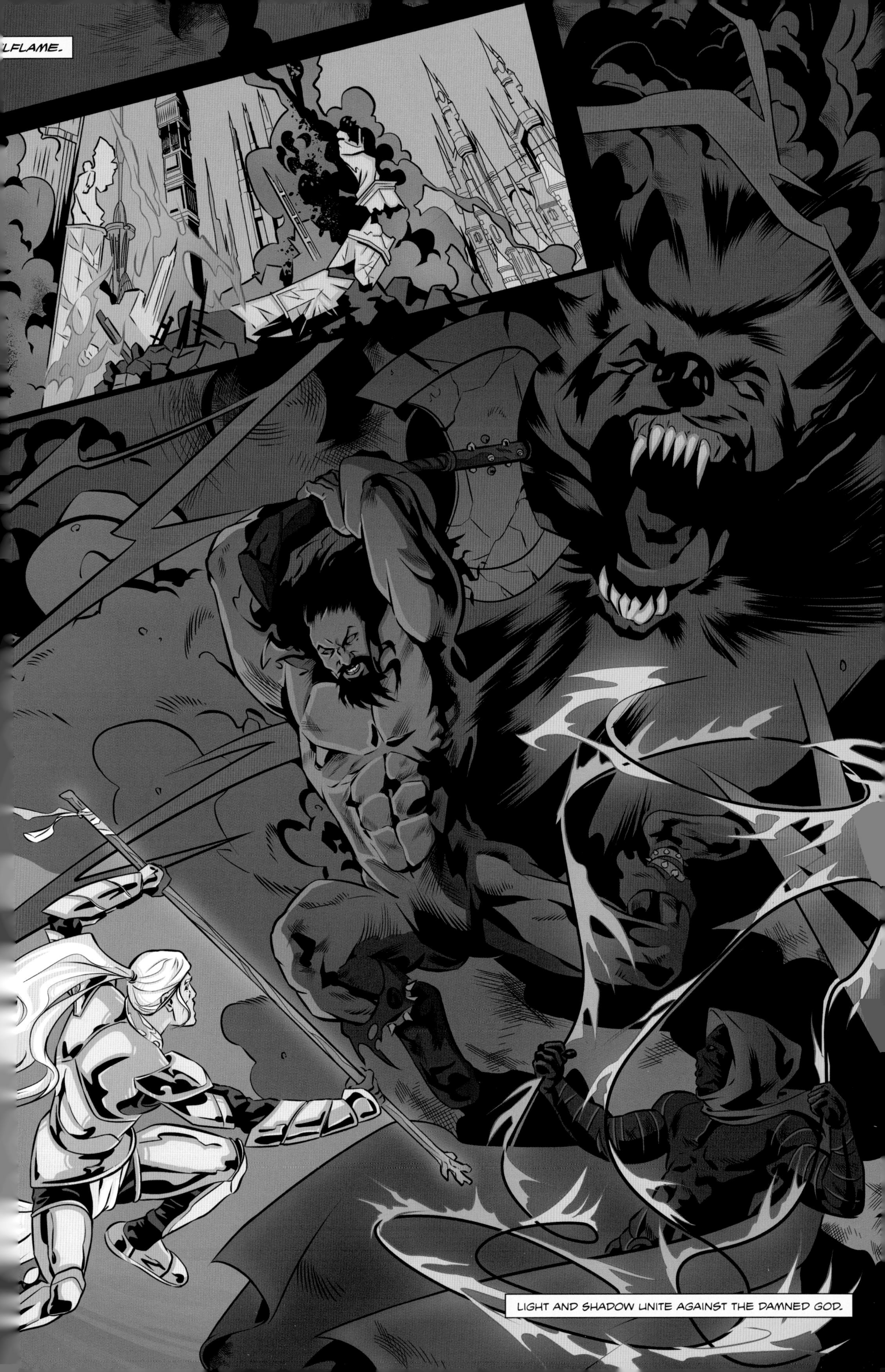

LFLAME.
LIGHT AND SHADOW UNITE AGAINST THE DAMNED GOD.

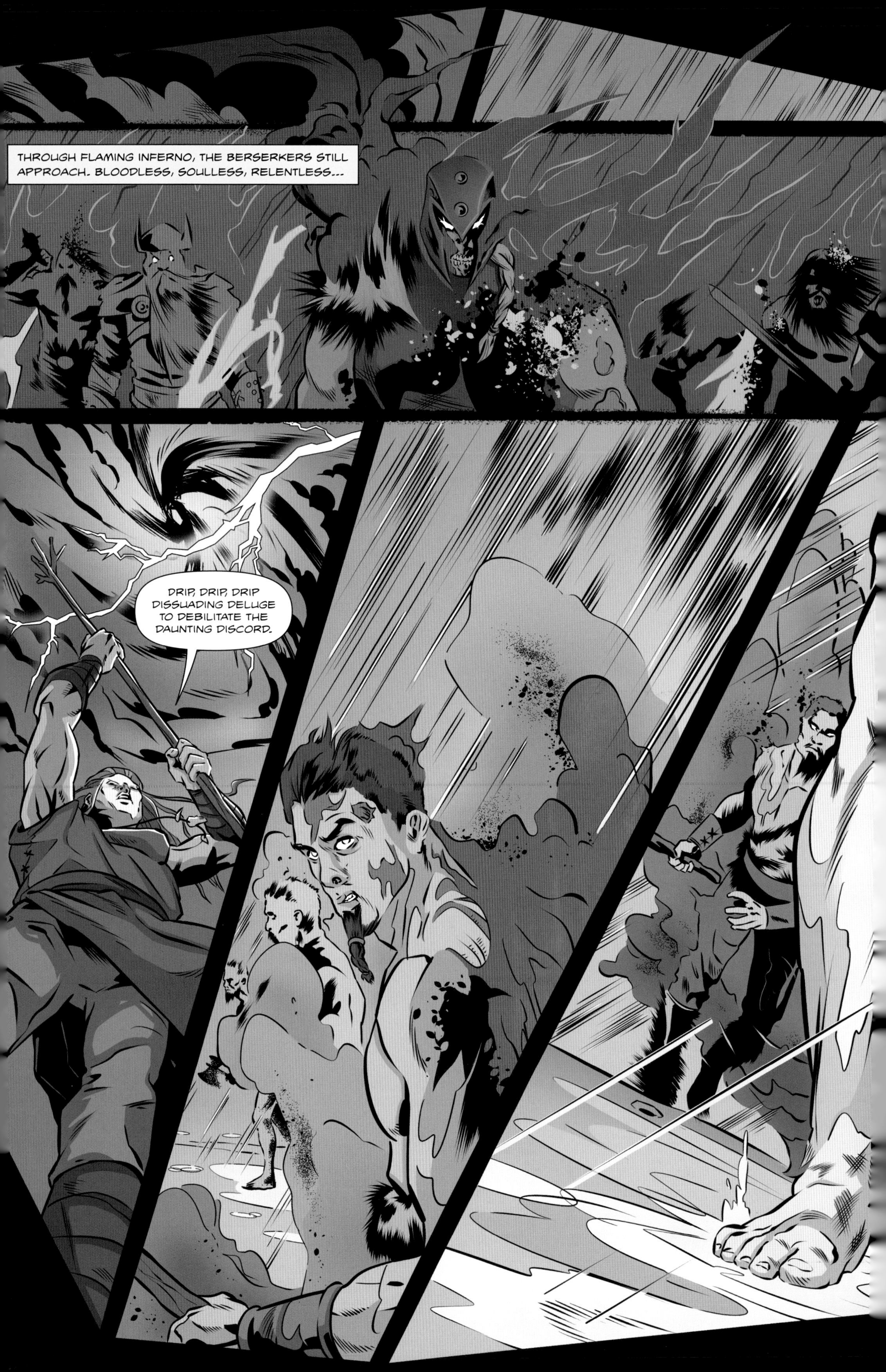
THROUGH FLAMING INFERNO, THE BERSERKERS STILL APPROACH. BLOODLESS, SOULLESS, RELENTLESS...
DRIP, DRIP, DRIP DISSUADING DELUGE TO DEBILITATE THE DAUNTING DISCORD.

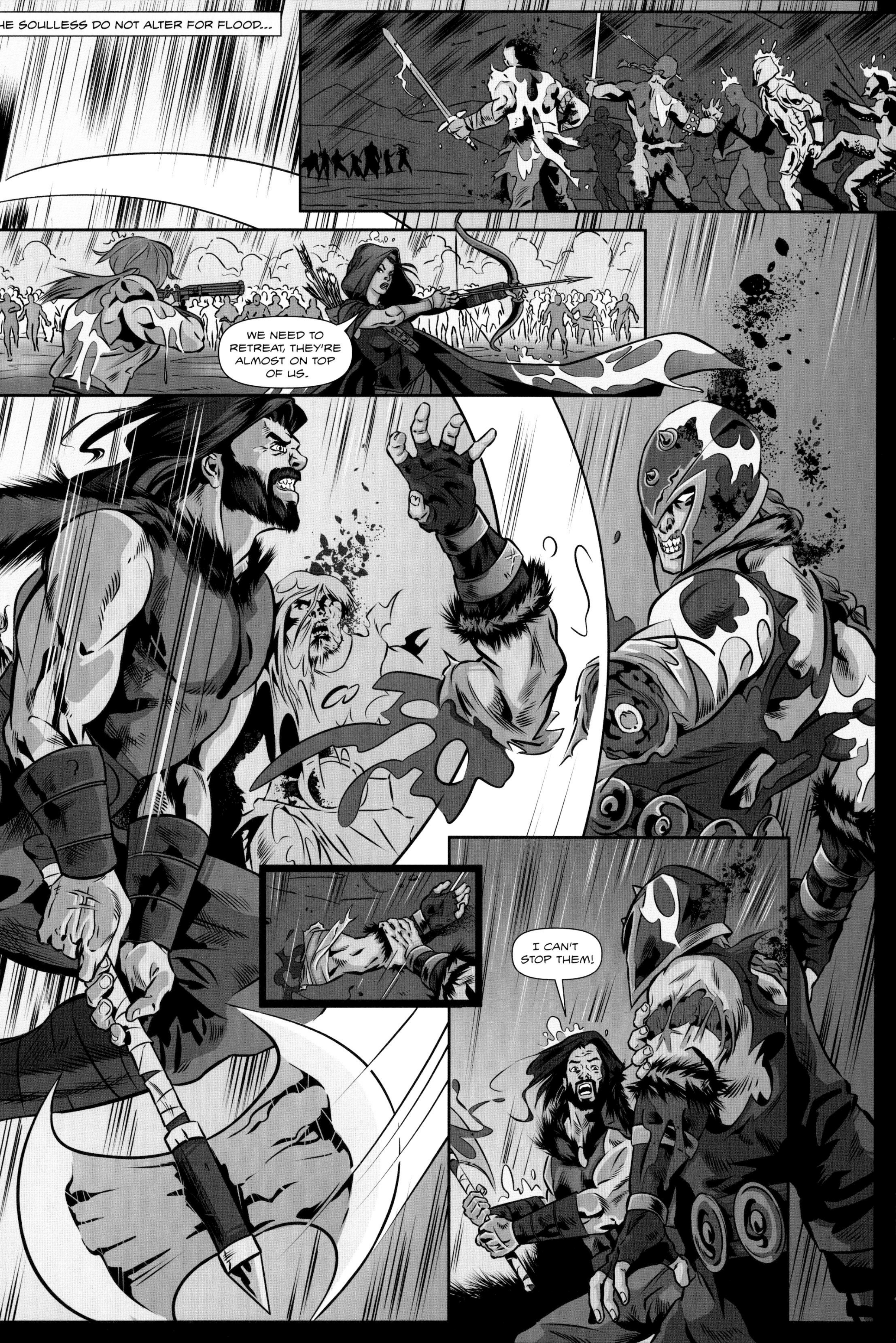
HE SOULLESS DO NOT ALTER FOR FLOOD...
WE NEED TO RETREAT, THEY'RE ALMOST ON TOP OF US.
I CAN'T STOP THEM!

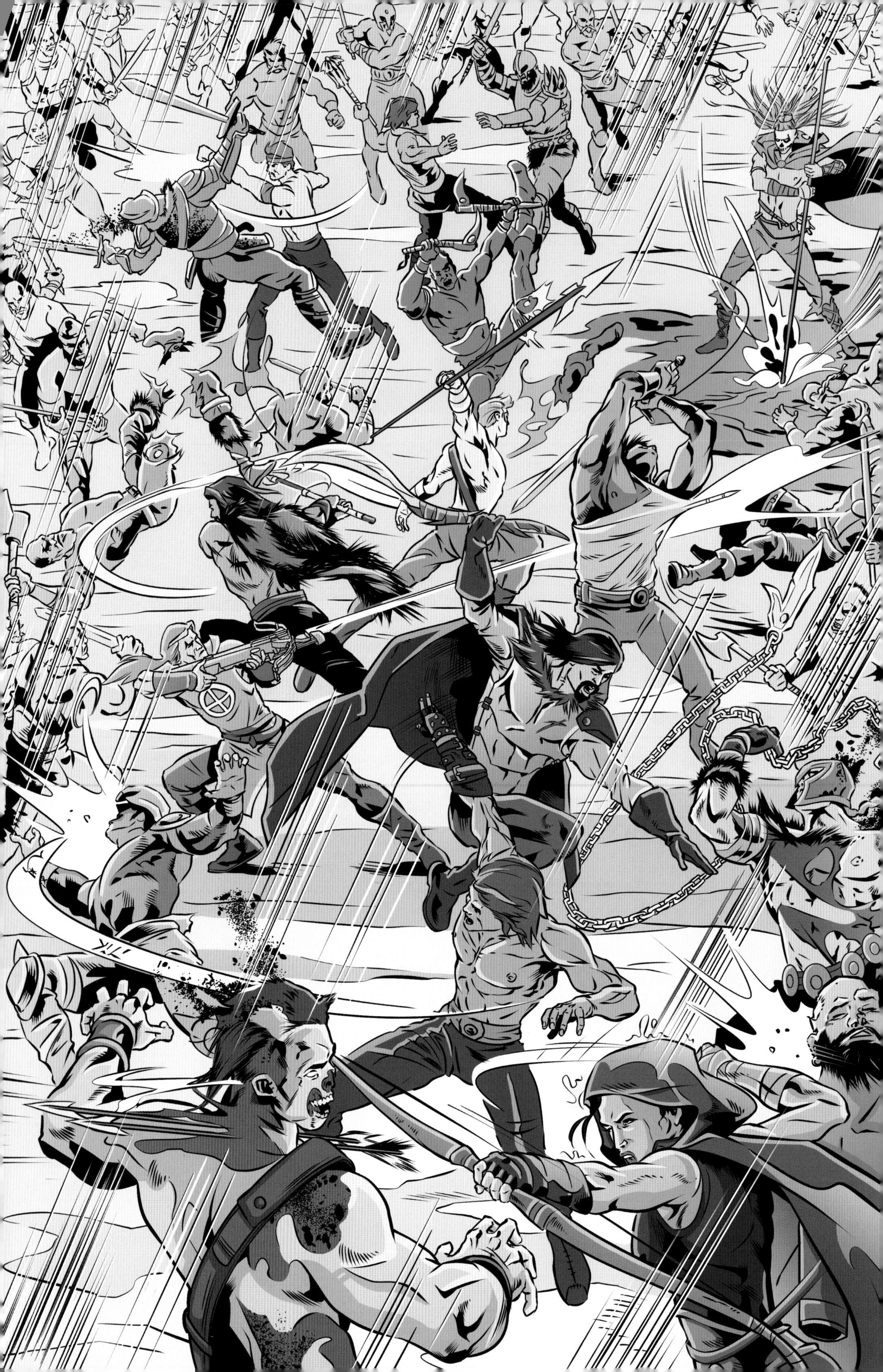

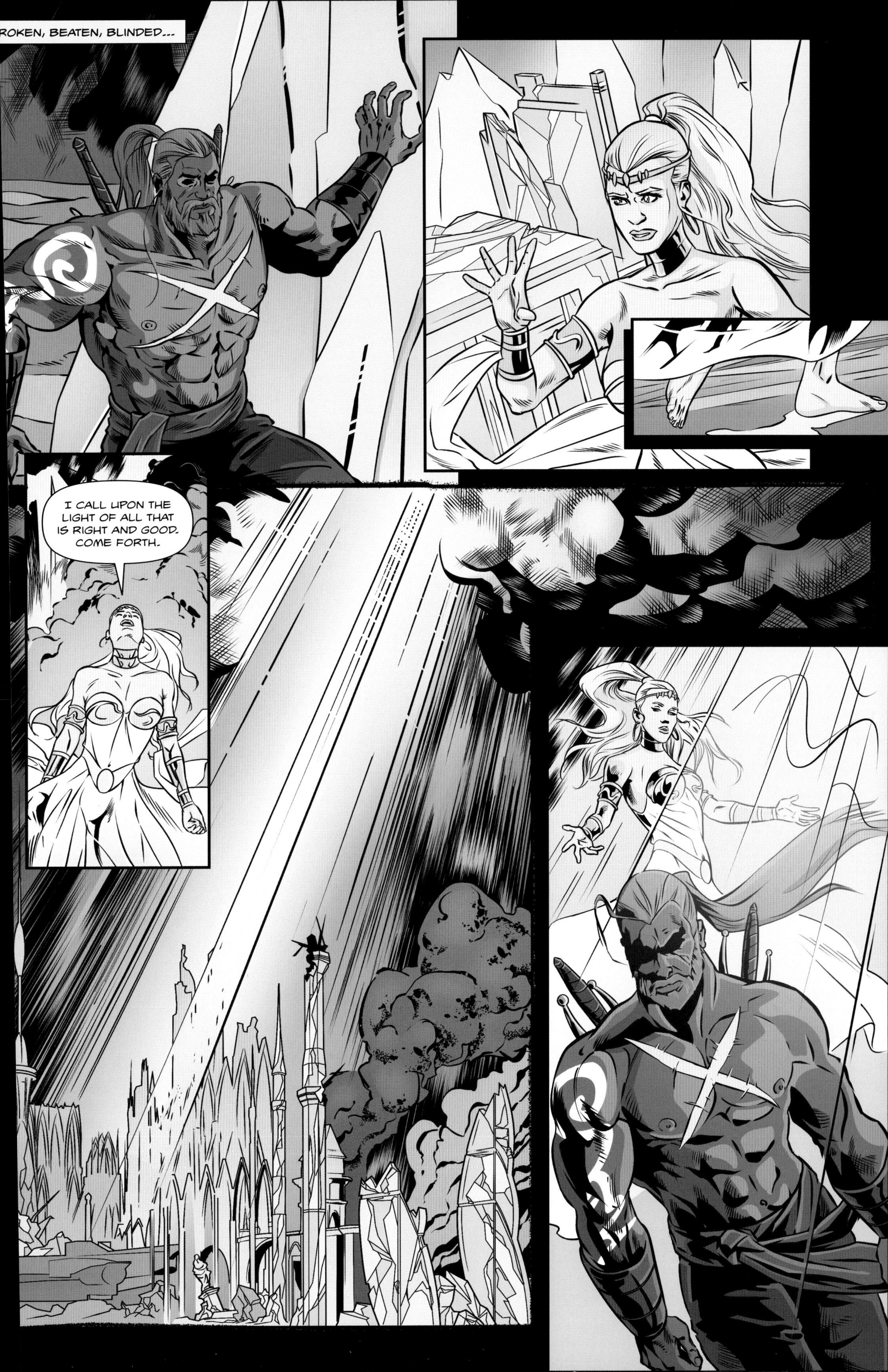
ROKEN, BEATEN, BLINDED...
I CALL UPON THE LIGHT OF ALL THAT IS RIGHT AND GOOD. COME FORTH.

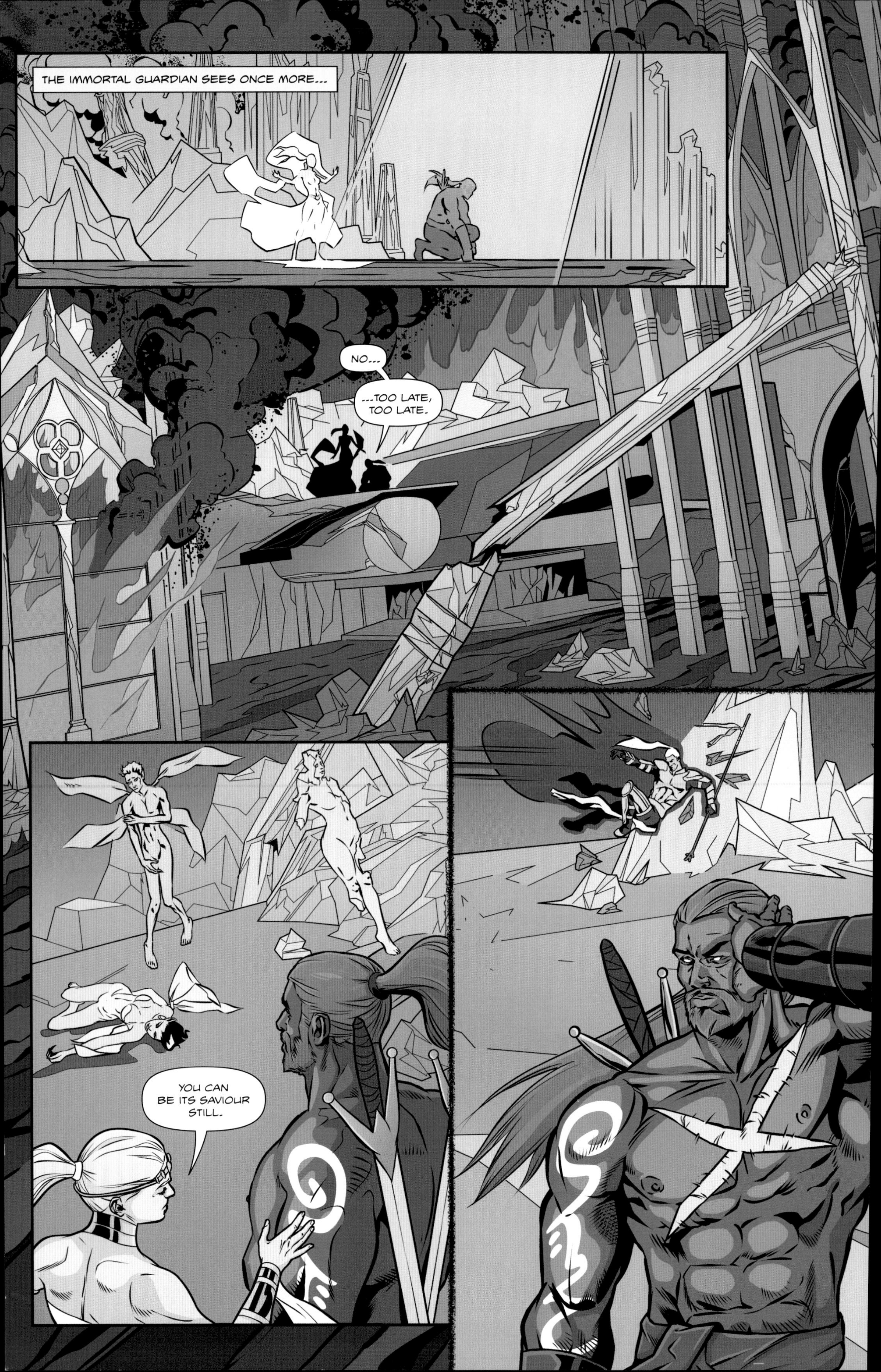
THE IMMORTAL GUARDIAN SEES ONCE MORE...
NO...
...TOO LATE, TOO LATE.
YOU CAN BE ITS SAVIOUR STILL.

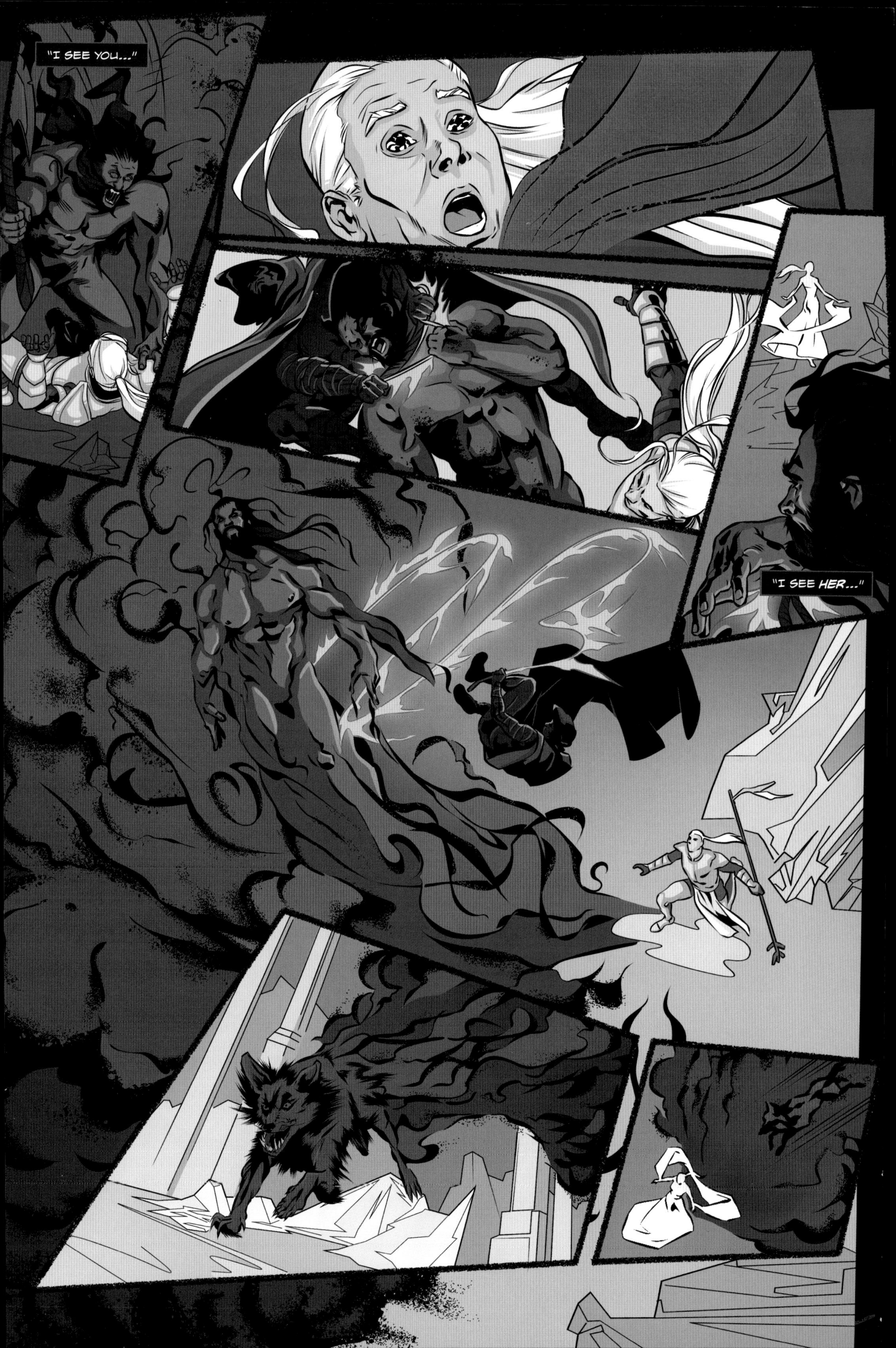
"I SEE YOU..."
"I SEE HER..."

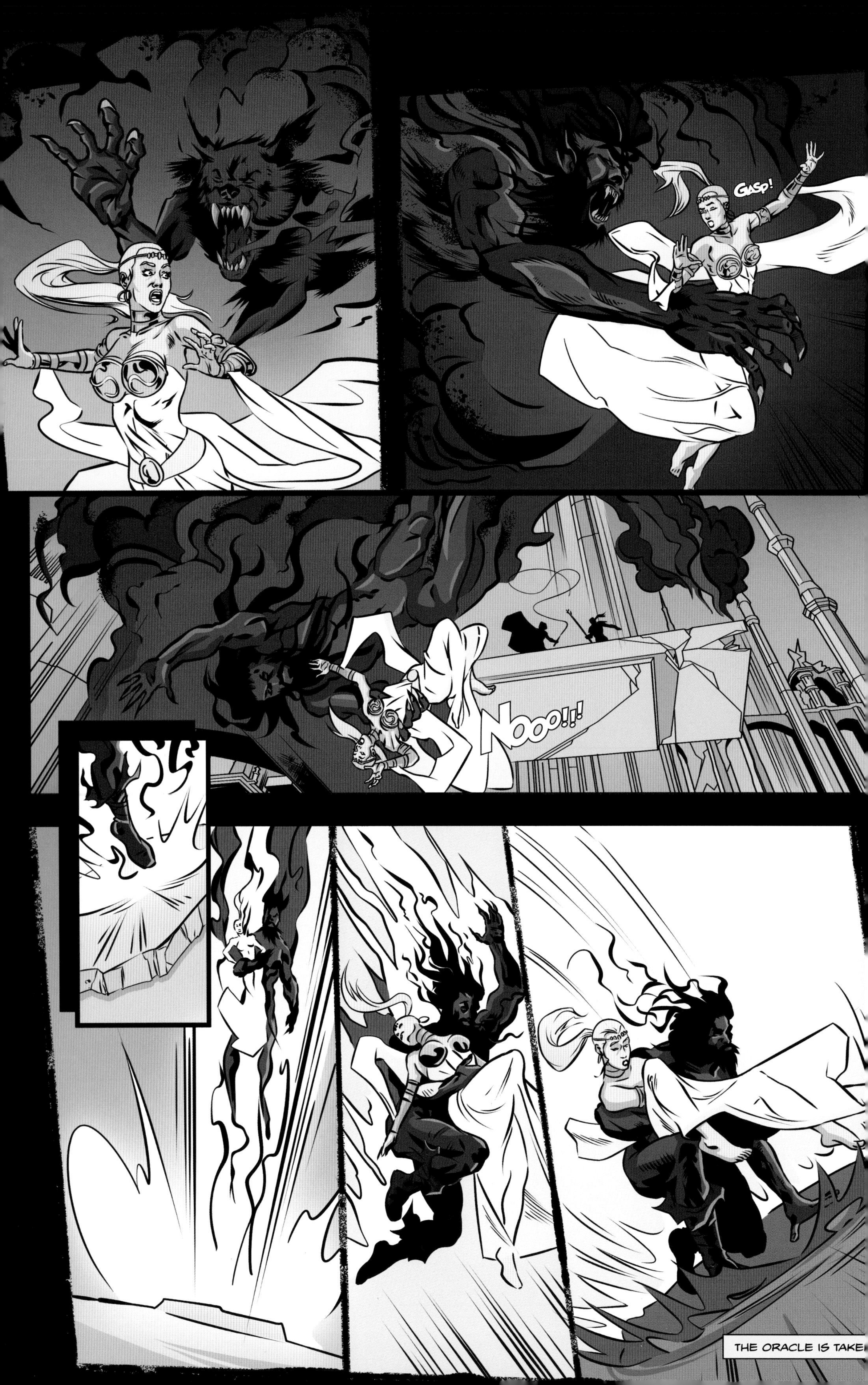
GASP!
NOOO!!!
THE ORACLE IS TAKE

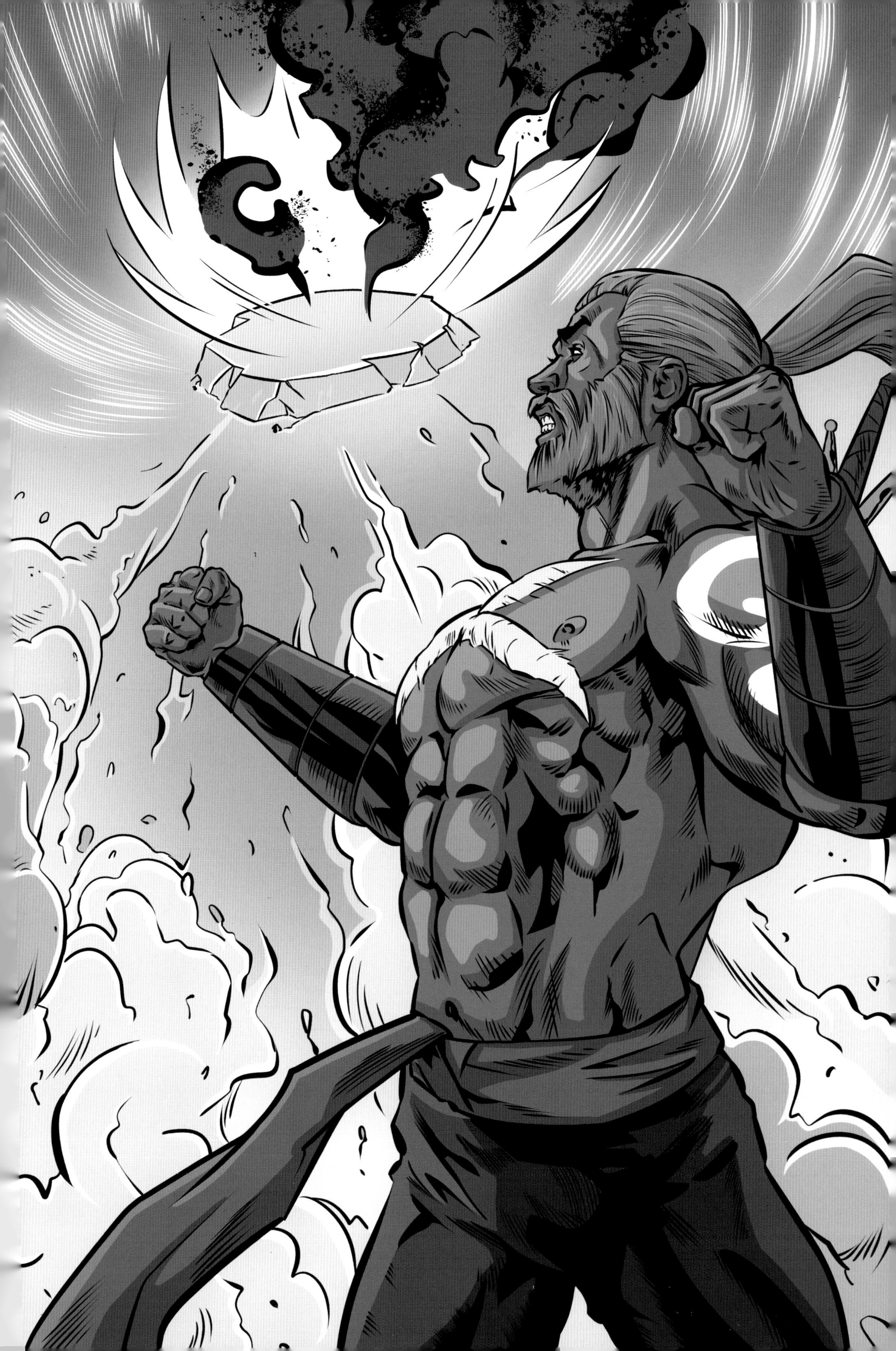

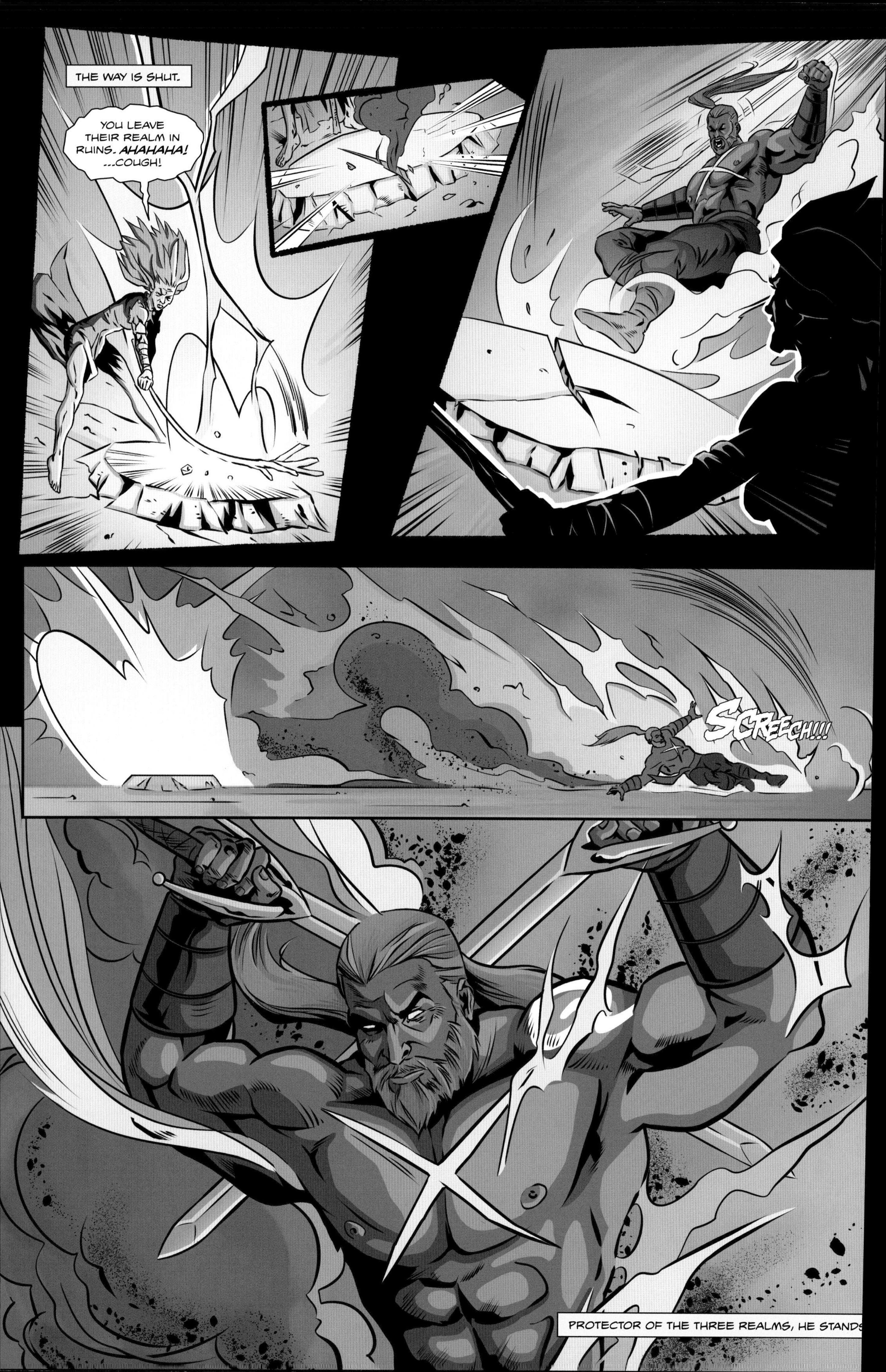

THE WAY IS SHUT.
YOU LEAVE THEIR REALM IN RUINS. **AHAHAHA!** ...COUGH!
SCREECH!!!
PROTECTOR OF THE THREE REALMS, HE STANDS

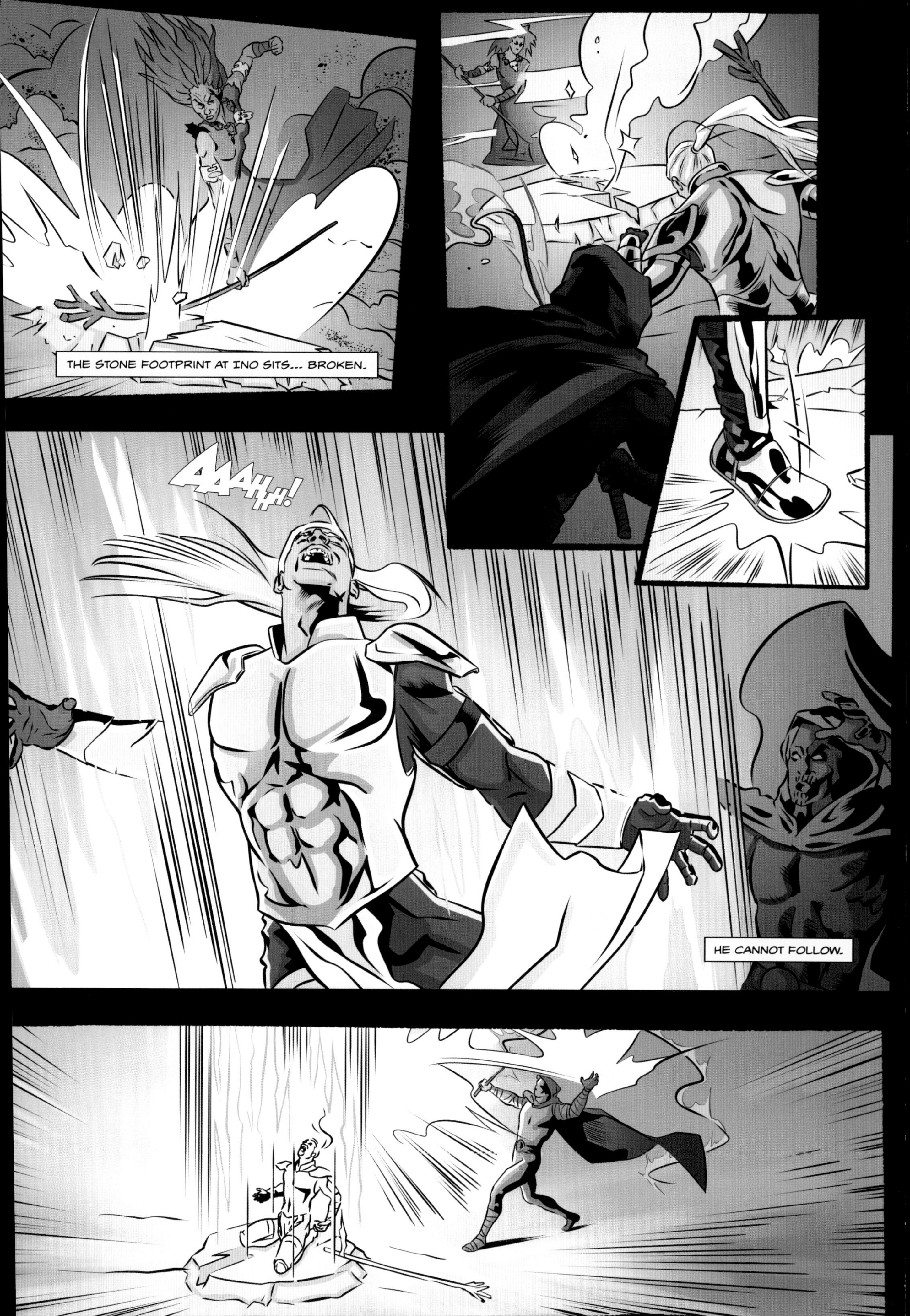
THE STONE FOOTPRINT AT INO SITS... BROKEN.
AAAAHHH!
HE CANNOT FOLLOW.

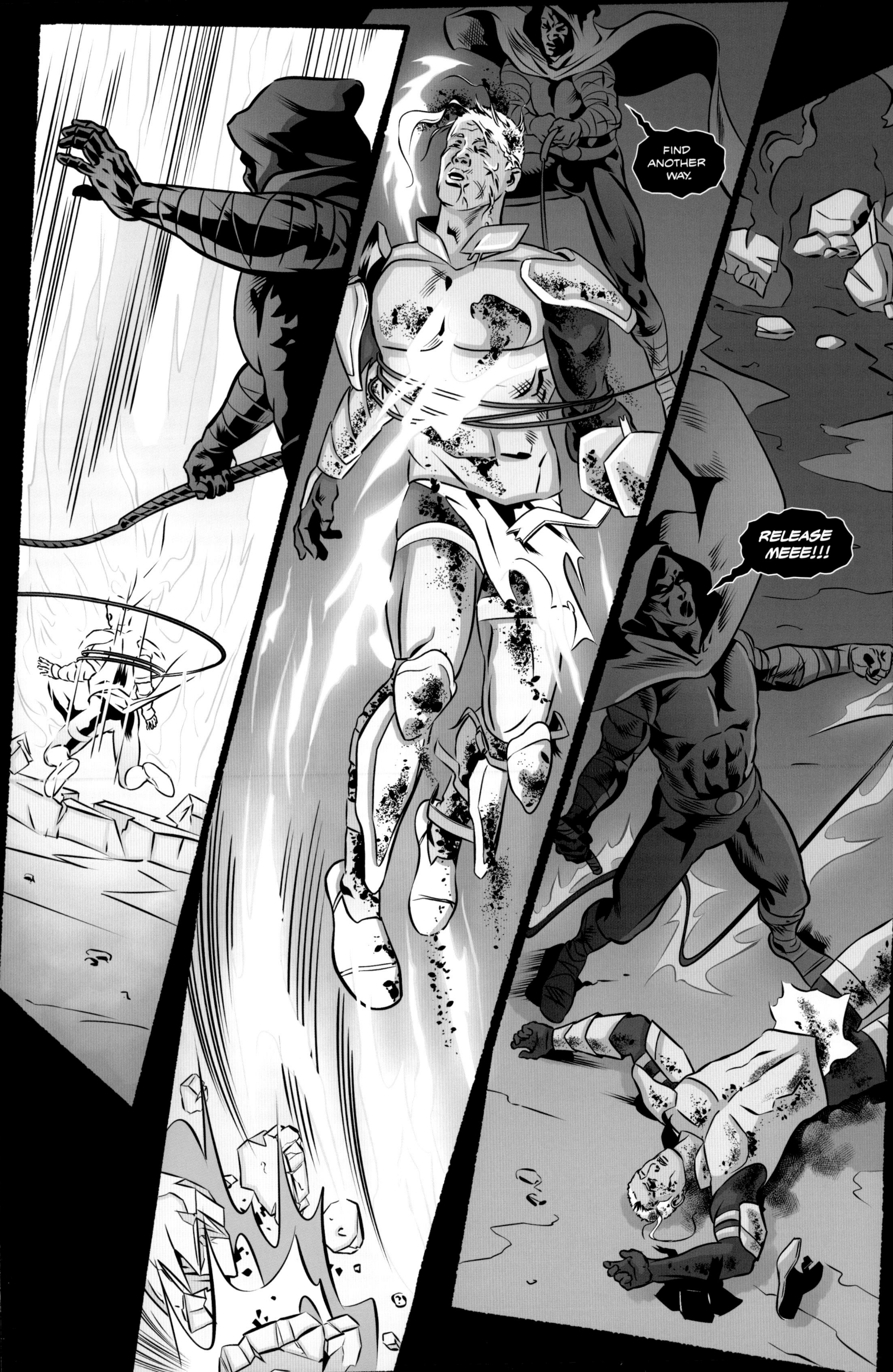
FIND ANOTHER WAY.
RELEASE MEEE!!!

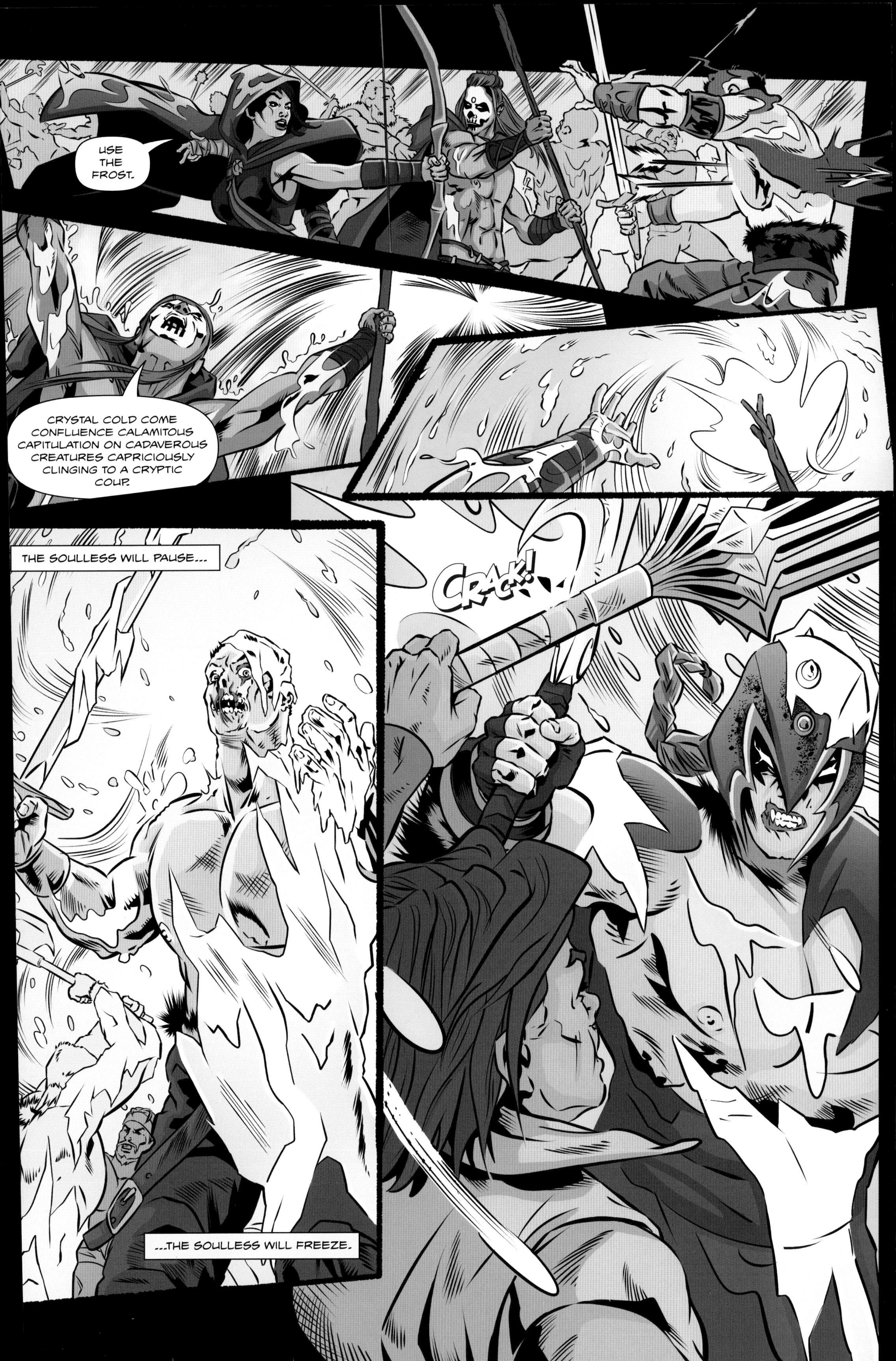
USE THE FROST.
CRYSTAL COLD COME CONFLUENCE CALAMITOUS CAPITULATION ON CADAVEROUS CREATURES CAPRICIOUSLY CLINGING TO A CRYPTIC COUP.
THE SOULLESS WILL PAUSE...
...THE SOULLESS WILL FREEZE.
CRACK!

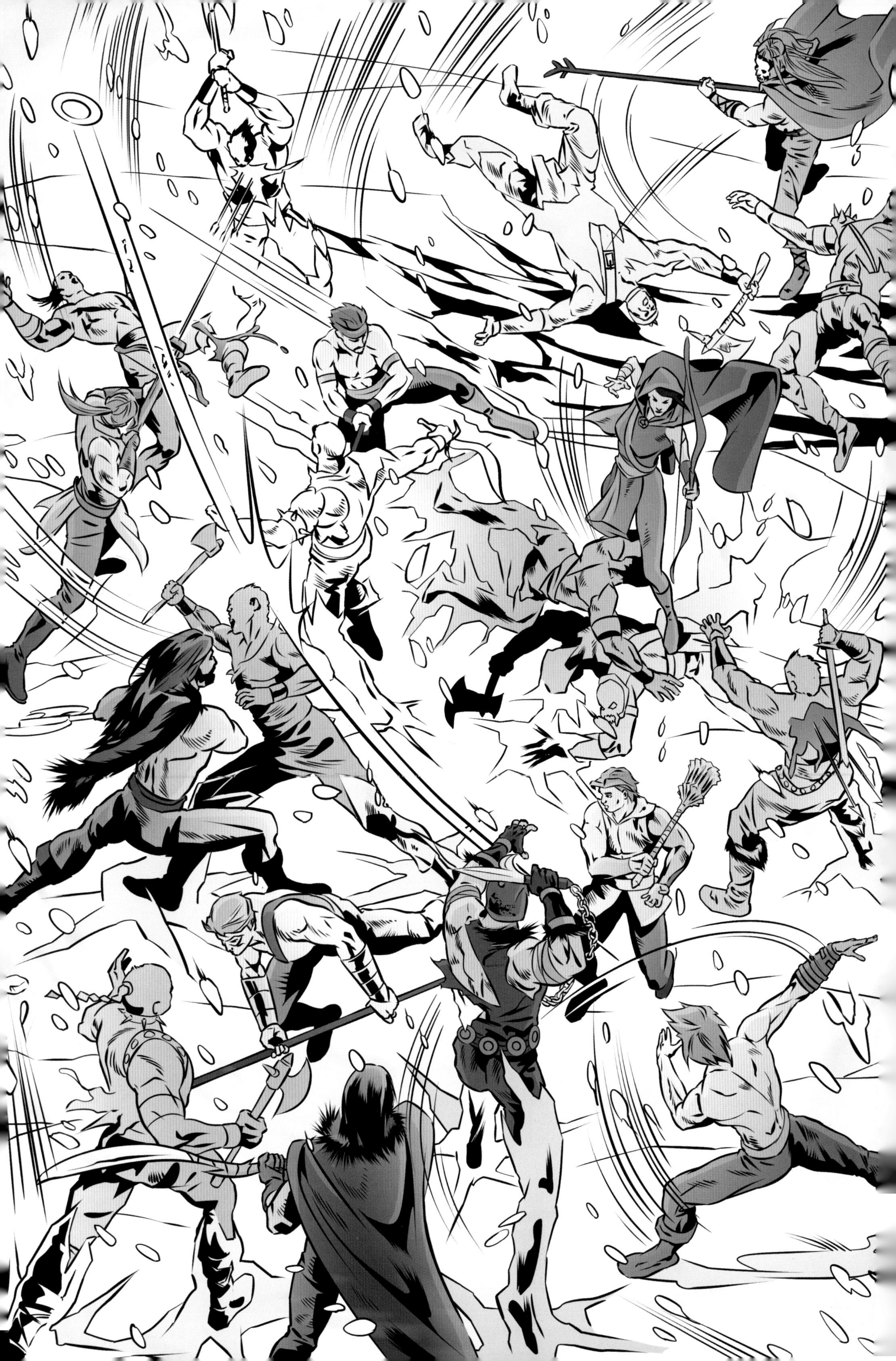

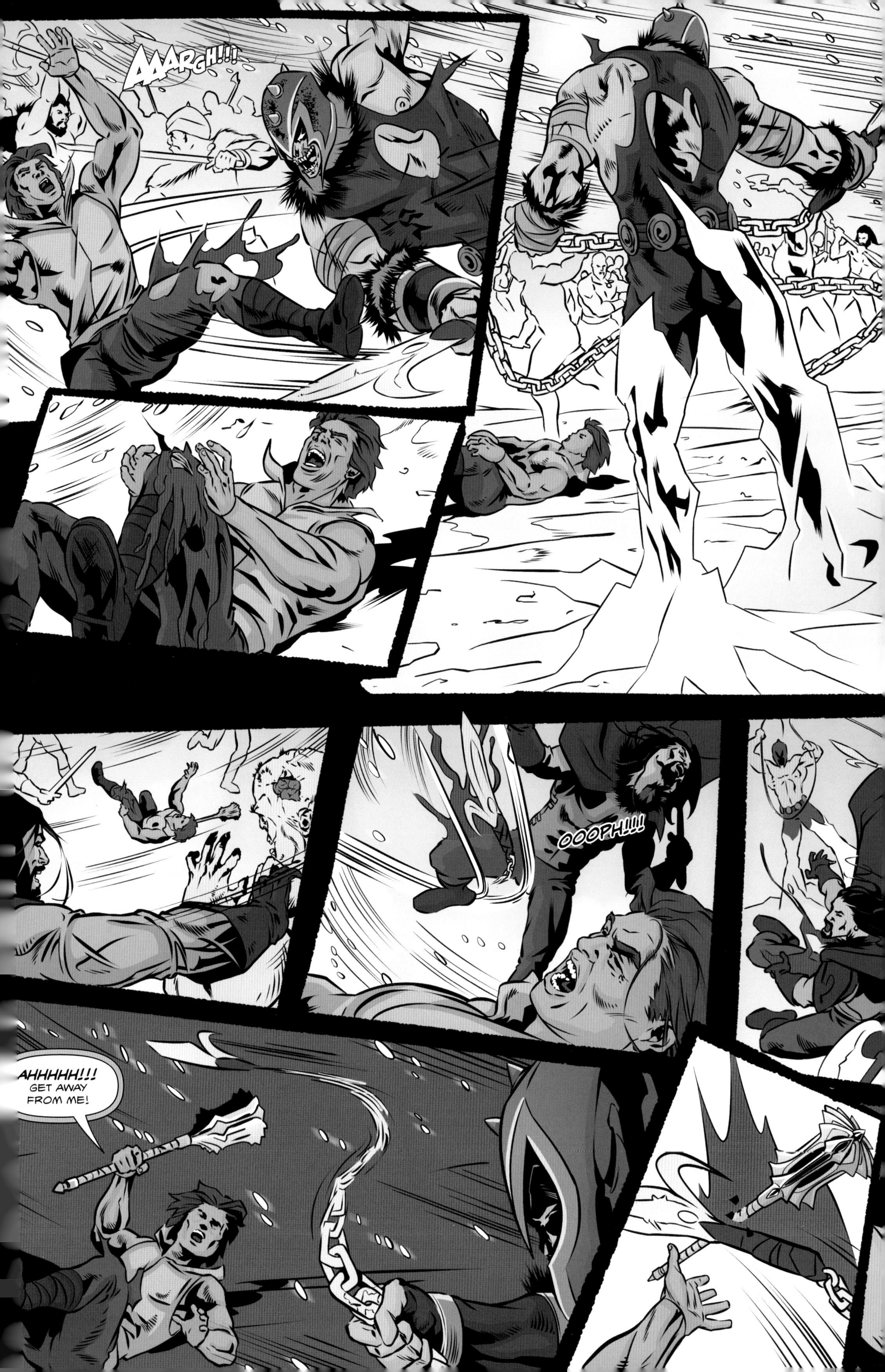
AAARGH!!!
OOOPH!!!
AHHHHH!!! GET AWAY FROM ME!

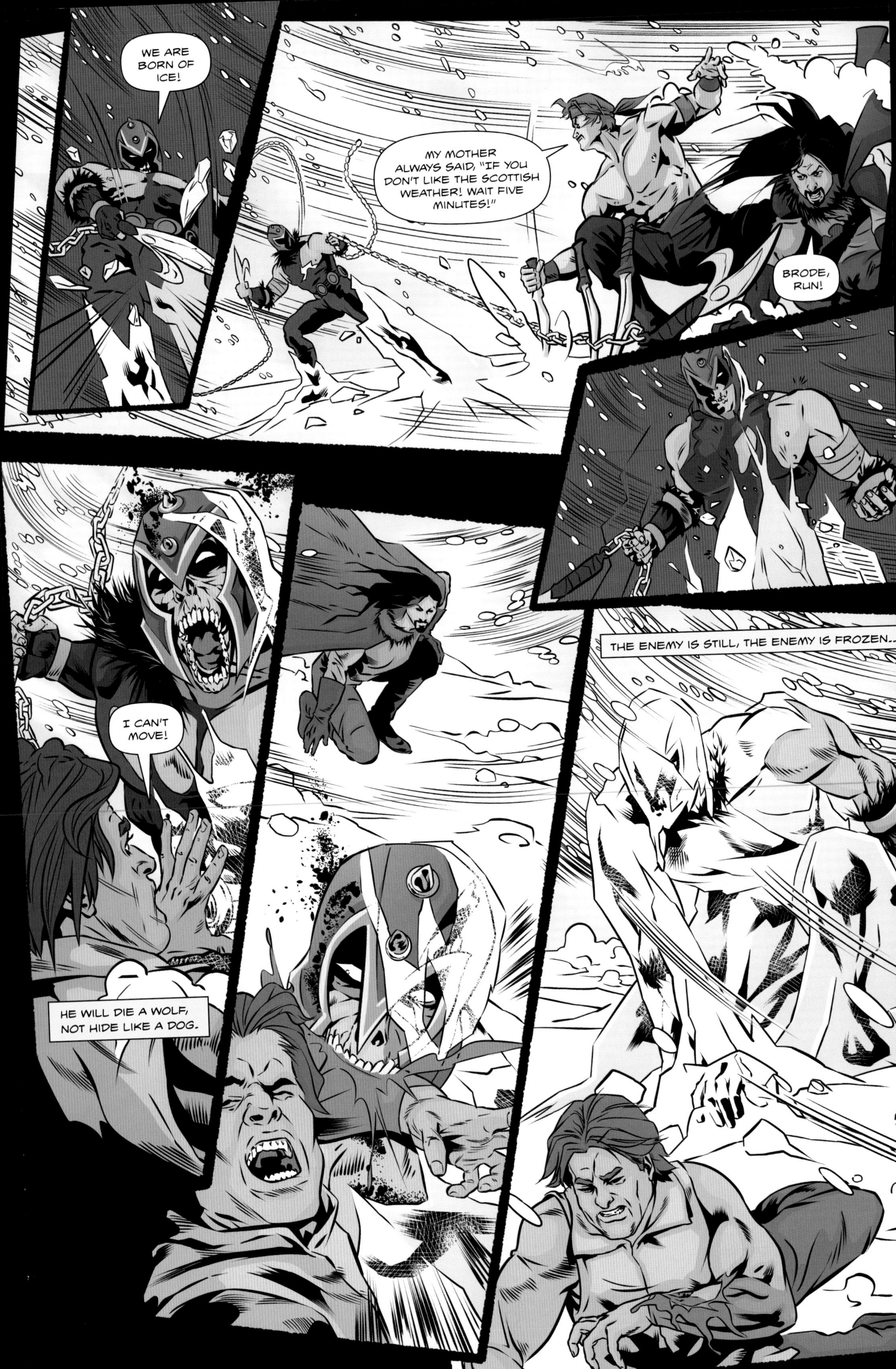
WE ARE BORN OF ICE!
MY MOTHER ALWAYS SAID, "IF YOU DON'T LIKE THE SCOTTISH WEATHER! WAIT FIVE MINUTES!"
BRODE, RUN!
I CAN'T MOVE!
HE WILL DIE A WOLF, NOT HIDE LIKE A DOG.
THE ENEMY IS STILL, THE ENEMY IS FROZEN...

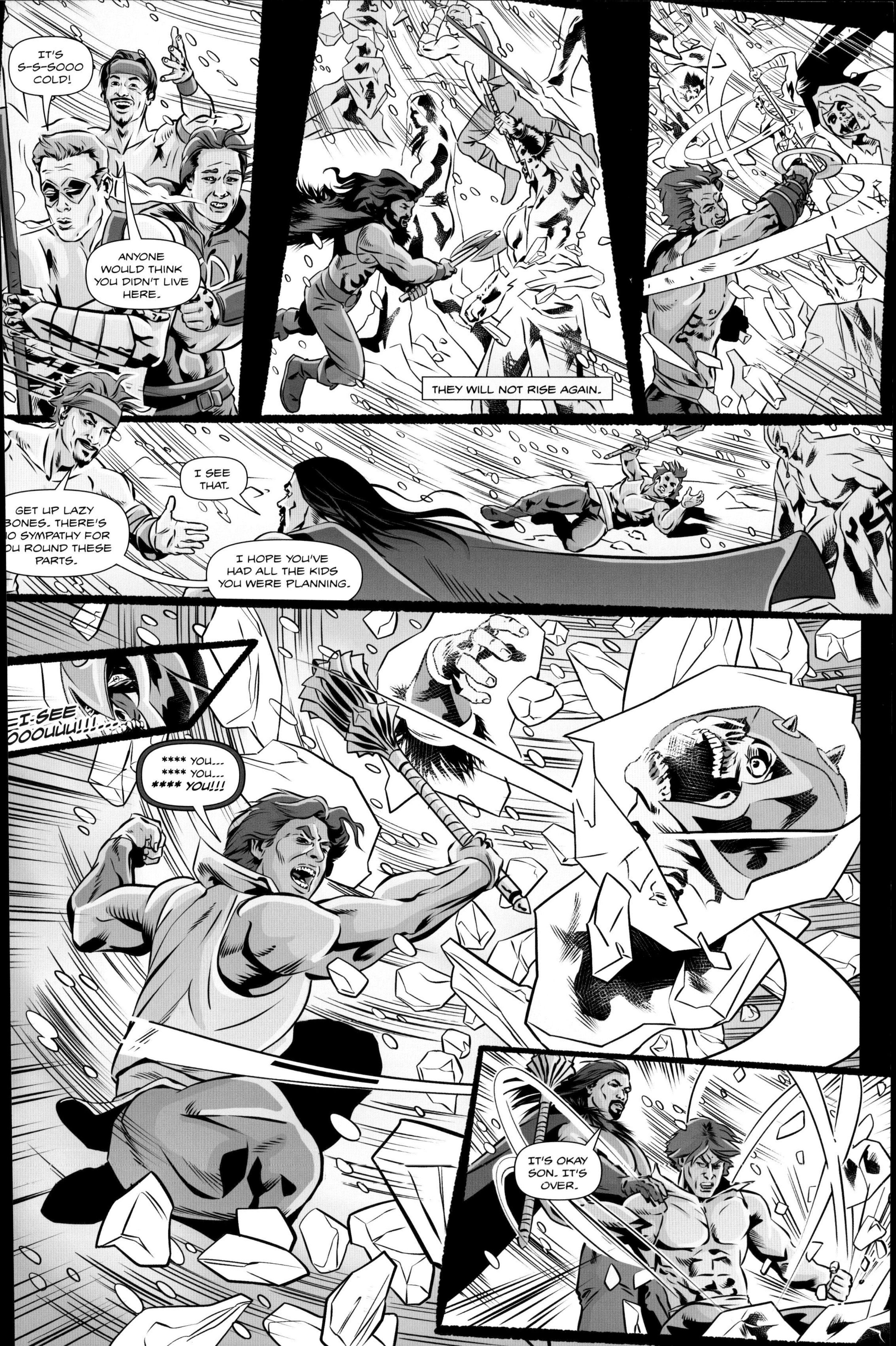
IT'S S-S-SOOO COLD!
ANYONE WOULD THINK YOU DIDN'T LIVE HERE.
THEY WILL NOT RISE AGAIN.
I SEE THAT.
GET UP LAZY BONES. THERE'S NO SYMPATHY FOR YOU ROUND THESE PARTS.
I HOPE YOU'VE HAD ALL THE KIDS YOU WERE PLANNING.
I SEE OOOUUUU!!!...
**** YOU... **** YOU... **** YOU!!!
IT'S OKAY SON. IT'S OVER.

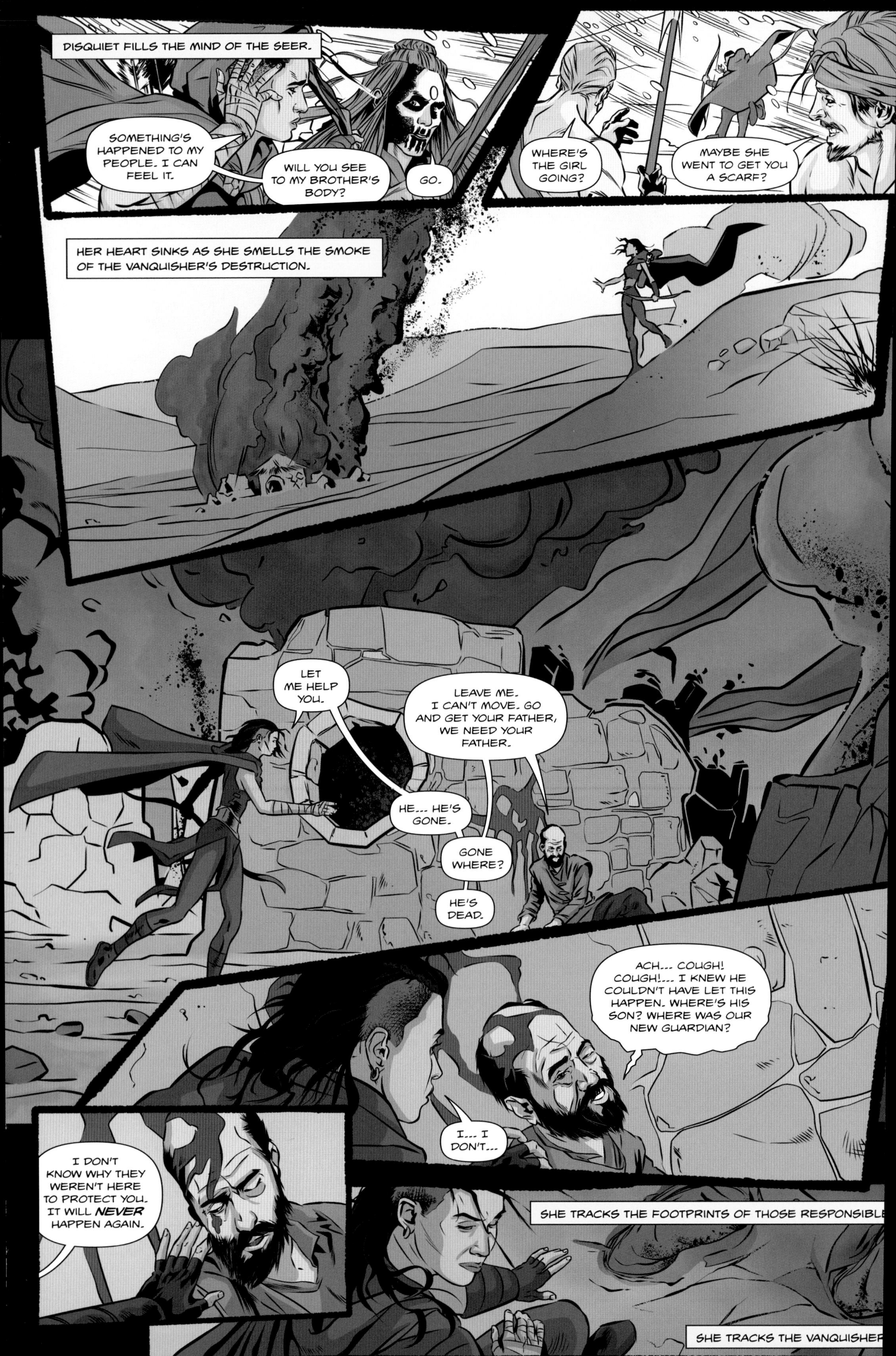

DISQUIET FILLS THE MIND OF THE SEER.
SOMETHING'S HAPPENED TO MY PEOPLE. I CAN FEEL IT.
WILL YOU SEE TO MY BROTHER'S BODY?
GO.
WHERE'S THE GIRL GOING?
MAYBE SHE WENT TO GET YOU A SCARF?
HER HEART SINKS AS SHE SMELLS THE SMOKE OF THE VANQUISHER'S DESTRUCTION.
LET ME HELP YOU.
LEAVE ME. I CAN'T MOVE. GO AND GET YOUR FATHER, WE NEED YOUR FATHER.
HE... HE'S GONE.
GONE WHERE?
HE'S DEAD.
ACH... COUGH! COUGH!... I KNEW HE COULDN'T HAVE LET THIS HAPPEN. WHERE'S HIS SON? WHERE WAS OUR NEW GUARDIAN?
I... I DON'T...
I DON'T KNOW WHY THEY WEREN'T HERE TO PROTECT YOU. IT WILL *NEVER* HAPPEN AGAIN.
SHE TRACKS THE FOOTPRINTS OF THOSE RESPONSIBLE
SHE TRACKS THE VANQUISHER

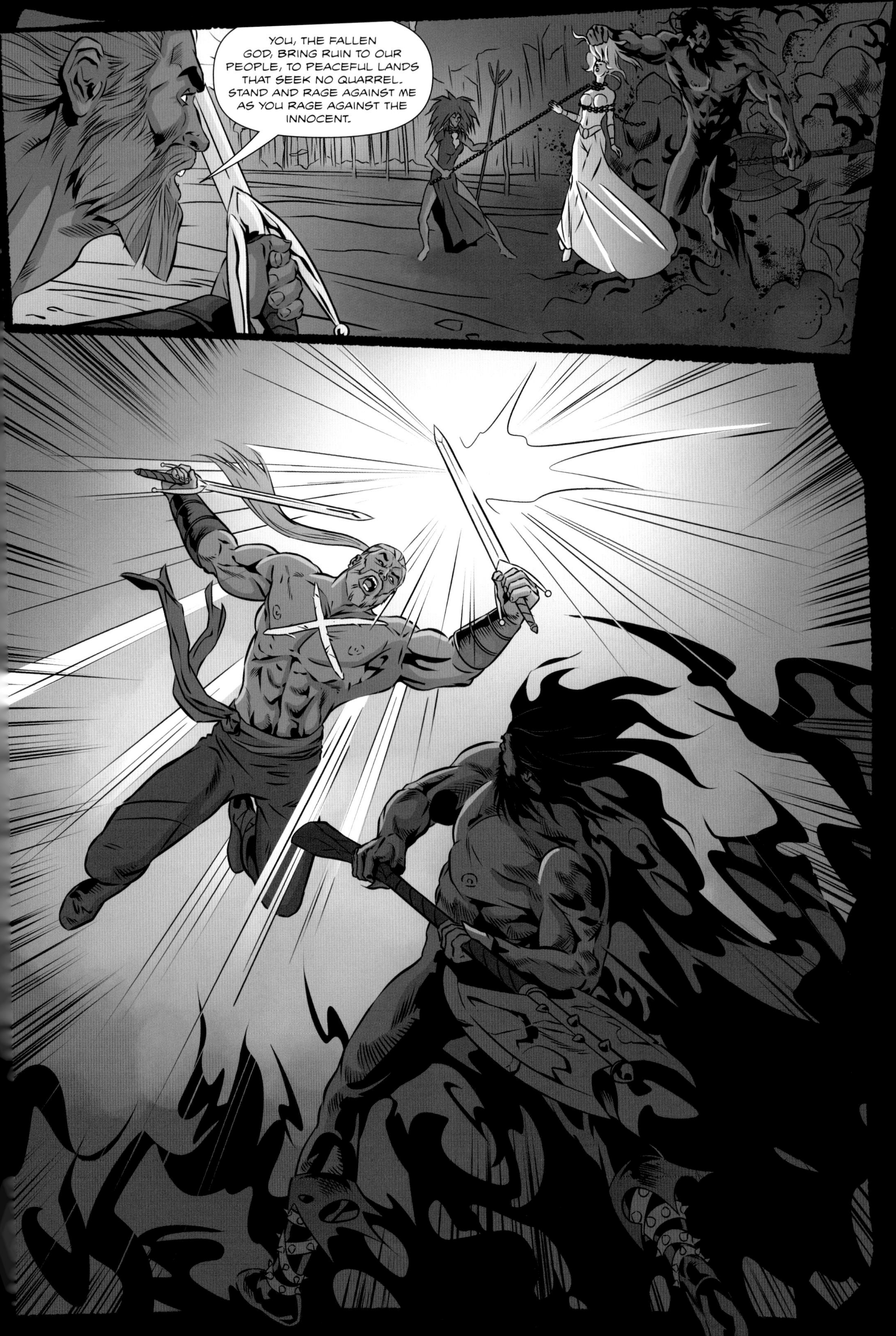
YOU, THE FALLEN GOD, BRING RUIN TO OUR PEOPLE, TO PEACEFUL LANDS THAT SEEK NO QUARREL. STAND AND RAGE AGAINST ME AS YOU RAGE AGAINST THE INNOCENT.

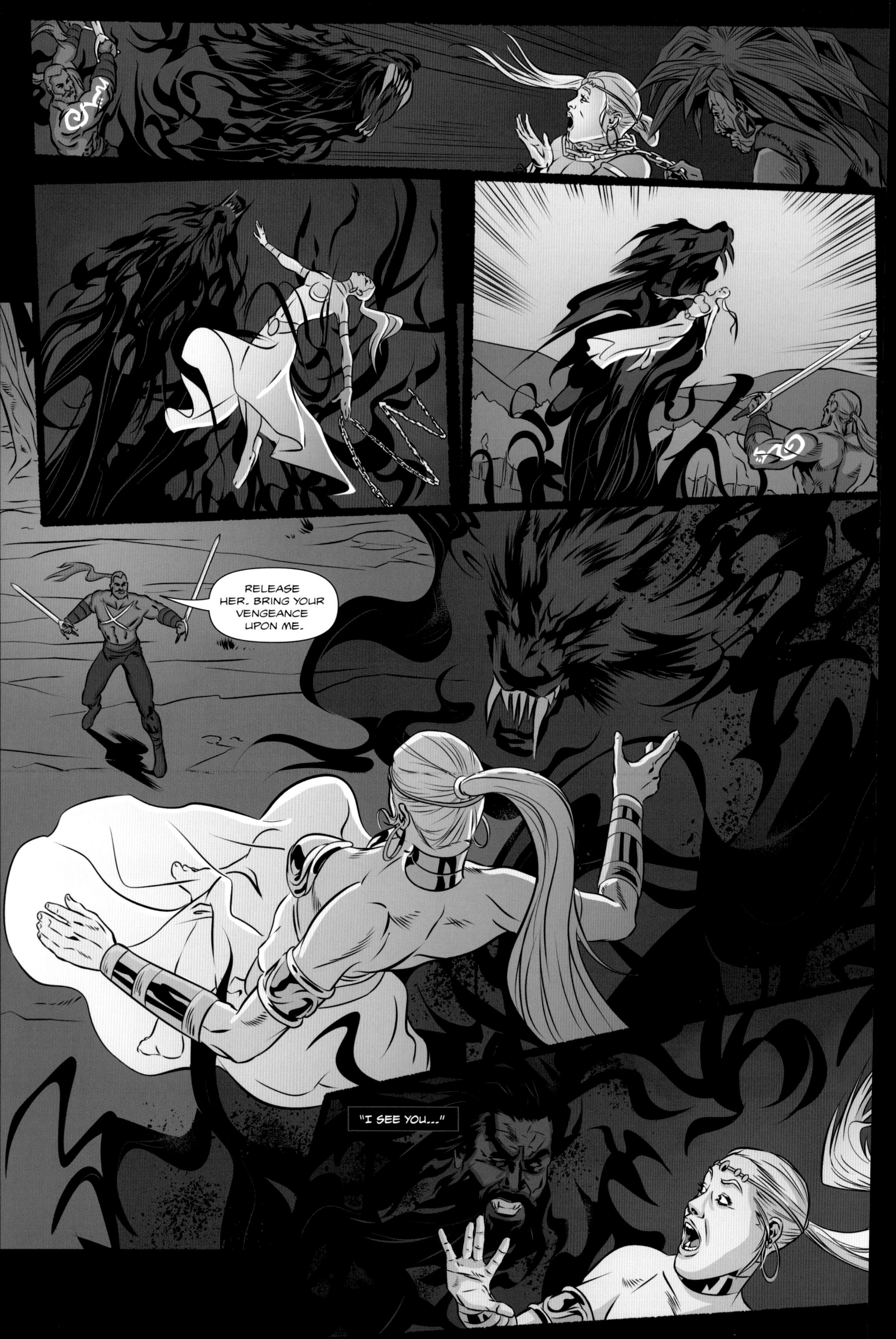
RELEASE HER. BRING YOUR VENGEANCE UPON ME.
"I SEE YOU..."

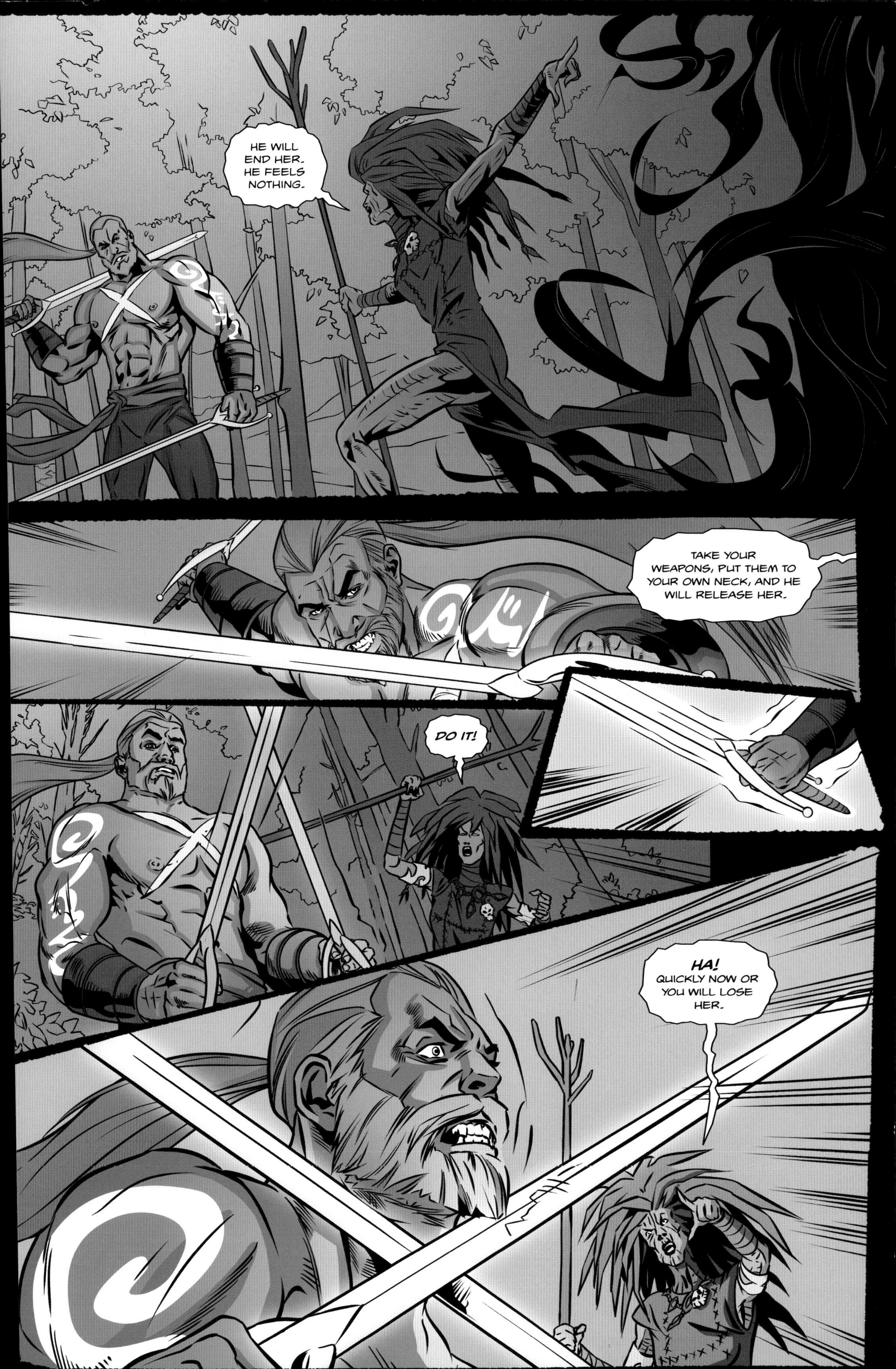
HE WILL END HER. HE FEELS NOTHING.
TAKE YOUR WEAPONS, PUT THEM TO YOUR OWN NECK, AND HE WILL RELEASE HER.
DO IT!
HA! QUICKLY NOW OR YOU WILL LOSE HER.

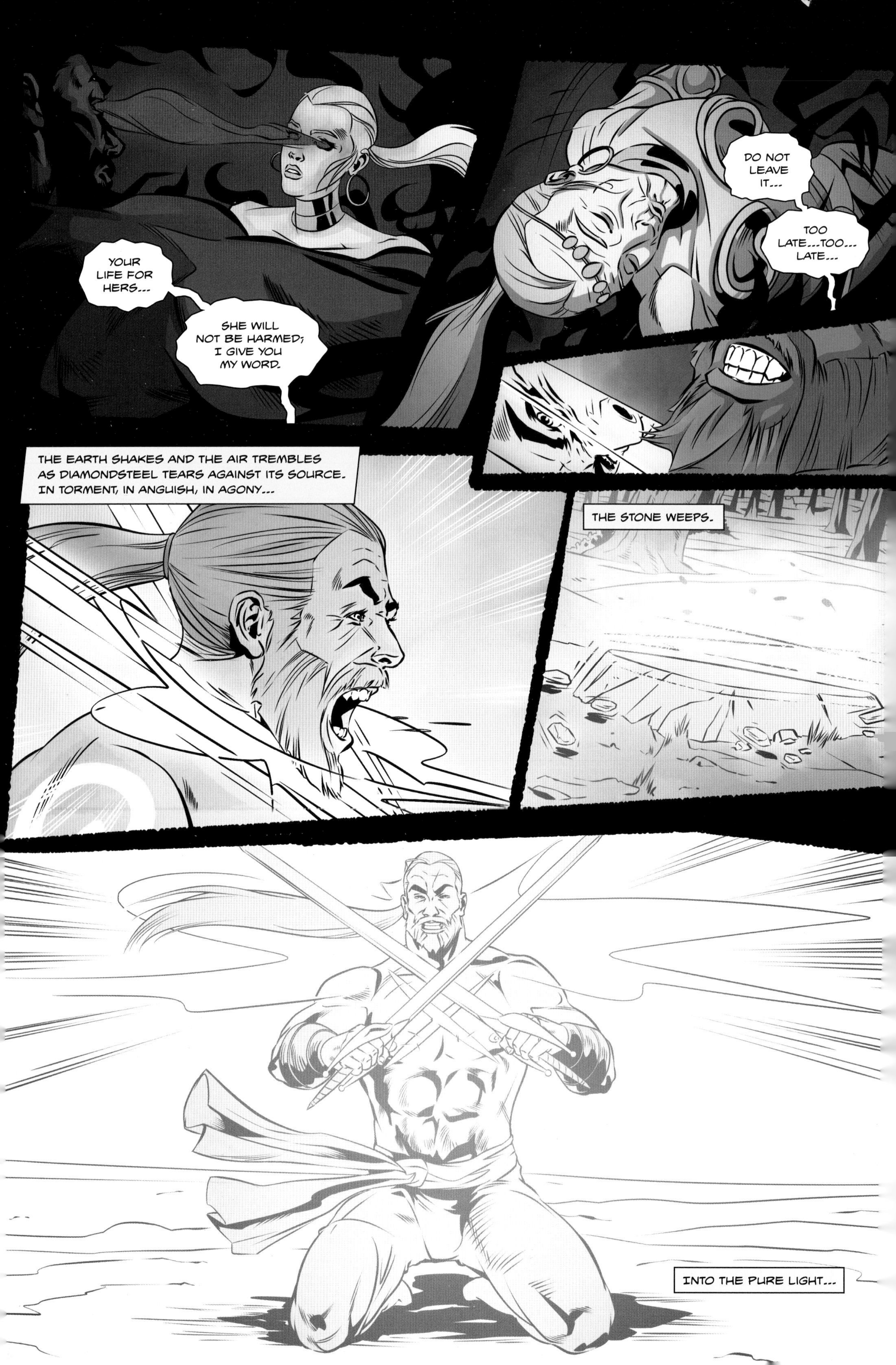
YOUR LIFE FOR HERS...
SHE WILL NOT BE HARMED; I GIVE YOU MY WORD.
DO NOT LEAVE IT...
TOO LATE...TOO... LATE...
THE EARTH SHAKES AND THE AIR TREMBLES AS DIAMONDSTEEL TEARS AGAINST ITS SOURCE. IN TORMENT, IN ANGUISH, IN AGONY...
THE STONE WEEPS.
INTO THE PURE LIGHT...

Chapter Six

Script: John Ferguson
Art: Toni Doya Heredia
Colours: Rebecca Horner
Letters: Phillip Vaughan
Editor: Clare Ferguson

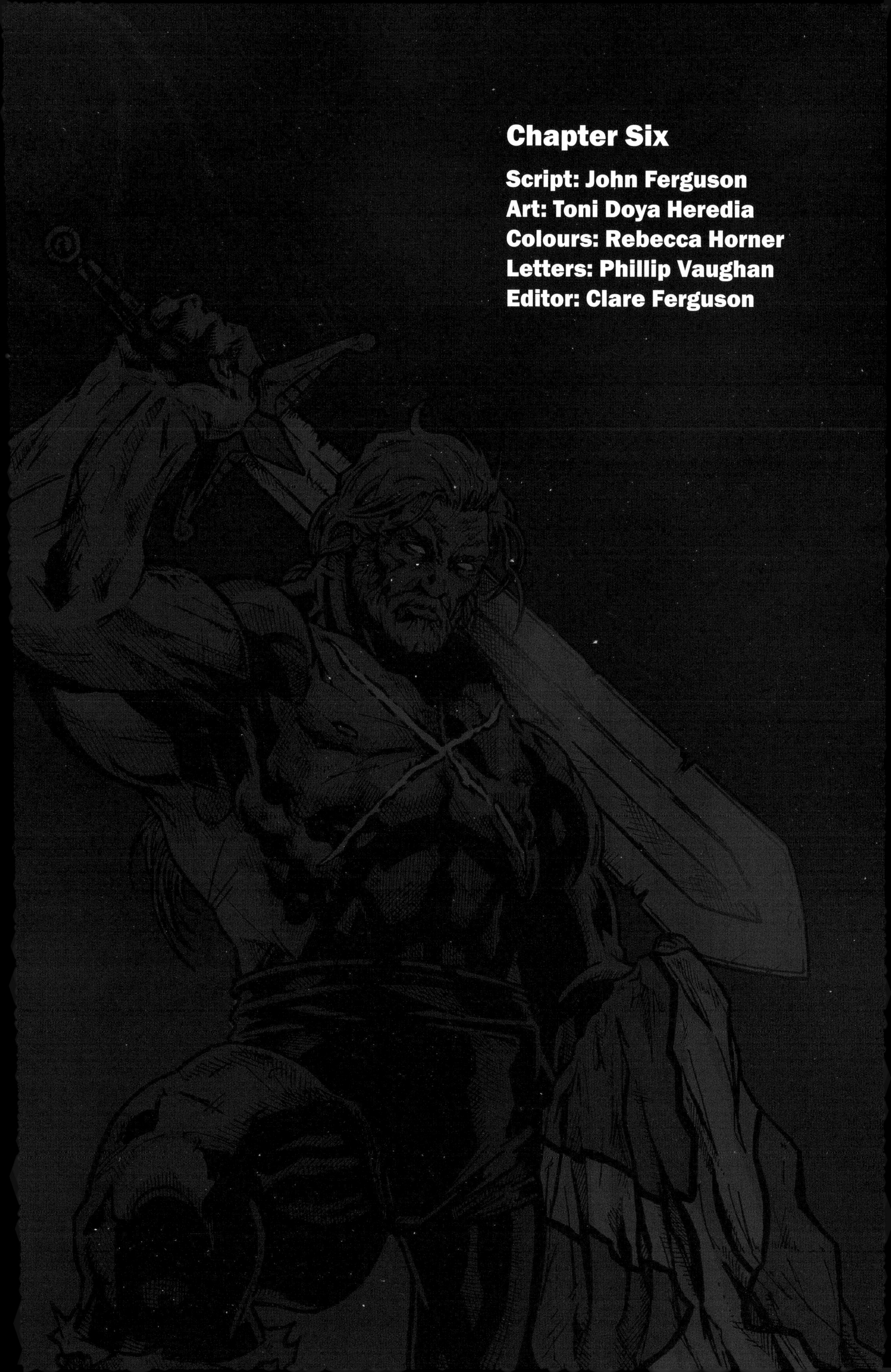

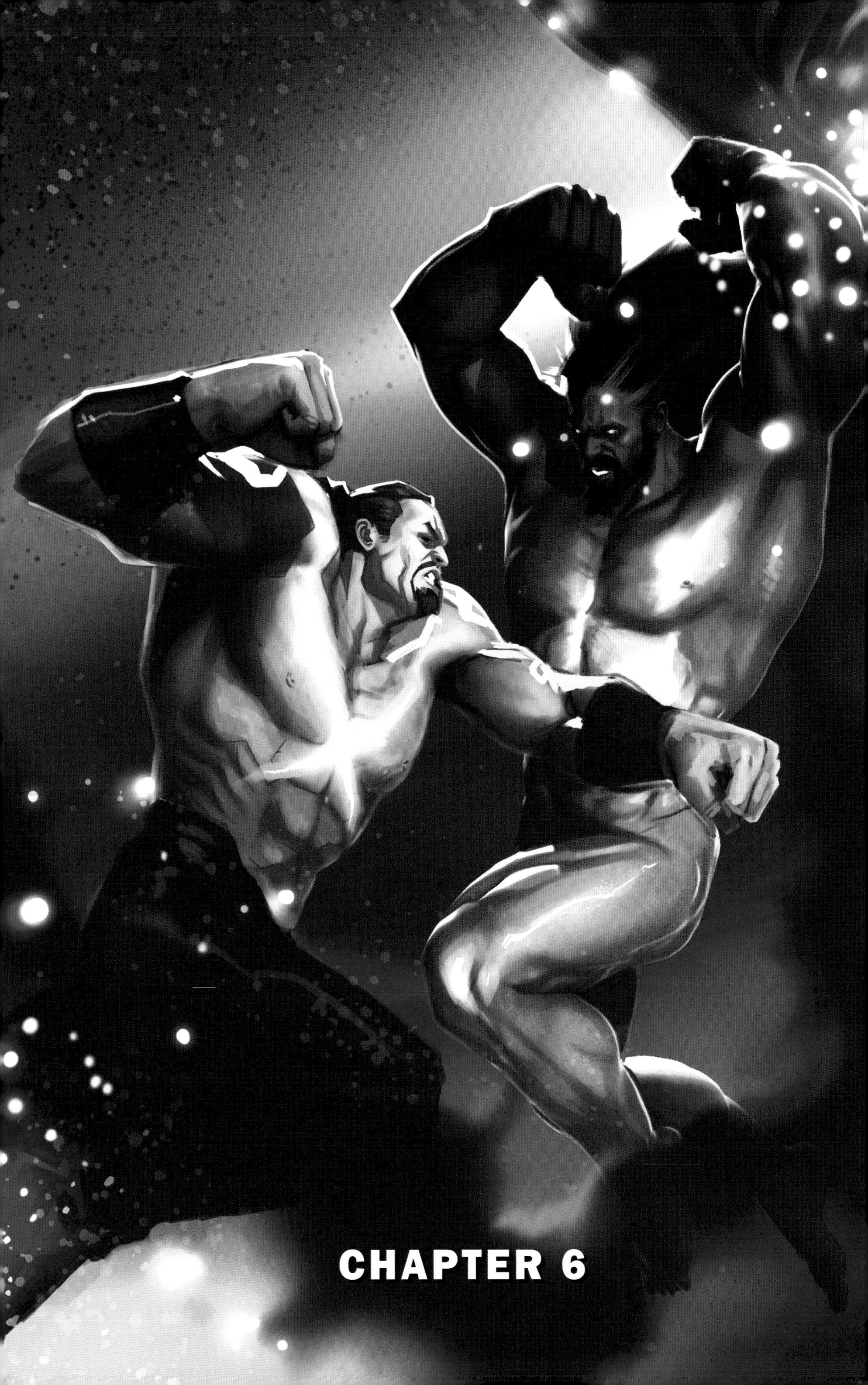

CHAPTER 6

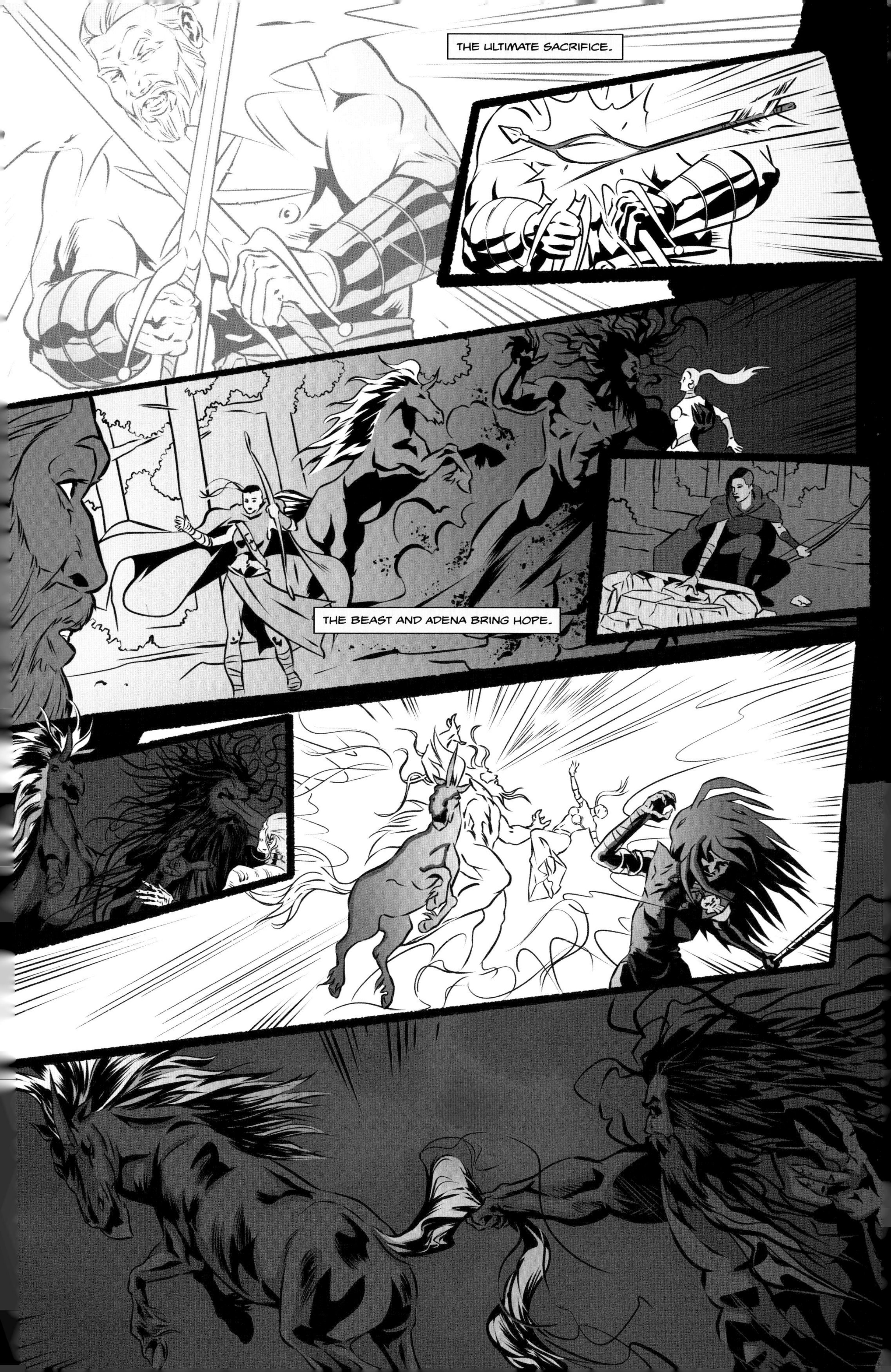
THE ULTIMATE SACRIFICE.
THE BEAST AND ADENA BRING HOPE.

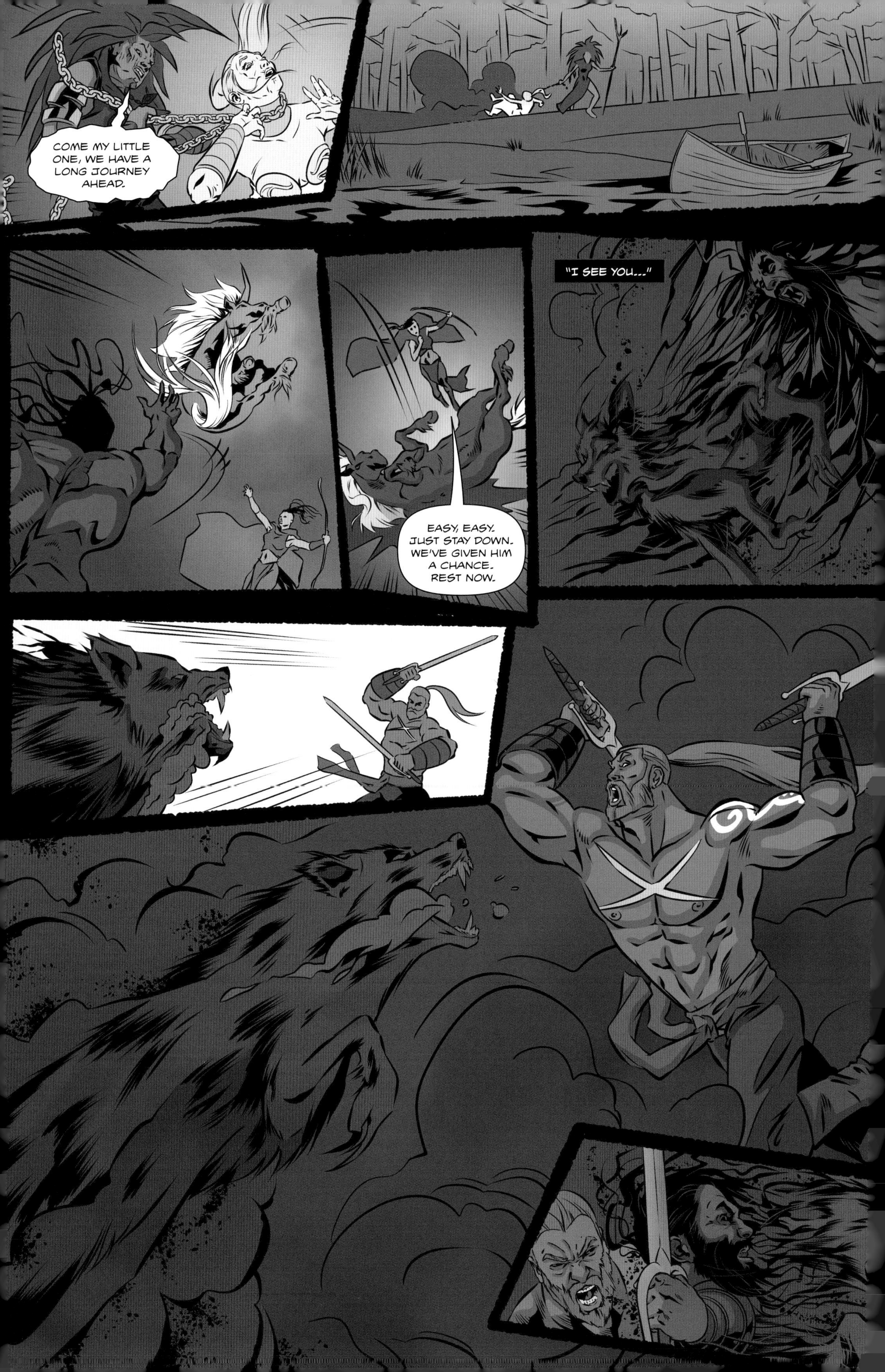
COME MY LITTLE ONE, WE HAVE A LONG JOURNEY AHEAD.
EASY, EASY. JUST STAY DOWN. WE'VE GIVEN HIM A CHANCE. REST NOW.
"I SEE YOU..."

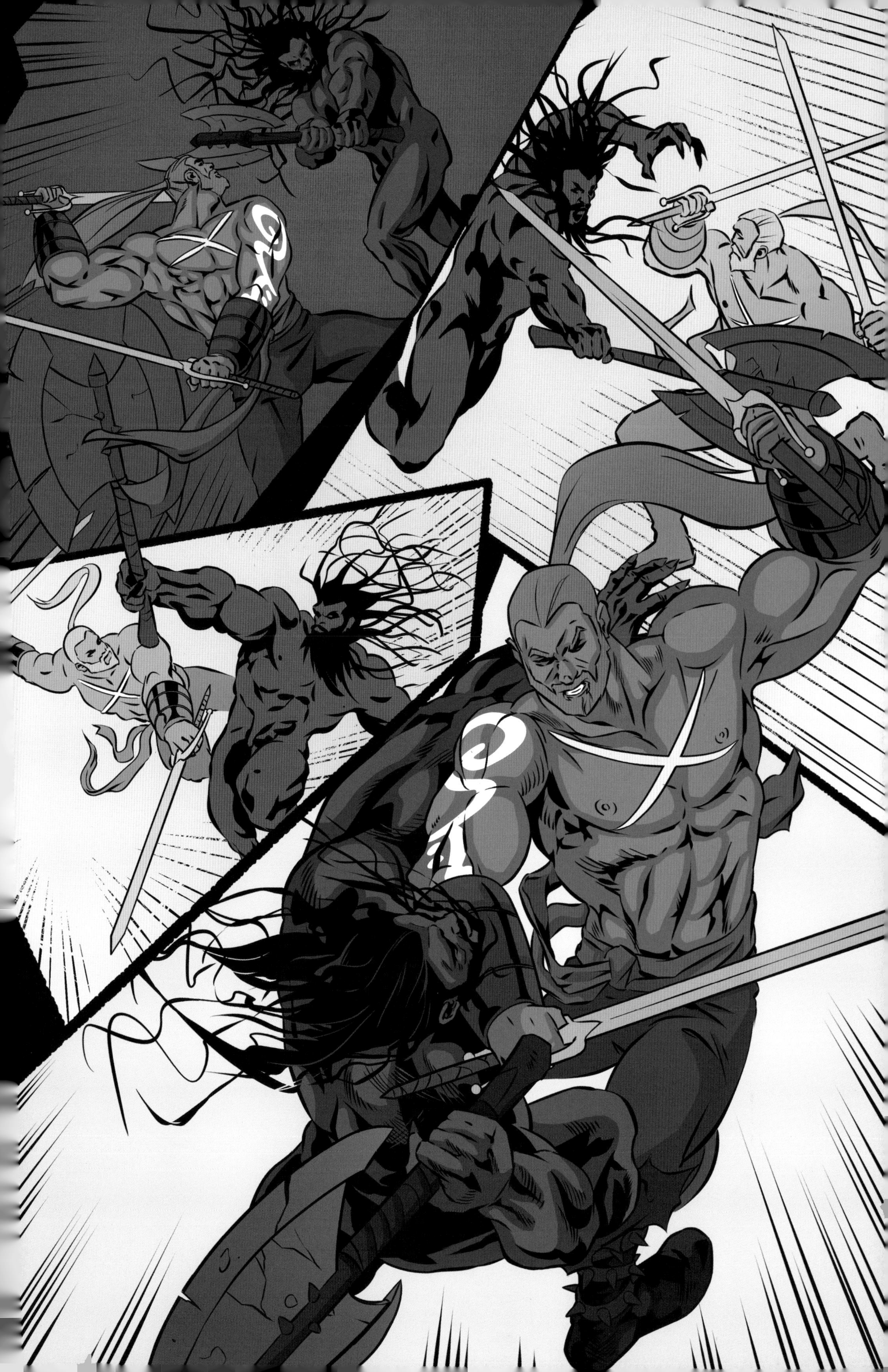

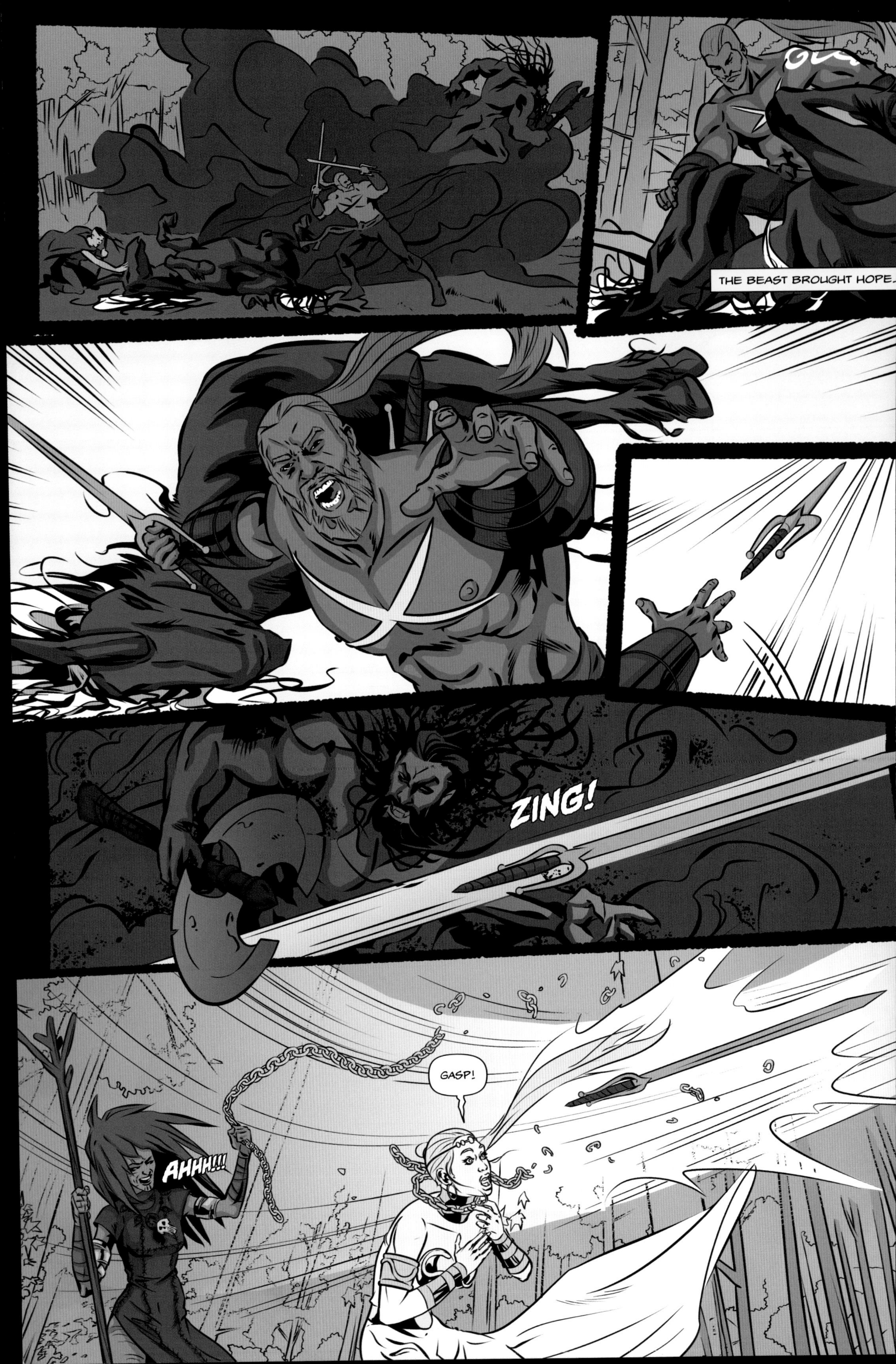
THE BEAST BROUGHT HOPE...
ZING!
GASP!
AHHH!!!

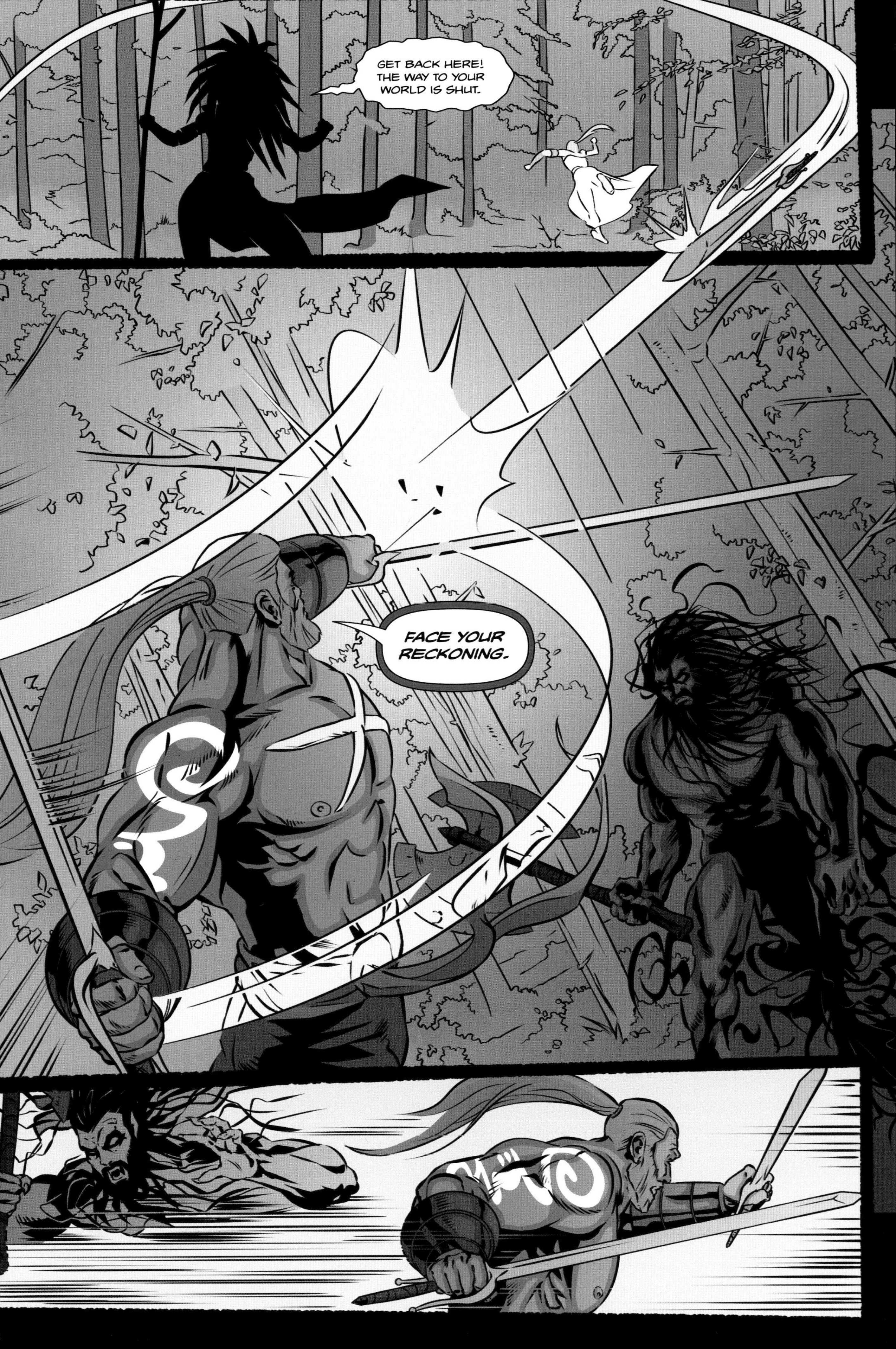
GET BACK HERE! THE WAY TO YOUR WORLD IS SHUT.
FACE YOUR RECKONING.

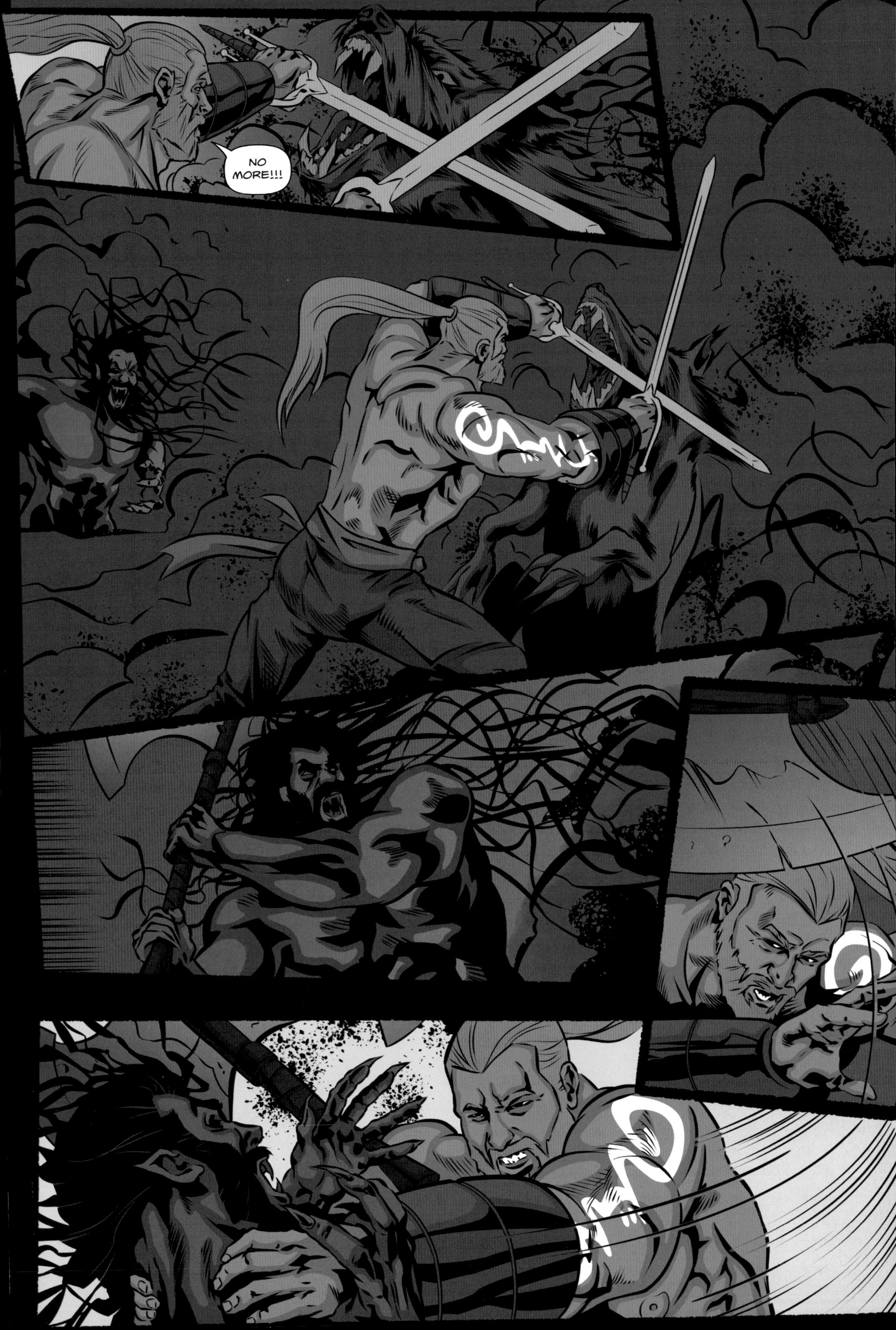
NO MORE!!!

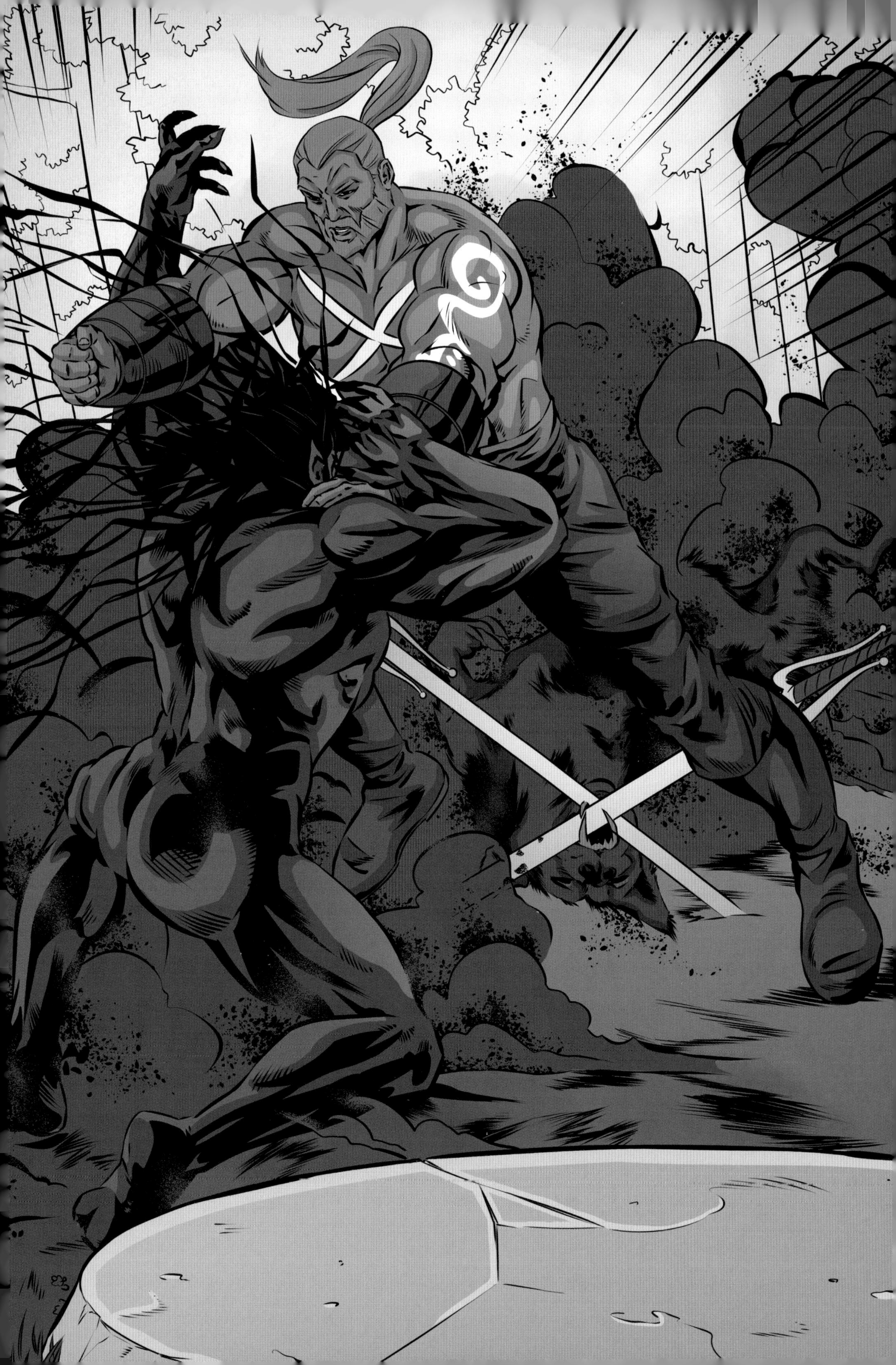

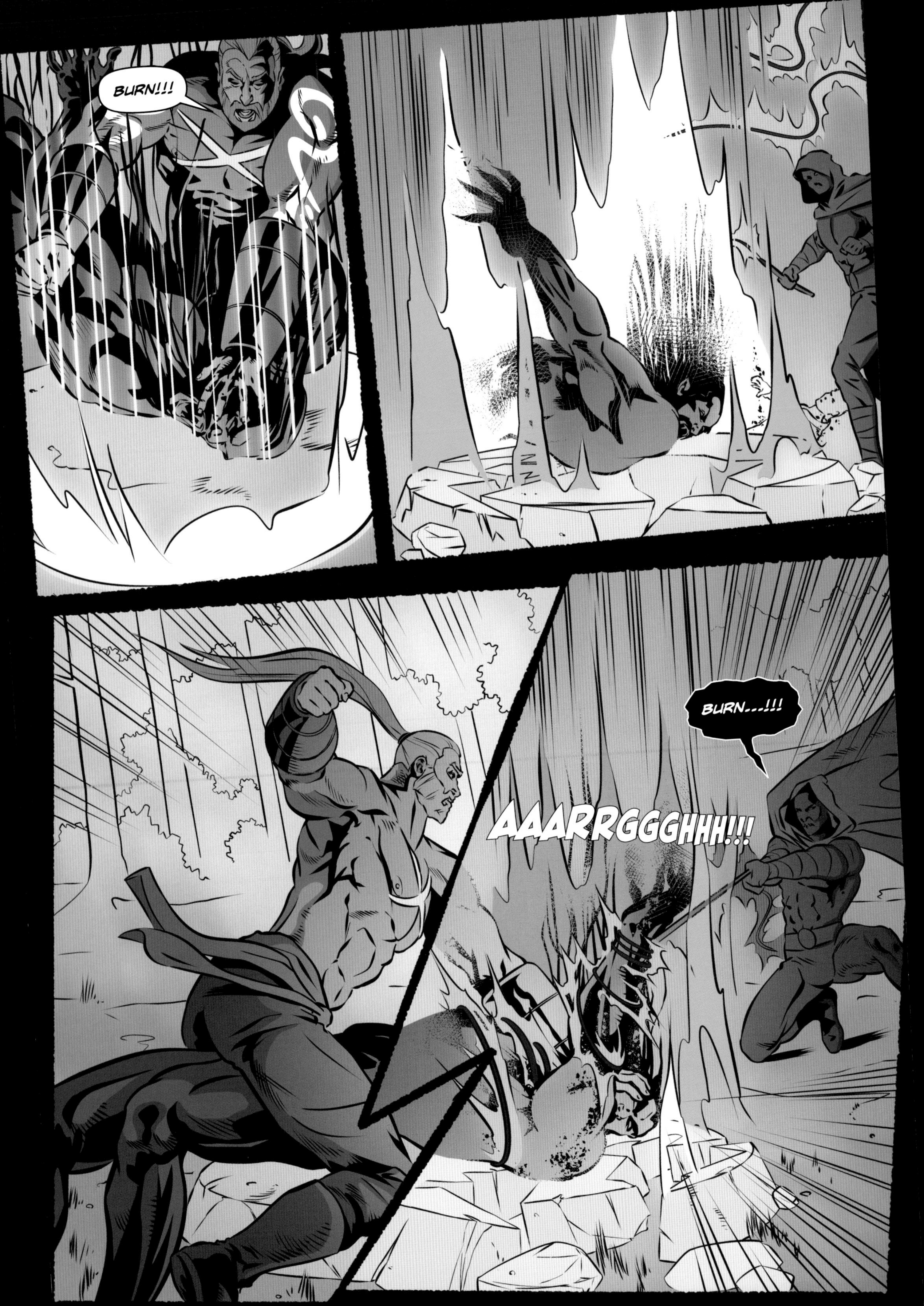
BURN!!!
BURN...!!!
AAARRGGGHHH!!!

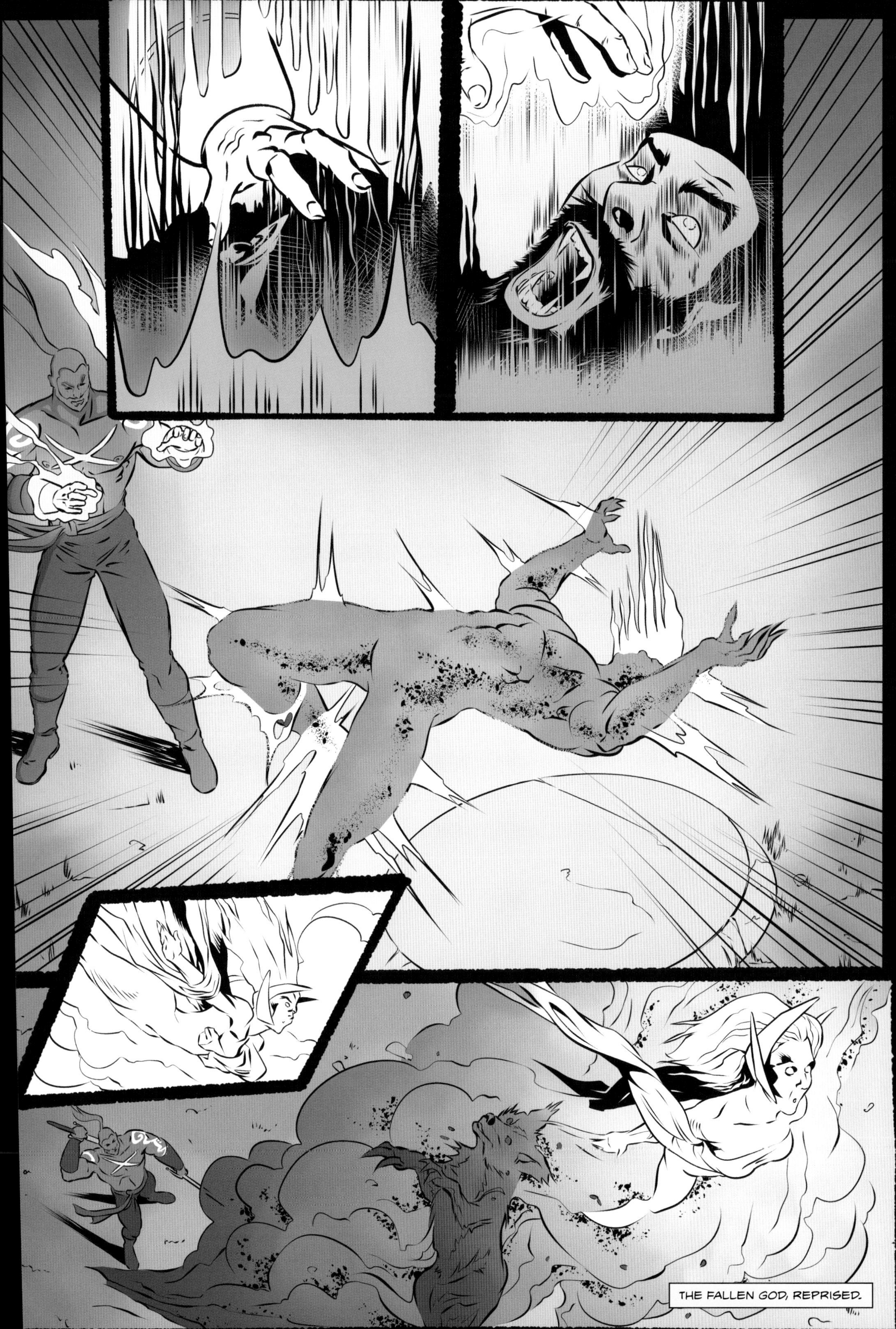
THE FALLEN GOD, REPRISED.

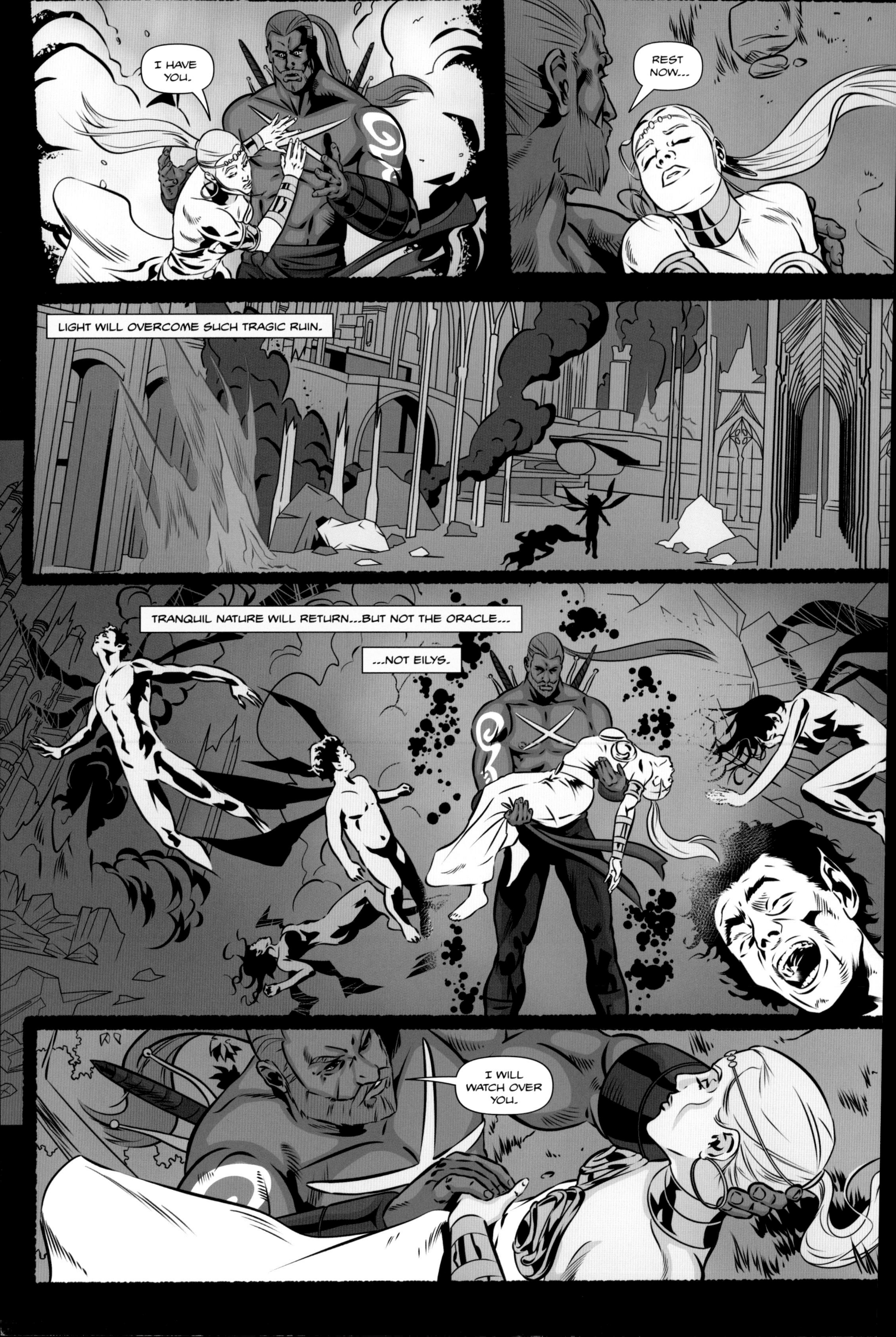
I HAVE YOU.
REST NOW...
LIGHT WILL OVERCOME SUCH TRAGIC RUIN.
TRANQUIL NATURE WILL RETURN...BUT NOT THE ORACLE...
...NOT EILYS.
I WILL WATCH OVER YOU.

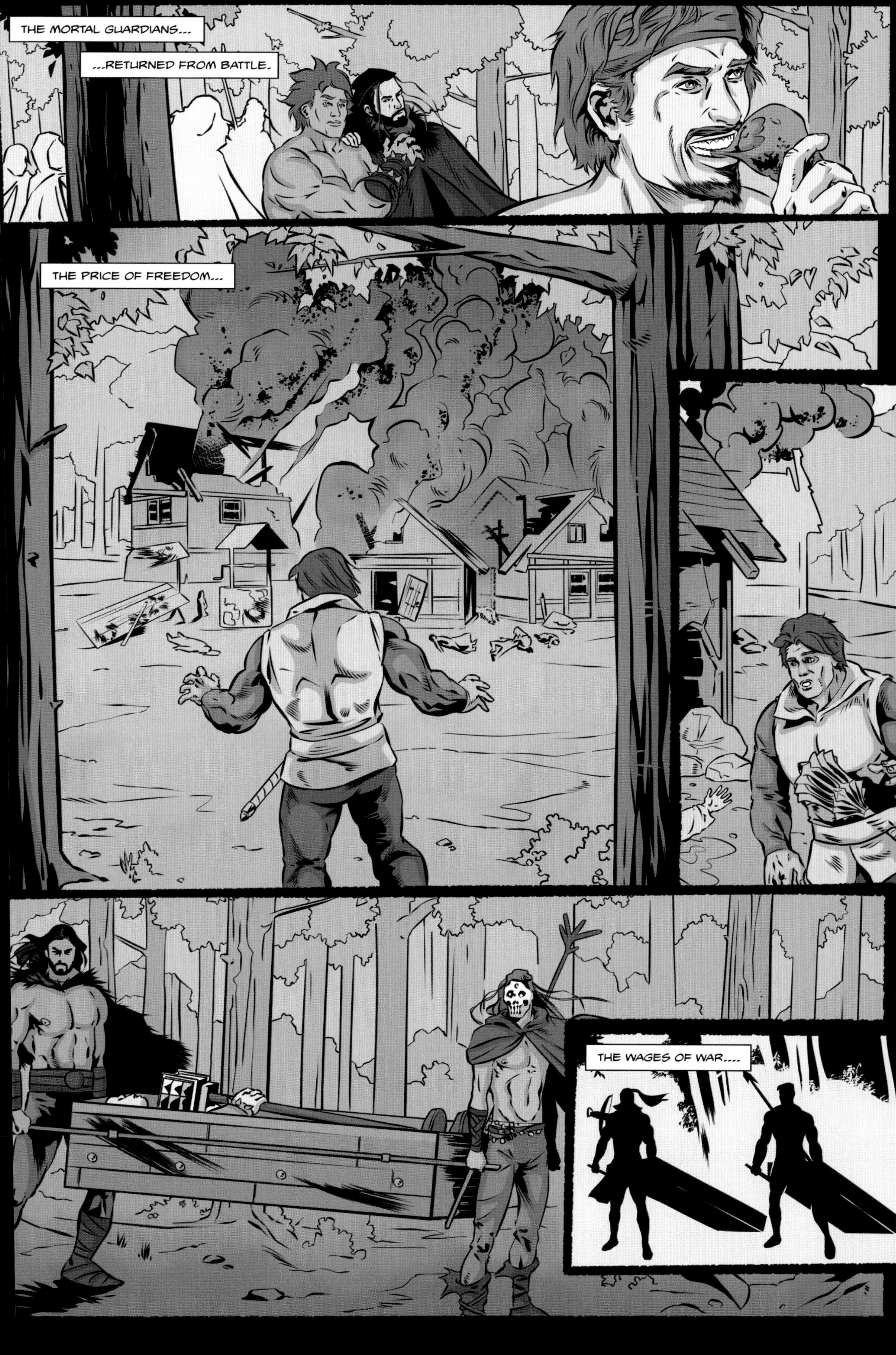
THE MORTAL GUARDIANS...
...RETURNED FROM BATTLE.
THE PRICE OF FREEDOM...
THE WAGES OF WAR....

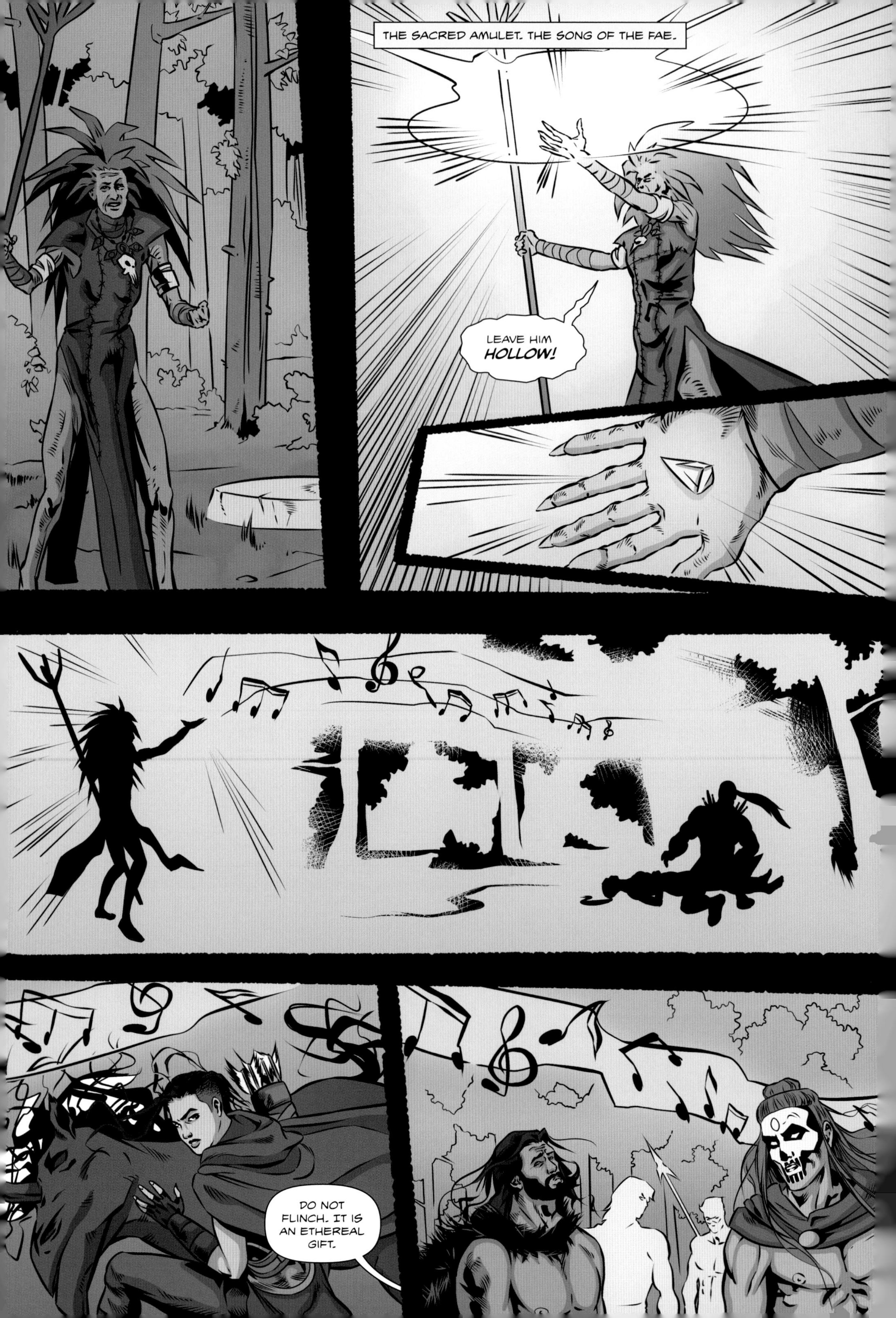
THE SACRED AMULET. THE SONG OF THE FAE.
LEAVE HIM HOLLOW!
DO NOT FLINCH. IT IS AN ETHEREAL GIFT.

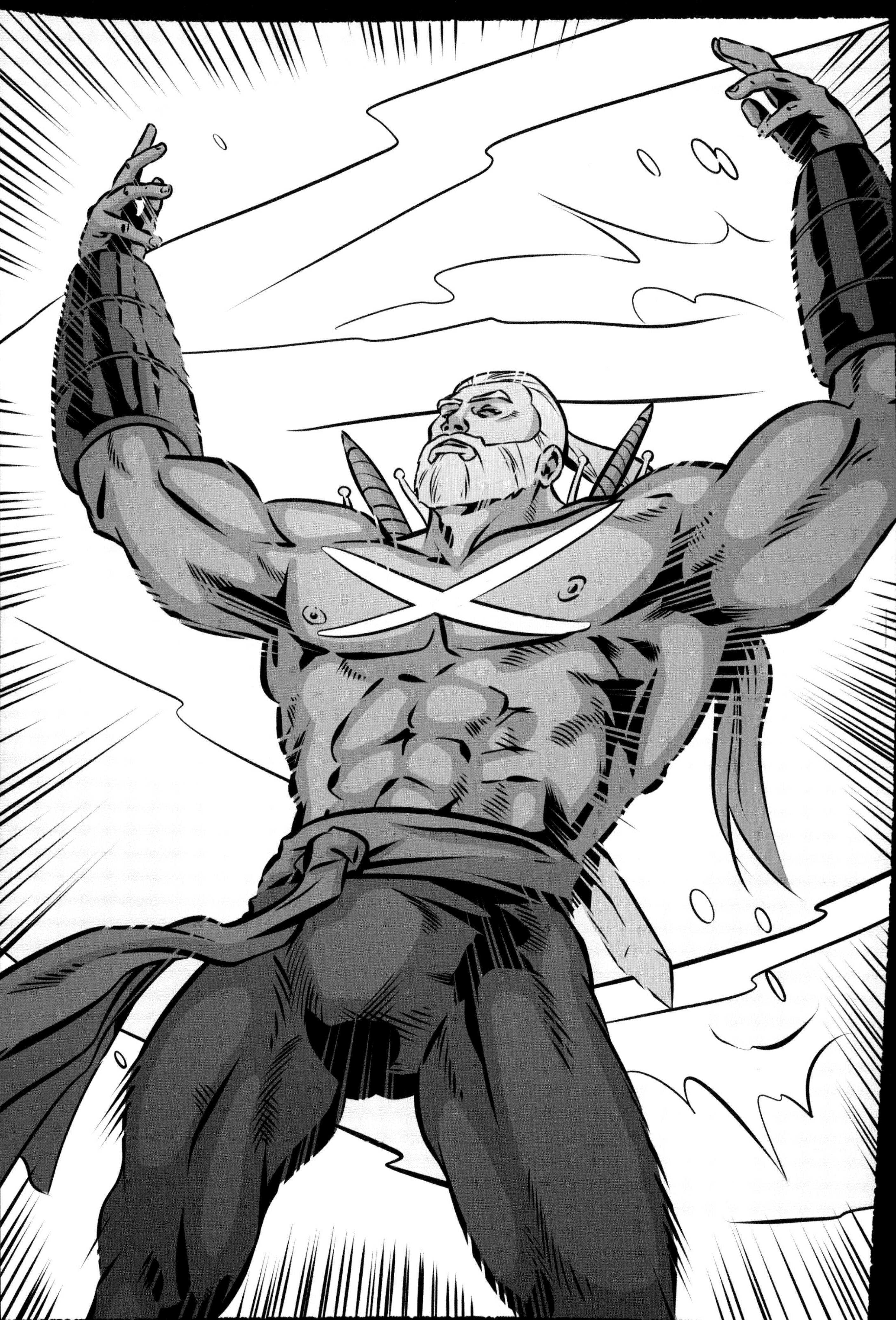

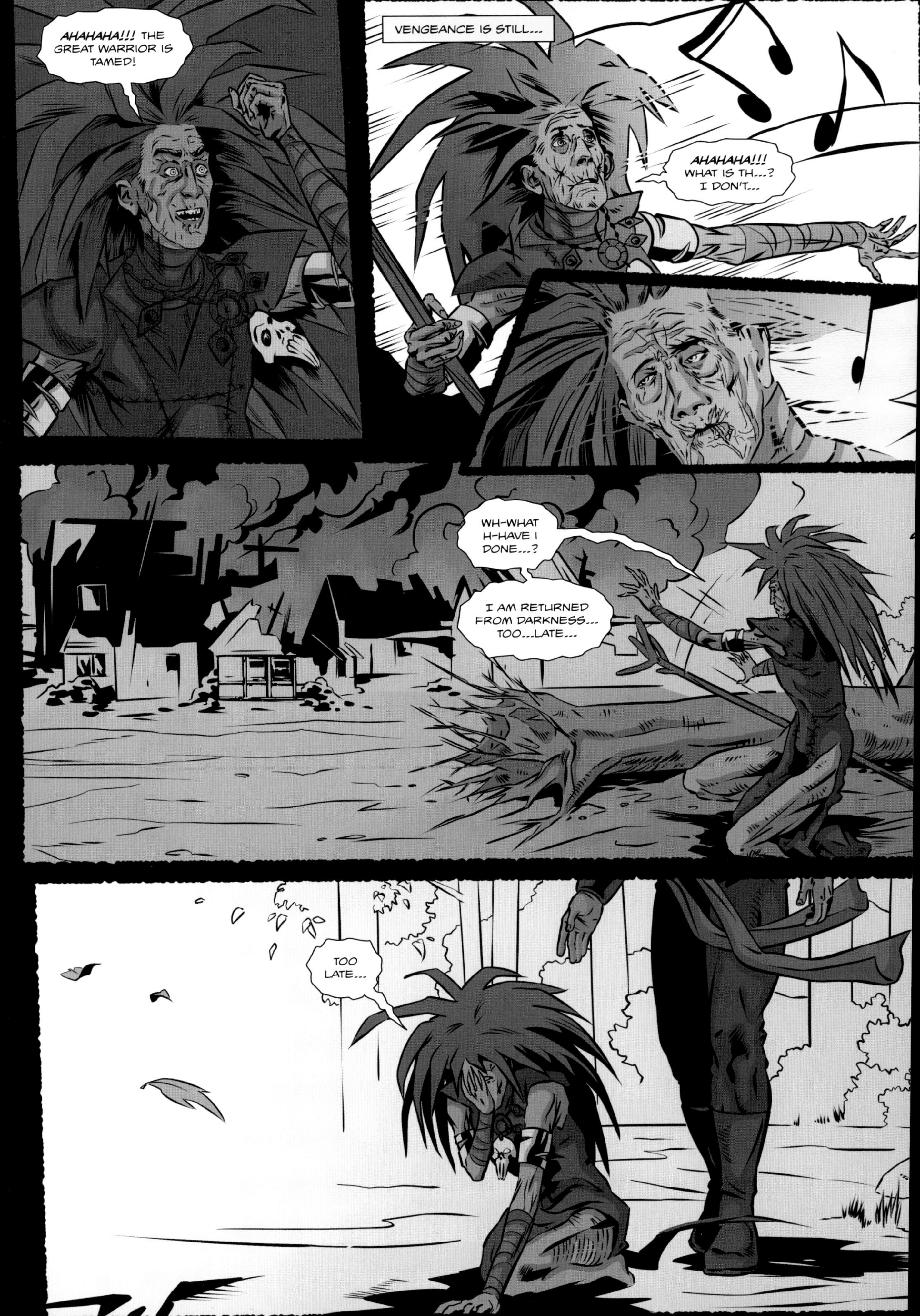
AHAHAHA!!! THE GREAT WARRIOR IS TAMED!
VENGEANCE IS STILL...
AHAHAHA!!! WHAT IS TH...? I DON'T...
WH-WHAT H-HAVE I DONE...?
I AM RETURNED FROM DARKNESS... TOO...LATE...
TOO LATE...

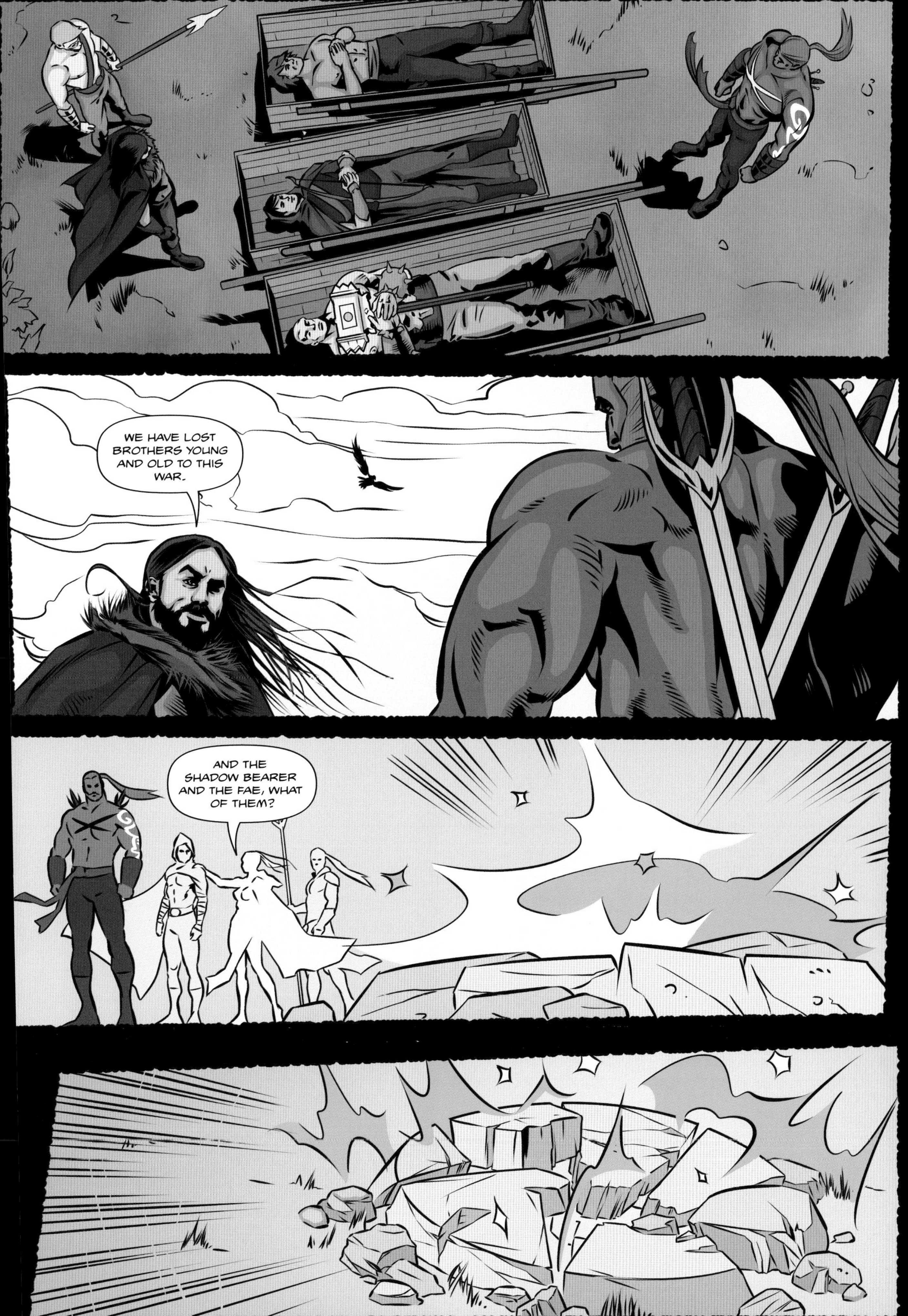
WE HAVE LOST BROTHERS YOUNG AND OLD TO THIS WAR.
AND THE SHADOW BEARER AND THE FAE, WHAT OF THEM?

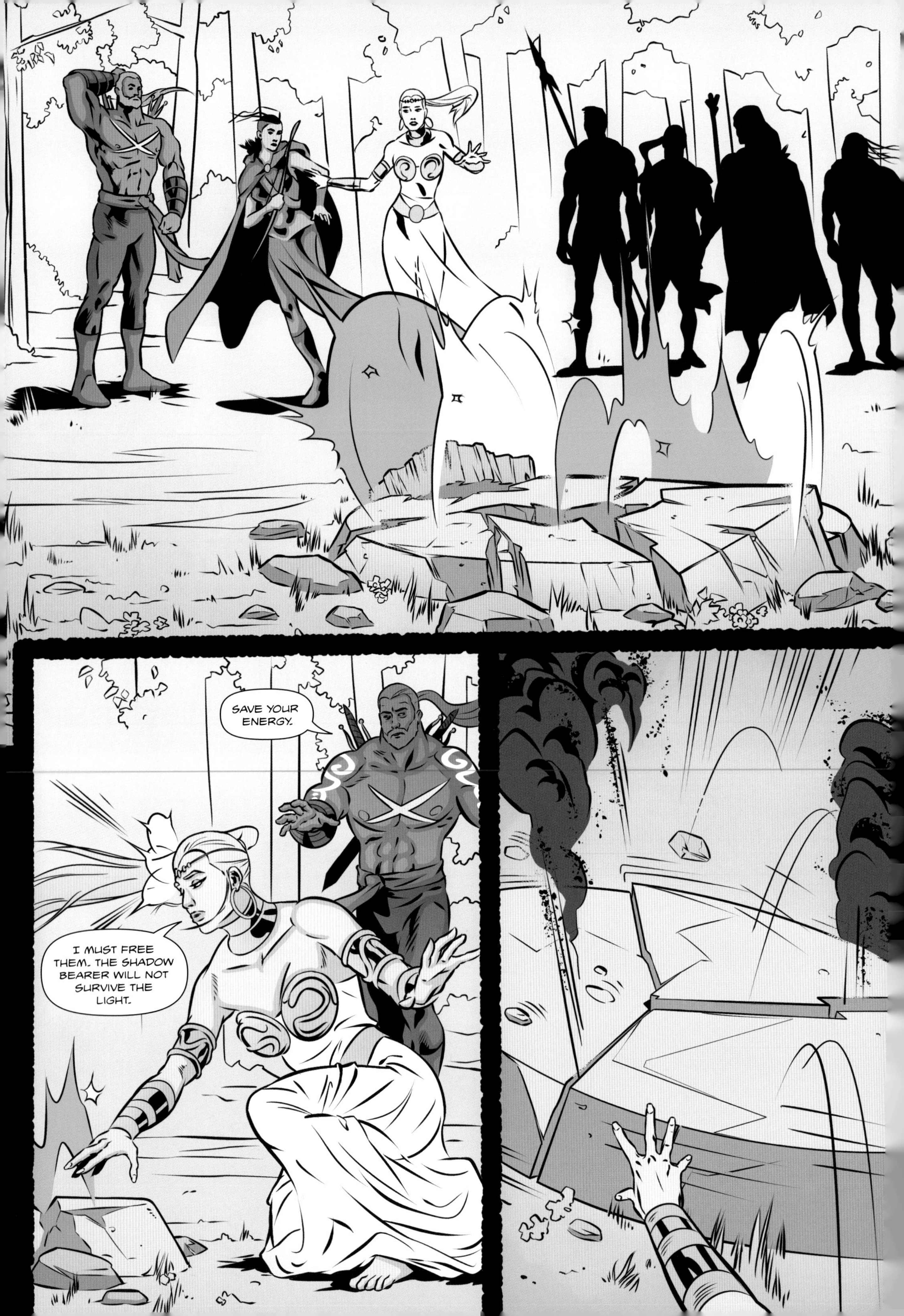
SAVE YOUR ENERGY.
I MUST FREE THEM. THE SHADOW BEARER WILL NOT SURVIVE THE LIGHT.

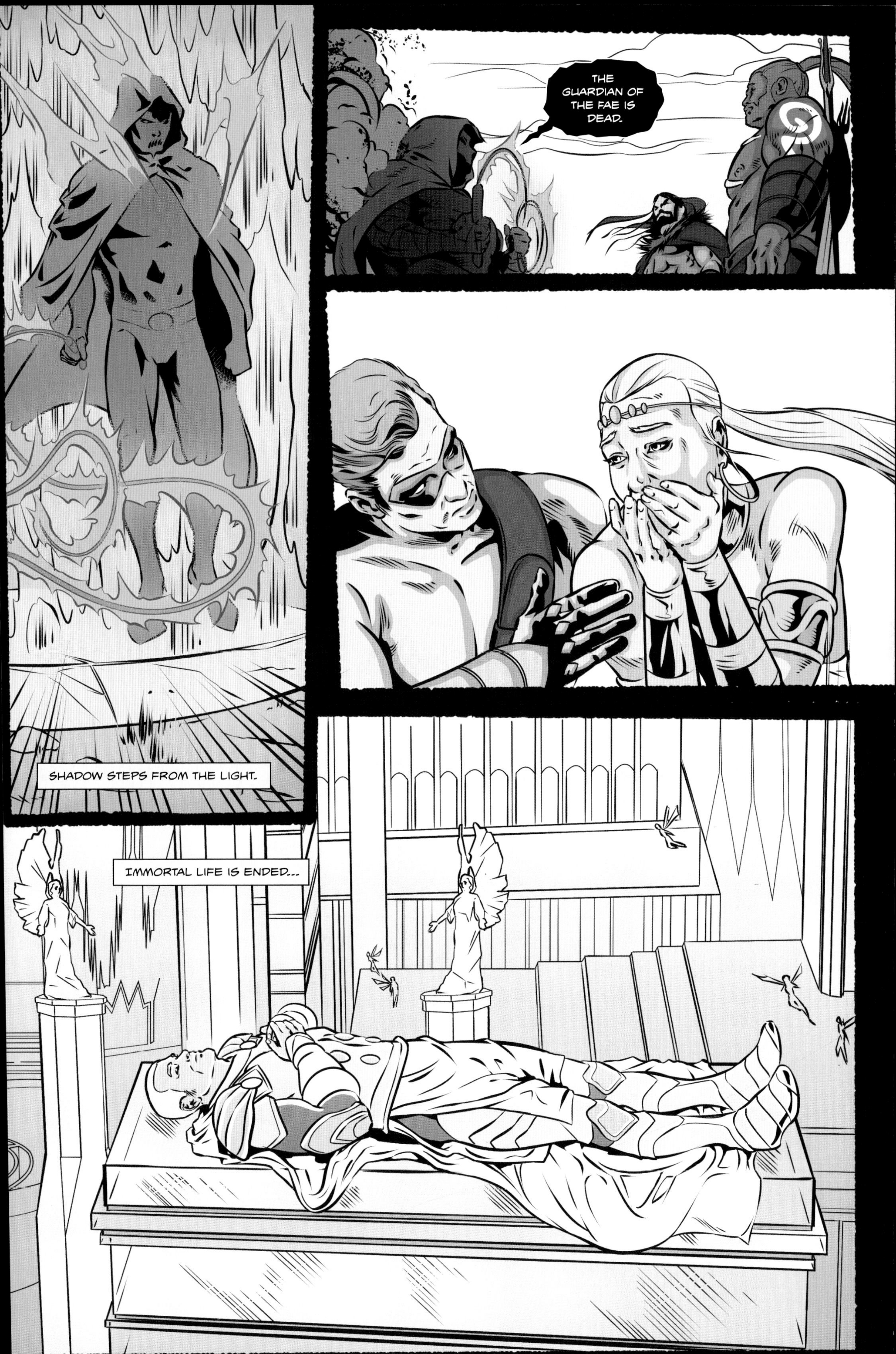
SHADOW STEPS FROM THE LIGHT.
THE GUARDIAN OF THE FAE IS DEAD.
IMMORTAL LIFE IS ENDED...

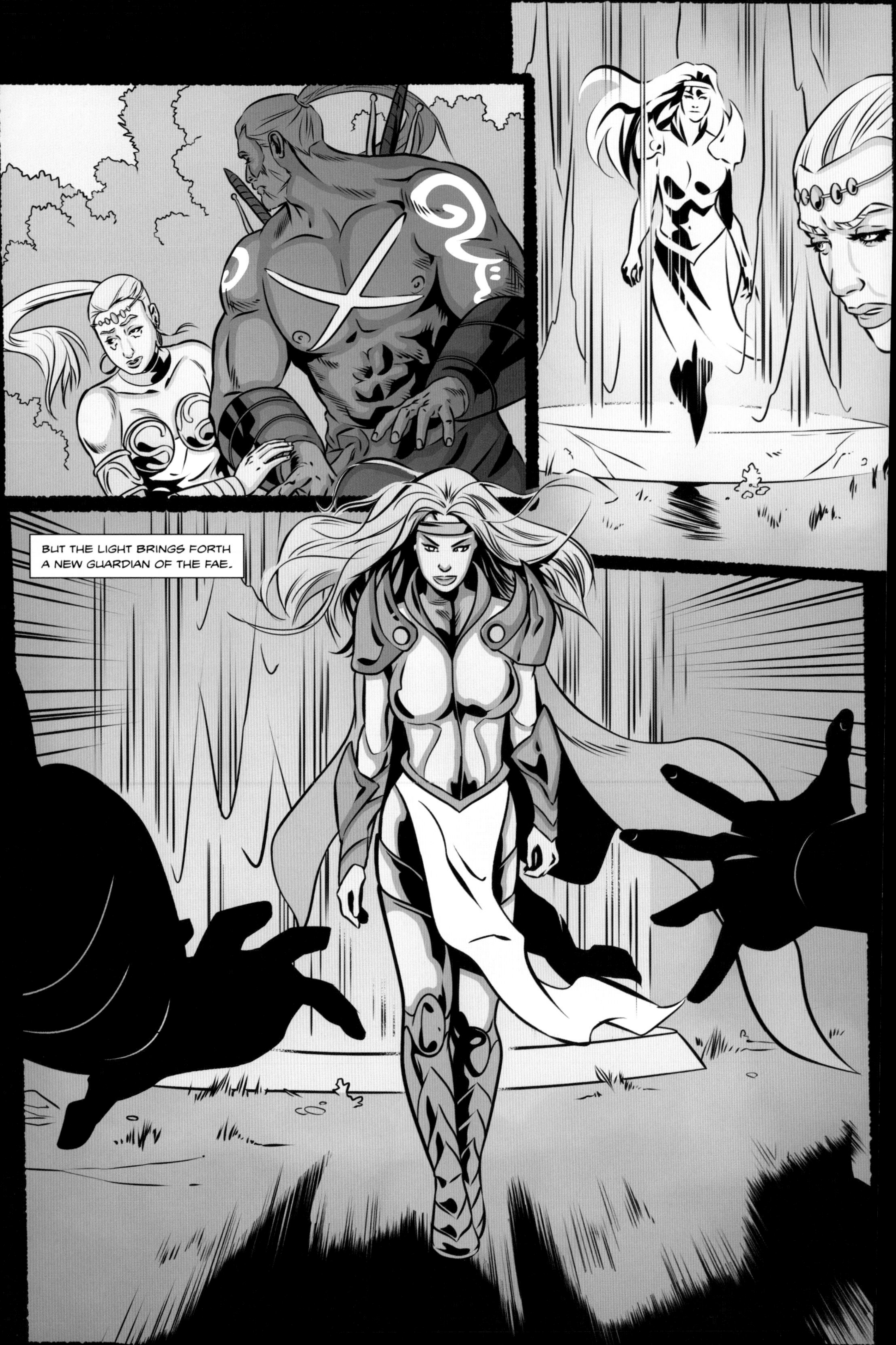
BUT THE LIGHT BRINGS FORTH A NEW GUARDIAN OF THE FAE.

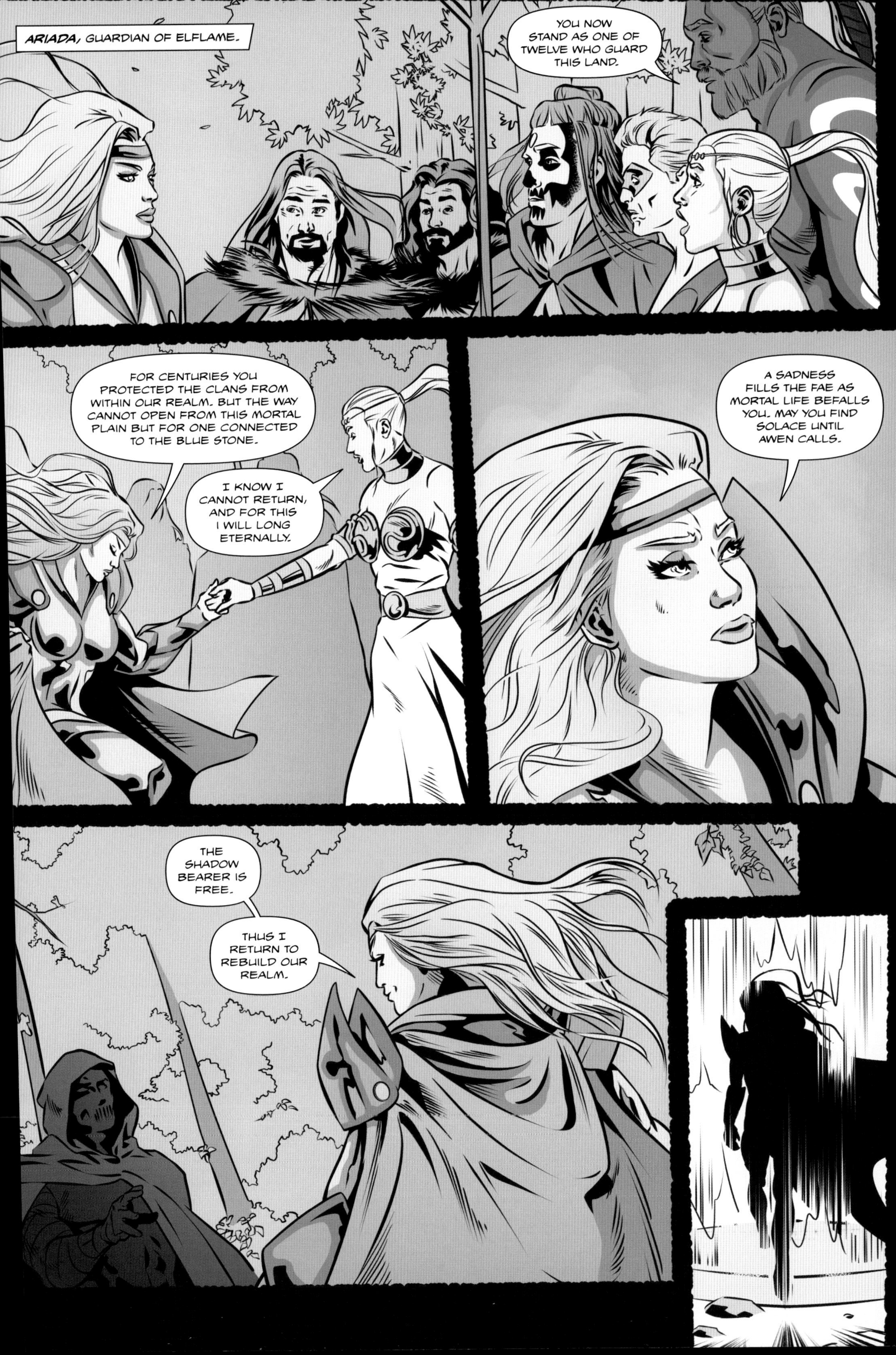
ARIADA, GUARDIAN OF ELFLAME.
YOU NOW STAND AS ONE OF TWELVE WHO GUARD THIS LAND.
FOR CENTURIES YOU PROTECTED THE CLANS FROM WITHIN OUR REALM. BUT THE WAY CANNOT OPEN FROM THIS MORTAL PLAIN BUT FOR ONE CONNECTED TO THE BLUE STONE.
I KNOW I CANNOT RETURN, AND FOR THIS I WILL LONG ETERNALLY.
A SADNESS FILLS THE FAE AS MORTAL LIFE BEFALLS YOU. MAY YOU FIND SOLACE UNTIL AWEN CALLS.
THE SHADOW BEARER IS FREE.
THUS I RETURN TO REBUILD OUR REALM.

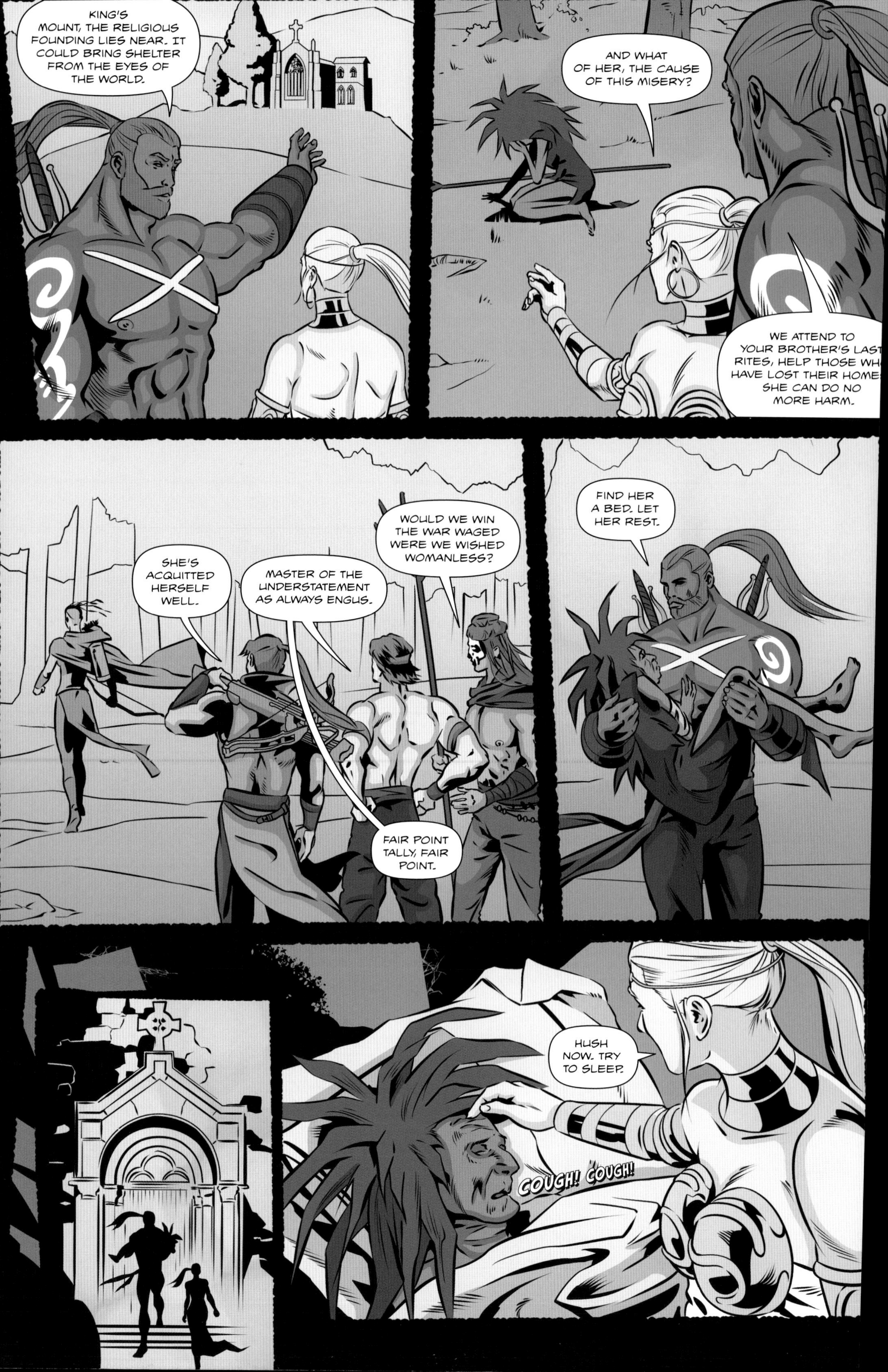
KING'S MOUNT, THE RELIGIOUS FOUNDING LIES NEAR. IT COULD BRING SHELTER FROM THE EYES OF THE WORLD.
AND WHAT OF HER, THE CAUSE OF THIS MISERY?
WE ATTEND TO YOUR BROTHER'S LAST RITES, HELP THOSE WH HAVE LOST THEIR HOMES SHE CAN DO NO MORE HARM.
SHE'S ACQUITTED HERSELF WELL.
MASTER OF THE UNDERSTATEMENT AS ALWAYS ENGUS.
WOULD WE WIN THE WAR WAGED WERE WE WISHED WOMANLESS?
FAIR POINT TALLY, FAIR POINT.
FIND HER A BED. LET HER REST.
HUSH NOW. TRY TO SLEEP.
COUGH! COUGH!

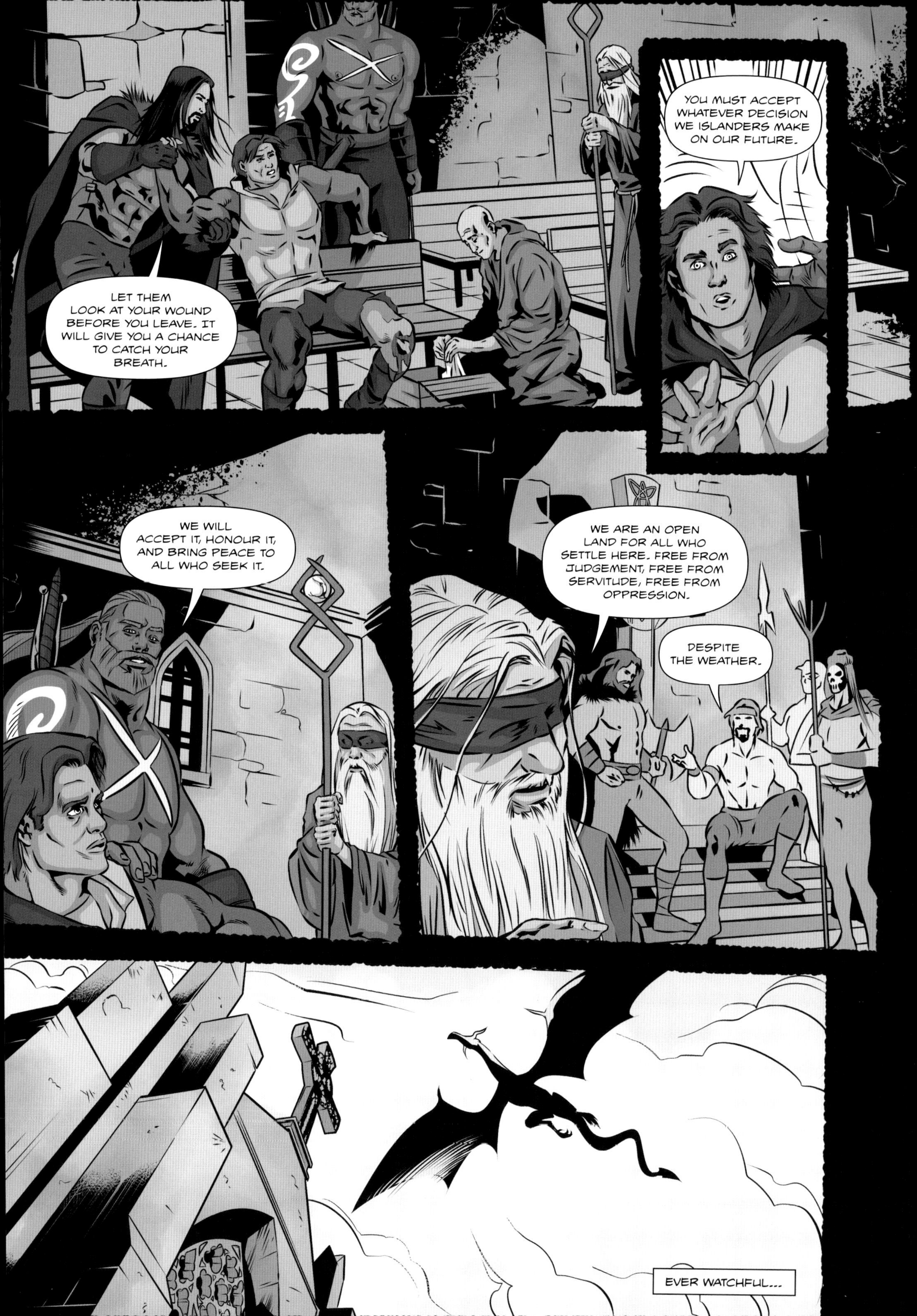
LET THEM LOOK AT YOUR WOUND BEFORE YOU LEAVE. IT WILL GIVE YOU A CHANCE TO CATCH YOUR BREATH.
YOU MUST ACCEPT WHATEVER DECISION WE ISLANDERS MAKE ON OUR FUTURE.
WE WILL ACCEPT IT, HONOUR IT, AND BRING PEACE TO ALL WHO SEEK IT.
WE ARE AN OPEN LAND FOR ALL WHO SETTLE HERE. FREE FROM JUDGEMENT, FREE FROM SERVITUDE, FREE FROM OPPRESSION.
DESPITE THE WEATHER.
EVER WATCHFUL...

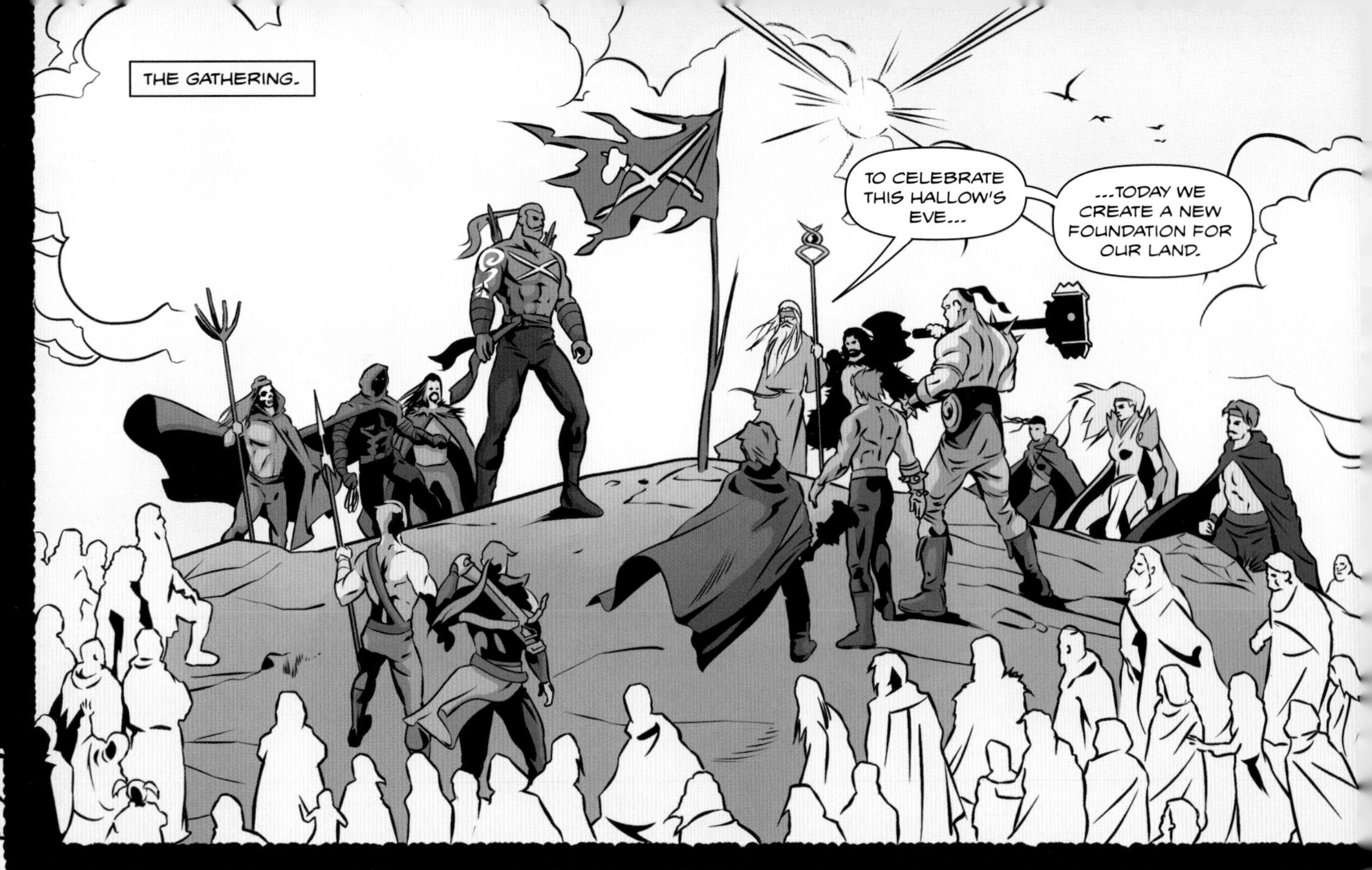
THE GATHERING.
TO CELEBRATE THIS HALLOW'S EVE...
...TODAY WE CREATE A NEW FOUNDATION FOR OUR LAND.

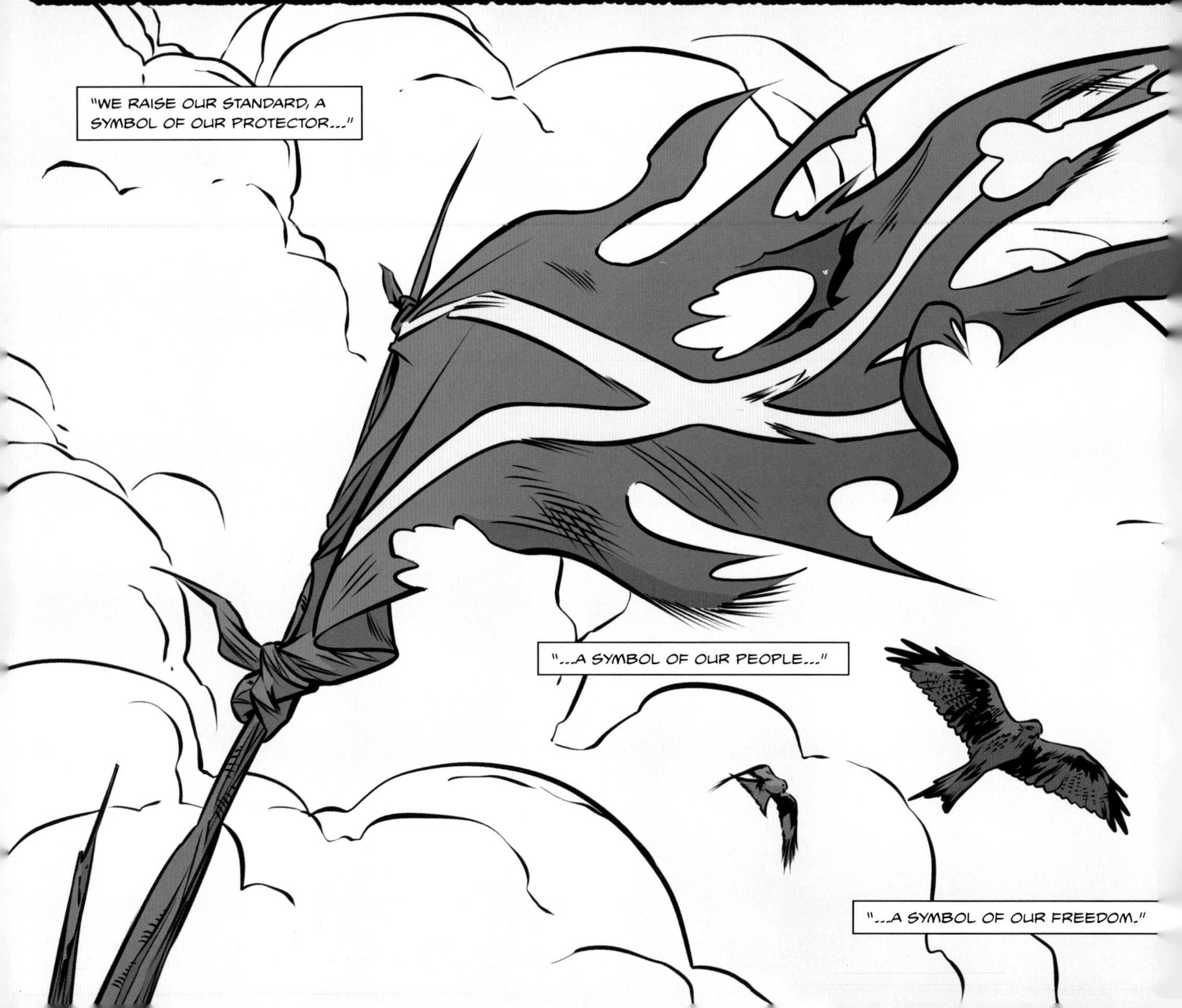
"WE RAISE OUR STANDARD, A SYMBOL OF OUR PROTECTOR..."
"...A SYMBOL OF OUR PEOPLE..."
"...A SYMBOL OF OUR FREEDOM."

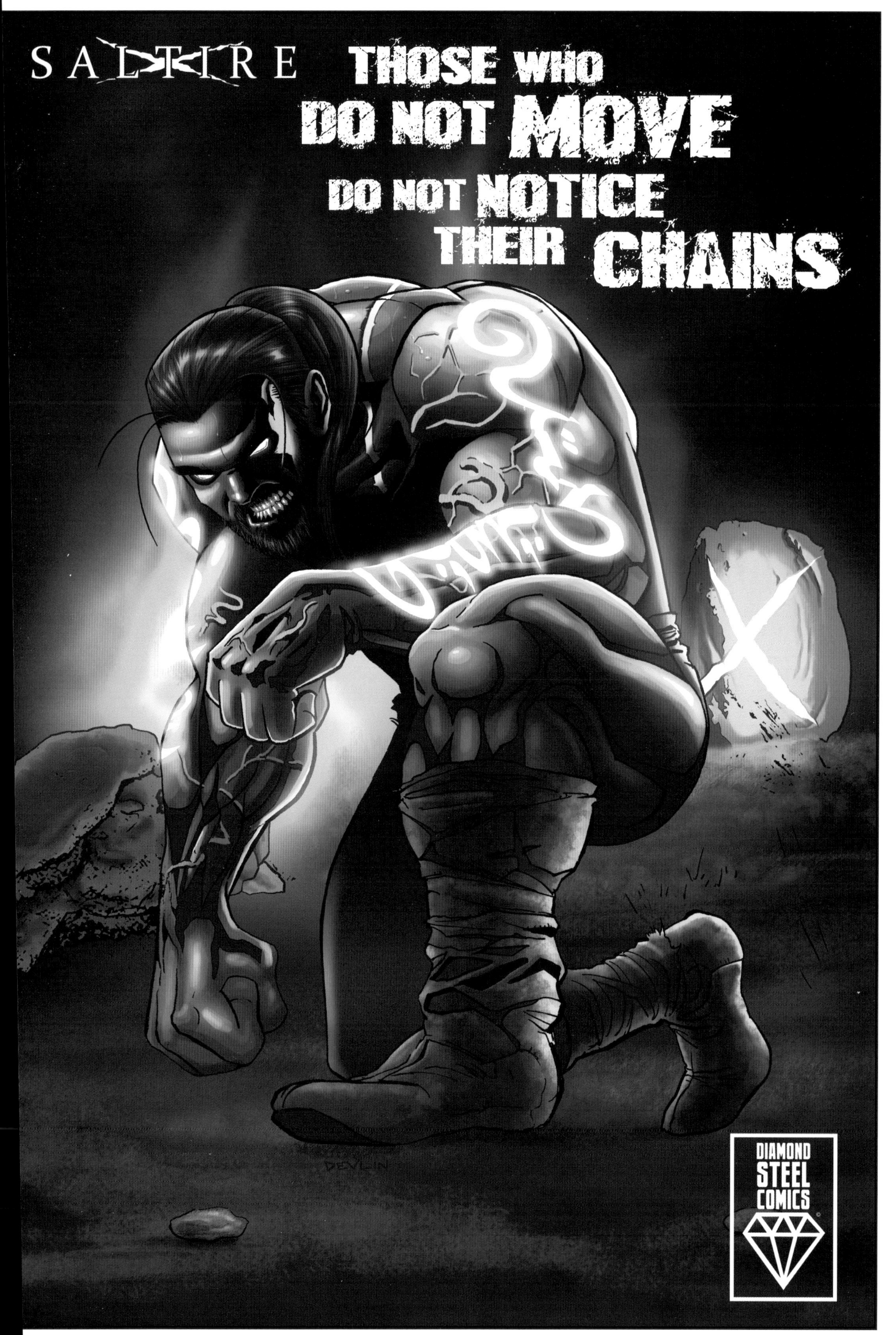

SALTIRE
THOSE WHO DO NOT MOVE DO NOT NOTICE THEIR CHAINS
DEVLIN
DIAMOND STEEL COMICS

work: Jimmy Devlin

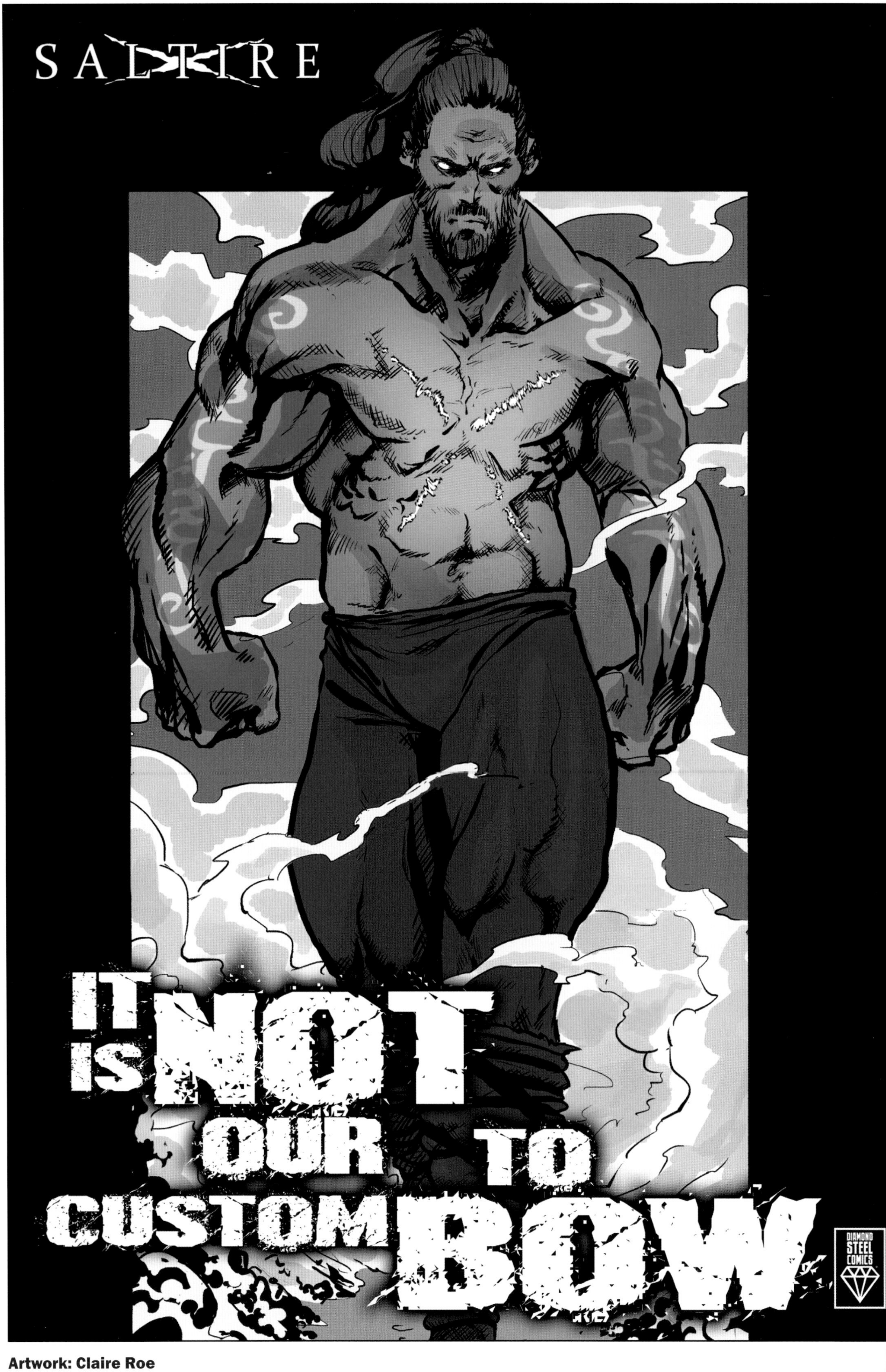
SALTIRE
IT IS NOT OUR CUSTOM TO BOW
DIAMOND STEEL COMICS

Artwork: Claire Roe

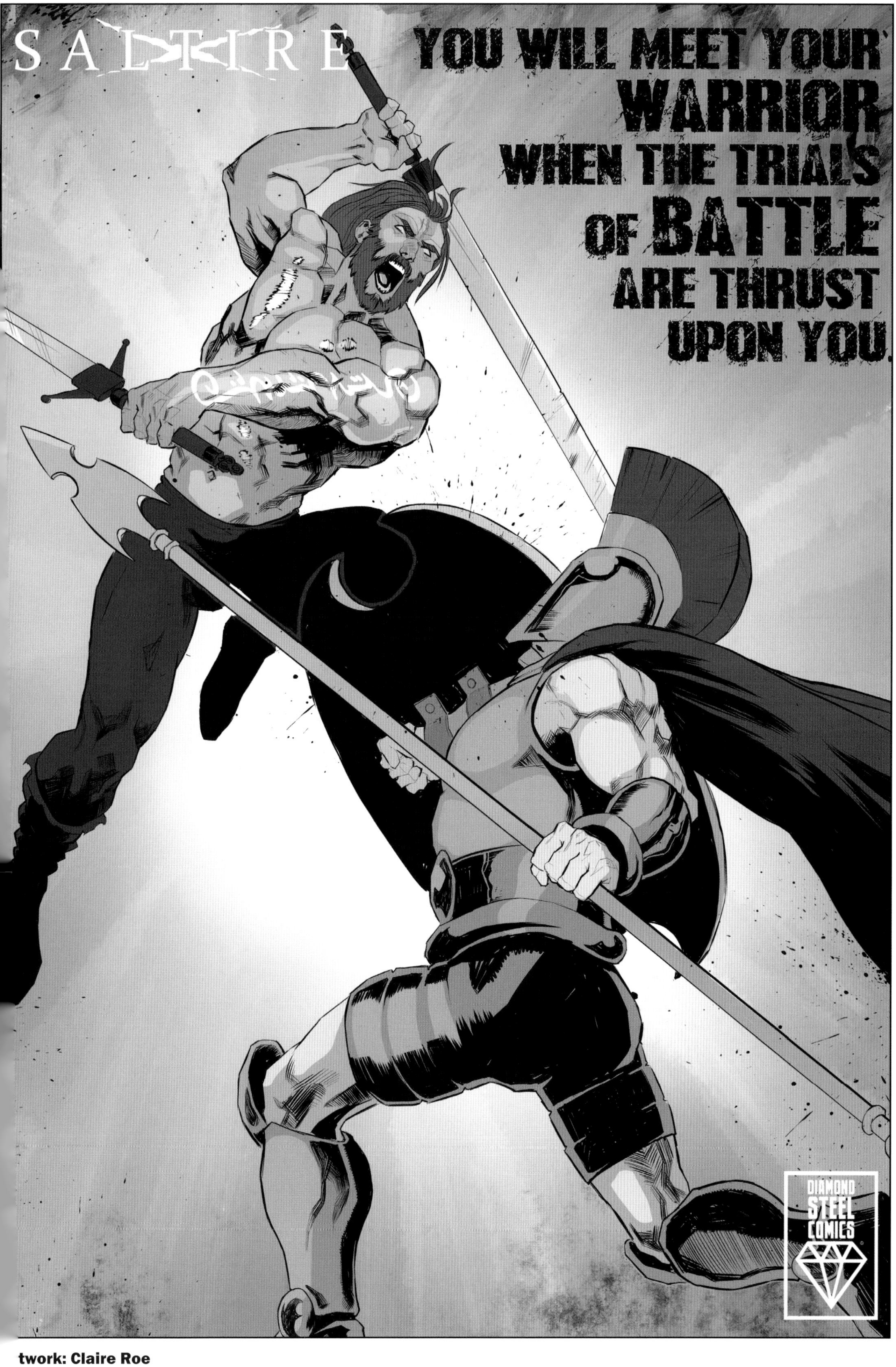
SALTIRE
YOU WILL MEET YOUR WARRIOR WHEN THE TRIALS OF BATTLE ARE THRUST UPON YOU.
DIAMOND STEEL COMICS

twork: Claire Roe

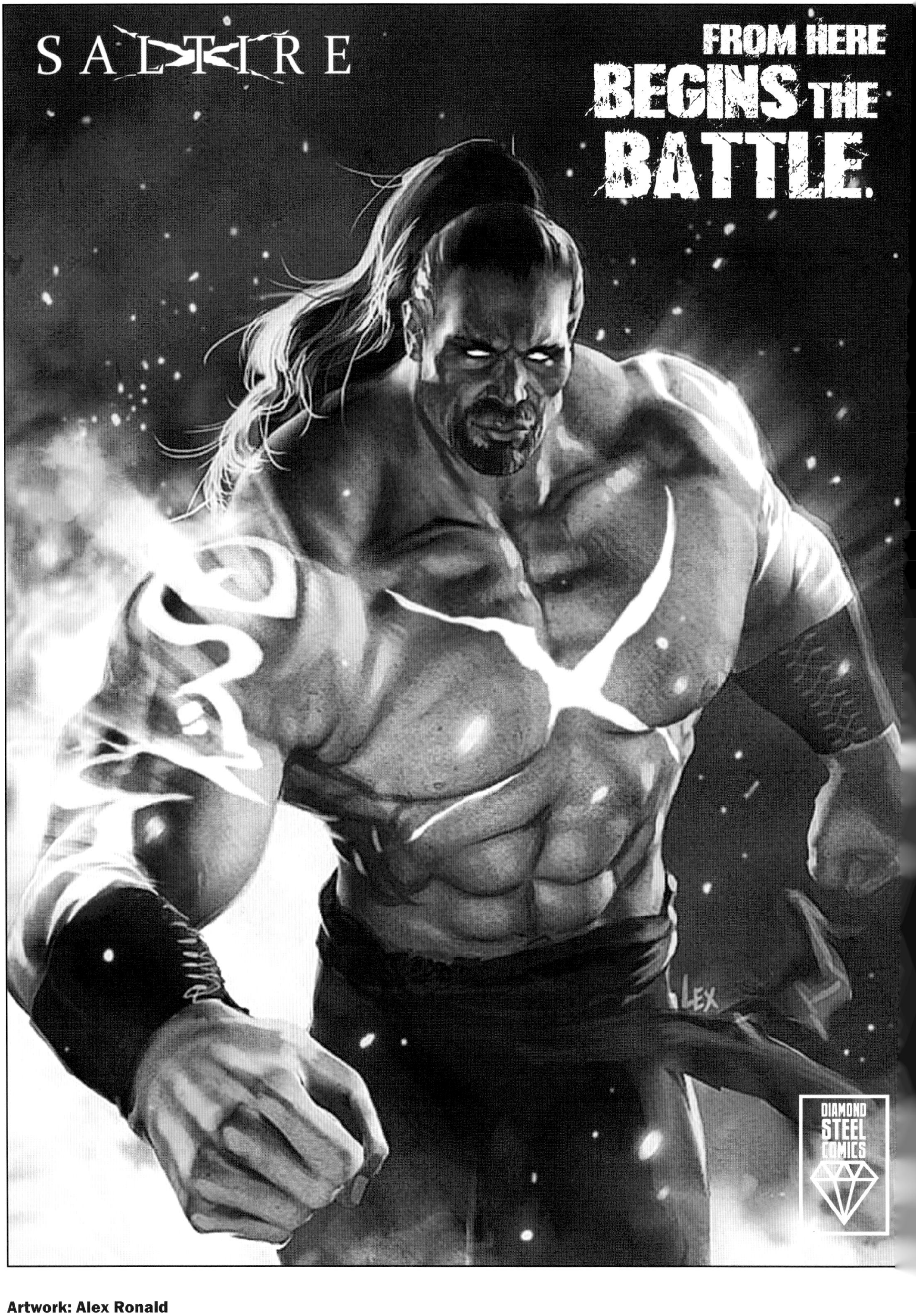
SALTIRE
FROM HERE
BEGINS THE
BATTLE.
LEX
DIAMOND
STEEL
COMICS

Artwork: Alex Ronald

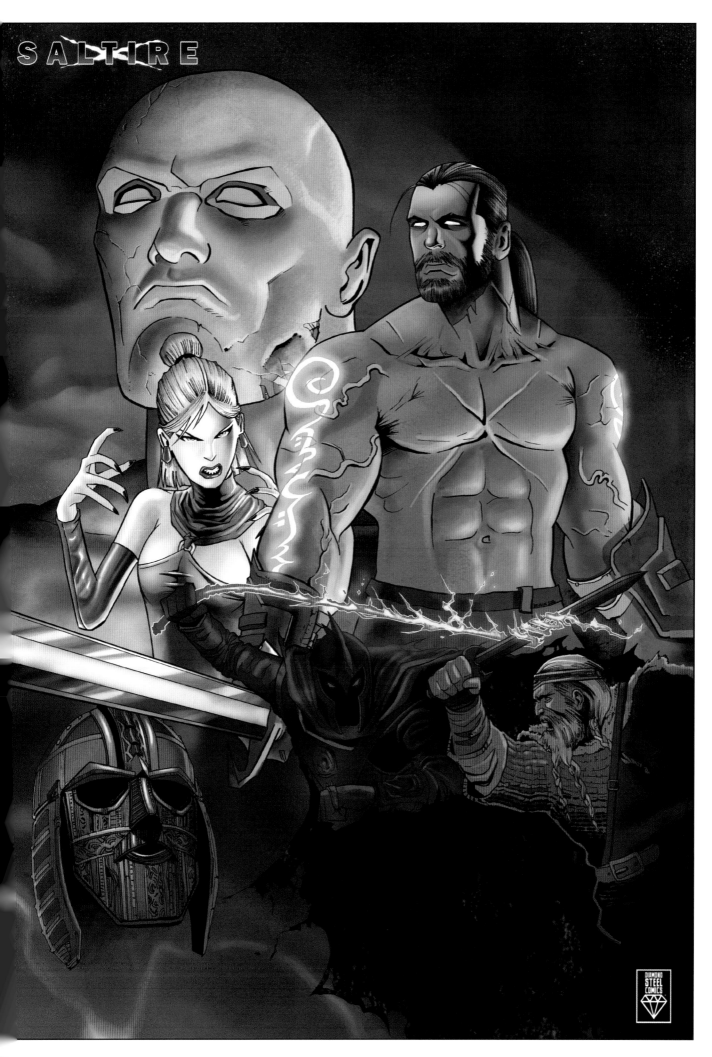

SALTIRE

work: Jimmy Devlin

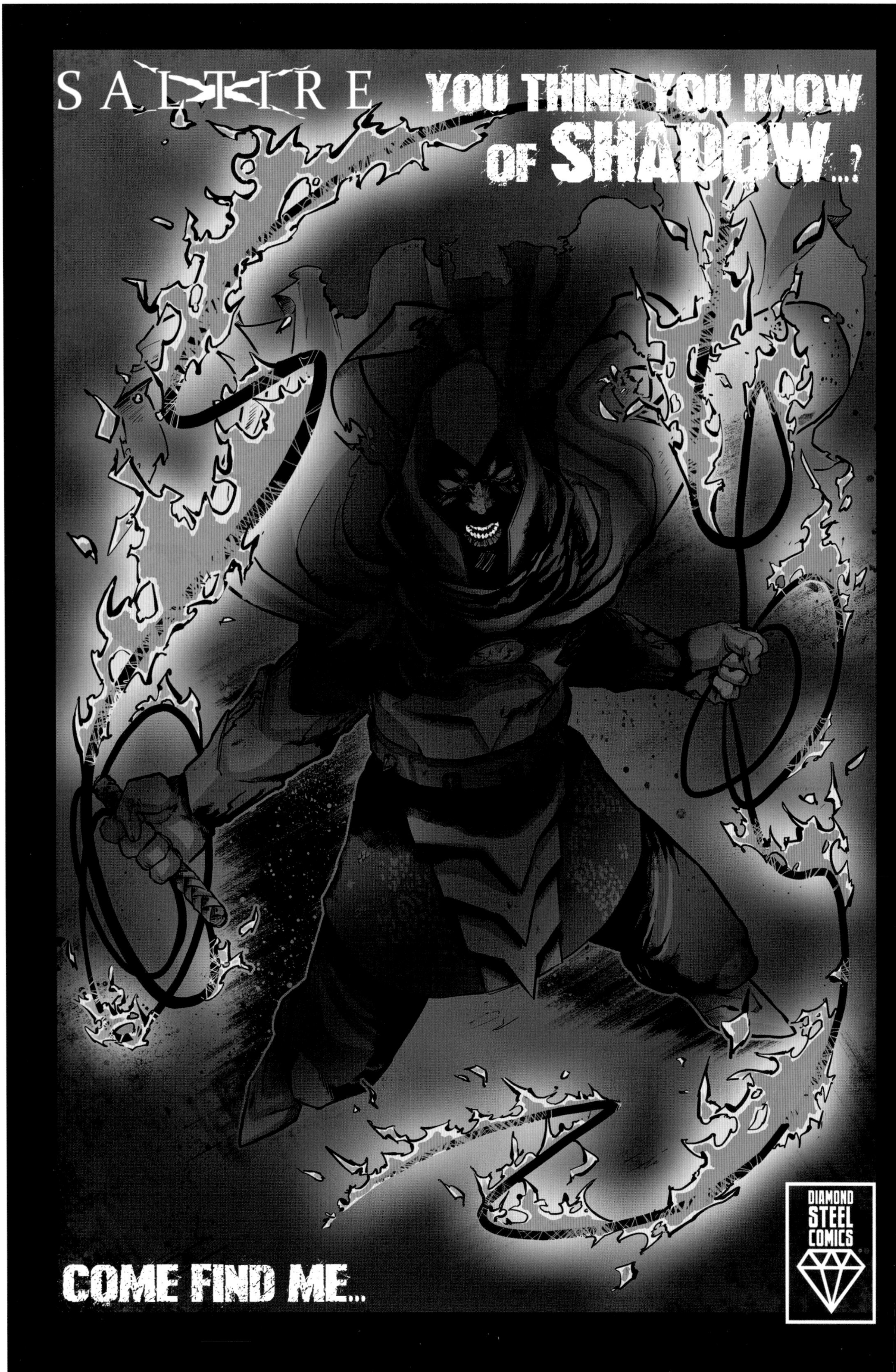

SALTIRE
YOU THINK YOU KNOW OF SHADOW...?
COME FIND ME...
DIAMOND STEEL COMICS

Artwork: Claire Roe

SALTIRE

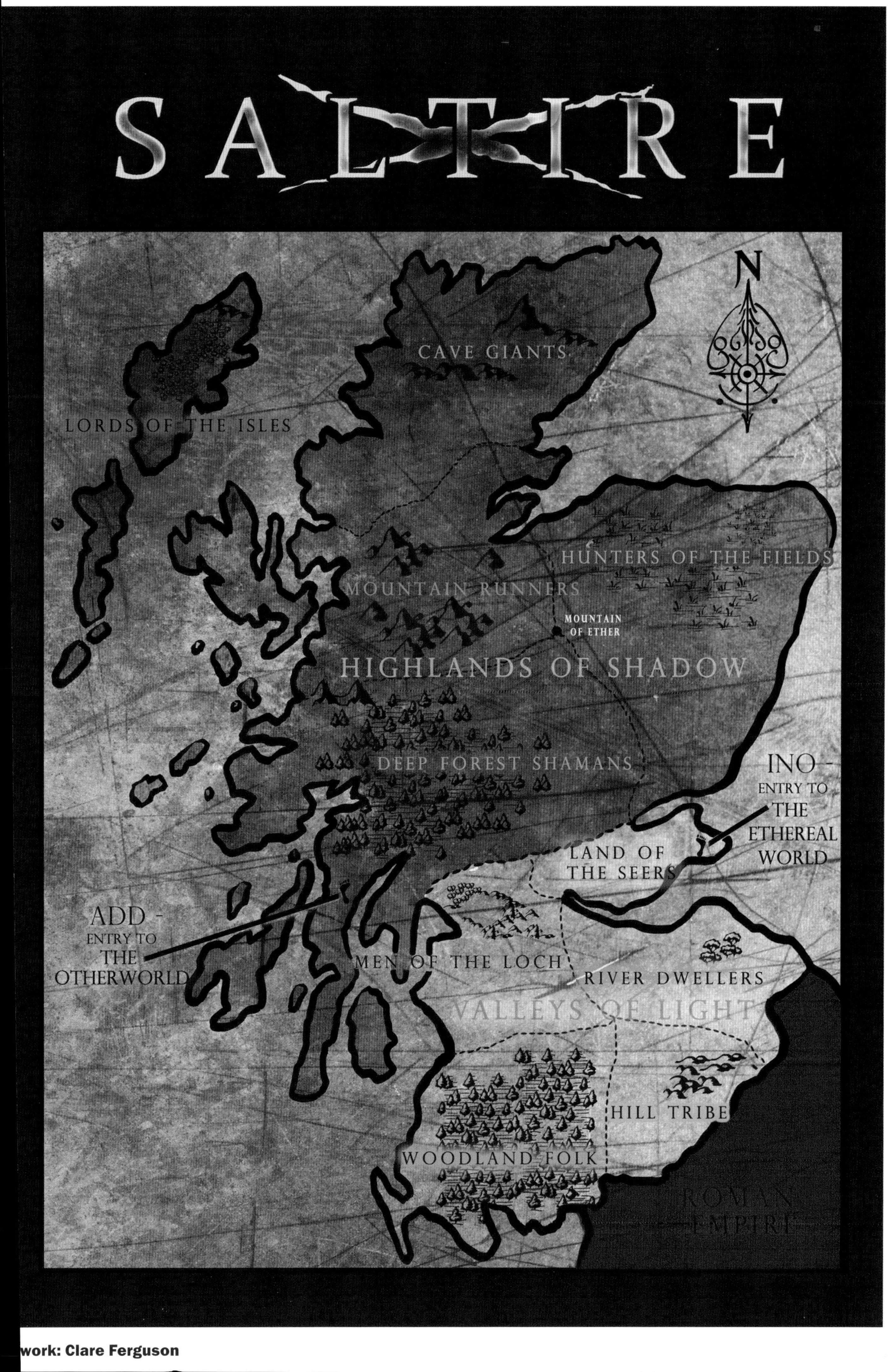
N
CAVE GIANTS
LORDS OF THE ISLES
HUNTERS OF THE FIELDS
MOUNTAIN RUNNERS
MOUNTAIN
OF ETHER
HIGHLANDS OF SHADOW
DEEP FOREST SHAMANS
INO -
ENTRY TO
THE
ETHEREAL
WORLD
LAND OF
THE SEERS
ADD -
ENTRY TO
THE
OTHERWORLD
MEN OF THE LOCH
RIVER DWELLERS
VALLEYS OF LIGHT
HILL TRIBE
WOODLAND FOLK
ROMAN
EMPIRE

work: Clare Ferguson

GUARDIANS OF THE
VALLEYS OF LIGHT

Riada - Fae of the Ethereal World
An immortal with elven features, he wears platinum armour and carries the Ethereal Staff that slows time for short periods and suspend objects in its beam. He has the ability to walk between worlds and will use diplomacy and reason before any resort to violence.

Cennet - Hill Tribe

Fast and deadly, he is the patient and vigilant protector of the southern border. Carrier of the Eagle Spear he is a hero to his clan. Gallan is a close ally. Ever watchful, he is often the first line of defence.

Trest - Men of the Loch
A formidable swimmer whose stamina is unparalleled. Master of the short blade he carries a belt of knives. Always found in or on the water with his industrious and cheerful nature. Banished the malevolence that became the Dark Man of The Moors from his position within the clan.

Gallan - Woodland Folk

A warrior of huge strength, wielding the two-handed Bear Claw axe. Legend tells of his ancestor uprooting and replanting the Tree Of Life that founded the clan. A close ally of Cennet.

Engus - River Dwellers
A thoughtful and spiritual warrior with incredible accuracy, he carries the driftwood crossbow. A storyteller and champion of the maidens, he pity's the water demon, Fidlash, who many believe should have been destroyed long ago.

Aden - Land of the Seers

A noble warrior of few words he has the gift of foresight (bestowed by the neighbouring Ethereal World). Unrivalled with his antler bow he will protect mortals from the secrets at Ino and understands the Fae better than most.

GUARDIANS OF THE HIGHLANDS OF SHADOW

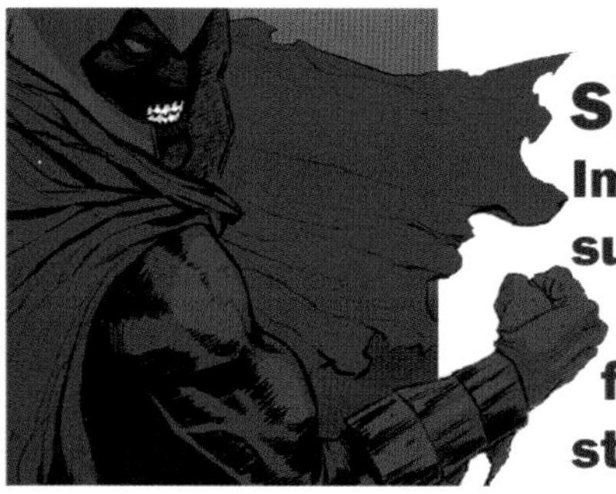

Sloan - Shadow Bearers of the Otherworld

Immortal and wearer of dragon scale armour he is surrounded by shadow magic and carries the Firelash, made from sinews of the dragon's tail. Has little regard for mortals and reveres power above all. Through the blue stone he walks between the worlds.

Talorgan - Deep Forest Shamans

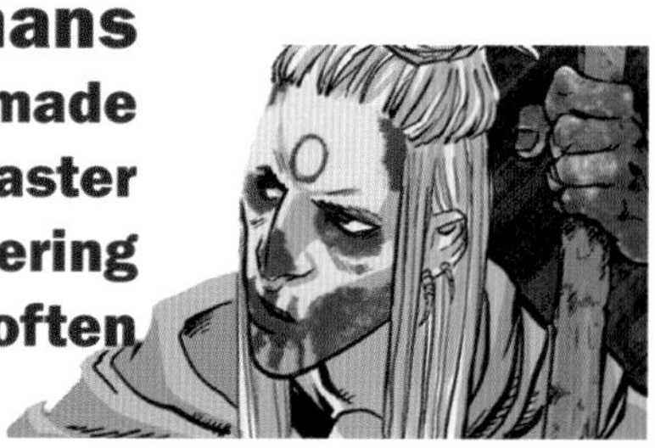

A warrior of great knowledge, he carries the Oak Staff made from the Tree Of Life (the roots hold nature's wisdom). A master strategist, he will observe and advise before ever entering combat. Of longer life than the other clan guardians he often saves the innocent from hypnotic Forest Daemons.

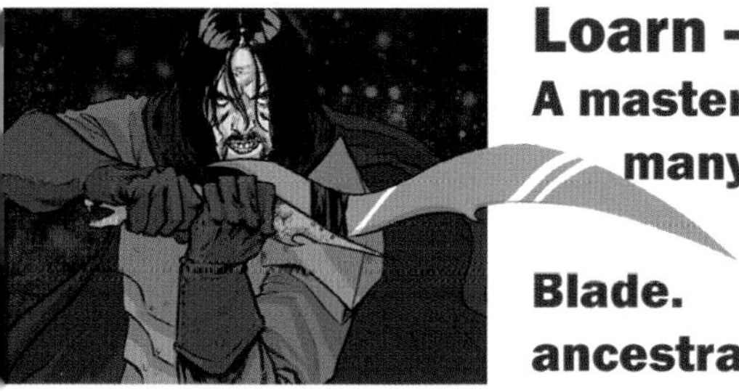

Loarn - Hunters of the Fields

A master swordsman who thrives in battle, he has slain many of the hideous creatures that blight the highlands. Silent and deadly he holds the powerful Serpent Blade. Carries the burden of having lost many of his ancestral clan to Ban Sith.

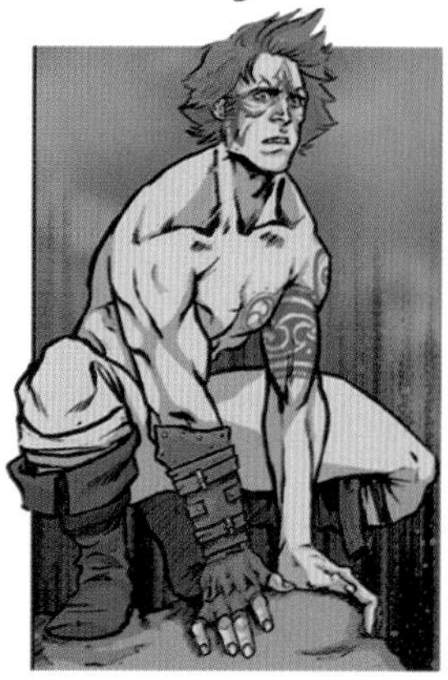

Domall - Mountain Runners

An unusual guardian, slight of build but unparalleled in acrobatic skills. Feline in mannerisms, he is lethal with the iron discus and prefers the solitude of the mountains. Defeated the Forest Daemon, Gunchann, in an epic struggle after the creature attacked the clan's children.

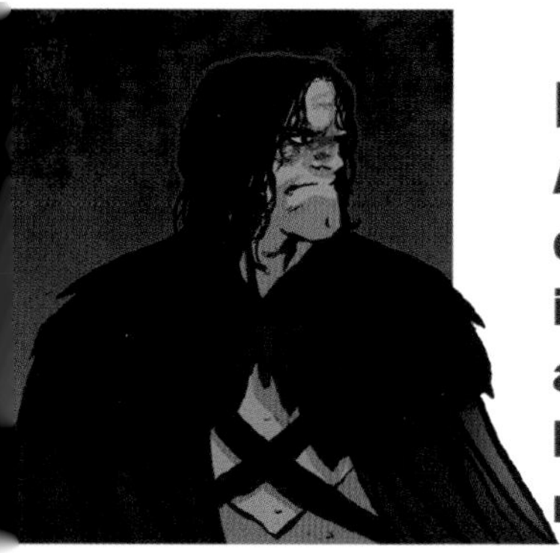

Brode - Lords of the Isles

A brooding warrior he is terse and curt. Carries the devastating lead mace and can create conflict where there is none. Years of drinking the Island whisky leave Brode's addiction affecting his actions. Devastated from losing his wife to the Water Wraiths he feels distant from the mainland.

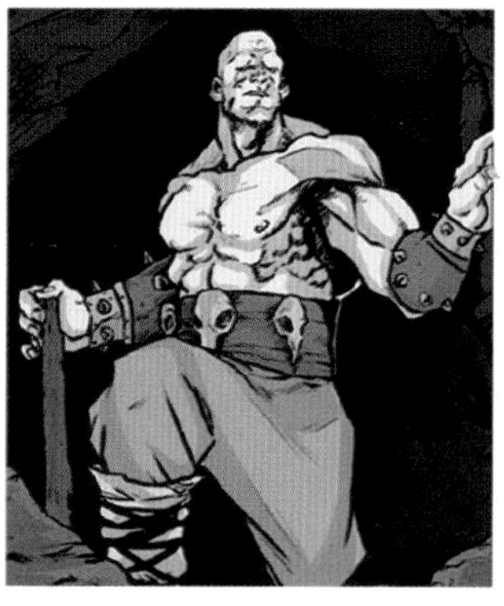

Cano - Cave Giants

Massive, pale skinned warrior and carrier of the mighty Wolf Hammer. Although isolated in the far north he will never back down from any challenge. He is often in conflict with the malevolent spirits of the Slaugh who fear the strike of his weapon.

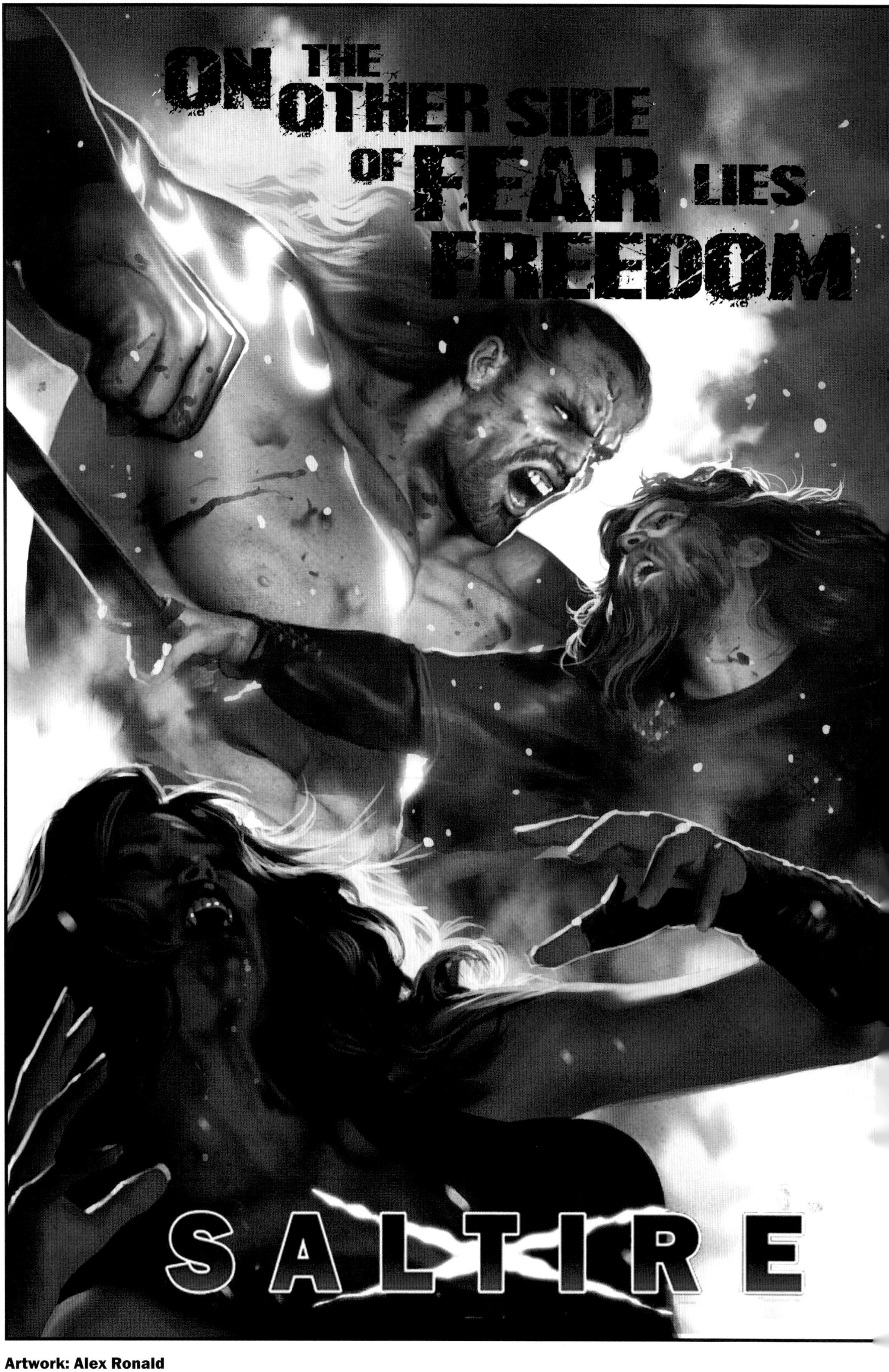
ON THE OTHER SIDE OF FEAR LIES FREEDOM
SALTIRE

Artwork: Alex Ronald

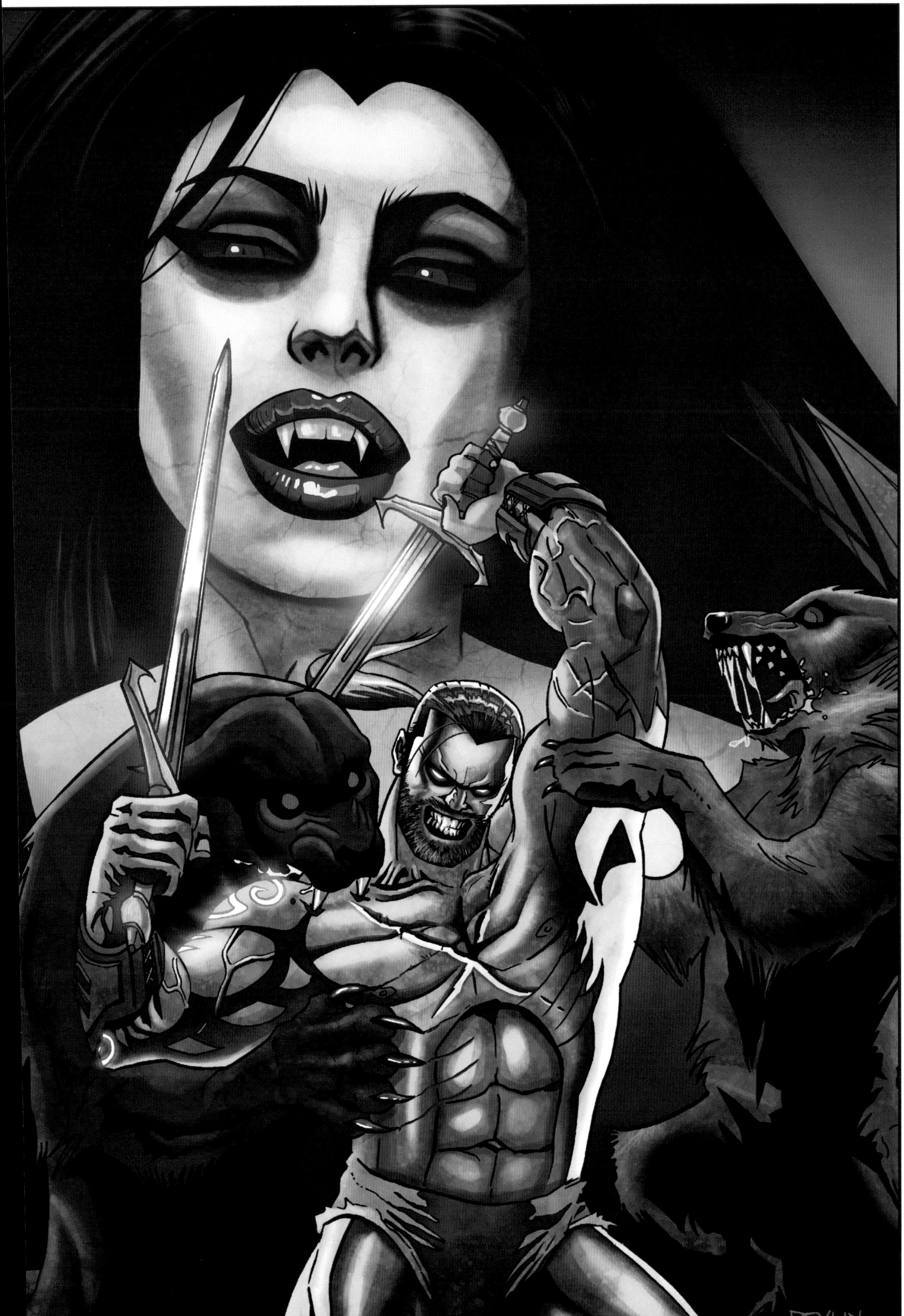
DEVLIN

work: Jimmy Devlin

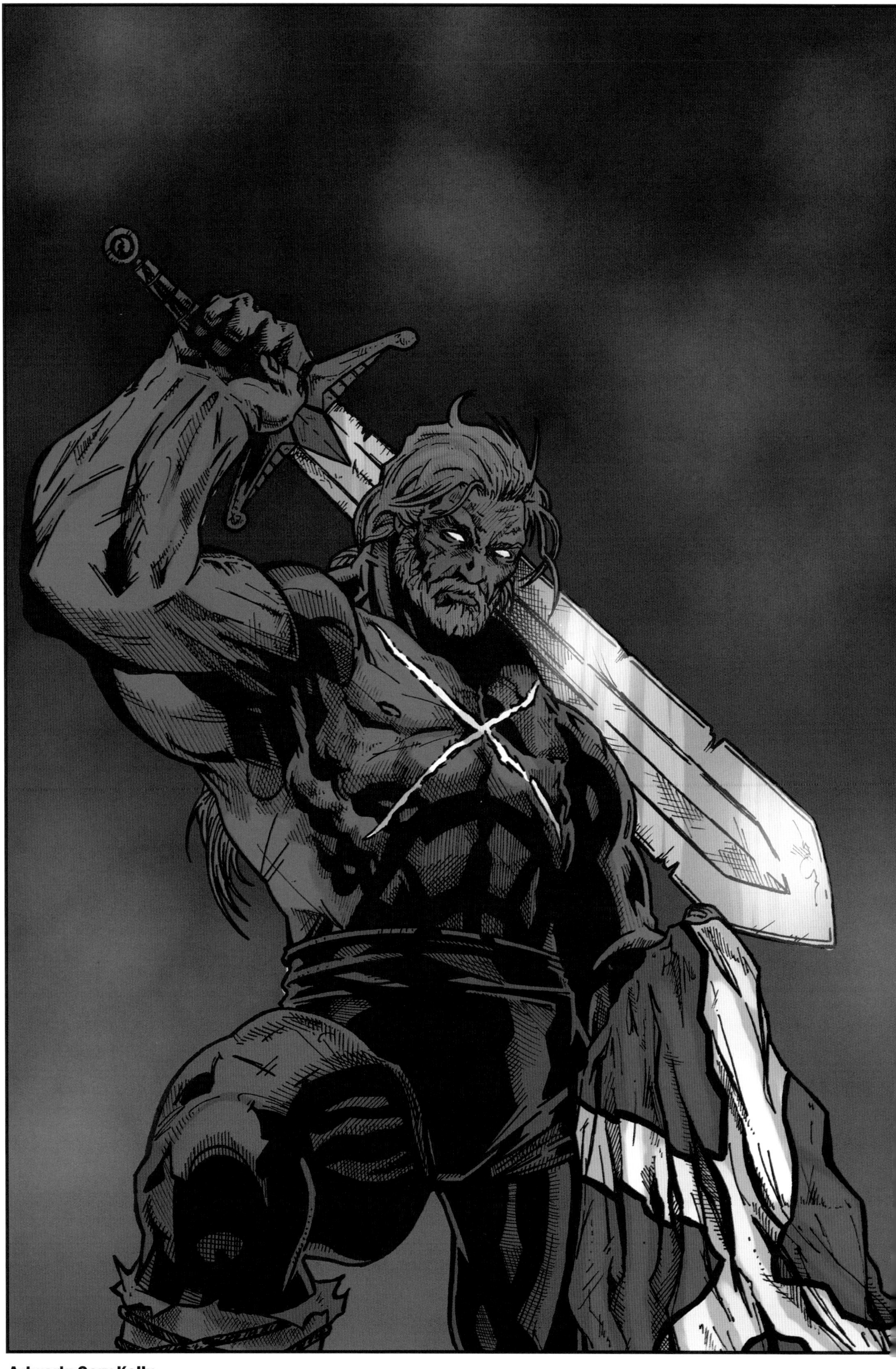

Artwork: Gary Kelly

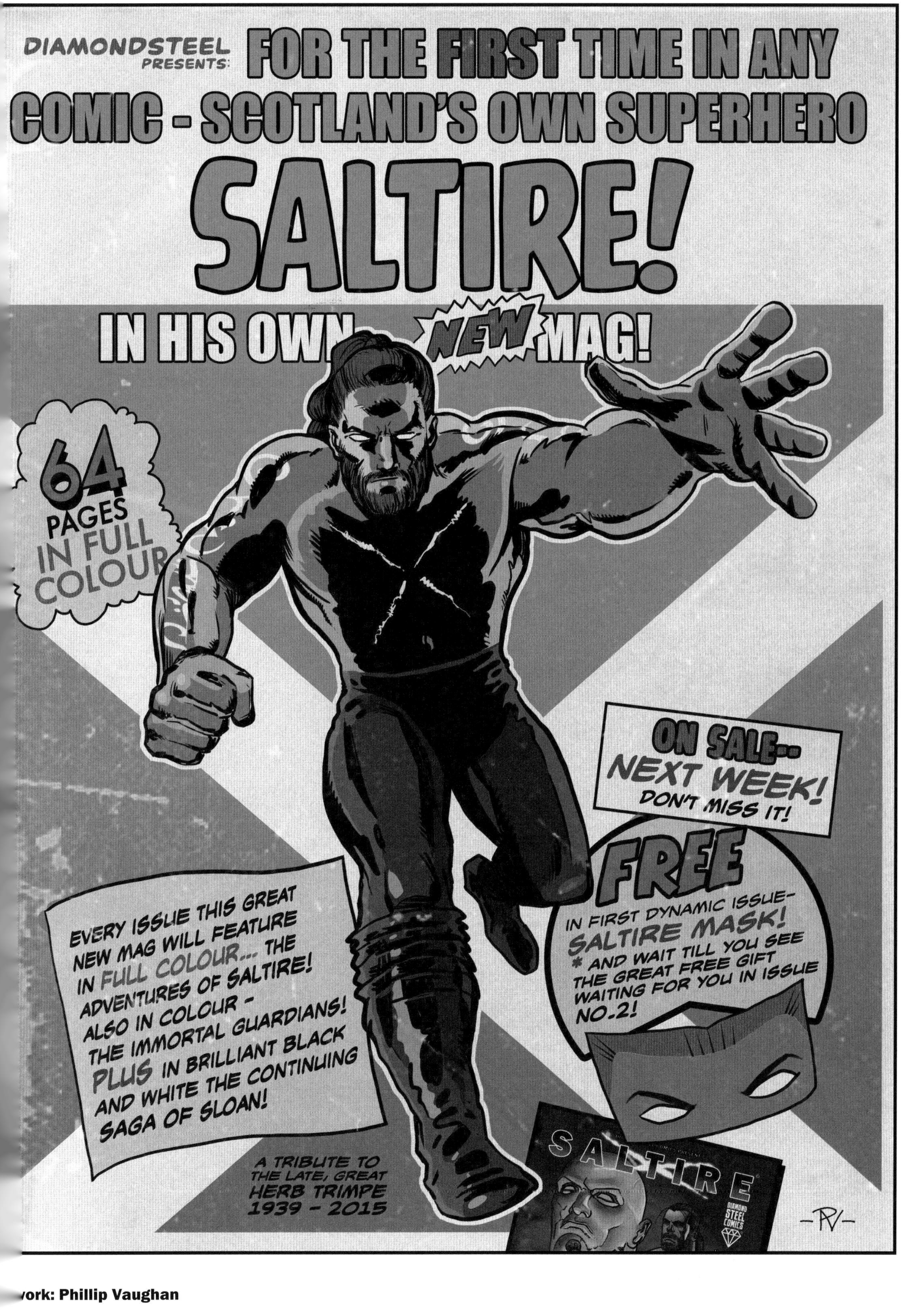
DIAMONDSTEEL PRESENTS:
FOR THE FIRST TIME IN ANY COMIC - SCOTLAND'S OWN SUPERHERO
SALTIRE!
IN HIS OWN NEW MAG!
64 PAGES IN FULL COLOUR
ON SALE.. NEXT WEEK! DON'T MISS IT!
FREE
IN FIRST DYNAMIC ISSUE- SALTIRE MASK! * AND WAIT TILL YOU SEE THE GREAT FREE GIFT WAITING FOR YOU IN ISSUE NO.2!
EVERY ISSUE THIS GREAT NEW MAG WILL FEATURE IN FULL COLOUR... THE ADVENTURES OF SALTIRE! ALSO IN COLOUR - THE IMMORTAL GUARDIANS! PLUS IN BRILLIANT BLACK AND WHITE THE CONTINUING SAGA OF SLOAN!
A TRIBUTE TO THE LATE, GREAT HERB TRIMPE 1939 - 2015
SALTIRE
DIAMOND STEEL COMICS
-PV-

work: Phillip Vaughan

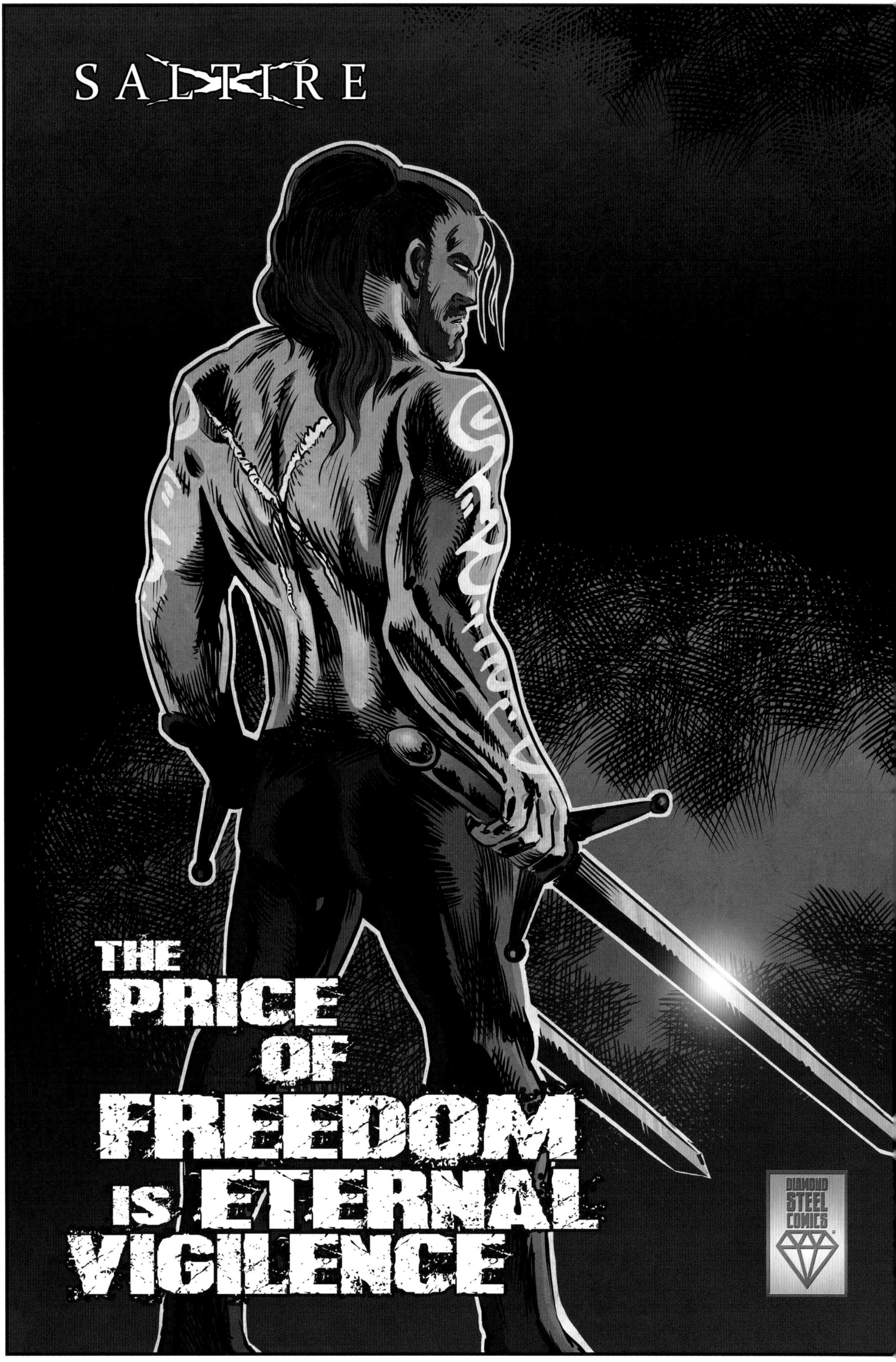
SALTIRE
THE PRICE OF FREEDOM is ETERNAL VIGILENCE
DIAMOND STEEL COMICS

Artwork: Tone Julskjaer/Phillip Vaughan

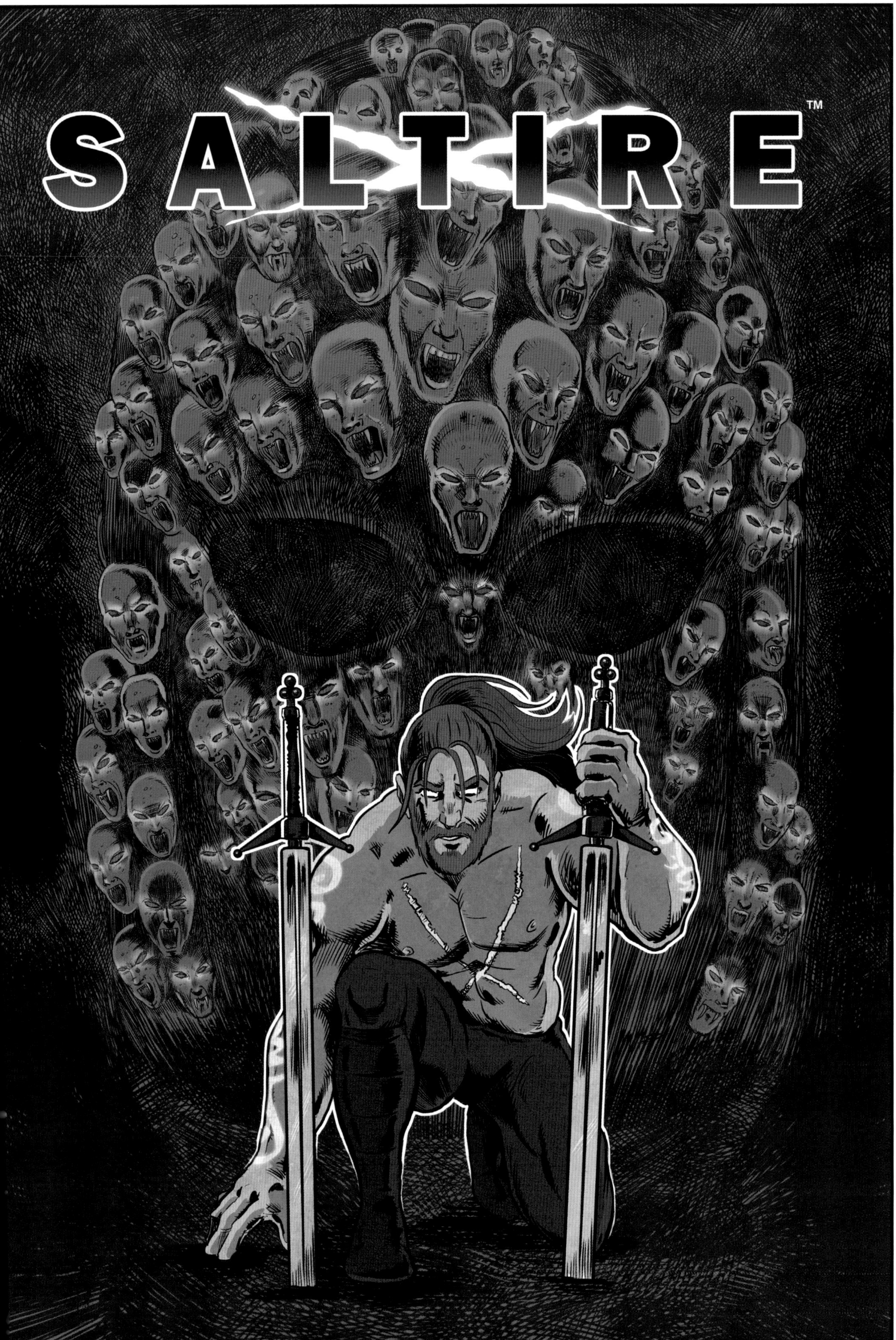
SALTIRE™

ork: Tone Julskjaer/Phillip Vaughan

MEET THE CREATIVE TEAM

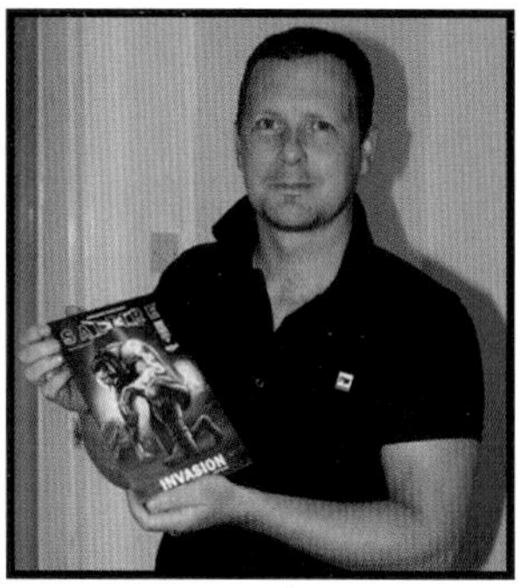
INVASION

John Ferguson - Creator & Writer
Born in Glasgow, Scotland, John now lives as a country gent with his wife and three children. Writing in various genres for many years including popular music magazines, he has written books on Scottish mythology and best selling graphic novels. He is best known as the creator of the Saltire graphic novels, a best selling and award nominated title with DC's Claire Roe. John is currently writing the Mean City noir comic book series and is about to release the Saltire graphic novel, Legend Eternal.

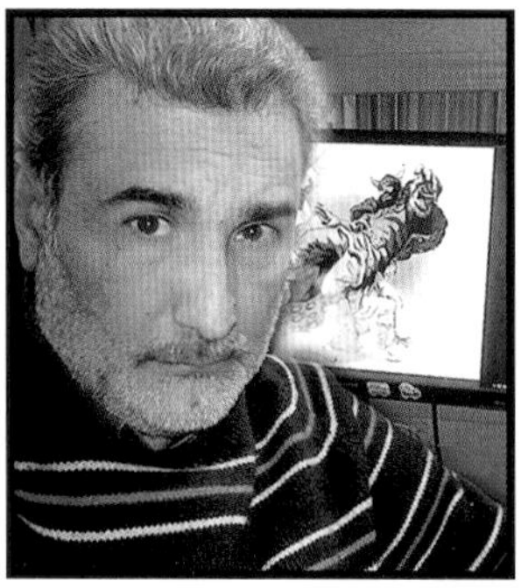

Toni Doya - Artwork
Toni, from Spain, started drawing from a very early age, but only recently embarked on his professional career in 2014 illustrating the first act of graphic novel, Cain: The First Born, followed by the graphic novel Ingress: Origins, for Cryptozoic. He then collaborated on Back to the Future for IDW and several independent titles. Since 2017 he has been working with Diamondsteel Comics on the Saltire graphic novel series.

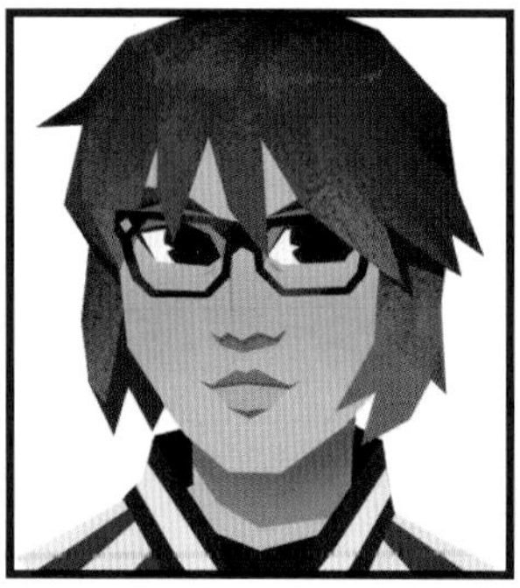

Lydia Praamsma - Artwork
Born and raised in Burbank California, Lydia is a world traveler, having lived in Holland, Taiwan, Scotland and now back to Southern California. She studied Animation at Duncan of Jordanstone College of Art and Design. Her family has long a history of industry work, from her grandparents at Hanna-Barbera and her aunts and mother at Disney Animation Studios in California. Lydia is available for freelance in Illustration, Concept Art and Design.

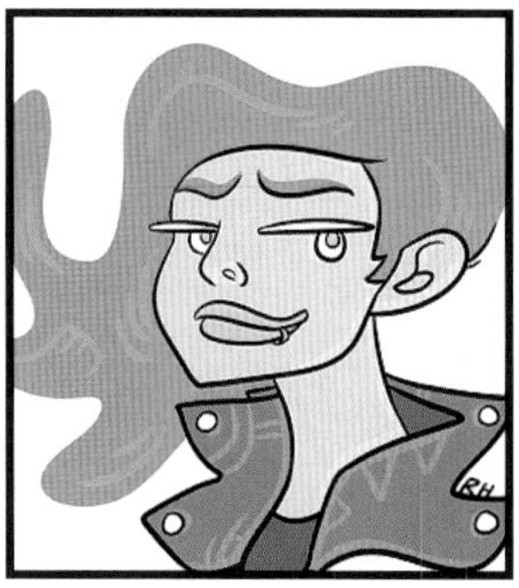
RH

Rebecca Horner - Colours
Rebecca is cartoonist and colourist at Ink Pot Studio, Dundee, and is also the studio manager for the space. She also works as a workshop coordinator at Dundee Comics Creative Space.
In 2017 Rebecca graduated from the new MDes in Comics & Graphic Novels at Duncan of Jordanstone College of Art, where she had also completed a BDes in Animation.

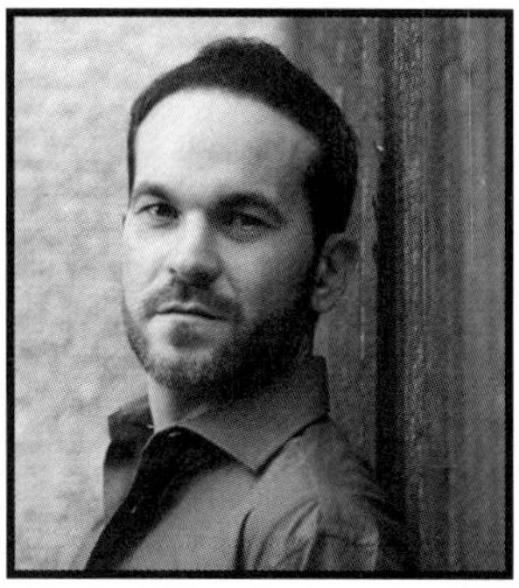

Phillip Vaughan - Lettering & Production Design
Phillip Vaughan is the Course Director for the MDes Comics & Graphic Novels course at the University of Dundee. He is also the creator of the Comic Art & Graphic Novels module at Duncan of Jordanstone. In 2015, he became the Art Director of the Dundee Comics Creative Space. Phillip has also worked as a animator and comics creator. He has worked on Superman for DC Comics, a No.1 selling App on iOS, and also created Bantah Six, with Rossi Gifford (Spirit Leaves), for David (V for Vendetta) Lloyd's Aces Weekly.